Society, Representation and Textuality

Society, Representation and Textuality
The Critical Interface

Edited by
Sukalpa Bhattacharjee
C. Joshua Thomas

◆SAGE www.sagepublications.com
Los Angeles • London • New Delhi • Singapore • Washington DC

Copyright © Sukalpa Bhattacharjee and C. Joshua Thomas, 2013

All rights reserved. No part of this book may be reproduced or utilized in any form or by any means, electronic or mechanical, including photocopying, recording or by any information storage or retrieval system, without permission in writing from the publisher.

First published in 2013 by

SAGE Publications India Pvt Ltd
B1/I-1 Mohan Cooperative Industrial Area
Mathura Road, New Delhi 110 044, India
www.sagepub.in

SAGE Publications Inc
2455 Teller Road
Thousand Oaks, California 91320, USA

SAGE Publications Ltd
1 Oliver's Yard, 55 City Road
London EC1Y 1SP, United Kingdom

SAGE Publications Asia-Pacific Pte Ltd
33 Pekin Street
#02-01 Far East Square
Singapore 048763

Published by Vivek Mehra for SAGE Publications India Pvt Ltd, typeset in 10/12 pt Times New Roman by Diligent Typesetter, Delhi and printed at Chaman Enterprises, New Delhi.

Library of Congress Cataloging-in-Publication Data Available

ISBN: 978-81-321-0953-2 (HB)

The SAGE Team: Neelakshi Chakraborty, Chirag Mohanty Samal and Vijay Sah

In memory of
Professor Goutam Biswas
who breathed life into all around him

Thank you for choosing a SAGE product! If you have any comment, observation or feedback, I would like to personally hear from you. Please write to me at contactceo@sagepub.in

—Vivek Mehra, Managing Director and CEO,
SAGE Publications India Pvt Ltd, New Delhi

Bulk Sales

SAGE India offers special discounts for purchase of books in bulk. We also make available special imprints and excerpts from our books on demand.

For orders and enquiries, write to us at

Marketing Department
SAGE Publications India Pvt Ltd
B1/I-1, Mohan Cooperative Industrial Area
Mathura Road, Post Bag 7
New Delhi 110044, India
E-mail us at marketing@sagepub.in

Get to know more about SAGE, be invited to SAGE events, get on our mailing list. Write today to marketing@sagepub.in

This book is also available as an e-book.

Contents

List of Illustrations	xi
List of Non-English Works	xiii
Foreword by Mrinal Miri	xxi
Introduction	xxiii

SECTION I: TEXTUALIZING SOCIAL DISCOURSE

1. Science and Literature: A Study of Rabindranath Tagore's Music   3
   Partha S. Ghose

2. Rabindranath Tagore's Philosophy of Art and Literature   13
   Goutam Biswas

3. The New Comparative Literature 'To Come' as a Critique of Cosmopolitanism   22
   Sourav Kargupta

4. Islam and Theodicy: A Critique of Ruqaiyyah Waris Maqsood's Theological Approach to Evil   41
   Mohammad Maroof Shah

5. Suturing of Selves Past: The Body in Revolution   63
   Anirban Das

6. Literature, Society and the Calling of Creative Public Spheres: Beyond Adaptation and Meditative Verbs of Transformations   78
   Ananta Kumar Giri

SECTION II: TEXTUALITY AND REPRESENTATIONS

7. Enugula Veeraswamy's Journal: A Study — 107
   Mohan G. Ramanan

8. Kafka: Literature, Law and Language — 121
   Franson Davis Manjali

9. Understanding Tribal World View: A Painter's Perspective — 133
   Sujata Miri

10. Reiterating Stereotypes?: Assessing the Role of Women in Contemporary *Jatra* — 143
    Somdatta Mandal

11. The Reinterpretation of Historical Trauma: Three Films about Partition — 162
    M. K. Raghavendra

12. Identity and Politics in the Songs of Contemporary African American Women — 175
    Ellerine Diengdoh

SECTION III: SOCIETIES, LITERATURE AND THE ETHNIC LIFE-WORLD

13. Transcribing Orality: A Study of *Ki Jingsneng Tymmen* — 189
    Esther Syiem

14. The Interface of Mizo Society and Literature — 202
    Margaret Ch Zama

15. Folklore and Folk Traditions as a Cohesive in Nepali Community in India — 209
    Utpala Ghaley Sewa

16. Singing the Nation: Pratima Barua Pandey, the Princess of the Lost Lores — 218
    Jyotirmoy Prodhani

17. The Revenant in Some Urban Legends of Shillong — 227
    Desmond L. Kharmawphlang

18. **Inter-Community Relations in Medieval Bengal as Reflected in Contemporary Bengali Vernacular Literature** 235
    Muhammad Shah Noorur Rahman

Select Bibliography 257
About the Editors and Contributors 264
Index 267

List of Illustrations

10.1	*Swapne Dekha Sukher Sangsar*	146
10.2	*Buro Khokar Kochi Bou*	147
10.3	*Aami Haridas Paler Bou*	149
10.4	*Aami Bonnhisikha*	150
10.5	*Roga Swamir Daroga Bou*	151
10.6	*Momotamoyeer Mostaan Cheley*	152
10.7	*Bouma Anna Bhiksha Dao*	154
10.8	*Nishidhha Premer Parinaam*	155
10.9	*Ruper Rani Swapner Raja*	156
10.10	*Abbajaner Hindu Meye*	158
16.1	Matia Bagh Summer Palace: Where Pratima Barua Pandey Lived	223
16.2	Pratima Barua Pandey (1935–2002)	224

List of Non-English Works

Chapter/Section	Title of Work (Poems, Books, Essays, etc.)	Kind of Work	Author/Editor/Producer/Director
Introduction	Différance	Chapter	Jacques Derrida
	Désistance	Chapter	
Chapter 1	Akash Bhora Surjo Tara	Poem	Rabindranath Tagore
	Anandalipi	Book	Rajat Chanda
	Biraat Srishtir Kshetre Atash Baajir Khelaa	Poem	Rabindranath Tagore
	Esho Esho Hey Trishnaaro Jal	Poem	
	Kakhon Baadol Chhonyaa Lege	Poem	
	Kabya O Bignaner Samanya—Rabindranather Bignan Manas	Book	Rajat Chanda
	Mon Je Bale Chini Chini	Poem	Rabindranath Tagore
	Neel Digante Oi Phuler Aagun Laaglo	Poem	
	Nrityeara Taale Taale	Poem	
	Praangane Mor Shirish Shaakhaye	Poem	
	Rabindra Racanāvali	Book	
	Rabindranath O Vijñān	Book	Dipankar Chattarji
	Visva Parichay **or** Visvaparicaya	Book	Rabindranath Tagore
Chapter 2	Prantik	Poem	Rabindranath Tagore
	Sangit Chinta	Book	

Chapter/Section	Title of Work (Poems, Books, Essays, etc.)	Kind of Work	Author/Editor/Producer/Director
Chapter 3	Des Tours de Babel	Chapter/Article	Jacques Derrida
	Abinirmān Anubād	Chapter	Gayatri Chakravorty Spivak
	Bānglā Upanyase 'Orā'	Book	Sibaji Bandyopadhyay
	Bānglāi Binirmān Abinirmān	Volume	Anirban Das (editor)
	Galpaguccha	Volume	Rabindranath Tagore
	Pārasye	Chapter/Article	
	Rabindra-Rachanābalī, Sulabh Samskaran, Ekādash Khanda	Book	
	Rabindra-Rachanābalī, Sulabh Samskaran, Dvadash Khanda	Book	
	Strīr Patra	Chapter/Article	
Chapter 5	Jeler Bhitor Jel	Book	Minakshi Sen
	Journal Sottor	Book	Raghab Bandyopadhyay
	Karagare Athero Bochhor	Book	Azizul Haque
	Mayabi Tantuja	Book	Ranjit Gupta
	Sei Doshok	Book	Pulakesh Mandal and Joya Mitra (editors)
Chapter 6	Byakti O Byaktitya	Book	Chitta Ranjan Das
	...Ebam Kadha	Book (collection of poems)	Rabi Narayan Dash
	Ebam	Book	Chitta Ranjan Das and Srinivas Udgata

Title	Type	Author
Achyutananda O Panchasakha Dharma	Book	Chitta Ranjan Das
Bhakta Charana Das	Book	
Biswaku Gabakha	Book	
Ethara Udiba Neta	Essay	
Gangadharanka Tapasya	Essay/Chapter	
Jatire Mu Jabana	Book	
Jangala Chithi	Book	
Le Troubadour	Poem	Francis Regis Bouquizabout
Ma Nishada **or** Maa Nishada	Book	Chitta Ranjan Das
Mitrashya Chakhusha: Prathama Sakala		
Odisara Mahima Dharma	Book	
Odiya Sahityara Ithihasa: Samajika-Sanskrutika Bhittibhumi	Book	
Odiya Sahityara Sanskrutika Bikashadhara	Book	
Pashyati Dishi Dishi **or** Pashyati Disidisi	Book	
Sahitya O **or** Sahitya O…	Book	
Sahitya O Srujanasilata	Book	
Sarjantmaka Sahitya Sameekhya: Abhimukhya O Angeekara	Essay	
Shukara O Socrates	Essay	
Utsa Nirupanara Roga	Book	
	Essay	
Jhankara	Journal	NA

Chapter/Section	Title of Work (Poems, Books, Essays, etc.)	Kind of Work	Author/Editor/Producer/Director
Chapter 7	Kasi Yatra Charitra	Book	Enugula Veeraswamy
	Pratapa Mudaliar Charitram	Book	Vedanayagam Pillai
	Rajasekhara Charitra	Book	Veeresalingam Pantulu
Chapter 8	Faux pas	Book	Maurice Blanchot
	La folie du jour	Book	
	La part du feu	Book	
Chapter 10	Aami Bonnhisikha	*Jatra* plays	NA
	Aami Haridas Paler Bou		
	Abbajaner Hindu Meye		
	Bhalobashar Karagare Bandini Sujata		
	Bouma Anna Bhiksha Dao		
	Brishtir Aaj Subhodrishti		
	Momotamoyeer Mostaan Cheley		
	Nishidhha Premer Parinaam		
	Ruper Rani Swapner Raja		
	Smashaney Holo Subhodrishti		
	Swapne Dehka Sukher Sangsar		

Chapter 11	Anmol Ghadi	Movie	Mehboob Khan (director)
	Anokhi Ada	Movie	–
	Bhuvan Shome	Movie	Mrinal Sen
	Deewar	Movie	–
	Dharti Ke Lal	Movie	K. A. Abbas (director)
	Gadar: Ek Prem Katha	Movie	–
	Garam Hawa	Movie	M. S. Sathyu
	Hum Log	Television series	–
	Karma	Movie	Subhash Ghai (director)
	Lagaan	Movie	–
	Mere Mehboob	Movie	–
	Nukkad	Television series	–
	Pinjar	Movie	Chandraprakash Dwivedi (director)
	Sara Akash	Movie	Basu Chatterjee
	Tamas	Television series	Govind Nihalani (director)
Chapter 13	Ki Jingsneng Tymmen	Book	Radhon Singh Berry
	Ki Jingsneng Tymmen Shaphang Ka Akor Khasi Ha Ka Rukom Rwai Phawar	Book	U. Radhon Singh Berry

Chapter/Section	Title of Work (Poems, Books, Essays, etc.)	Kind of Work	Author/Editor/Producer/Director
Chapter 16	Dine Dine Khasia Paribe Rangila Dalaner Mati	Ballad/Song	NA
	Era Bator Sur	Movie	Bhupen Hazarika
	Hudum Deo	Song	NA
	Kati Puja	Song	NA
	Mahut Bandhu	Movie	Bhupen Hazarika
	Mukti	Movie	Pramathesh Barua
	O Mor Hai Hastir Kanya Re	Song	NA
	Sona Rai	Song	NA
	Axom Nandini Pratima Barua Pandey Bhumika	Book	Prafulla Barman
	Ganor Pratima, Pranor Pratima	Poem	Girija Shankar Ray
	Goalparar Jana Itihax	Book	Suriti Sarma Brahmachoudhury
	Goalparia Loka Sanskriti Aru Loka Geet	Book	Shanto Barman
	Goalparia Loko Sahitya Samaj Jibanor Protifolon	Book	Dhiren Das
	Mahut Bandhure: Pratima Barua Pandey - Jiban O Gaan	Book	Shashi Sarma
	Manishi Thakur Panchananer Bani	Book	Shaymal Chakraborty
	Manishi Thakur Panchananer Jiban Katha	Book	Shri Upasu (Editor)
	Panchanan Smaranika	Book	Shri Upasu
	Rajbanshi Bhasha Sahitya Aru Iyar Unnanyan	Book	Dhirendranarth Das
	Rajbanshi Bhasha Tattva	Book	D. N. Bhakat
	Rajbanshi Kavita Sankalan	Article/Chapter	Amanatulla Khan Choudhury
		Book	Binod Bihari Barman and Jatin Burma (Editors)
	Setu Bandhane Loka Shilpi Tagar Adhikary	Book	Sudhanshu Shekhar Aditya
	Surendranath Basunia: Karma Jiban O Sangeet Sadhana	Book	Ramendranath Adhikary

Chapter 17	Ka Dak Bangla	Book	Remy Phankon
Chapter 18	Baharistan-i-Ghaibi	Book	Mirzanathan
	Bangali Sanskriti Prasanga	Book	Gopal Haldar
	Bangla Sahityer Itihas	Book	Sukumar Sen
	Banglar Baishnab Bhabapanno Musalman Kavir Padomanjusha	Book	J. M. Bhattacharjee
	Banglar Itihas Samhandhe Kayakti Katha	Essay	Bankim Chandra Chattopadhyay
	Bharatchandra Granthabali	Book	Brajendranath Bandyopadhyay and Sajanikanta Das (Editors)
	Bibidh Prabandha	Book	
	Dhakurpala Part	Book	Ghanaram Chakraborty
	Dharma Mangal	Poem	
	Gangastak	Verse	Daraf Khan
	Gopichander Sannayas	[Book]	Sukur Mahmud
	Goroksha Vijaya	[Book]	Faizullah
	Jnan Chautisa	Treatise	Sayid Sultan
	Jnan-Pradip	Treatise	Sayid Sultan
	Kavikankan Chandi	Poem/ Devotional Verse	Mukundaram Chakraborty
	Madhaya Yugar Bangla Sahitye Hindu-Mussalmaner Samparkhya	Book	Musa Kalim
	Manasa Mangal	Poem	Ksemananda
	Meinsat (Mayna Sati)	Poem/ Devotional Verse	Mian Sadhan

Chapter/Section	Title of Work (Poems, Books, Essays, etc.)	Kind of Work	Author/Editor/Producer/Director
	Mymansingh Gitika	Book/Collection	Dinesh Chandra Sen
	Mrigavat	Poem/Verse	Qutban
	Nabi-Vamsa	Poetic work	Sayid Sultan
	Nurunneha O Kaborer Katha Pala	Ballad	Not Known
	Padma Purana	Book	Vijay Gupta
	Padmavat	Poem/Verse	Alaol
	Padmavat	Poem/Verse	Malik Muhammad Jaisi
	Purba Banga Gitika	Book/Collection of verses	Dinesh Chandra Sen
	Rasul Vijay	Poetic work	Sayid Sultan
	Sati Mayna	Poem	Daulat Qazi
	Satya Narayan	Ballad	NA
	Satya Pir	Ballad	NA
	Srimad Bhagabata	Book	NA

Foreword

It gives me great pleasure to write this brief foreword to *Society, Representation and Textuality: The Critical Interface*, edited by Sukalpa Bhattacharjee and C. Joshua Thomas. The book brings together papers from various critical perspectives of the humanities and social sciences. The Introduction by the editors spells out the theoretical framework within which the book has been conceived and planned. The work attempts to (*a*) take stock of the recent developments in critical theory and cultural studies, (*b*) determine the impact of these developments on the understanding of social reality and the human predicament in India and (*c*) bring together scholars from North-east India who are engaged in the project of understanding society and communities in their chosen intellectual practices.

I have been associated with the editors since the inception of this project and I am indeed very glad that this work will be available to a critical audience interested and engaged in similar projects.

Mrinal Miri
Chancellor, Rajiv Gandhi University,
Itanagar, Chairman, ICPR,
Member of Parliament (Rajya Sabha) and
Former Vice Chancellor,
North-Eastern Hill University, Shillong

New Delhi
10 November 2011

Introduction

Sukalpa Bhattacharjee
C. Joshua Thomas

The intimate connection between society, representation and textuality is both genetic and epiphanic. It is genetic in the sense of society being an originary cultural and historical source of creative subjectivity. The connection is epiphanic in the sense of unveiling the originary experience of the 'social' in the realm of representables in the language of text. The epiphanic possibilities interrupt and forestall the steady narrative of the event and bear the witness of the flesh. Theorization about society as an over-determination, which arises with any description of oneself and another, conceives of 'the primacy of the social' over any other cognitive and epistemic source such as 'perceptual', 'bodily' or any other naturalizable entity. Indeed any source of creativity is socially qualified and any description of its origin lies in an *a priori* 'social world', which in turn gets identified with the specific mode of its knowing. An *a priori* social world consists of constituting oneself in the midst of another that produces a continuous striving towards life. Much of what the creative subject does is unknown to the subject, as acts of creativity have more sense than what the agent or subject can know. This is how the genetic aspect of the social world opens up the possibility of a conscious representation in a given description or in a given text. The text is a 'social object', but not an object in the sense of being merely available, as its 'senses' cannot be exhausted in its constitutive elements. The constitution of texts as 'social objects' arises from creative actors engaged in competing conceptions of the social that is grounded in the 'representation' of the common will or in the 'contract' that binds justifications given to interpretations of text.

Such justifications can also be characterized as an accumulation of various routes of signification that can affirm, interrupt or negate an aesthetically sublime and fictional stratum of narrative occurrences. Such narrative occurrences act as reassuring significations of the social that aims at subjectification of one kind or another and at each moment of its occurrence and reoccurrence, it attempts to recuperate the 'text', which is without an object. The text is already caught in the web of interpretations and decodifications such that its signifying territory can be recovered from any source of appropriation. The source of appropriation is the creative personalization or transfiguration of the very act of interpretation into an embodied subjectivity. Creative subjectivity is wrenched by the experience of constituting the sociality of the text and thereby it is decoded and deterritorialized in the polysemic social which again materializes into experience. Experience here has double meaning: one, the familiar and the known and the other, the unfamiliar and the new. Indeed the second meaning implies an encounter with the 'new' which is an interruption and refutation of the global assembly of signifieds and in that sense, can be called 'negativity of experience'. This negativity of experience in the decoded domain of the social is curiously productive as it throws up new significations. These new significations give the creative subjectivity a sense of the sublime, as it surpasses the usual and the known, continually constructing a realm of the beyond to which any experience looks inadequate. The criticality of this function of inadequacy lies in the subject not knowing any longer what they do, so that interpretations, acts and discourses that used to be taken for granted by the subject now become problematic, risky and challenging. This creative lack in the subject produces sublimity as an affect of the experience that resists the abstract semiotic drive of creating the familiar. This provides a great strength to the act of interpretation to recover subjectivity from its purported sublimation to a stable signifying order. The idea of the social arises beyond semiological redundancy of interpretative possibilities, as it breaks through the 'fusion of horizons' between actors to arrive at a superior degree of sublimation that moves beyond the pleasure and pain of creation. Isn't this a 'syncopation' of creative consciousness in the 'flesh' of the text, which itself is reproduced from the 'social world'? This syncopation is necessarily related to the agency of the subject as the experience wrenches the subject out of itself and places it in the midst of the humdrum of composition, to which it is obligated not just by action but by the codes of writing that present, expose and speak of the world that is already situated in the 'conflicts' centring around the social. This is a substitution of the world by a commitment to present the world in the bodily act of composition of the text in place of the object, indicating the subreption[1] of creative subjectivity in the possible creation of deterritorialized symbolic, material and social ensembles of meaning. In this way creative subjectivity overcomes the bounds of syncopatic discourse and remains situated between a critique of textual meanings and the content of the world as an unsublimated sublime. An illustration of this unsublimated sublime is the pure negative freedom that literature ushers in, in which nothing can count as literature. How then is literature possible?

Syncopation simultaneously haunts modern literature and it reproduces a critique of the social world in the text by way of an *a priori* technique of judgement, justification and contract. This is how the sense of literature remains immanent in the presentation and representation of the social. The metaphoric and metonymic movements of language go to the service of literary and cultural imagination, which is most often termed 'political' or 'sociological'. Metaphors of space, community and signifying discourses separating an ontology of 'being-in' and 'being-in-common' mark a process of anticipation of the 'other'. Such anticipations in language remain at the exterior of literature to produce an imaginary effervescence. The stylistic labour that displaces form to content is a total absorption of the negativity of experience into subjective and objective abysses. These abysses, for the presence of the other, are the origin of activity of the other directed actor, who now can endow its relation to itself into a moment of speculation. Such speculation also produces a temporal distance with the subjectivity of the other. Can politics strike its roots in this mediation between self-relation and otherness of the subject? Is the event of otherness a sufficient social relation that can be captured in an attempt to make sense of the temporal distance between the 'self' and the 'other'? Is an attempted textualization a mere prosthetic attachment to the distance between the 'self' and the 'other'?

Making an interdisciplinary examination of this critical interface between society, representations and textuality through several scholarly chapters, the collection of essays in this book seeks to enlarge the scope of both literary and cultural studies on the one hand and creative social sciences on the other, problematizing issues of representation, realism, self and the other. This would project how critical disciplinary transactions begin at the moment of critical dialogue between society and its subjects of representation, which in the words of Edward Said (1983) may be described as the interface between the "text and the world."

Textuality thrives on two very important functions—the 'representational' and the 'hermeneutic', which derive their resources from the idea of the 'social world'. These two fundamental functions of the text have been also understood as 'explanation' and 'interpretation'. Explanation is "referred to the model of intelligibility borrowed from natural sciences and applied to the historical disciplines by positivist schools; interpretation on the other hand was a derivative form of understanding" (Dilthey 1976: 248),[2] which was a fundamental characteristic of the human sciences as different from other sciences. As far as interpretation is concerned, Gadamer conceptualizes it on the basis of a shared pre-understanding in a tradition of interpretation and performance based on shared norms and values. Gadamer (2004: 310) considers that such a sharing happens within an already constituted horizon with which one must have the "ability to open ourselves to the superior claim the text makes and to respond to what it has to tell us." In this way, understanding becomes a process of 'handing down' and it proves to be an event. Understanding a text based on its interpretation by the subject as "the interpreting word is the word of the interpreter; it is not the language and the dictionary of the interpreted text" (Gadamer 2004: 468) and thereby granting the subject an interpretative freedom that marks a shift from mere 'methodological consciousness' of the subject encountering the text. Thus Gadamer (2004: 468) contends:

> The intimate unity of understanding and interpretation is confirmed by the fact that the interpretation that reveals the implications of a text's meaning and brings it into language seems, when compared with the given text, to be a new creation, but yet does not maintain any proper existence apart from the understanding process.

Understanding, therefore, is not a mere correctness of technicality of interpretation, but is an encounter with what a specific tradition tells us, is a genuine experience (*Erfahrung*), which is an encounter with something that asserts itself as "truth." (Gadamer 2004: 483). Charles Taylor, another philosopher of human sciences advocates the role of understanding to be 'epiphanic' (Taylor 1991:122) as it discloses the entire domain of self-consciousness as an event of truth seeking and arrival upon a discursive self-definition. Such a disclosive self-definition in the mode of encounter with the text and the world construes the basic relevance of human sciences. The inner depth of such an encounter is recognized in "complementarity ways we recognize our common life" (Taylor 1991: 122) that understand social and cultural identity with "the ideal of authenticity" (Taylor 1991: 58).

Introduction **xxvii**

In the backdrop of such representational and hermeneutic possibilities, one can examine realism, which has been a key concept in literary and cultural production. It has undergone significant changes based on the variations in the perception and lived experiences of the 'real', of a 'self' in its relationship to society (Williams 1961). The relationship assumes its significance in an encounter with the other. As the other pervades the manifold of sense, there are contrary ways to think about this encounter, different from what realists have fixed as a given frame of linguistic and cultural reference. Such a fixed frame marks the insignificance of 'still-life' as it is only confined to the 'causal order of the world of representation'. The odyssey of the self outside of itself in order to "face the obscure, subterranean and nonsensical world of thing-in-itself: the meaningless world of naked will-to-life" is the lived experience of the real that surpasses any account of reality referred to by the self (Rancière 2009: 29–30). In a sense, there is a participation in the contrary of the real and reality, knowing and not knowing, action undertaken and pathos undergone, which shape a frame of reference that never identifies itself with the subject (Rancière 2009). It is for this reason that understanding and interpreting human sciences in an aesthetic mode assumes that the expression of real is no longer caught up in an entanglement with reality; it is rather engaged in textualization and effectively exiles the life of the self-presence. The subject then requires a transformation from the non-philosophical real to break the "bewitchment" by the world to reconstitute itself as reality through a struggle against the real (Srnicek 2011: 171–72). This is how the primacy of the subject as a social being over its representation is established, while such a possibility is ingrained in the very being of knowledge and representation of reality. Reality arises only after its representation by the subject, who constitutes herself as an 'effect' of an already given language and its received and new interpretations that belong to praxis.

What becomes important in such a moment of critical transformation operative between the 'text and the life' is the production of decisions, reasons and meanings as textual experience that is not 'dictated by the text'. Rather, the text is the space where a reader deciphers what J. Hillis Miller (1986: 1) calls the "ethical moment ... which is neither cognitive, nor political, nor interpersonal but properly and independently ethical."[3] The reader's role becomes important in the concrete situation of reading a text when her subject's position interrupts the context of the life-world represented in the text. Every text is the subject of a law where life negates itself only to affirm itself in the impossibility of testimony, experience and the ethical. So the reader of a text sometimes has to read against the text in order to remain faithful to the text. In other words, every text has a life-world which differs from itself, defers itself and operates itself as *différarce* (Derrida 1982). Every text remains as a yet-to-come without taking a hold on itself, but by being mediated by acts of reading, interpreting and understanding.

Thus, hermeneutic function of, and in, the text or the interpretation of it, as an act of deciding the meaning of a text, encounters multiple possibilities of meaning, not as an intended consequence but as an inevitable directedness to a referential frame,[4] which cannot be determined by the text or the interpretation. This undecidability of the referential frame acts as a source of multiple interventions on the text, which simultaneously provides support to the text as well as reorders it from a critical position allowing for intertextuality. Culler (2002: 103) therefore states:

> Intertextuality is less a name for a work's relation to particular prior texts than a designation of its participation in the discursive space of a culture. Study of intertextuality is not the investigation of sources and influences as traditionally conceived, it casts its net wider to include anonymous discursive practices, codes whose origins are lost, that make possible the signifying practice of later texts.

In a related context, Roland Barthes (1977: 109) identifies the literary text as network of "multiple writings" which come from a variety of sources and discourses already in circulation in some form or other. To him, the writer is a synthesizer who deliberately reworks and echoes other texts because "the text is a tissue of quotations drawn from the innumerable centers of culture." The domain of intertextuality sometimes extends temporal and spatial limits in the sense that even intertextual and allusive connections between two or several texts may not lead to full understanding of the texts; rather, intertextual closeness between one text and another may be determined by their exploration of, or representation of, similar issues, motifs and characters. Intertextual closeness may also be noticed in the writings of two authors who have never known or heard of each other or lived in the same place and generation. According to Paul Ricoeur (1991: 109), "Each text is free to enter into relation with all the other texts which come to take the place of circumstantial reality referred to by living speech. This relation of text to text engenders the quasi-world or texts of literature."

In the context of textuality and representation, particularly in literature, it might be useful to recall what Edward Said (1982: 20) states:

> The organized study of literature ... is premised on the constitutively primary act of literary (that is artistic) representation, which in turn absorbs and incorporates other realms, other representations secondary to it. But all this institutional weight has precluded a sustained, systematic examination of the coexistence of and interrelationship between the literary and the social, which is where representation—from journalism, to political struggle, to economic production and power—plays an extraordinarily important role. Confined to the study of one representational complex, literary critics accept and paradoxically ignore the lines drawn around what they do.

Here, Said is particularly critical of a depoliticization of literary production by severing its connection with life and society. The institutionalization of literary studies has created a further gap between the production of knowledge and the production of culture, alienating the discipline from the 'subject' to whom it belongs. Umberto Eco (1984) also makes a distinction between the 'open text' and 'closed text' and shows how in semiotic analysis an open text is a text that allows multiple or mediated interpretation by the readers. In contrast, a closed text leads the reader to one intended interpretation.[5]

Therefore, what Paul Ricouer (1991: x) calls "Text to Action" is actually the transformative powers of the journey through the text in the encounter between the text and the world of human agency. The issue of ethics and politics looms large here as the world of human agency uses representational modes that constitute the poetics of textuality, which again in its essence is inseparable from ethics and politics. Ricouer (1991: x), arguing that the formal properties of the text, "distantiation, autonomy and free variation" have their bases in the idea of human freedom, states that social discourse and textuality can themselves be forms of "meaningful action." Such meaningful action in a disciplinary context produces docile and yet free bodies through a series of practices, discourses and bodies of knowledge that assume their identity and freedom in the very process of desubjectification (Agamben 2009: 19–20). The textual practices involve a moment of desubjectification that is implicit in the moment of subjectification in the practices related to the text. It is also a relationship with text that marks a disjunction and anachronism with the text. Such a disjunction and anachronism is "the experience of the ineluctable"—"double constraint", "double law, knot and caesura of a divided law, the law of the double" (Derrida 2008: 224-25). The law of the double lies in writing oneself that desists the self from its identification with itself. The narcissistic and the Oedipal law that is presupposed in writing the self, is altered in the opposition between presence and non-presence.

The chapter by Partha S. Ghose, drawing on the apparently oppositional representational mode between science and literature, describes the literary or literature as incessant murmur. Ghose, in the course of his discussion, states that great literature and great music are indestructible because they are revelatory of a background web of murmurings. The background of this web lies in nature, of which our society and we are products or parts. Drawing on the works of Tagore in particular Ghose discusses how literature and music not only reveal what lies deeply hidden in society but also what lies deeply hidden in nature and science as a whole, establishing our relationships with nature in a way that science by itself cannot. There is a tension between the particular and the universal, and a continual process of reconciliation between the two is going on in all true art, in both literature and science through revelatory murmurings. According to Ghose, no one has stirred these revelatory murmurings about nature and science more effectively than Rabindranath Tagore. Both literature and science are texts in the sense that science demands the relativity of the frame of reference to be included in the object of study. In this context it might be pertinent to remember what Barthes (1977: 155) says:

> What History, our History, allows us today is merely to slide, to vary, to exceed, to repudiate. Just as Einsteinian science demands that the relativity of the frames of reference be included in the object studied, so the combined action of Marxism, Freudianism and structuralism demands, in literature the relativization of the relations of writer, reader and observer (critic). Over against the traditional notion of the work for long ... and still ... conceived of in a, so to speak Newtonian way, there is now the requirement of a new object, obtained by the sliding or overturning of former categories. The object is the Text.

In 'overturning' conventional categories of history, truth and realism the relation between the textuality of literary text and representations of society is also explicable by crossing the boundary of ordinary semantics so far as the definitions and/or descriptions of the concepts of truth and fact are concerned, affirms Goutam Biswas in his discussion on the art and philosophy of Tagore. He elaborates on how notions of poetic truth and justice are different from truth in its ordinary sense and realism represented in literary texts does not conform to the 'real' of the ordinary life and world but is in a hyphenated and deferential sociocultural landscape. The philosophy of literature therefore must rest not on ordinary semantics and the hermeneutics centring it but, as Tagore would like to put it, upon the aesthetic upbringing of the 'surplus' in the human. Aesthetic truth is therefore not the propositional kind or grounded upon a one-to-one correspondence between what is said and what is the case. Art, as Heidegger depicted, is "the setting-into-work of truth." This setting-into-work of truth, for Heidegger (1975:75),

> thrusts up the unfamiliar and extraordinary and at the same time thrusts down the ordinary and what we believe to be such. The truth that discloses itself in the work can never be proved or derived from what went before. What went before is refuted in its exclusive reality by the work.

According to Biswas what art founds can therefore never be compensated and made up for by what is already present and available in the text and the world. Therefore, the chapter by Sourav Kargupta asks, "What remains between the text and the world? What shields the one from the other, what tempts the one into the other?" According to him any thinking of the literary object has to address this very central problematic. In dealing with the 'real' and the 'representational' one cannot ignore ideology which intervenes between the 'real' and the 'represented' in the representation of the subject's consciousness which is associated with 'false consciousness' according to some strains of Marxist theory. In his opinion if the subject is seen as produced through her practical coping with the world of objects, consuming dominant representative patterns, then ideology can be understood, following Antonio Gramsci, as "a practice producing subjects" (Mouffe 1979: 187).[6] A theory of ideology, therefore, resists any model of representation that does not problematize the gap between the real and the representational. Kargupta's chapter critically reads into the theoretical and textual dimensions of the transaction that goes on between the 'world' and the 'word' and the process through which the self-contained closure of the 'book' is replaced with the open-endedness of the 'text'.

Thus an ideological reading of any text, literary, social or religious, challenges and interrogates accepted notions of truth, justice and evil by problematizing the 'real' and the 'representational'. Such a problematic takes the form of an apophatic discourse that traverses through stages of symbolic theology and positive predication of the secular world. The chapter by Mohammad Maroof Shah discusses the problem of evil that constitutes the apophatic and cataphatic discourse of theistic worldviews. According to him, it is the changed perception or cognizance of evil that differentiates modern humanist secularist worldview from the traditional theistic worldviews. Such a position can pose a serious challenge to traditional theology in modern times. Both from a religious and political standpoint any attempt to secure a rational foundation for religion in a secular context in modern times must seriously reckon with the problem of dialectics of presence and non-presence. From Shah's point of analysis theodicy thus becomes a notoriously difficult job for any theologian in modern times because usual theological apologies or answers are hardly convincing and have resulted in intra- and inter-community conflicts. Rather, the traditional metaphysical approach presented in the writings of the school of perennialists' thought to the problem convincingly refutes major critiques of theism and formulates a viable theodicy. His chapter makes a critical appraisal of Ruqaiyyah Waris Maqsood's partially theological reading of the Islamic view on evil to bring home the transformatory dialogue between the text and the world.

In encountering the critical interfaces of the dialogue between the societal and the textual, the individual versus the collective on the anvil of ideology the role of memory becomes very important. Does individual memory contest and interrupt dominant events and ideologies? Again, is the act of remembering and forgetting socially and culturally determined and ideologically governed? The chapter by Anirban Das tries to address these questions through an exercise of how memories written as texts bring out certain itineraries of the acts of writing. He says that as one goes on to produce (write) new texts in reading the earlier ones, one becomes—yet one more time—aware of the infinitude of the radical act of producing supplements which disrupt accepted or known descriptions. Memories of revolution exceed the history of revolution and memories of the body of the revolutionaries in turn, inscribed upon by events and ideologies interrupt these ideologies and produce events. However according to him all writings of memories do not enact the breaks. Such enactments need ideological work, which involves descriptive categories of the social sciences and the performative agencies of the literary.

However, the chapter by Ananta Kumar Giri discusses how meaningful action might be possible through a transcendental move beyond the descriptive categories of the social sciences and the performative agencies of the literary. He shows how literature is not only a mirror of society but also a field of conflictual expressions and confrontations, which breaks through conventional descriptions of society and creates new languages of self and collective realizations. This is what Derrida (2008: 224–25) calls "law of the double" that produces an ongoing dialectic between conflict and its reconciliation. According to Giri, both literature and society are not only fields of adaptation but also fields of transcendence and transformations in which individuals and groups strive to go beyond adaptation and interrogate the existing logic of both literature and society. Therefore, in exploring the relationship between literature and society the language of interdisciplinary transaction is not enough; rather, what is needed is "transdisciplinary cultivation ... beyond adaptation and meditative verbs of transformations."

Such a transdisciplinary cultivation, for instance in deciphering the relationship between historicity and textuality, shows that there is only a thin line dividing fact from fiction, which is reflected in both literary and historical texts. Mohan G. Ramanan, in his chapter, states that all writing is in a profound way fiction because writing implies selection of material and narrative deployment, emphases and foregrounding of one thing at the expense of another. Ramanan reads into a travel narrative by an early modernist called Enugula Veeraswamy, a Telugu gentleman whose journey from Madras to Kasi and back is the subject of the text first written in the 1830s. One is aware that the rise of the genre of diary writing, journal keeping, memoirs and confessions and the novel are all part of the modernizing tendency after the European Renaissance and these texts have also been read as alternative histories. Ramanan shows how historical consciousness along with self-consciousness have been attributes of that intellectual movement and the writing of history and the writing of novels are part of the manner of articulating this new knowledge. In Veeraswamy's narrative one can see critical interfaces of the encounter between a modern mind and the forces of history which also calls for a re-examination of the relationship between the individual and the collective, societal realities and textual representations.

Again, language is crucial both for constituting representational agencies and therefore the issue of language as a means of representation figures very prominently in the thematic discussion of the book. The variations in the use of critical language in humanities and its allied disciplines are particularly interesting to note. As mentioned earlier, language is put to the service of literary and cultural imagination, which is most often termed 'political' or 'sociological'. Correspondingly, fictional and poetic presentations of textual, intertextual and intersubjective 'forms' of reality alter sensibilities about society, as the self-reflexive creator produces a no-second version of her political and sociological imagination. This is what arises in the relation between text and world, 'a world joins, plays, speaks and shares: this is its sense, which is not different from the sense of 'making sense'" (Nancy 1997: 78).

Franson Davis Manjali, in his chapter, shows how from Blanchot's perspective the trajectory that literature takes is very clear. In his view just as one's own death is an impossibility, one encounters the impossibility of the language of literature, and of literature itself. This is where literature can be spoken of as an 'incessant murmur' in and of language, and this is where one can discern the movement of what Foucault (1977) calls "language to infinity." Manjali explains this ambivalence through his study of Kafka's portrayal of his characters. He ponders over the relationship of literature to "society" on the one hand, and to "community" on the other and finds that community has been relegated to the background. For instance, in the classic work of modern linguistics, *Course in General Linguistics*, Ferdinand de Saussure (1978) speaks of language extensively in relation to society. Saussure, assuming a socially consistent knowledge of the system of signs conceived of 'semiology' as a branch of 'social psychology', which itself would pertain to a 'general psychology'. What is of interest to Manjali is the question of the coexistence as well as the covariance of the elements of language and the elements of society or community. Following the emergence of modern nations, a language is taken to be coextensive with a society or a community. He finds that literature, paradoxically, is both an affirmation of the language of a given society or community, and a denial and a defiance of it. Like Giri, Manjali also finds that literature is the transgression of, and an invitation to transgress, the boundaries that circumscribe the (coextensive) coexistence of language (discourse) and society privileging one representational mode over the other.

Although a distinction is made between 'work' and 'text' it is not meant to privilege one representational mode over the other but to establish interdisciplinarity between different disciplines. Barthes (1977: 155) further explains the difference between text and work:

> The work is a fragment of a substance, occupying a part of the space of books (in a library for example), the text is a methodological field ... the one is displayed, the other demonstrated ... the work can be held in hand, the text is held in language, only exists in the movement of a discourse ... the text is not the decomposition of the work, it is the work that is the

imaginary tail of the Text; or again, *the Text is experienced only as an activity of production.*

Julia Kristeva, who also engaged for several decades in understanding what such an 'activity' involves, tries to describe textuality as a "heterogeneous practice" that establishes dialogic encounters between old texts with new texts, between readers and "*writing subject* who is again a subject constituted by several forces, of history, ideology, the unconscious, and the body...." The work closes on a signified; ... its field is that of the signifier" (Becker-Leckrone 2005: 13).

Textuality as "heterogeneous practice" also establishes a dialogic encounter between orality and painting as a representational mode without hierarchizing the written over the oral or vice versa. Such a non-hierarchical "sensible infinity beyond language" calls for forgetting and resisting the narrator (Kristeva 2005: 268–69). This further calls for empathy and reconstruction of transitionality of language (Kristeva 2005: 147). Although Paul Ricouer (1991) says that the text is any discourse fixed by writing which means that a text has to be written out, all writing have been preceded by speaking and therefore the relationship between text and speech marks the transitionality of language. It implies choice between various strategies of interpretation available to the interpreter. Writing only places in linear script what has already been articulated orally. Therefore writing is only an act of 'fixation', enabling conservation of oral articulations. Writing is fixed speech. Speech can also mark another transition to narration without words, but in images. Sujata Miri, through her reflective paintings, attempts to articulate her own views on the tribal life-world, particularly of that of India's north-eastern region with which she has been engaged over several years. She argues that while in the case of the more complex, for example, the so-called civilized societies, there is available, for the social scientists to study, traditional written texts along with their 'hermeneutical' interpretations, the same is not true for most of the so-called primitive societies. According to her, an existence of a written intellectual tradition, however, should not lead to the conclusion that the written word somehow lends an element of unchangeability to the tradition. A written tradition is just as vulnerable to historical contingencies as an oral tradition. A worldview in her opinion represents a more or less flexible framework of concepts and a great variety of carriers of meanings (for example, symbols, metaphors, stories, songs, artefacts of different kinds, etc.), which offer answers to questions such as, 'Who am I?', 'Who are others?', 'What is my relationship to others?' World-view contains guidelines about man–God, man–woman, man–child and man–nature relationships. Contrary to the Kantian rationality paradigm, Miri holds that tribal world-views have a coherence and a completeness that can be ascertained by gaining an access to the inner life of the people. An interesting fact to note is that one can discover in traditional tribal religions and worldviews strong sanctions for the preservation of their ecology, which is reflective of their unquestioned reverence for nature, man and animal.

A critique of the privileging of the written word in general and the literary text in particular is also put forth by Somdatta Mandal in her chapter on the role of women in contemporary *jatra* of Bengal. She discusses how, as a consequence, the diverse cultural production of a large part of the postcolonial world falling outside the verbal has been excluded from the category of culture. Again, in the age of new media, which is dominated by the visual and the aural, there is always a competition between literature and representations of the postcolonial experience in film, television, music and theatre. As part of the folk tradition, the *jatra* of Bengal has always been looked upon as a poor competitor of the theatre, run commercially mainly in the rural areas of West Bengal and Bangladesh. Mandal shows how through its textuality, the *jatra* continues to pose a challenge to mainstream representational modes like theatre and films by reflecting several sociocultural issues of our contemporary society.

Thus, the creative yearning for the call of the beyond in the social and the textual is both historical and trans-historical. The dominant narratives of history and other social and natural sciences are being interrogated on the basis of literary narratives that demystify canonical stereotypes in these disciplines. Again, the complex relationship between the self, memory and forgetting of an event vis-à-vis a historical documentation of a collective experience done on the basis of empirical data collection is reflected through a sociological imagination of the literary text which provides a space for a deconstructive reading of both the social and the textual. Such a practice does not simply negate society and literature as opposites, either in antithesis or in dialectical overcoming, but explores new possibilities of 'seeing' and 'reading'. It is not only about the literary figures and philosophers, but one might as well ask about the psychologists, historians and social scientists that study the links between society, representational modes and textuality. In the discipline of performance studies, much critical energy has been exerted to ensure the privileging of the live event over the literary theatre text. For some—most often, actors and directors, the text is merely a script or starting point (albeit, an essential and necessary starting point); while for others—not surprisingly, many playwrights and literary critics, the text is holy writ. Across such a continuum, this hard technology intervenes in cultural and economic contexts as an object attributed with varying degrees of symbolic capital (Webb, Schirato and Danaher 2002). In his chapter, M. K. Raghavendra claims that the partition of India occupies the same position in the Indian consciousness that the Holocaust does in the consciousness of the West but mainstream Indian cinema has not given it the position that Hollywood has accorded to the Holocaust and yet Indian mainstream cinema has a singular relationship with history. Raghavendra thinks that the value of works like the Holocaust lies in the paradigm of mourning and its emphasis on the importance of replaying the past is rooted in a traditional notion of history associated with the elegiac tradition, enacting the mourning process and hence reaffirming beliefs about providence. Such a valorization leads to an uncritical and ahistorical attachment to experience, failing to transform the agency of mourning or remembering of the past into creative energy, which could have highlighted the political significance of the partition in Indian cinema that goes beyond grief at occurrences of the past. In this manner the representational modes in a mainstream medium like commercial films mostly reiterates the canonical cinematic position. A similar problem in this context can be examined in the field of music as well. Ellerine Diengdoh states that black female contributions in the field of music have been sadly neglected, because scholars have been lax in mining black women's lyrics for the cultural and gendered values embedded in them. She argues that before Angela Y. Davis' *Blues Legacies and Black Feminism* (1998), songs written and performed by black women have seldom been contemplated in a theoretical context. The reason behind this she thinks is the belief that any analysis of popular songs lacked scholarly objectivity because songs are emotional, ephemeral, physical and accessible. In recent years however new disciplines like ethnomusicology and jazz studies have witnessed the proliferation of research dedicated to black music analysis, yet only a few published materials in these fields have focused on the songs or lyrics of African American women. The textuality of music produced by African American women holds immense interdisciplinary possibilities, as the domain of folklore studies in general and African American studies in particular, can be enriched by better examination of black female contributions in the field of music.

When one reads a text or witnesses it enacted, one sees how the 'word' intervenes into the person's embodied experience, irrespective of it being interpreted or understood as a fiction be it a theatre text or fiction, the producer of the text has little or no control over where the text is travelling and who is exposed to it. John Durham Peters (1999), in his analysis of the idea of communication, revisits the anxieties of the ancient Greek scholars with regard to written texts. He argues that Socrates explicitly articulates what remains a key concern in contemporary performance, namely, the longing for living contact or connection with other human beings. Whereas oral speech almost invariably occurs as a singular event shared by the parties privy to the discussion, writing allows all manner of strange couplings: the distant influence of the near, the dead speak to the living and the many read what is intended for the few. The conflict between orality and written script has been a feature of societies in northeast India and authors and creative writers from this region have been able to articulate an alternative language of resistance and representation. The chapter by Esther Syiem's on the paradox of *Ki Jingsneng Tymmen* is a reiteration of the argument that authors from north-eastern India attempt to recast memory and tradition in their own terms, which provide them an autonomous aesthetic horizon beyond the *desi–margi* dichotomy. Syiem clarifies at the very outset that the interface between the social and the literary in Khasi society is at the level of the oral although for obvious reasons critical and literary discussion often centre around the written version. She tries to look at *Ki Jingsneng Tymmen* as a vital extension of the social, an outgrowth of the oral that has defined the Khasi way of life. She examines how it serves as a coalescence of Khasi thought and many of the dos and don'ts found in *Ki Jingsneng Tymmen* are still functional in modern everyday life, "the anchor that, ironically, seems to assuage but not alleviate much of the confusion in an increasingly complex society." Syiem states that *Ki Jingsneng Tymmen* reflects the vital chords of a society that has always believed in the existence of one supreme deity, *U Blei Nongbuh Nongthaw*, "God the Creator and God the Maker" and the life concurrent with such a belief that the Khasi has come to this world only to *kamai ïa ka hok* or to "work for righteousness." This she finds is intimately connected with the elevation and installation of the oral to a position of centrality that was consequent upon the mythical loss of the written script. The oral or the spoken word, *ka ktien*, rationalizes the ultimate meaning of existence in a way that is geared towards the preservation of a mystical sense of life where the *rngiew* or the aura that radiates from an individual and even the entire community must be kept alive.

Margaret Ch Zama also makes a critique of the interface of Mizo society and its literature after the advent of its transition from a pre-script culture to one that received what it did not have before—both script and institutionalized religion in 1894, through its first missionaries, "all in one package as it were." She opines that the dominance of literacy and writing post-1894, which textualized Mizo literature through Christian oriented discourse, reveals an interesting tension:

> First, the failure to diminish the influence and relevance of many of the oral folk traditions and cultural practices in spite of the new faith, and second, the convenient fusion of attitudes and mindsets of the old and new, on issues especially of gender and patriarchy.

Through the reading of two short stories *Chhingpuii* (published in 1939) and *Lali* (published in 1937) in her chapter, Zama attempts to show how creative work can be seen as a social activity, as a receptacle of rich and old legacies, but more importantly, of how this can be a thriving, alive technique for the exploration and depiction of the complex interface of contemporary issues as well.

Another site for complex interface of the social and the textual is evident in folklore, particularly the urban legend, which throws light on contemporary issues. Desmond L. Kharmawphlang examines how a dominant urban legend of Shillong city is impacting the social milieu in the city. It is interesting to see how these legends set in everyday life are charged with a sense of peril that is often accentuated with an ironic twist. While these stories reside in the present and are regarded as disputable truth, they contain elements of ancient myths. Kharmawphlang examines how urban legends, sometimes as contemporary stories, continually reinvent events and create shared memories among the members of a society. They contribute to the reconstruction and reaffirming of community identities and help reinforce social bonds through elaboration of the psychosocial communicational mechanism spawned at their narration. Folklore as a text is a very powerful medium of problematization of memory and identity in most diasporic societies. Utpala Ghaley Sewa examines the functions of folklore in a diasporic society like the Nepali, which according to her, through mythic revisiting of the imaginary homeland, stands reinforced by its conscious and continuing practice of folklore and folk traditions. She examines how these practices have helped create in this diasporic, vastly dispersed community, the sense of cohesion that is both temporal as well as actual by "locating the community in the imaginary homeland that centralizes, binds and keeps alive awareness of identity beyond the flux, confusion and loss of actual homeland." In the light of the writings of Rapport and Dawson (1998), Sewa substantiates her claim as to how folklore attempts to pre-empt forgetting and alienation from the remembered home through generations and so prevents sociocultural dilution where "being rootless, displaced between worlds, living between a lost past and a fluid present, are perhaps the most fitting metaphors for the journeying modern consciousness" (Rapport and Dawson 1998: 23). This statement is especially true of the Indian Nepalis of North Bengal, namely the Darjeeling Hills, the people who came with the land when it was annexed to India and made a part of West Bengal. Likewise, the chapter by Jyotirmoy Prodhani on the effect of Pratima Barua Pandey's music in the reconstruction of a geopolitical region called "Goalpara" also begins by examining the creative strength of folklore and folk music. He says, "Pratima Barua Pandey occupies a unique position for she is more than just a folk artist; she has been a provider of a cultural address to a community desperately seeking space of its own in the geo-cultural space of its habitation." The attendant awareness of a community, region and nation, according to Prodhani, emerges through a collective experiential understanding of the self, which is again essentially informed by the rediscovery of native cultural nuances. Prodhani looks at the identity construction of the Rajbanshis, a major ethnic community living in west Assam and North Bengal in West Bengal—a community with the odd historical compulsions to continually justify their own existence in the respective geopolitical context of the two territories. They had to opt for a voluntary revocation of their native selves. In the process they lost their tongue. Ironically, despite having a glorious history to look back to, they found it was not locatable in the official versions of history. Their claim in history became seemingly inauthentic; their political articulations provisional, which caused the dwindling of their cultural and social credibility following their dislocation from the most intimate physical locale—land. Interestingly, Muhammad Shah Noorur Rahman, interrogating canonical history writing in his chapter, claims that medieval Bengal has neither any authoritative nor any continuous contemporary sociocultural historiography except Mirzanathan's *Baharistan-i-Ghaibi*. This, according to Rahman, is a work on political history, which hardly throws light on the social conditions of Bengal. It deals with the expansion of the Mughal Empire in Bengal, Kamrup and Assam. Asserting that British historians were not free from bias, Rahman quotes Bankim Chandra Chattopadhyay (322):

> The works of history composed by Englishman are not true histories of Bengal.... What is required is the history of Bengal, otherwise there is no

hope for Bengal. Who will write it? You will write, I will write, all of us will write. Come; let us all write the history of Bengal.

Therefore, Rahman makes an attempt to focus inter-community relations, mainly, Hindu–Muslim relations in medieval Bengal as reflected in the contemporary Bengali vernacular literature, namely *Mangal Kavya, Vaishnava Sahitya, Anubad Sahitya, Islami Bangla Sahitya, Purba Banga Gitika, Mymansingh Gitika, Punthi Sahitya, Atharo Bhatir Panchali, Sufi Sahitya* and *Pir Sahitya* to reconstruct an alternative social history.

Mainstream research in humanities and social sciences, which tries to establish a logical and heuristic connection between society, representational agencies and textuality in the form of disciplinary norms and competitive structures of research, needs to open up a dialogic space for intellectual encounters and interdisciplinary transactions. Homogenization of knowledge and knowledge systems through specialization is a matter of great concern for researchers across humanities and all other disciplines in human sciences, which want to decentre knowledge claims of researchers in their institutional ghettos. Late-twentieth-century universities overemphasize the production of 'mini-me' academics who ignore their own proclivities in favour of pre-professional training and 'sky-high' theory. Forgetting the liberal arts tradition, our institutions produce students who read only the latest journal articles by the hippest theorists or those who are conditioned to expect a fee-for-credit educational service industry that sells 'McNuggets' of knowledge. The situation calls for a different and revisionary look at established academic practices connecting the social and the textual. An intellectual critique oriented towards concrete social realities such as issues of marginality, aesthetic and representation in terms of classes, races, castes, tribes and other such categories of understanding needs to be carried out with a spirit of academic interrogation. The book has tried to address such issues through scholarly essays that throw light on the theme from different disciplinary perspectives.

A promise to return to the primacy of sociality through representation is a possible outcome of listening through the language of pain in the domain of creative and transformative experiences. Such an act of listening moves through the registers of literal, figural and fantastic. Indeed, such registers are plural and interminable as the cry of pain and the inevitability of bringing life to an 'end' surges within the responsive subject. The collection of essays builds on multifarious possibilities of such an engagement with languages that can produce a first-hand perspective on the ties between society, representation and text. The social relations implicated in a textual representation get naturalized in an inquiry about the interrelationship between society, representation and text. This inquiry requires that one put into language the experience that one undergoes in language. This requirement needs to be kept in mind in setting out connections between discourses, ideas and events, all as part of the lived experience of language. It is a limit of experience that lies in the secret place of thought that no thought can order and bring into the system. In human and social sciences, such a secret place of thought produces a circuitous relationship between events and ideas. This collection looks for these relations that open up the very act of thinking to the redemptive fulfilment of repositioning the interfaces that are 'mystic' and 'anarchic', but enriched by an intuitive fulfilment of senses that are immanent in the passage from society to representation to textuality. This fulfilment often borders on traces of a time that is still unrepresentable and hence shows itself up in silence and in an ineffable way. This is the moment when silence acts as the very possibility of dialogue between the text and the world—a moment of iterability, a moment where opposites are opposed. This is also the disappearance of the subject in the world to witness its own disappearing gaze. One may call it an annulment of existence, a labyrinth of philosophical loss (Nancy 1997: 79–80). This is touching the subject at its limit where it sees and shows itself with a vision of itself. The book is an attempt to mark out such a vision.

Notes

1. Subreption is a concept deployed by Immanuel Kant in his *Critique of Judgment* to indicate that aesthetic imagination cannot be subjected to pure or practical reason, as the notion of sublime cannot be grasped by any human faculty, it can only be intuited with a sense of wonder and awe.
2. Quoted in Ricoeur (1991).
3. Quoted in Critchley (2007: 44).
4. Representation is not possible without being a noneist, as claimed by Graham Priest (2005: 76). This implies that one has to imagine the world in a certain way to make representation possible, although imagining the world in that way does not ensure that the corresponding thing subsists in the world. Undecidability arises from the frame of reference to picking up the intended reference in the world.
5. The concept of the "open text" originates from Umberto Eco's collection of essays, *The Role of the Reader: Explorations in the Semiotics of Texts* (1984), but also has reference to Roland Barthes' distinction between "readerly" (*lisible*) and "writerly" (*scriptible*) texts as elaborated in his essay, 'The Death of the Author' (1977).
6. Quoted in Das (2010: 4).

Introduction **xliii**

References

Agamben, Giorgio. 2009. *What is an Apparatus? And Other Essays*. Translated by David Kishnik and Stefan Pedatella. Stanford, CA: Stanford University Press.

Barthes, Roland. 1977. 'The Death of the Author', in *Image—Music—Text*. Edited and translated by Stephen Heath. New York: Hill and Wang.

Becker-Leckrone, Megan. 2005. *Julia Kristeva and Literary Theory (Transitions)*. Hampshire & New York: Palgrave Macmillan.

Biakliana. 2004. 'Lali', in *The Heart of the Matter: Handpicked Fictions from Meghalaya, Manipur, Mizoram, Assam and Nagaland*. New Delhi: Katha.

Chattopadhyay, Bankim Chandra. 'Banglar Itihas Samhandhe Kayakti Katha', in Brajendranath Bandyopadhyay and Sajanikanta Das (eds), *Bibidh Prabandha*. Kolkata.

Critchley, Simon. 2007. *The Ethics of Deconstruction: Derrida and Levinas*. Motilal Banarsidass Publisher.

Culler, Jonathan D. 2002. *The Pursuit of Signs: Semiotics, Literature, Deconstruction*. Revised Edition. Ithaca, NY: Cornell University Press.

Das, Anirban. 2010. *Toward a Politics of the (Im)Possible: The Body in Third World Feminisms*. London: Anthem Press.

Davis, Angela, Y. 1998. *Blues Legacy and Black Feminism*. New York: Pantheon Books.

Derrida, Jacques. 1982. 'Différance', in *Margins of Philosophy*, pp. 3–27. Trans. Alan Bass. Chicago, IL: The University of Chicago Press.

———. 2008. 'Désistance', in Peggy Kamuf and Elizabeth Rottenberg (eds), *Psyche: Inventions of the Other*, pp: 224–225. Stanford, CA: Stanford University Press.

de Saussure, Ferdinand. 1978. *Course in General Linguistics*. Translated by W. Baskin. Glasgow: Fontana.

Dilthey, Wilhelm. 1976. 'The Development of Hermeneutics', in *Selected Writings*. Edited and translated by Hans Peter Rickman. Cambridge, UK: Cambridge University Press.

Eco, Umberto. 1995. *The Role of the Reader: Explorations in the Semiotics of Texts*. Bloomington: Indiana University Press.

Foucault, M. 1977. 'Language to Infinity', in *Language, Counter-Memory, Practice: Selected Essays and Interviews*. Trans. D.F. Bouchard and S. Simon. Ithaca, NY: Cornell University Press.

Gadamer, Hans-Georg. 2004. *Truth and Method*. London: Continuum.

Heidegger, Martin. 1975. *Poetry, Language and Thought*. Harper Colophon Books.

Kant, Immanuel 1973. *Critique of Judgment, Encyclopedia of Philosophy*. Vol. 4. Macmillan.

Kaphleia. 2004. 'Chhingpuii', in *The Heart of the Matter: Handpicked Fictions from Meghalaya, Manipur, Mizoram, Assam and Nagaland*. New Delhi: Katha.

Kristeva, Julia. 2005. *Hatred and Forgiveness*. Translated by Jeanine Herman. New York: Columbia University Press.

Miller, J. Hillis. 1986. *The Ethics of Reading: Kant, de Man, Eliot, Trollope, James, and Benjamin*. New York: Columbia University Press.

Mouffe, Chantal (ed.). 1979. *Gramsci and Marxist Theory*. London: Routledge.

Nancy, Jean-Luc. 1997. *The Sense of the World*. Translated by Jeffrey S. Librett. Minneapolis, MN: University of Minnesota Press.

Peters, John Durham. 1999. *Speaking Into the Air: A History of the Idea of Communication*. Chicago, IL. The University of Chicago Press.
Priest, Graham. 2005. *Towards Non-Being: The Logic and Metaphysics of Intentionality*. Oxford, UK: Clarendon Press.
Rancière, Jacques. 2009. 'The Aesthetic Revolution', in *The Aesthetic Unconscious*. Trans. Debra Keats and James Swenson, pp: 29–30. Cambridge, UK: Polity Press.
Rapport, N. and A. Dawson. 1998. *Migrants of Identity: Perceptions of Home in a World of Movement*. Providence and Oxford, Berg Publishers.
Ricoeur, Paul. 1991. *From Text to Action: Essays in Hermeneutics, II*. Trans. Kathleen Blamey and John B. Thompson. Evanston, Illinois: Northwestern University Press.
Said, Edward W. 1982. 'Opponents, Audiences, Constituencies and Community', *Critical Inquiry*, Vol. 9, No. 1 (September).
———. 1983. *The World, the Text, and the Critic*. Harvard University Press.
———. 1989. 'Opponents, Audiences, Constituencies and Community', in Philip Rice and Patricia Waugh (eds), *Modern Literary Theory: A Reader*. London: Arnold.
Srnicek, Nick. 2011. 'Capitalism and the Non-Philosophical Subject', in Levi Bryant, Nick Srnicek and Graham Harman (eds), *The Speculative Turn: Continental Materialism and Realism*. Melbourne: Re.Press.
Taylor, Charles. 1991. *The Ethics of Authenticity*. Cambridge, MA: Harvard University Press.
Webb, Jen, Tony Schirato and Geoff Danaher. 2002. *Understanding Bourdieu*. London: SAGE Publications.
Williams, Raymond. 1961. 'Realism and the Contemporary Novel', in *The Long Revolution*. New York: Columbia University Press; London: Chatto & Windus.

SECTION I
Textualizing Social Discourse

1
Science and Literature
A Study of Rabindranath Tagore's Music

Partha S. Ghose

Great literature and great music are indestructible because they are revelatory of a 'background web of murmurings' (Miri 2010). This background web is, in general nature, of which human beings and society are products or parts. Literature and music not only reveal what lies deeply hidden in society, they can also reveal what lies deeply hidden in nature as a whole and in science, and describes one's relationships with nature in a way that science by itself cannot. There is a tension between the particular and the universal, and a continual process of reconciliation between the two is going on in all true art, literature and science through revelatory murmurings. No one has perhaps stirred these revelatory murmurings about nature and science more effectively than Rabindranath Tagore. There is something quite unique about him in this regard. From a Tagorean perspective, one could attempt to illustrate the relationship between science and literature.

Sir Michael Atiyah, one of the leading mathematicians of the day, could be cited in order to make a common distinction between science and the arts. Atiyah (2010: 8) says:

> Science deals with the hard facts of existence while the Arts exist only in the human mind; 'beauty lies in the eye of the beholder.' Science is objective, Art is subjective, the two dwell in parallel planes and never meet. This naïve distinction fails to grasp the nature of science....

Perhaps I can end by reproducing the only poetic passage I have ever written. It is entitled 'Dreams' and appears in *The Unravelers*, a book produced by the IHES.

In the broad light of day mathematicians check their equations and their proofs, leaving no stone unturned in their search for rigour. But, at night, under the full moon, they dream, they float among the stars and wonder at the miracle of the heavens. They are inspired. Without dreams there is no art, no mathematics, no life.

The same is, of course, true of great creative scientists like Darwin and Einstein. This is what Darwin writes in *The Origin of Species* (1859: 106):

There is grandeur in this view of life, with its several powers, having been originally breathed into a few forms or into one; and that, whilst this planet has gone cycling on according to the fixed law of gravity, from so simple a beginning endless forms most beautiful and most wonderful have been, and are being, evolved.

Pais A writes (1994):

A knowledge of the existence of something we cannot penetrate, our perceptions of the profoundest reason and the most radiant beauty, which only in their most primitive forms are accessible to our minds—it is this knowledge and this emotion that constitutes true religiosity; in this sense, and this alone, I am a deeply religious man.

Einstein called this 'cosmic religious feeling'. He goes on to say:

How can cosmic religious feeling be communicated from one person to another, if it can give rise to no definite notion of a God and no theology? In my view, it is the most important function of art and science to awaken this feeling and keep it alive in those who are receptive to it. (Pais A 1994: 118–120)

Now one could think of Rabindranath's song *Akash Bhora Surjo Tara* (Tagore 1931: 430) and the sense of 'wonder' (*bismay*) he expresses in it.

> The sky studded with the sun and stars, the universe throbbing with life,
>   In the midst of all these have I found my place—
>   In wonder whereof gushes forth my song.
> The blood that courses through my veins can feel the tug
> Of the sway of time and the ebb and flow that rocks the world—
>   In wonder whereof gushes forth my song.
> Stepped have I gently on the grass along the forest path,
> My mind beside itself with the startling fragrance of flowers.
>   The bounty of joy lies spread all around—
>   In wonder whereof gushes forth my song.
> I have strained my ears, opened my eyes, poured my heart out on the earth,
>   I have searched for the unknown within the known—
>   In wonder whereof gushes forth my song.
>
> (Translated by this author.)

It is clear that there is no fundamental difference between scientists like Einstein and Darwin and a poet like Rabindranath in the quality of the 'wonder' created in the mind by the universe. How wonderfully the poet delineates the essential character of pure science in the line, "I have searched for the unknown within the known"! The problem is that science is too often identified with its utilitarian aspect alone and its deeper spiritual aspect remains unnoticed, unknown.

In the preface to his only book on science, *Visvaparichaya* (An Introduction to the Universe), dedicated to the scientist Satyendranath Bose, Tagore (1937) writes about his fascination for science from his childhood—how his teacher Sitanath Datta used to thrill him with simple demonstrations like making the convection currents in a glass of water visible with the help of sawdust. The differences between layers of a continuous mass of water made obvious by the movements of the sawdust filled him with a sense of wonder that never left him. According to him, this was the first time he realized that things that we thoughtlessly take for granted as natural and simple are, in fact, not so—this set him wondering.

The next wonder came when he went with his father, Maharshi Debendranath, to the hills of Dalhousie in the Himalayas. As the sky became dark in the evenings and the stars came out in their splendour and appeared to hang low, Maharshi would point out to him the constellations and the planets, and tell him about their distances from the sun, their periods of revolution around the sun and many other properties. Rabindranath found this so fascinating that he began to write down what he heard from his father. This was his first long essay in serial form, and it was on science. When he grew older and could read English, he started reading every book on astronomy that he could lay his hands on. Sometimes mathematics made it difficult for him to understand what he was reading, but he laboured through them and tried to absorb their gist. Sir Robert Boyle's book he liked the most. Then he started reading Huxley's essays on biology. He writes in the "Preface" (Tagore 1937: 5):

> It is extremely important for those who have just started their learning process to enter right from the beginning, not perhaps into the store house of science, but into its courtyard....
>
> The universe has hidden its micro-self, reduced its macro-self or shelved it out of sight behind the curtain. It has dressed itself up and revealed itself to us in a form that man can perceive within the structure of his simple power. But man is anything but simple. *Man is the only creature that has suspected its own simple perception, opposed it and has been delighted to defeat it.* To transcend the limits of simple perception man has brought near what was distant, made the invisible visible, and has given expression to what is hard to understand. He is ever trying to probe into the unmanifest world that lies behind the manifest world in order to unravel the fundamental mysteries of the universe....
>
> It is needless to say that I am not a scientist, but from childhood my strong desire to enjoy the *rasa* of science knew no bounds.... My mind was exercised only with astronomy and life science. That cannot be called proper knowledge, in other words, it does not have the sound foundation of scholarship. But constant reading created a natural scientific temper in my mind. My lack of respect for the stupidity of blind faith has, I hope, saved me from the extravagance of cleverness to a large measure. Nevertheless, I have never felt that it hurt my poetry or imagination in any way.
>
> Today, at the end of my life, my mind is overwhelmed with the new theory of nature—scientific *māyāvāda*. What I read earlier I did not understand fully, but I kept on reading. Today also it is impossible for me to understand everything of what I read, as it is for many specialist pundits too.
>
> (Translated by this author; italics added.)

This is how Rabindranath characterizes the nature of science in *Personality* (Tagore 1917: 90–91):

> Science has a materialistic appearance, because she is engaged in breaking the prison of matter and working in the rubbish heap of the ruins. At the

invasion of a new country plunder becomes the rule of the day. But when the country is conquered, things become different, and those who robbed act as policemen to restore peace and security. Science is at the beginning of the invasion of the material world and there goes on a furious scramble for plunder. Often things look hideously materialistic, and shamelessly belie man's own nature. But the day will come when some of the great powers of nature will be at the beck and call of every individual, and at least the prime necessaries of life will be supplied to all with very little care and cost. To live will be as easy to man as to breathe, and his spirit will be free to create his own world.

All this involvement with and understanding of science helped him develop his own interpretation of the Upanishadic philosophy of nature to which he was introduced at an early age by his father. The originality of his interpretation must have become clear to the leading European scientists of his time. Einstein wrote to him in 1926 expressing a desire to meet him. Werner Heisenberg came to Calcutta in 1928 to meet Rabindranath shortly after his discovery of the 'uncertainty principle', which is at the root of the breakdown of determinism at the level of individual events in quantum mechanics. According to D. M. Bose, quoted in Sen (1985: 41):

Heisenberg appeared one day without any previous introduction in the University College of Science. Some of us ... arranged a lunch at Firpo's for Heisenberg. Rabindranath was in Calcutta at that time. Heisenberg having expressed a desire to see him, it was arranged that we were to take him the same afternoon to Jorasanko (the poet's residence). On arrival, we found that [the poet's son] had arranged a fine tea for us. We left Heisenberg to have a talk with the poet. I do not remember what was the substance of his talk, but Heisenberg was very much impressed by the poet's illuminating personality which reminded him of a prophet of the old days.

The substance of the talk was later revealed by Heisenberg himself in an interview he gave to Fritjof Capra who writes (1988):

In 1929 [1928] Heisenberg spent some time in India as the guest of the celebrated Indian poet Rabindranath Tagore, with whom he had long conversations about science and Indian philosophy. This introduction to Indian thought brought Heisenberg great comfort, he told me. He began to see that the recognition of relativity, incommensurability, interconnectedness and impermanence as fundamental aspects of physical reality, which had been so difficult for himself and his fellow physicists, was the very basis of Indian spiritual traditions. "After these conversations with Tagore," he said, "some of the ideas that had seemed so crazy suddenly made much more sense. That was a great help for me."

(Parenthesis added; the year mentioned by D. M. Bose was 1928.)

This involvement with modern science and its implications engrossed his mind when he delivered the Hibbert lectures in Oxford in 1930.[1] These lectures were later published as the *The Religion of Man* (Tagore 1931). The book begins with the following paragraphs:

Light, as the radiant energy of creation, started its ring-dance of atoms in a diminutive sky, and also the dance of the stars in the vast, lonely theatre of time and space. The planets came out of their bath of fire and basked in the sun for ages. They were the thrones of the gigantic inert, dumb and desolate, which knew not the meaning of its own blind destiny and majestically frowned upon a future when its monarchy would be menaced.

Then came a time when life was brought into the arena in the tiniest monocycle of a cell. With its gift of growth and power of adaptation it faced the ponderous enormity of things, and contradicted the unmeaningness of their bulk. It was made conscious not of the volume but of the value of existence, which it ever tried to enhance and maintain in many-branched paths of creation, overcoming the obstructive inertia of Nature by obeying Nature's law.

But the miracle of creation did not stop here in this isolated speck of life launched on a lonely voyage to the Unknown. A multitude of cells were bound together into a larger unit, not through aggregation, but through a marvelous quality of complex inter-relationship maintaining a perfect coordination of functions. This is the creative principle of unity, the divine mystery of existence, that baffles all analysis. The larger cooperative units could adequately pay for a greater freedom of self-expression, and they began to form and develop in their bodies new organs of power, new instruments of efficiency. This was the march of evolution ever unfolding the potentialities of life.

But this evolution which continues on the physical plane has its limited range. All exaggeration in that direction becomes a burden that breaks the natural rhythm of life, and those creatures that encouraged their ambitious flesh to grow in dimensions have nearly perished of their cumbrous absurdity.

Before the chapter ended Man appeared and turned the course of evolution from an indefinite march of physical aggrandizement to a freedom of a more subtle perfection. This has made possible his progress to become unlimited, and has enabled him to realize the boundless in his power....

The process of evolution, which after ages has reached man, must be realized in its unity with him; though in him it assumes a new value and proceeds to a different path. It is a continuous process that finds its meaning in Man; and we must acknowledge that the evolution which Science talks of is that of Man's universe. The leather binding and title-page are parts of the book itself; and this world that we perceive through our senses and mind and life's experiences is profoundly one with ourselves.

The divine principle of unity has ever been that of an inner inter-relationship. This is revealed in some of its earliest stages in the evolution of multicellular life on this planet. The most perfect inward expression has been attained by man in his own body. But what is most important of all is the fact that man has also attained its realization in a more subtle body outside his physical system. He misses himself when isolated; he finds his own larger and truer self in his wide human relationship. His multicellular body is born and it dies; his multi-personal humanity is immortal. In this ideal of unity he realizes the eternal in his life and the boundless in his love. This unity becomes not a mere subjective idea, but an energizing truth. Whatever name may be given to it, and whatever form it symbolizes, the consciousness of this unity is spiritual, and our effort to be true to it is our religion. It ever awaits to be revealed in our history in a more and more perfect illumination.

What is striking is the utter sincerity and conviction with which he embraced scientific truths within an all-embracing energizing philosophy. To him scientific truths were not mere abstractions and formulas or hypotheses but concrete, living and unifying truths that inspired him to write great poems and compose wonderful songs.

If one reads and listens to some of his most popular songs with this background, it would become at once clear how profoundly he was influenced by the modern scientific view of the universe at large and the evolution of life on earth, and how he assimilated and internalized these scientific truths and weaved them into the very fabric of his philosophy and his artistic creations.[2] So complete was the fusion that the songs stand by themselves as great musical creations far removed from the world of science. However, when the veil of lyrical and musical beauty is removed from them through translation into a different language, particularly English, which is so different from Bengali, their inspiration and meaning stand revealed. Deconstructed in this manner, this is how some of them appear. The first one, *Nrityeara Taale Taale* (Tagore 1931: 543) and *Akash Bhora Surjo Tara* were obviously inspired by a cosmic view of the universe and the last two, *Kakhon Baadol Chhonyaa Lege* (Tagore 1931: 453) and *Mon Je Bale Chini Chini* (Tagore 1931: 521) by evolution on earth.

Nrityeara Taale Taale (partial):

Unshackle, unshackle, unshackle all bonds, O Nataraj, with the rhythm of your dance,
Banish sleep, awaken the rhythm of free flowing melody in my mind.
Let the gentle wind of your feet
Through the ages and time, music and rhyme
Stir the ripples on the lake of Saraswati's mind
And conjure up the enchanting fragrance of the pure lotus.
Salutation to thee, Salutation to thee, Salutation to thee,
May your dance fill my mind with its unbounded riches.

....

The rebellious atoms are spellbound by your dance into beautiful forms.
The sun and the moon ring out like bells of your luminous anklets.
The benumbed world awakens in consciousness with the enlivening touch of your dance.
Through the ages and time, music and rhyme
Your eternal bliss breaks into waves of happiness and sorrow.
Salutation to thee, Salutation to thee, Salutation to thee,
May your dance fill my mind with its unbounded riches.

(Translated by this author.)

Kakhon Baadol Chhonyaa Lege:

Who knows when with the touch of rain
    Green clouds invade the bare fields.
The soft glow of the dense grass cools down the earth—
They come with the gush of life
    Bursting forth like songs suddenly sung.
They are the warriors who won the battle of life on deserts,
    My acquaintance with them dates back to the earliest of times.
No wonder my eyes are drawn so inexorably to their playfields—
    My heart rocks at the sight of their swaying.

(Translated by this author.)

Mon Je Bale Chini Chini:

> I recognize, I do, says my mind,
> The fragrance that wafts with the wind.
> Who says she is a stranger, the summer night's *chameli*.
> She has left her imprint in my blood,
> In dreams have we visited each other,
> I remember not in which remote past,
> In which pathways of the wind,
> In which forest, on which sea shore.
> The sound of her flute reaches my heart today
> In so distant an alien home,
> And the old bird in me has responded to the call—
> The *bhairavi* of tears wells up in my mind.
>
> (Translated by this author.)

Needless to say, there must be many, many more songs that can be cited. Mention may be made of only three of them that are particularly significant in the discussion on the relationship between science and literature, *Praangane Mor Shirish Shaakhaye*, (Tagore 1931: 579) *Neel Digante Oi Phuler Aagun Laaglo* (Tagore 1931: 531) and *Esho Esho Hey Trishnaaro Jal* (Tagore 1931: 431).

Finally, one could think of the poem Rabindranath wrote on the afternoon of 3 February 1941 at "*Udayan*," his house in Santiniketan, just about six months before his death.

Biraat Srishtir Kshetre Atash Baajir Khelaa: (Tagore 1983)

> This gigantic creation
> Is a fireworks display of
> Suns and stars across the skies
> On a cosmic time scale.
> I too have come from the eternal and the imperceptible
> Like a spark in a tiny remote corner of space and time.
> Today as I enter the final Act of departure,
> The flame weakens,
> The shadows reveal the illusory character of the play,
> And the costumes of grief and happiness begin to slacken.
> I see the colourful costumes
> Left over by hundreds of actors and actresses across the ages
> Outside the arena of the theatre.

I look up only to find
Beyond the backdrop of hundreds of extinguished stars
Nataraj, silent and lonely.

(Translated by this author.)

Notes

1. For a more comprehensive account of Rabindranath's involvement with science, the reader may wish to look at Chattarji (2000) and Lahiri (2009).
2. A similar view, covering a wider area of poems has been expressed by Chanda (2009).

References

Atiyah, Michael. 2010. 'The Art of Mathematics', *Notices of the American Mathematical Society*, 57 (1): p. 8.
Capra, Fritjof. 1988. *Uncommon Wisdom*. Bantam.
Chanda, Rajat. 2011. 'A synthesis of the Arts and Sciences: Rabindranath's Poetic Vision', in 'Rabindranath Tagore: A Timeless Mind', pp. 36–47. The Tagore Centre UK in collaboration with the Indian Council for Cultural Relations.
Chattarji, Dipankar. 2000. *Rabindranath O Vijñān* (Rabindranath and Science). Calcutta: Ananda Publishers Private Ltd.
Darwin, Charles. 1859. *The Origin of Species*. London: John Murray.
Lahiri, Ashish. 2009. 'Rabindranath Tagore and the Two Cultures', in Amiya Deb (ed.), *Science, Literature and Aesthetics*, PHISPC, Volume XV, Part 3, pp. 815–36. Delhi: The Centre for Civilization.
Miri 2010. 'Society and Literature: Interdisciplinary Transactions', Professor Mrinal Miri's keynote address at the National Seminar organized by the Department of English in collaboration with ICSSR-NERC, held at North-Eastern Hill University Shillong, India between 16–18 March 2010.
Pais A. 1994. *Einstein Lived Here*, Oxford: Clarendon Press, pp. 118–120.
Sen, Dibakar. 1985. 'Rabindranath and Dr. D. M. Bose', in *Dr. D. M. Bose Birth Centenary Celebration Commemoration Volume 1885–1985*. Calcutta: Bose Institute.
Tagore, Rabindranath. 1917. *Personality*. Bombay: Macmillan.
———. 1931. *The Religion of Man*. Macmillan.
Tagore 1983. 'Arogya' ('Recuperation'), in *Rabindra Rachanavali* (The Complete Works of Rabindranath), Vol. 3, Nov. 1983 edition, page 126.
———. 1937. *Visvaparichaya*, in *Rabindra Racanāvalī*, Vol. 15. Calcutta: Visva-Bharati.

2
Rabindranath Tagore's Philosophy of Art and Literature

Goutam Biswas

The relation between literature and society is explicable by crossing the boundary of ordinary semantics so far as the definitions and/or descriptions of the concepts of truth and fact are concerned. Truth in literature is not the truth in its ordinary sense. Facts in literary texts are not facts of the ordinary life and world but are in a hyphenated and deferential sociocultural landscape the meaning of which suffers from un-decidability. The philosophy of literature therefore must rest not on ordinary semantics and the hermeneutics centring it but, as Tagore would like to put it, upon the aesthetic upbringing of the 'surplus' (Tagore 1978) in the human. Aesthetic truth is therefore not the propositional kind or grounded upon a one-to-one correspondence between what is said and what is the case. Art, as Heidegger depicted, is "the setting-into-work of truth." (Tagore 1978). For Heidegger (1975: 75), this setting-into-work of truth,

> thrusts up the unfamiliar and extraordinary and at the same time thrusts down the ordinary and what we believe to be such. The truth that discloses itself in the work can never be proved or derived from what went before. What went before is refuted in its exclusive reality by the work. What art founds can therefore never be compensated and made up for by what is already present and available. Founding is an overflow, an endowing, a bestowal.

This is perhaps a modernist version of freedom of art from all types of practicability as well as responsibility, whereby induction of responsibility in the domain of art is considered tantamount to making art essentially didactic. The usual opprobrious attitude to the concept of art and literature as didactic is also an index of modernity. The question that needs to be addressed is: can a Tagorean philosophy of literature be conceived with this notion of freedom as its reference point? The question is important for two reasons: (*a*) Tagore belonged to the so-called modern era of literature and had sufficient exposure to what we today understand as modern and (*b*) he believed in the freedom of writer and artist and never vouched for any straightway correspondence between artistic truth and statements of fact in the world. So far as these two aspects of Rabindranath Tagore's preoccupation with art and literature are concerned, he may not stand too far from the modernist's ethos. However, alongside this proximity of Tagore to the equation of aesthetic freedom with art production and his agreement on the distinction between truth and fact, we should also take note of his emphasis upon the relationship between art and human nature in terms of art being essentially an expression of human 'surplus' and his placement of art and philosophy in close proximity with the cultural trajectory of public life and its tradition.

Art activity for Tagore, with all its spontaneous character, is a concerted effort too for the production of something that is not sheer repetition, and aesthetic experience must be non-reductive in nature. Unlike the evolutionists he would not prefer judging the value of an artistic creation with reference to its physical and mental skills and fundamentals, as the beauty of a grown-up tree cannot be judged with reference to its seed. The evolution that Tagore emphasized is the one that initiates human history through a manifestation of the 'surplus in man' after the completion of physical evolution. In this emphasis his purpose is to point out that evolution in case of the human and human life cannot be complete in the sense of bringing a 'closure' at the physical and outer level alone. Tagore (1994: 13) says:

> Before the chapter [of evolution] ended Man appeared and turned the course of evolution from an indefinite search of physical aggrandizement to a freedom of a more subtle perfection. This has made possible his progress to become unlimited, and has enabled him to realize the boundless in his power.

The divinity of man, according to Tagore, lies in his humanity. Humanity emerges by going beyond evolution at the physical plane and lies even beyond the development of intelligence that is required by animals as well. What is important for man, for Tagore, is the development of consciousness as it gives man his own identity in freedom and infinity. He says (1978: 152–58):

> What is unique in man is the development of consciousness, which gradually deepens and widens the realization of his immortal being, the perfect, the eternal. It inspires those creations of his that reveal the divinity in him—which is his humanity—in the varied manifestations of truth, goodness and beauty, in the freedom of activity which is not for his use but for his ultimate expression.

This is the inner being of man, which, for Tagore, cannot be slurred over in silence by any theory of evolution. Thus, the concept of evolution offered by Tagore provides a major clue to understanding what he meant by tradition. The domain of art activity and art experience centres around the inner life of the human—the life that is not simply fact-ridden. In this context, Tagore's distinction between 'true' and 'real' is to be recalled. By 'real' Tagore meant what is fact-oriented, and the 'true' is the inner being of the human, which is expressed in the realm of art. According to Tagore:

> In order to gain himself truly, he is moved towards self-creation and self-transcendence. In the image of the Ideal, man makes himself.... Transcending himself that is his local and limited self, he seeks for objects that will endure as well as satisfy the deep human hunger for the not-yet. His arts and literature are but symbols of that greater, unrealized self.... It is only in the realm of contemplative life that man recovers his lost heritage and becomes truly Man, *Chirakaler Manus*. Where there is disrespect for the dreamer, man becomes less than human. This we will see all around us all the time, everywhere, in the subordination of the true to the real.... In other words, he is more than fact, he is true. The building of man's own world, a living world of truth and beauty, is the function of art. (1978: 155)

By 'lost heritage' of man, Tagore means heritage of this *Chirakaler Manus* or the 'oblivion of the inner being of man' that is the 'surplus' expressed in the realm of art beyond the domination of the world of facts. In this sense the objects of art are of eternal value; they are not sheer facts. To speak in the terminology of K. C. Bhattacharya, they are not 'meanable' and 'spoken' but 'significant' and 'speakable'. Art objects as speakable and significant entities, in contradistinction to what is known as 'meanable' and 'object' in the empirical sense in the world of facts, add to the exteriority of human heritage and tradition by pointing to the inner being of man, that is, the truth of man. The concept of tradition thereby becomes explicable in terms of a tension between the inner and the outer. The inner enriches the outer and the outer world provides the space to the inner being of man. The tension thereafter becomes a relation of complement. Thus an art object is not measured with reference to external and factual criteria, but with reference to some unique criteria based upon this complementarity. When the outer world becomes resistant and refuses to provide the space to the inner being of man, the inner proclivity of the artist goes to construct an alternative world. Even in this latter case this alternative world becomes a major addendum to the realm of art as a witness to the agony of failure to be remembered in human history or the history of the individual. Art objects are thus autonomous entities or in Mikel Dufrenne's term, "quasi for themselves" (1973: 351); for Tagore they are the emblems of the 'surplus' in man. Tradition thus becomes non-stereotype from the standpoint of aesthetics. The preservation of tradition, from the standpoint of the artist, need not take any paternal gesture. He sustains it perhaps in a more sensible way. We may remember what K. G. Subramanyan (1987: 7) says in the context of what he understands as 'living tradition':

> Tradition is to be understood here not merely as a mechanical relay of thought and action stereotypes from generation to generation, but as one that incorporates due reassessments and innovations by each generation; reviewing continually the norms and methods of a previous generation; the innovations proving once for all the health and vigour of the tradition which otherwise would have degenerated into flaccidity and inertia.

This positive meaning of tradition is founded upon a critique of it, and the critique comes rather spontaneously from the artist. Tagore paved the way for this positive meaning of tradition by providing a critique of it as well as a critique of modernity. About Indians harping on tradition Tagore (1994: 76) observes:

> We Indians have had the sad experience in our own part of the world how timid orthodoxy, its irrational repressions and its accumulation of dead centuries, dwarfs man through its idolatry of the past. Seated rigid in the center of stagnation, it firmly ties the human spirit to the revolving wheels of habit till faintness overwhelms her. Like a sluggish stream choked by rotting

weeds, it is divided into shallow slimy pools that shroud their dumbness in a narcotic mist of stupor. This mechanical spirit of tradition is essentially materialistic; it is blindly pious but not spiritual, obsessed by phantoms of unreason that haunt feeble minds in the ghastly disguise of religion.

This over-allegiance to tradition consists of a selfish passion for upholding the glory of one's past that yields an unfortunate alienation not only from those who are outside this past but also from all time to come. It is not morally commendable either. This over-allegiance is manifest when tradition is institutionalized and comes in direct conflict with new values and modernity. S. N. Ganguly (1977: 53–54) says:

> Tradition, being a very generalized value scheme, is highly pliable and therefore when needed, it readjusts itself to the changing circumstances; that is, the superstructure is visibly modified. It is only when tradition is institutionalized that we cry a halt to such progress.... The reason why tradition is not antagonistic to modernity is ... due to the fact that tradition gives us the most pervasive and generalized value scheme in terms of which our further social progress is directed. That is why creativity is more intimately connected with tradition than any descriptive form of communication. A creator or an artist produces values and unless he has an implicit value scheme to start with, he is inevitably stymied.

One could interpret Tagore's critique of Indian tradition as a critique of its institutionalized form that dogmatically resists any creative interference and emancipatory force of human beings. With reference to Tagore's approach to tradition, Subramanyan (1987: 33) says:

> Art was to him an essential proof of man's personality, an inevitable outgrowth of his emotional surplus; it was what singled out man from the other species of creation.... He accepted tradition, but as a channel that helped the forward flow of culture, not as something that clogged it up; in his view change was in the very nature of art as it belonged to the procession of life making constant adjustment with surprises.

While the concept occupies a central position and becomes a matter of concern in Tagore's reflections on art and aesthetics we cannot perhaps dissociate it from his philosophical anthropology, which has always shown a thematic–problematic tension in viewing the human self and the world that it interacts with. In a sense, Tagore's philosophical anthropology is essentially thematic for nurturing and vindicating an axiological dimension of what he explicated as the 'surplus in man'. This for him constitutes the aesthetic and moral consciousness of man. At the same time he posited his problematic vision of the world as the wretched earth replete with violence, absurdity and evil—as a challenge to his thematic. He did not deny the evil, but rejected the idea of permanence of the evil. The "overwhelming consciousness of evil," in Ayyub's opinion (1973: 23), inspired a great poet and artist like Baudelaire to depict the world as one of ugliness, full of vices that can be catalogued in the most perfect phrases—as the world the walk over which has to be psychosomatically crippled. This is a vision of the world that Tagore would not like to give an enduring image and a permanent citadel in his world of art. From his thematic–problematic angle, it could at most be allotted a transient time and considered a passing phase of life. Even in his later poems, as well as in some of his paintings, where his consciousness of evil or dark side of the human world was provided a space, the thematic was consciously nurtured. He did not deny the possibility of aesthetic images and imageries underpinning the vision of the wretched earth; but consistently with his thematic he denied this vision as an alternative at all—an alternative to the life and world integrally related to each other through the 'surplus', ever expressive in the process of the 'being' of man as distinguished from 'having'. The idea of finality of the world of vices and ugliness is perhaps an outcome of a sense of unfulfilment, dissatisfaction and personal failure of aspirations tending towards disenchantment. Tagore experienced it, but transcended its border showing that human tradition cannot end up with this slice of so-called 'modernity'. One can trace a new meaning of 'modernity' minus this image of the world or modernity in terms of the thematic–problematic tension in his later poems, as below. Tagore writes (1986: 53):

> Serpents are hissing poisoned breath on every side.
> The gentle words of peace sound like futile mockery
> Before I leave
> I send forth my last call
> To all who are preparing, night and day,
> For the fight against the demons.

In fact, the thematic comes back in the later poems of Tagore in absolutely new attire. Here, 'the guileful one' Tagore (1986: 55) is recognized as very close to life, but the poet is still not oblivious of his thematic; on the contrary the thematic becomes one with his life and the problematic receives a new face. As Tagore (1986: 55) says:

> Truth he earns
> In his inner heart washed
> With his own light.
> Nothing can deceive him
> The last reward he carries
> to his treasure house.
> He who has easefully borne your wile
> gets from your hand
> the unwasting right to peace.

Who could be more modern in the then Indian context or even now? This particular stipulation of 'modernity' without losing faith in the thematic had the potentiality to revise the meaning of 'tradition' too, which was not sheer 'handing over' to the next generation, but a gift to be contemplated upon in all creative exercises. Indian tradition defies any kind of encapsulation. Tagore recreated Indian tradition in a certain sense. Niharranjan Ray (1961: 223) said:

> One of the measures of greatness as much in creative thought and action as of individual personality is the measure of greatness, in depth and extension, of the integration and synthesis one achieves of the tradition which one inherits with the responses to the challenge of the time and space to which one belongs. The manner and method one adopts to interpret the tradition and to recreate and revitalize it to enable to flow towards the future is also a part of the measure.

An explication of the value of harmony, primarily as an aesthetic concept in Tagore's discursive writings and artistic creations, as well one he thought to be extendable further to other spheres of human life may provide an important clue in this connection. We should remember that the union of the virtual and real, that is, the aesthetic leading towards a deprofanization of the real life situation, was a serious aspiration of Tagore as an artist. The concept of harmony, which Tagore borrowed from music and mathematics, had for him serious ramifications in the domain of art and literature. Its impact in this realm certainly demands an interweaving of the Dionysian and the Apollonian approaches to art or a synthesis of them. 'Harmony' in the ambience of Tagore's philosophy of art is a telos and being experiential conveys a mystical sense of unity; it does not consist in mere absorption of differentials or divergent components of something within one principal concept or presiding rule. If one speaks of a principal concept within the purview of Tagore's philosophy then there is no one such principal concept. However, if it is not sheer absorption, what does it consist of? Interestingly Tagore does not use any hierarchical term to explain what harmony is. For him it consists of interrelationship. The creative spirit of man, that is, his inner being, discloses itself through interrelationship with the world and other creatures including humans; this interrelationship is contemplated upon by the creative spirit again and again to come up with unique forms in literature, painting and music. Each such form is unique. Tagore (1994: 87–88) moves on to little abstraction in giving an analysis of the concept of harmony in terms of interrelationship with particular examples of music and mathematics:

> When taken out of its concrete associations and reduced to symbols, it [mathematics] reveals its grand structural majesty, the inevitableness of its own perfect concord.... Yet there is not merely a logic, but also a magic of mathematics, which works at the world of appearance, producing harmony—the cadence of interrelationship. This rhythm of harmony has been extracted from its usual concrete context, and established through the medium of sound. And thus the pure essence of expressiveness in existence is offered in music.... It is the magic of mathematics, the rhythm which is in the heart of all creation, which moves in the atom and, in its different measures, fashions gold and lead, the rose and the thorn, the sun and the planets. These are the dance steps of numbers in the arena of time and space, which weave the *Maya*, the patterns of appearance, the incessant flow of change, that ever is and is not. It is the rhythm that churns up images from the vague and makes tangible what is elusive. This is *Maya*, this is the art in creation, and art in literature, which is the magic of rhythm.

The harmony that music and mathematics speak of is the ideal for Tagore to be followed in the domain of art as one that has the potentiality to map onto the human life world. In his reflections on Herbert Spencer's view on music, Tagore once commented, "A time will come when we all will speak through music" (Tagore 1994: 87).

Though Tagore's philosophy of art and literature does not carry didacticism as its essence, it deviates from the conception of literary or aesthetic self being in an eternal flight from reality or perennially alienated from the world and reality or segregated from its own being as multiple signatures in public language games. Multiple or infinite number of self-identities can come to dialogical terms amongst themselves in art and literature without necessarily conceiving themselves as nothing but inscriptions in the institution of language.

References

Ayyub, Abu Sayeed. 1973. *Poetry and Truth*. Jadavpur University.
Dufrenne, Mikel. 1973. *The Phenomenology of Aesthetic Experience*. Translated by Edward Casey. North-Western University Press.
Ganguly, S. N. 1977. *Tradition, Modernity And Development: A Study in Contemporary Indian Society*. Madras and New Delhi: The Macmillan Company of India Limited.
Heidegger, Martin. 1975. *Poetry, Language and Thought*. New York: Harper Colophon Books.
Ray, Niharranjan. 1961. 'Rabindranath Tagore and the Indian Tradition', in *A Centenary Volume: Rabindranath Tagore*, pp. 223–32. New Delhi: Sahitya Akademi.
Subramanyan, K. G. 1987. *The Living Tradition: Perspectives on Modern Indian Art*. Calcutta: Seagull Books.
Tagore, Rabindranath. 1978. 'The Real and the True', in Sisirkumar Ghose (ed.), *Angel of Surplus*: *Some Essays and Address on Aesthetics*. Calcutta: Visva-Bharati.
———. 1986. 'Prantik'. Translated by Sisirkumar Ghose. *Rabindranath Tagore*. New Delhi: Sahitya Akademi.
———. 1994. *The Religion of Man*. Indus Publication.
———. *Sangit Chinta*. Visva-Bharati.

3

The New Comparative Literature 'To Come' as a Critique of Cosmopolitanism[1]

Sourav Kargupta

Introduction: The Text and the World

What remains between the text and the world? What shields one from the other, what tempts one into the other? Any thinking of the literary object remains haunted by this very central problematic. One might even say, in an aside, that the literary aesthetic has had a developed 'theory of ideology' long before the Marxist intervention. The ideological, if one remembers, is the screen that intervenes between the 'real' and the 'represented' in the representing subject's consciousness, being associated with 'false consciousness' in some strains of Marxist theory. If the subject is seen as produced through her practical coping with the world of objects, consuming dominant representative patterns, then ideology can be understood, following Antonio Gramsci, as "a practice producing subjects" (Mouffe 1979: 187, quoted in Das 2010: 4). A theory of ideology, therefore, resists any model that assumes a clean cut between the real and the representation, or any foregrounding of a fully present subject. In the field of the 'literary', a thinking of this 'screen', likewise, problematizes the transaction that goes on between the 'world' and the 'word' as well as replaces the self-contained closure of the 'book', with the open-endedness of the 'text'.[2] Interestingly, as one might notice, in the case of the literary, this tripartite model (of world–mediation–text), does assume a certain continuity between the 'world' and the 'text', since any proposition of a radical break between the two would makes it difficult to articulate them in the same register. In the same gesture, this continuity proposes a difference (for otherwise there would be no point in proposing a continuity within the same thing; 'sameness' would preclude that), between the text and the world, between that which is literary and that which is not (if we narrow the scope of the 'text' further to literary text only). But is there anything exclusively literary in the structure of textuality, or, to put it in other words, does literariness have any central position in the matrix of textuality? Following Jacques Derrida, one might say that literariness cannot be posited as an 'intrinsic property' of the textual, and that there is no text that is 'literary in itself' (Derrida 1992a: 44). Rather, it is like an 'intentional layer,' (Derrida: 1992a: 44) like a membrane that is touched every time one tries to touch a text. This layer is not of the text, not of the object so to say and not even of the subject (the reader), but comes 'in between' in the very act of conceiving the object (that is, in the act of reading). It is like an 'implicit consciousness' of 'rules', of the 'conventional' and of the 'institutional'—indeed of the 'social' (Derrida 1992a: 44). Derrida is careful to differentiate this 'implicit consciousness' from being a mere projection or a positive attribute of the subject in the sense of the 'caprice of each [individual] reader.' (Derrida: 1992a: 44) Therefore, contrary to common belief, there are not as many texts as there are readers! Instead, this subjectivity is 'non-empirical and linked to an intersubjectivity' (Derrida 1992a: 44). What Derrida calls transcendent reading, which is also the reading of a text 'as literature', must always face this in-between, this inscription, which is the object's being–literary. One has a very fundamental ontological vision of the 'literary' here. This literariness is posited not to annul literary value, which is shaped by national, linguistic or generic allegiance of a text, but to bring them into sharper focus. "There is no literature," Derrida would remind us, "without a suspended relation to meaning and reference" where 'suspended' means not only suspense but 'dependence' as well (Derrida 1992a: 48). Therefore, a text might exist in several registers, in the generic, in the national, in the linguistic, each of which must be kept in mind while peeling the scales of it, but still, a thought of the basic literariness might be activated at any moment to critically question the primacy of all the other registers. One has this thought, of a basic literariness, disrupting any claim of essence or rootedness, working as the general premise in the ensuing discussion.

It has already been indicated how the production of the subject can be thought of in relation to that of the text; at a basic level both remain subjected to a certain sense of law. Law as such, that confers subjectivity as well as literary value to a text. But what of the one who comes from the other side of the divide, the 'guest' who comes and demands hospitality or the text-as-guest which does not conform to the existing rationality of reading, but which still claims a 'just' reading? The perusal of the figure of this 'other text', or other as text, remains crucial if we keep in mind the Spivakian note that "without the reading of the world as a book, there is no prediction, no planning, no taxes, no laws, no welfare, no war" (Spivak 1987: 95). But along with this critical caution, that even if an individual can be read as a text, the opposite is not possible. Having made this detour through the text and the world, and the screen of the 'literary' in-between, I can now go into the main discussion.

Literature and Cosmopolitan Law

According to Derrida (2000: 75):

> *Pas d'hospitalité*: no hospitality, step of hospitality. We are going. We are moving around: from transgression to transgression but also from digression to digression. What does that mean, this *step too many*, and the transgression, if, for the invited guest as much as for the visitor, the crossing of threshold always remains a transgressing step? And if it even has to remain so? And what is meant by this *step to one side*, digression? Where do these strange processes of digression lead?.... It is as though we were going from one difficulty to another.... It is as though hospitality were the impossible: as though the law of hospitality defined this very impossibility.

Chiefly in his later works, Jacques Derrida has often underlined how it is imperative to think of hospitality in terms of one single step, underlining the immense responsibility contained in the moment of decision. But what is it to cross a border, to the other, other's territory? How to pose a critique of the existing international laws of conditional hospitality determined by its Kantian legacy, which presupposes finite closures, in the line of a deconstructive critique that poses the aporia not as a closure but as an impasse which one 'must' cross, but responsibly, always failing in economising between the self and the other? In his late essay on 'perpetual peace' Immanuel Kant posited the right of hospitality both as natural and juridical.[3] The Kantian proposal radically called for an ethics that would go beyond 'philanthropy' (see note 4) and situate hospitality as a 'right' (*Recht*) common to all. But the Kantian notion of 'universal hospitality' (see note 4) is also limited, where only a right of 'visitation' (*Besuchsrecht*) (see note 4) is secured, and not of permanent residence (*Gastrecht*).[4] It is this very restriction, articulated in the last of the three "definitive articles for perpetual peace among states" (quoted in Benhabib 2004: 26), which has come under severe critical review in the recent past. For Seyla Benhabib, what separates the right of visitation from the right of residence is nothing less than an 'unbridgeable gap' (Benhabib 2004: 38). Benhabib shares this point with Derrida. To both, the Kantian legacy in its restrictiveness pervades most of the legal articulations of hospitality prevalent in modern times. Derrida tells us that "it is this limitation on the right of residence" that still "remains for us debatable" (Derrida 2005: 22). In the "Kantian sense," he goes on to remark, "hospitality, whether public or private is dependent on and controlled by the law and the state police" (Derrida 2005: 22). To put it schematically, in this context, the postmodern shift would lie in moving from the expression 'ethic of hospitality' to 'ethics is hospitality', pointing to the limits of the Kantian articulation of the cosmopolitan law. Ethics as hospitality would not wait for the other to visit as other, outside and alien; rather, it is the recognition of the irreducible and intimate presence of the other in self, that makes the self un-homely, with hospitality as a way of being–there. But, how to understand this ethical shift in the context of the tension between the universal and the particular in the field of the literary? How to retain the irreducible specificity of a (culturally located) event without losing the responsibility towards the other, as well as to a universality that ensures the possibility of this very passage, this very translation? In an address on human rights Derrida mentioned that the problematic of 'universal human rights' is one of translation.[5] How to form a viable critique of a conditional hospitality, which always economizes between 'yes' and 'no' in answering the visitor's call, through Derrida's reading of translation as the double bind between translatability and untranslatability of a particular text?

Related to this is my other thematic, crossing of borders, especially in literature, or, in other words, Comparative Literature.[6] My question here would be simply, what is the location of Comparative Literature? What is its place with respect to the social sciences as well as single literature disciplines? In the universities, literature disciplines are always marked by national or linguistic markers, 'single literatures' in shorthand, and a sense of naturalness informs this situation. Sisir Kumar Das, a sympathizer of the discipline of Comparative Literature and an untiring compiler of the voluminous history of Indian literature had to admit rather timidly that "comparative literature differs from single literatures not in method, but in matter, attitude and perspective," and then added, "its aim is the literature of the whole world. Its strength and its weakness lie in its cosmopolitanism" (Dev and Das 1989: 97). This is rather an encyclopaedic vision of Comparative Literature in the model of 'world literature.' One can already hear the usual suspicious quips: literature of the world! Can one, even a group of scholars grasp it all? Ever? Is it possible to read texts embedded in different languages and cultures with the same method, and ultimately, can one compare two dissimilar objects, even if both are literary?[7] Then again, in locating Comparative Literature at the site of the world instead of the national, one needs to perform the difficult task of crossing borders. Borders that keep closures. "Is it not a retrograde step?" asks Das in the same essay, "to propose an Indian Literature as far as the [basic] framework of comparative literature is concerned?" But he only goes on to justify the move to an Indian literature on the ground of 'shared historical fact' of an Indianness (Dev and Das 1989: 97). But who shares? Not in the sense of sharing any 'thing', or any fact with a claim to 'presence', but 'shares as such', to form a collectivity? In what axis must one imagine a collectivity? And why must the crossing of borders stop at any point, why must imagination stutter when it reaches the fold of the nation, history must end at the state form, even if, one can very well imagine the next border is always only one step away.

This study is broadly divided into two movements. The opening delineates the building blocks of the central argument. Here, in dealing with the questions already mentioned, this chapter tries to make at least two moves crucial to its central argument. One, it proposes to read the problematic of cosmopolitanism, that is, territorial border crossing in alignment with the thinking of a literature as such upstream from national/single literatures, or, border crossing in literature. Without reducing one to the other, the suggestion is to read the world as text, and texts as containing 'worlds' in them, with cultural/genre-specific/national borders to be crossed. This move questions the essentialist model of belonging, of a text, or an event, in one genus: nation, language or national literature. It calls for a specific kind of reading, reading without constraint, which I try to outline following the Derridean approach to translation and law. The second move is to propose that this opening to the other, in the spirit of deconstruction, is viable only in the way of a certain notion of literature. This point refers back to the first move, which already presupposes a crossing over between two seemingly disparate registers: textual and real. Surely, this crossing over, which Derrida would call an act producing 'intense pleasure,' can be approached without literature. "But literature is also, 'in life', in its way, in 'real life'", in a way that it might not be possible to distinguish 'calmly' between the two (Derrida 1992a: 56). Here one brings in the notion of the literature as such, or the universal in literature, and tries to think the aporia of undecidability one faces when this universal tries to reconcile itself with a particular, a text from the periphery for instance. How does one disrupt the universal reason for reading and give the 'other text' a different reading, a culturally specific reading that is its due? On the other hand, the re-presentation in circulation of the global is in terms of graphs, maps and international borders, and thus ironically, already available as a text in its finitude, a finitude which is also one of the basic imperatives for Kant in thinking cosmopolitan law ("earth's surface is not infinite but *limited* by its own configuration," (Kant 1991: 137; italics added). This study poses, after Gayatri Chakravorty Spivak, a thinking of the planet beyond plotting, collectivity beyond closure, the programme of a 'new Comparative Literature to come'. If entry–exit in a closed genus is controlled with a logic of calculation, collectivity works with the incalculable. One could try to flesh out the Spivakian programme in the latter half of this chapter where comes the question of the singular event in thinking of a literature without condition, which would open itself up to the other, other texts, bodies, words.

Building Blocks of an Argument

In approaching the theoretical building blocks of a notion of the literature as such one could follow two related registers in which Derrida talks about the philosophy of translation, aligning them side by side with two articulations of law in the Derridean oeuvre. Derrida talks about translation in several of his texts.[8] He posits translation as the movement that works in between translatability and untranslatability. To follow this argument, I propose only this, that it might be worthwhile to follow the consistent in Derrida, recurring pulse of the arguments stretched over these texts, holding forth to its revealing moment, when the pulse is heard, felt, and passing over the interval when it threatens never to appear again. These bits/bites of stability would nevertheless be grouped under various broad movements.

Translation, Law and 'Literature as Such'

In 'Des Tours de Babel', Derrida shows how translation works in between two extreme poles, the radical untranslatability of a text and the full translatability of it, between yes and no. He explains this with the fabulous tale of the Tower of Babel (Gen. 11:1–9).

The sons of Shem, in desiring to build the tower of Babel, did not only aim at reaching the heavens, but also tried to force one single tongue/lip[9] on all men, a violent endeavour in itself. The project was not to invent a universal language to which all would have equal access (colonial promise, we might recognize), but to impose a language on everybody by the virtue of being 'the master with most force' (Derrida 1982: 101; colonialism in action). When God deconstructs the tower (it 'is' deconstruction, one is told), and imposes his own name on the world, the act imposes a double bind in effect. God's name must be (insufficiently) translated to make it understood, to proclaim the law. The proper noun belongs to language, it is 'in language', but it is also beyond it. To be beyond, it must (re)claim its authority through translation. It craves this journey, to continue. It is a plea/command, the translator answers this call. This, if one follows Derrida, is also the basic structure of law as such. One is reminded of his reading of Franzz Kafka's short story *Before the Law*, where the logic of law is construed as a series of concentric layers, each having an 'opening' that stands for the promise part of the law. But, these doors are guarded closely by fearsome sentries personifying the forbiddance that law issues in the same gesture to the one who is 'before the law.' Translation operates with this general structure as well, it becomes "the law, duty and debt, but the debt one can no longer discharge" (Derrida 2007: 199).

God ordains plurality of language, his proper name promises singularity. Translation between languages is possible 'only because' there is one promised language. The translator works before that horizon of fully just translation 'to come', or a language which would annul the need for translation altogether. But what happens if we substitute language with literature in this argument, and rewrite a famous Derridean formula: "We only ever write/read one literature" to "We never write/read only one literature."

This is an anticipation, of a literature that is one, the 'one' which makes 'many' possible. But, in the same breath it is also about the (im)possibility of translation between two literatures, texts; indeed, impossibility of the very relevance of the literary as such. Following this argument, we might investigate the status of a discipline that must rely heavily on studying literatures in translation. It has been proposed against the discipline of Comparative Literature that studying literatures in translation cannot claim to be a serious reading practice, that this method ignores the nuances of the original text that get irrecoverably lost in translation. But what if Comparative Literature does not simply assume a fluid transaction between literatures; rather, it questions the very claim of one literature dwelling exclusively in one language. Therefore, it is never one-to-one comparison between two 'separate' literatures, for literatures cannot claim to dwell in closures constituted by single languages. Instead the literature–language relation is constituted by a fundamental disjunction, they are always already in translation. Comparative Literature only underlines this fundamental homelessness of specific literatures before the literary horizon (which I have called 'literature as such'), a law that also validates the taking place of these specific literatures. It is a way of positing the universal and the particular in literature.

One needs to clarify here the way the two terms, 'comparison' and 'translation' have been used in this study. They are not used interchangeably, and yet as two stages of the same movement. As explained below, any comparison between two different things assumes a certain violence. A violence that makes both come to a level ground where the operation of comparison can take place. This involves a *defférance* a (forced) transformation, which is another name for translation. The translated carries the mark of this violence, of comparison. Thus, the two terms are posited as stages that are not to be understood in the way of any temporal succession but as two movements of the same structure.

Confronting the Particular

But still, how to read, how to go about it? How to read a text, this text that is on my desk, printed on this paper, this paper that one touches, here at this very moment? A text that demands that its reading be an event, an event of reading, also a singular reading, for it is still one, closed upon itself. A text that might come from the side of the other and call for its right, a text from the periphery that might defy universal laws of reading. It is here that one refers to the other register in the Derridean approach to translation. If 'Des Tours de Babel' (2007) posited translation as a responsibility placed between a yes and a no, translatability and the exact opposite of it, then in "What is a "Relevant" Translation?" (2001b) Derrida confronts the possibility of translation at work, a decision that economizes between the two poles. It is the confrontation of this economical in translation and its ruin that he follows in reading William Shakespeare's comedy *The Merchant of Venice* (1596–98). Derrida points to the transaction that is at the very heart of the play and asks whether it is possible to imagine the exchange of two dissimilar objects as a kind of translation? This knotty problem is raised in the way of giving a seemingly obvious example: "Everything in the play can be retranslated into the code of translation and as a problem of translation.... as, for example, between a pound of flesh and a sum of money" (Derrida 2001b: 183). But immediately we are warned that it is nothing short of "an incalculable equivalence" (Derrida 2001b: 184), between a materiality (of the flesh) and a fluid sign (money) that is, and that this incalculability has a parallel in the Jew's conversion to Christianity, which was "forced" (Derrida 2001b: 184). But the first instance (exchange between flesh and money), forced is it not as well,[10] and a moment of violence? But how to decide what is just (lawful) faced with such an incalculability?

In 'Force of Law' (Derrida 1992b), where one tries to see the parallel of this second register in talking about translation, Derrida (in our reading) likewise moves from law as such, to focus more on one of its articulations, law as legality (a universal in itself), and also on the singularity of individual instances. "How are we to reconcile the act of justice that must always concern singularity ... with rule, norm, value or the imperative of justice which necessarily have a general form, even if this generality prescribes a singular application in each case?" (Derrida 1992b: 17). Here he uses a term borrowed (and modified) from Immanuel Levinas: equity, which is different from equality. Equality means "calculated proportion, equitable distribution of distributive justice," whereas 'equity' on the contrary would signify, "absolute dissymmetry" (Derrida 1992b: 22). It is this equity as different from any (forced) equality that a new Comparative Literature must keep as its watchword. Reading, within this argument that I propose, would then be seen as a responsible decision, a way in approaching 'justice'. This reading would always try to give room to anxiety, to broken, unassailable meanings that might spring from a text as other. Justice in this sense, as a decision to give in to the rhythm of infinite reading, or 'justice as such' is incalculable, non-deconstructible. But justice approached through law would be within calculation. There, in fact, it would demand more calculation than anything, infinite calculation. What is resisted here is not reading/translation as an act, but the economy that satisfies itself in the most relevant transference of meaning, in the most eligible guest. What is critiqued is this impatience. Of force. In waiting, in staying with open-ended calculation, this evasion of anxiety and suspense. "This moment of suspense, this period of *epoché*, without which, in fact, deconstruction is not possible, is always full of anxiety, but who will claim to be just by economizing on anxiety?" (Derrida 1992b: 20). But how to perform this truly differential reading in the way to a new Comparative Literature, reading here–now, reading the here–now? How to approach a text from the margins of cosmopolitanism, how to read the margin?

Approaching the "New Comparative Literature 'To Come'"

Sometimes, texts situated in the global south, Spivak reminds one, would need the decision on the readers' part of a reading different from the universal reason of reading (Spivak 2003). For, Spivak also warns, denying them this due, of a different reading, this rupture from the universal reason of reading, might mean a failure in learning to learn from below, that the discipline (of Comparative Literature) cannot do without. The universal is therefore constituted through the right of difference accorded to the particular as other. This is a way out of the commonsensical notions of democracy and the rhetoric of uncritical, contractual equality, equality that, a Marx would say, goes well with property and Bentham in the space of the market (see Marx 1982: 280), as well as a critique of restricted cosmopolitanism.

Collectivity

Against restricted cosmopolitanism, Spivak's motto is 'collectivity'(Spivak 2003), which can disrupt those borders that close and open 'on condition', both in time and space. One proposes to read the Spivakian collectivity in its Derridean purport. In this reading, one would pass over the irreducible differences between the two positions and read one signature into the other, Spivak and Derrida. The way again would be a bias towards the consistent, the rhythm of similarity, the pulse. One hopes to come up with something that is within the law of both the signatures and also outside of each.

In "Law of the Genre", Derrida (1992a: 221–52) proposes that any genus is bound by a differential "re-mark" (not "mark" which is always already re-markable). This (re-)mark, is not like a tag, although that might have been easier to understand, rather it is a constitutive lack. The re-mark gives many particulars a similarity, as well as separates them as a whole from an outside. Each of the particulars might belong to the remarkable genus, but the re-mark itself, belongs nowhere. Derrida's example is of the literary genre. Where exactly is that distinguishing feature that lets one identify a novel as one? Can it ever be separated from the body of the text as novel? And yet, that sign does not belong to the text or to the novel as genre, it is a groundless, un-marked gap. Like the blink of an eye, which makes seeing possible, through its surreptitious insertion in (and) between seeing, opening. Which opens at the close. Theoretically (and not temporally) the (re-)mark can be said to have a priority. It is 'before' the law of genre in the sense of standing outside, and prior to it (Derrida 1992a: 221–52).[11] Collectivity can, one might conjecture, be thought of in this way. The (re-)mark connects one to a community of 'others', unexpected ties are formed, unknown faces may hover around, haunting and being haunted, but the crux of the matter would lie in that very uncertainty. Like the re-mark, no text (can the two be separated?) can dwell in a genus, in the sense of dwelling in it with a claim of propriety. It is upstream from a 'nation' with a set calculus of inclusion and exclusion, as well as from any exclusive archive as national literature. It is where no precondition or control would work. It is, in Derrida's formulation, more an interdict than a choice. Clearly this is beyond the economy of conditional cosmopolitanism and hospitality. It is in this rhythm that Spivak (2003: 26) writes, "If we are serious about ... Comparative Literature, we have to ask the question of the formation of collectivities without necessarily prefabricated contents." Spivak's new Comparative Literature is in line with Derrida's 'new international' (Derrida 1994b) even if not a mirror image of it. It bases its claim on a horizon of futurity, a literature (as such) to come and opens itself up to an aporia which is strictly different from 'open' or 'closed' border. An aporia is a non-passage, but it is still permeable, one must pass through it.[12] Against this permeability with all its stake on responsibility that a deconstructive move tries to retrieve with relentless rigour, the 'global' poses 'restricted permeability' (Spivak 2003: 16). "Borders are easily crossed" from metropolitan centres, but the reverse flow is not as smooth, roadblocks are put in the form of 'bureaucracy' or 'police' (Spivak 2003: 16). If this structure is based on a conditional 'yes', a yes tempered by 'no', then the deconstructive move is but a deferral of the yes, only to flesh it out bit by bit from the trivialities of the given, of the mundane here–now, but still, it is condemned to work precisely in the site of the here–now. Therefore, contrary to the popular image, deconstruction works with the affirmative, it is a poetics of affirmation through and through. If one is permitted to cite a parallel from literary theory, it reminds one of the Lukácsian definition of the novelistic hero, who searches for authentic values in a setting that is demonic, where this search must force him to go through the demonic as well, without end.[13] Towards that which Derrida would call the 'infinite desire', visible at the horizon but only as 'miraculous and spectral' (Derrida 1998: 22). For which one must reach only by way of the tiniest of displacements, gathering relentlessly the infinitely smallest of meanings. It is like a habit, this ever so imperceptible but persistent displacement, which is another name for the possession of a language, the (native) language we think we dwell in. Like breathing we forget it, but the moment we try to remember, to (re)claim, we end up creating a distance, a remoteness without which both possession and dispossession cannot be understood. One must, theoretically speaking, go by the way of creating this 'place of fantasy' which stays always already at an 'ungraspable distance' (Derrida 1998: 42). This distance is beyond cartographic imagination through which most of the global is governed, as well as upstream from that blueprint of an encyclopaedic world literature that just adds up single literatures to make a monstrous inventory.

Against Cartographic Closures: The "Planet"

It is palpably this fantastic distance that Spivak conjures in thinking 'planetarity' (as against the 'global'): "It is as an alternative to such timid and placatory gestures, as well to the arrogance of the cartographic reading of world literature in translation as the task of Comparative Literature, that I propose the planet" (Spivak 2003: 73). Planet beyond graphs and maps.[14]

Spivak recounts her experience of flying from the direction of Baghdad, making a "clandestine entry into 'Europe'" (Spivak 2003: 93). Looking down through the window she wondered about that immense border which separates, or the invisibility of it. The distance blurs the cartographic imagination, but the monitor on-board still shows the borders plotted on a map. "Planetarity cannot deny globalization," (Spivak: 2003: 93). but it can promise a 'writing over'. In a very similar situation, in the still early years of civil aviation, another poet felt comparable emotions on his way to Baghdad; such is the coincidence. He recounts in his travelogue, how the immense height severs the connection of the land below one's senses reduced to sight only (Tagore 1991a). "Within the closures of finite time and space, creation manifests itself in different forms," Rabindranath Tagore writes in 1932, only years before the Second World War, "[but] as these borders get blurred, creation slides into impending doom." When man comes out flying in his machine, says the poet, to "drop lethal weapons" on the ones below, "then he might become violent without remorse" since he flies above "the logic of calculation"[15] (Tagore 1991a: 629)[16] (translated by the author).

The coming of the planet in its disruptive, one proposes, trembles between these two competing gazes, one opens to promise, the other to violence. One is the blink for the other. The work of the new Comparative Literature, like deconstruction, would "find itself between these two poles" (Derrida: 1992b: 22), confronting both desire and responsibility.

The Coming of the Loser

"Only events without arrivals. From these sole 'arrivals', and from these arrivals alone, desire springs forth." (Derrida: 1998: 61).[17]
The desire to cross borders, guarded by so many jealous guards, blocked by "so many tax levied." (Derrida: 1992a: 36) But still the 'subject' of this essay, and why not of Comparative Literature in the spirit of deconstruction, a "suspended subject of pure performance" (Derrida 1992a: 36) must hear the call of her 'contemporaries', philosophers and friends of the future, and march ahead to that (im)possible horizon; as Derrida (1998: 57) says:

> Compatriots of every country, translator-poets, rebel against patriotism! Do you hear me! Each time I write a word, a word that I love and love to write; in the time of this word, at the instant of a single syllable, the song of this new International awakens in me. I never resist it, I am in the street at its call, even if, apparently, I have been working silently since dawn at my table.

These are not exactly dispassionate words. But precisely what an argument which keeps close to the 'literary' would aim at. As Spivak would tell us, knowledge in the humanities retains the "vague", the "unverifiable", the "iterable" (Spivak 2003: 101). This opening to the radically different vis-à-vis the subject of social sciences is imperative for humanities, since it must ever remain "responsible, responsive, answerable" (Spivak 2003: 102). In the spirit of this literary, then, I graft two fragments into each other, one from Spivak, the other from Derrida: "If we want to compete with the hard 'science'(s) and the social sciences at their hardest as 'human science,' we have already lost, as one loses institutional competition. In the arena of the humanities as the uncoercive rearrangement of desire, he who wins loses" (Spivak 2003: 101). "It therefore begins before beginning. That is the incalculable origin of a rhythm. Everything is at stake, but may the loser win" (Derrida 1998: 48). The economy that governs cosmopolitanism, controls at check posts, would not let this figure of the "loser" in, entry would be forbidden to the one who does not conform to the logic of verifiability. But one untranslatable word, one text from the periphery, one obstinate little block would always resist reduction, this opening to economics. But it is also that which makes that very opening possible, at least the pretence of it, the check posts are made for this figure, translation justifies itself in the untranslatable. Precisely there lurks the double bind. It saves and it kills. It is a 'gift'. It would question the neatness of borders, fullness of dwelling, startle the economy of cosmopolitanism, smooth circulation of the optimism of it.

Conclusion: Working Under a Banner

All along this chapter I have tried to argue under the shorthand of "Comparative Literature" even if palpably, in several moments of the argument, it has come to seem interchangeable with concepts like "(new) humanities" and "literature as such". It would be useful to end with a statement of purpose which would both separate Comparative Literature from other related concept–metaphors as well as indicate their shared space. I would like to do that by introducing yet another analogous term, in the way of putting this space in sharper focus. This shared space, which is also a space of urgent action, of decision, is the space of the university, both in its real institutional embodiment and as a concept. To refer back to the cosmopolitan law, the most prominent legal manifestation of it in the present world has been in the site of human rights. The international court gets its validity almost solely based on this single assumption, that the basic humanness has a universal claim to protection and justice beyond all cultural differences. If we remember, the Kantian ploy was to present a structure of cosmopolitanism with two basic nodal points. An unattainable ideal horizon in perpetual peace and a very basic first step to it, minimum possible measure in the form of conditional hospitality. That minimum step seems to have congealed at present in the form of universal human rights. Thus the importance of thinking, what is proper to 'man'. The new horizon of cosmopolitanism must be worked out from this new measure. According to Derrida (2001a: 25), "the concept of man, of what is proper to man, of human rights, of crimes against the humanity of man, organizes as we know such a *mondialisation* or worldwide-ization." This key concept of the human, Derrida seems to say, is to be questioned, indeed must be made subject to indefinite questioning from within the university without condition,[18] and "above all in the humanities" (Derrida 2001a: 25). I have, in the course of my argument, already extended this logic to the space of the literary, or have read Spivak as making this logical move. The thinking of the new Comparative Literature thus, is not necessarily upstream from Derrida's use of the term "new humanities", just as the new humanities is not a departure from or perfection on the concept–metaphor 'university'. I am trying to get to, again, the measure of a concept, the basic unit of it. The new Comparative Literature would be that single step, of the university without condition, and not prior to it in any way. As a signature, it is in the university and also beyond it in representing a proper name.

But Comparative Literature has another crucial significance, coming from its difficult history as a discipline in the realpolitik of the university structure, especially in India. Its very existence has been a point of unease, as its validity as a discipline has been questioned both internally and externally over the years.[19] In many ways it has been something like a 'rogue discipline', a discipline without the necessary closure, that is, a discipline without a disciplinary boundary as such. Therefore when one chooses to use this name consciously, makes a point of labouring under this dissident signature, one takes part in a politics. It is the move of sharing a banner, of choosing to work for a radical mark. It is in this same spirit that a Gustave Flaubert (1980: 234) declares, "*Madame Bovary, c'est moi*" ("Madame Bovary is myself"), or a Rabindranath Tagore undersigns the "Strīr Patra" (Wife's letter, 1914; see Tagore 1991b). Normally a signature comes at the end of a work, representing a proper name, claiming authority and responsibility for the work. But where does the signature 'take place' in the case of this short story, taking responsibility for the monologue of the woman/wife (*strī*)? Where does that ultimate circumference lie? In the signature of the woman, '*mrināl*' (proper name), or in the authorial signature external to it, 'Rabindranath Tagore'? The work cannot totally subsume the signature, neither can it deny. It is before the signature's law and also outside of it. The work takes part in the signature, by re-forging it, re-staging it, declaring it. The formation of the unconditional collectivity, the way it has been explicated in this chapter following the cue from Spivak, can only be understood in terms of this idea of the 'signature'. For the signature of choice does not claim any necessary allegiance, it is open. In a recent article published in the *New York Times* titled "We Are All Egyptians", the special correspondent from Cairo reports his experience with the protesting crowd:

> The lion-hearted Egyptians I met on Tahrir Square are risking their lives to stand up for democracy and liberty, and they deserve our strongest support—and, frankly, they should inspire us as well. A quick lesson in colloquial Egyptian Arabic: *Innaharda, ehna kullina Misryeen*! Today, we are all Egyptians!

(Krist of 2011)

Notwithstanding the flashy use of words like democracy and liberty we might note the main thrust of the report in the motto, "*Innaharda, ehna kullina Misryeen*" (Today, we are all Egyptians). It reminds one of the famous Bengali slogan of the 1970s: "*amār nām tomār nām vietnām*" (my name, your name, Vietnam). In both cases, nobody is really claiming any inheritance related to property, any inalienable right to a name or to a territory, but forming a collectivity, which takes shape when one decides to stay with a work, a work that opens up a politics of the incalculable. It is a deeply political choice, this 'being possessed' by the mark of dispossession, this nearness to the signal of distance and dissidence, this giving in to the law of an unlawful signature. The new Comparative Literature is one such signature, to come.

Notes

1. A shorter version of this chapter was presented at the Cultural Studies Workshop 2011, which took place in January 2011 in Jaipur, organized by the Centre for Studies in Social Sciences, Calcutta. I thank Anirban Das for his suggestions and criticisms at the time of writing the chapter (that came before as well), and also Saumyabrata Choudhury for

his incisive comments made on the paper presented at the Cultural Studies Workshop. The segment on the theme of translation, which I merely touch upon here, is elaborated in Kargupta (2011).
2. See Spivak (1994: xii) for an account of the 'text' in its interrelation with the 'book'.
3. See Benhabib (2004: 25–31). Also see Kant (2006).
4. See Benhabib (2004: 25–31) and Kant (2006).
5. Original occasion: Jacques Derrida and Alan Montefiore in conversation, Oxford Amnesty lectures, 1992. Video Uploaded by 'flame0430', on 21 May 2008. Duration: 10:17 Min.
6. In writing 'Comparative Literature', I have used capital letters throughout this chapter, following the rule generally used in the *Jadavpur Journal of Comparative Literature*, as well as that used by Spivak in Spivak (2003). But I have left the phrase appearing within quotations from other texts unchanged.
7. "Even if." The question turns back on itself, it grafts certain hesitation, ambiguity into the utterance, something or someone speaks in between, surreptitiously inserting an element of disruption (see Fink 1995: 38–41). The thought of the 'if' is also closely related to Jacques Derrida's formulation of the new humanities (see Derrida 2001a: 31–57).
8. There is a fragment of the Derridean corpus: 'Des Tours de Babel' (Derrida 1985/2007) where Derrida 'reads' (he is himself the model diligent reader) Walter Benjamin's much read 1923 introduction to a Baudelaire translation (1973) in 'What Is a "Relevant" Translation?' (Derrida 2001b) and parts of *Monolingualism of the Other; or, The Prosthesis of Origin* (Derrida 1998) along with cues from some other texts written by Derrida and others (Derrida cannot be the only signatory of the Derridean corpus).
9. In Hebrew the word for tongue is 'lip' (Derrida 2007: 193).
10. See Marx (1982: 344) in the chapter on 'The Production of Absolute Surplus Value': "There is here therefore an antinomy, of right against right, both equally bearing the seal of the law of exchange. Between equal rights, force decides."
11. Here I am deviating from what would be a more obvious interpretation of the (re-)mark, if there can be one.
12. Gayatri Chakravorty Spivak translates aporia as *apāriyā* in Bengali and puts it impeccably in 'Abinirmān Anubād': "The experience of thought is [nothing but a] translation without [reaching] another side. Therefore [aporia/] *apāriyā*" (Spivak 2007: 54; translated by this author).
13. I am drastically simplifying both Derrida and Lukács here. See Lukács (1971).
14. Evidently Spivak here is up against Franco Moretti's project as delineated in his article 'Graphs, Maps, Trees: Abstract Models for Literary History—1' (2003). See also Moretti (2000), along with the ensuing debate in the *New Left Review*.
15. '*hisāber anka*', see Thakur (1991a).
16. Sibaji Bandyopadhyay has discussed this moment in several of his texts and unpublished lectures. See for example Bandyopadhyay (2002). I also remember his lectures on post-structuralism, delivered as part of the Post-Graduate programme of Department of Comparative Literature at Jadavpur University, during the 2001–03 session.
17. Compare this with the quote from the much-earlier *Of Grammatology* (Derrida 1994: 217): "All language in general *springs forth when passionate desire exceeds physical need*, when imagination is awakened, which awakens pity and gives movement to the supplementary chain." (Italics added.)
18. About the university without condition, Peggy Kamuf (2004) writes, "I am referring to 'The University Without Condition', which is above all a profession of faith, declared

as such, *in* the university, and within the university in the Humanities as space for a writing and thus for events of signature." (Italics in original.)
19. There is a vast literature that exists on the disciplinary problematic. For an introduction, see Bernheimer (1994), Melas (2006) and Saussy (2006).

References

Bandyopadhyay, Sibaji. 2002. *Bāmlā Upanyase 'Orā'* (The 'They' in Bengali Novels). Kolkata: Papyrus.
Benhabib, Seyla. 2004. *The Rights of Others: Aliens, Residents and Citizens*. Cambridge, UK: Cambridge University Press.
Benjamin, Walter. 1973. 'The Task of the Translator' in *Illuminations*, 69–82. London: Collins (Fontana).
Bernheimer, Charles. 1994. *Comparative Literature in the Age of Multiculturalism*. Baltimore and London: The Johns Hopkins University Press.
Das, Anirban. 2010. *Toward a Politics of the (Im)Possible: The Body in Third World Feminisms*. London: Anthem Press.
Dev, Amiya and Das, Sisir Kumar (eds). 1989. *Comparative Literature: Theory and Practice*. Shimla: Indian Institute of Advanced Study in association with Allied Publishers.
Derrida, Jacques. 1982. *The Ear of the Other: Otobiography, Transference, Translation*. New York: Schocken Books.
———. 1985/2007. 'Des tours de Babel' in *Psyche: Inventions of the Other*, Volume I. Stanford: Stanford University Press.
———. 1992a. *Acts of Literature*. Ed. Derek Attridge. London: Routledge.
———. 1992b. 'Force of Law', in Drucilla Cornell, Michel Rosenfeld, David Gray Carlson (eds), *Deconstruction and the Possibility of Justice*), pp. 3–67. London: Routledge.
———. 1994. *Of Grammatology*. Trans. Gayatri Chakravorty Spivak. Delhi: Motilal Banarsidass.
———. 1998. *Monolingualism of the Other; or, The Prosthesis of Origin*. Stanford, CA: Stanford University Press.
———. 2001a. 'The Future of the Profession or the University without Condition (Thanks to the "Humanities," What Could Take Place Tomorrow)', in Tom Cohen (ed.), *Jacques Derrida and the Humanities: A Critical Reader*, pp. 24–57. New York: Cambridge University Press.
———. 2001b. 'What Is a "Relevant" Translation?' *Critical Inquiry*, 27 (2, Winter): 174–200.
———. 2000. *Of Hospitality*. California: Stanford University Press.
———. 2005. *On Cosmopolitanism and Forgiveness*. London and New York: Routledge.
———. 2007. *Psyche: Inventions of the Other*, Volume I. Stanford: Stanford University Press.
Fink, Bruce. 1995. *The Lacanian Subject: Between Language and Jouissance*. Princeton, NJ: Princeton University Press.
Flaubert, Gustave. 1980. *The Letters of Gustave Flaubert, 1830-1857*, Vol. 2. Translated by Francis Steegmuller. Cambridge and Massachusetts: Belknap Press of Harvard University Press.

Kafka, Franz. 1971. "Before the Law" in Nahum N. Glatze (ed.), *Franz Kafka: The Complete Stories*. New York: Schocken Books Inc. 1971.
Kamuf, Peggy. 2004. 'The University in the World it is Attempting to Think' in *Culture Machine*, 6. Available at: http://www.culturemachine.net/index.php/cm/article/viewArticle/3/2 (accessed 12 January 2011).
Kant, Immanuel. 1991. 'The Metaphysics of Morals', in H. S. Reiss (ed.), *Kant: Political Writings*, pp: 131–175. Cambridge, UK: Cambridge University Press.
———. 2006. *Toward Perpetual Peace and Other Writings on Politics, Peace, and History*. Ed. Paula Kleingeld. New Haven and London: Yale University Press.
Kargupta, Sourav. 2011. 'Jacques Derrida and the Gift of Translation', *Jadavpur Journal of Comparative Literature*, No. 47: 97–110.
Kristof, Nicholas D. 2011. 'We Are All Egyptians', *The New York Times*, 3 February. Available at http://www.nytimes.com/2011/02/04/opinion/04kristof.html?_r=0 (accessed 4 February 2011).
Lukács, Georg. 1971. *The Theory of the Novel: A Historico-Philosophical Essay on the Forms of Great Epic Literature*. Cambridge, MA: The MIT Press.
Marx, Karl. 1982. *Capital: A Critique of Political Economy*, Vol. 1. Trans. Ben Fawks. New York: Penguin Books and *New Left Review*.
Melas, Natalie. 2006. *All the Difference in the World: Postcoloniality and the Ends of Comparison*. Stanford, CA: Stanford University Press.
Moretti, Franco. 2000. 'Conjectures on World Literature', *New Left Review*, 1 (January–February): 54–68.
———. 2003. 'Graphs, Maps, Trees: Abstract Models for Literary History—1', *New Left Review*, 24 (November–December): 67–94.
Mouffe, Chantal (ed.). 1979. *Gramsci and Marxist Theory*. London: Routledge.
Saussy, Haun (ed.). 2006. *Comparative Literature in an Age of Globalization*. Baltimore : The Johns Hopkins University Press.
Shakespeare, William, 2005. *The Merchant of Venice (Norton Critical Editions)*. Ed. Leah S. Marcus. New York: New York: W. W. Norton & Company.
Spivak, Gayatri Chakravorty. 1987. *In Other Worlds: Essays in Cultural Politics*. London: Routledge.
———. 1994. 'Translator's Preface' in Jacques Derrida, *Of Grammatology*. Translated by Gayatri Chakravorty Spivak, pp: ix-xc. New Delhi: Motilal Banarsidass.
———. 2003. *Death of a Discipline*. New York: Columbia University Press.
———. 2007. 'Abinirmān—Anubād' (Deconstruction—translation), in Anirban Das (ed.), *Bāmlāi Binirmān Abinirmān*. Calcutta: Ababhas.
Thakur, Rabindranath. 1991a. 'Pārasye', in *Rabindra-Rachanābalī, Sulabh Samskaran, Ekādash Khanda*, Vol. 11, pp. 623–67. Kolkata: Visva-Bharati.
———. 1991b. 'Strīr Patra' [Wife's letter] in 'Galpaguccha' (Bouquet of stories), *Rabindra-Rachanābalī* (Complete Works of Tagore.), *Sulabh Samskaran, Dvadash Khanda*, Vol. 12, pp 329–35. Kolkata: Visva-Bharati.

4
Islam and Theodicy
A Critique of Ruqaiyyah Waris Maqsood's Theological Approach to Evil

Mohammad Maroof Shah

The problem of evil is arguably the most difficult problem for all theistic worldviews. Modern age is characterized by the extreme obtrusiveness of evil and it could well be argued that it is the changed perception or cognizance of evil that differentiates modern humanist secularist worldviews from the traditional religious worldviews. The problem constitutes perhaps the foremost challenge to traditional theology in modern times. Any attempt to secure a rational foundation for religion in modern times must seriously reckon with the problem. And theodicy has become a notoriously difficult job for any theologian in modern times. It has been a canker in the heart of theism. The usual theological apologies or answers are hardly convincing and have been subjected to searching criticisms from various quarters. However, the traditional metaphysical approach, presented in the writings of the perennialists, to the problem convincingly refutes major critiques of theism and formulates a viable theodicy. This chapter will attempt a critical appraisal of Ruqaiyyah Waris Maqsood's more or less theological (as distinct from the metaphysical approach of the perennialists) reading of the Islamic view on evil.

Ruqaiyyah Waris Maqsood's *The Problem of Evil* could well be seen as representative of the position of literalist dualistic (exoteric) theologians. Although it well captures certain dimensions of the issue of evil and makes quite bold statements and rightly highlights certain distinctive elements of the theological genius of Islam, it lacks the profundity of perennialist and Sufi approaches. It does not reckon with the complex theological and metaphysical problems concerned. It reads the scripture too literally and attributes certain dogmatic assertions of the author herself to the Koran. Modern criticisms of theodicy or discussions of the problem are more or less ignored or superficially reckoned with and dismissed. It also either ignores or caricatures other than Islamic approaches (such as those of Christianity, Buddhism and Hinduism) to the problem. It only tangentially touches the mystical corpus of Islam in this connection. Sufistic reading of the scripture is either ignored or suspected of heterodoxy. It asserts too much without sufficient warrant for the same. It hardly dares to face the problem squarely and resorts to various marginalizing and dodging stratagems to dilute the force of the challenge. It shifts the focus of the discussion to side issues. Ignoring much of the traditional wisdom of Islam (the prerogative of Muslim philosophers and mystics) it stands on very vulnerable ground. It is riddled with many contradictions as I will presently point out. It could be critiqued on both the traditionalist orthodox and certain modern grounds. It cannot convincingly refute major modern criticisms of theology or theodicy. Its tone and style is more rhetorical than logical and rational. Needless to say it does not convince on the whole, though its significance for the general audience and literalist masses cannot be doubted.

Maqsood, like Iqbal, accepts the usual Epicurean formulation of the problem and then attempts to answer it. This is the problem with this position. Once one accepts this traditional format, one is hard put to silence the critics while fully subscribing to the traditional theistic paradigm. She thus expresses the problem, revealing her questionable metaphysical and theological assumptions in this process (Maqsood 2000: 2–3):

> Now, if God is All-Powerful, then He must be able to do anything and everything; and if he is All good, then he cannot wish to see pain and suffering and evil in the world. Yet evil and suffering undoubtedly do exist—so this must mean that either God is powerless to stop them (in which case He is not All-Powerful) or He is not aware that they are happening, (in which case He is not All knowing) or He does not care if they happen (in which case He is not All-Loving or All Good). Clearly if God can do anything, and yet in fact produces a cosmos in which there is suffering and evil, then there must be something wrong with His intentions. Conversely, if He is good, and there is nothing wrong with His intentions, and yet He produces an environment in which there is evil and suffering, then there must be something deficient in His power. Both conclusions are repugnant to Muslim doctrine as they are also to Christian and Jewish doctrine that

preceded the Muslim. The faith revealed to all three Peoples of the Book is that God is both supremely good and is indeed the source of all values, and also that God created the universe out of nothing—a doctrine that emphasizes God's Omnipotence.

After cataloguing many causes of physical and moral evils Maqsood expresses the problem in these words: "A human father who loves his children does not inflict suffering upon them gratuitously. Yet, if God is truly the creator, He does" (Maqsood 2000: 3). Although the author does not obviously blame God, she forfeits many ways of exonerating Him. She lands indeed in a very precarious position.

One cannot miss the personalist anthropomorphist assumptions in the above quoted formulation of the problem. It presupposes very simplistic notions about God's nature. It does not distinguish between Being and Beyond-Being that is so crucial in accounting for evil, as Schuon (1976) says. It assumes the veracity of populist or commonsensical understanding of God's attributes of omnipotence and foreknowledge. It attributes only goodness to God leaving evil outside His decree or dominion.[1] It attributes the doctrine of ex nihilo creation to the Koran in exclusivist fashion as if the doctrine of emanation is irreconcilable with it.[2] It implies a mechanical conception of God and His relation to the world. Creation is something external to God, as if it lies outside His infinitude. Any organic or necessary connection between God and the world seems to be ruled out. God is as if a spectator, watching it from outside. The world has a beginning in time. Souls too are mechanically manufactured. They too have a beginning in time. God is responsible for creation. Onus lies on personal God. It is as if a suit could be filed against God and His innocence needs to be defended or argued for. It puts God in very poor and difficult positions. It assumes man can judge God. It imagines God in one's own image. It is a simplistic understanding of the knotty and weighty issues of theology, indulging in what Schuon (1976) calls bad metaphysics. It is no easy matter to argue for consistent theodicy, and no dogmatic assertions will come to our rescue.

Maqsood then proceeds to examine various proposed answers to the problem. Her own answer is presented not quite systematically but interspersed in her observations on these various approaches to the problem. First, I will examine her critique of the Biblical or Judeo-Christian approach to the problem. She seems to offer a typical Muslim theological (exclusivist exoteric) reaction. She caricatures the traditional Christian approach, repeating the usual platitudes and rhetoric. Her approach is more or less dismissive of the Christian tradition in this connection (of course, after its reinterpretation she accepts it). She makes a caricature of the ideas of original sin and the Fall, and has no use for them in theodicy. She does not see any warrant for such a doctrine in the Bible either. She finds Jesus' healing ministry of central importance in the Christian attitude towards evil. She concludes from these narratives of healing the sick that "sickness cannot have been inflicted as the will of God in the first place, for if it had been the will of God, then nothing Jesus said or did could have made any difference" (Maqsood 2000: 46).

The traditional Christian approach, not unlike the Islamic approach, has centred around the sovereignty of God's will and man's submission to it, but that has not implied passive acceptance of suffering and not taking active measures to decrease it. The traditional Christian notions of original sin and the Fall could be understood in such terms as man's instinctual proclivity to evil; his being created weak and frail and prone to wickedness. The Fall need not be interpreted as a once-upon-a-time event. It happens daily in our lives. It has been interpreted in existential terms. Man's proclivity to sin and the fact of being placed outside the divine centre cannot be denied. Adam is not the name of historical man only. Man is created of the vilest of clay although he is nobler than angels also. He is weak-willed, impetuous, frail and prone to corruption. He is created in difficult conditions indeed. Most men are surely in the loss, except the chosen few who are saved and enter heaven. The dark reality of sin and evil, so acutely and poignantly portrayed by Christian theologians and some philosophers and many modern writers and such religions as Buddhism, cannot be ignored. Adam's sin or the original sin may imply nothing more than this. The presence of the devil in our veins and what is called as the passional self or *nafs-i-amara* may be interpreted as the Islamic appropriation of the notion of original sin. Of course the exoteric literalist Christian understanding of the whole narrative of Genesis may be critiqued on various grounds, not least on the grounds of universal orthodoxy. The Koran too narrates the story of eating the forbidden fruit and the resultant fall from the Eden Garden. There is an agreement on the basic narratives of Adam's fall in the Bible and the Koran. Man has eaten the forbidden fruit in both cases and this is a fact of momentous consequence in the history of mankind. The doctrine of the Fall, consequent on a certain kind of sin, is common to both Islam and Christianity. Islam differs from Christianity in positing that this sin was not communicated to posterity but if this original act of sin or *zulm* were reinterpreted in universal existential or psychological terms then this fact of transmission hardly affects the import of the main doctrine. If Adam symbolizes man rather than the concrete historical human individual then the symbolism in the story of Genesis holds universally and trans-historically. The Christian scheme of salvation is closely linked to the idea of a saviour, or a dying and rising God-man, who takes on himself the sins of the world and thus transmutes them. This idea is crucial to Christian theodicy. Maqsood finds no warrant for such a doctrine either on rational or scriptural grounds. There is no doubt that in the usually understood exoteric sense the idea of saviour and atonement is at variance with the Koran. However, in the perennialist traditionalist approach, the issue appears in a very different light. Islam rejects incarnationist theology, yet at the esoteric level there is discernable correspondence of perspectives on the notions of devil, sin, grace, heaven and hell and some sort of redemption (called *shifaat* in Islam).

Maqsood builds her account of Christian theodicy from the parable of the wheat and the tares. She says that this parable indicates one reason why God did not simply just "weed out" (Maqsood 2000) of our worldly life all that caused suffering amongst us. The parable (Matthew 13: 24–30 [*The Holy Bible* 2007]) teaches us that the 'farmer', God, had an enemy, the devil, and he was responsible for the evil and suffering in the world. She says that God certainly knew it was there, and left it there. And she asks why He left it there. "Two reasons it seems. Firstly, to give the evil person the greatest possible opportunity to reform and change and secondly because to destroy all evil persons would be terribly hurtful and damaging to the good those who loved them" (Maqsood 2000: 54, 55). It is a very crude understanding of Satan that one sees here. She rightly sees Satan as the key figure in the problem of evil but her presentation and construction of Satan is not convincing for the modern mind and philosophers of religion. The way she presents the devil complicates rather than solves the problem, as will be seen later in her discussion of the Koranic view on the problem of evil.

Maqsood herself invokes the 'Christian' notions, especially in the last pages of the book, to console sinful, God-abandoned bereaved souls. She emphasizes God's forgiveness and love and their redeeming power. To keep steadfast faith in God in all circumstances is her answer to despair. The background psychology of Christian faith in Jesus' redeeming power and her belief in God's boundless forgiveness for sinners is not very different. The following passages could well have been written by a Christian theologian or priest.

> Love works unremittingly for the redemption of all that is imprisoned in hatred, terror and ignorance, all that is perverse, unclean and imprisoned in

chains of resentment and fear. Love can never rest until all God's creatures are free to receive the life-giving power. He wishes to bestow upon us.

Let us believe in God's love, in his faithfulness. He is always at work in our hearts. He never slumbers nor sleeps. His grace takes hold of every heart that really desires it, however poor and weak that heart may feel.

We cannot see God, but we can welcome the gift of His presence. His presence begins our awareness and opens the way to his love that love remains with us, even when we cannot feel it, even in the dark times when we have no doubts. (Maqsood 2000: 126–27)

We should be amazed that Allah loves us, and never be fooled into thinking that His love could fail us. We should have the humility to see that our wretchedness, however great, cannot be an obstacle to the power of God. It does not matter if we do not understand everything. If we truly believe in Him, if He truly means everything to us, we have only to turn in His direction. We should offer ourselves to Him in all our weakness and insecurity with nothing but our desire to obey Him and let Him work on us. (Maqsood 2000: 125)

She repeatedly emphasizes that faith in the God of love and mercy saves; our moral worth does not. Faith in God and faith in Christ, who symbolizes love, are hardly distinguishable as far as the basic psychology of the believer and the effect of it is concerned. The Prophet of Islam said that it is only God's *Fazl* or grace that saves and not our deeds. *Iman* stands for the alchemy of love. Evil is conquered by love, and by our conviction that God forgives; He is merciful and compassionate. Christian dogma is geared towards making this point as the perennialists point out. The dimension of God's justice and His being a hard taskmaster (demanding purity of heart and conduct from those who want to enter His kingdom) is not lost sight of in the Bible. The Koran testifies rather than whitewashes or nullifies the previous revelations. Essentials for salvation or entering the kingdom of God are faith in God and purity of conduct and these things are emphasized by both Islam and Christianity. No thoughtful Christian or Muslim takes God's mercy or grace or love to mean that licence is granted to sinners. We are all sinners if we keep the highest moral ideal before us. So God's grace and forgiveness is crucial to our salvation. Although Maqsood is very critical of Christianity for its heresies or theological errors, she succeeds in bringing home the point that the theodicies as formulated in the Koran and the Bible are essentially the same. Both offer similar panaceas against evil. Both take refuge in the same God of Love against the devil. However, it needs to be pointed out that there is a way to interpret Christian dogma in such terms that do not negate the Islamic perspective. Christian Orthodoxy could well be orthodox on its own terms in its own way, as the perennialists point out. It may be cashed in profitably, in reckoning with the nagging problem of evil.

Maqsood's appraisal of the story of Job is admirable. She rightly emphasizes the similarity between the Old Testament and the Koran in this connection. Her own answer to the problem of evil is indebted to the Book of Job. One can see that the Koranic perspective colours her treatment of the Old Testament. The story of Job has been much commented upon by religious as well as non-religious scholarship. It is central to Biblical theodicy. Modern man finds Job greatly relevant. He himself is passing through a similar predicament. He feels abandoned by God. The devil has overpowered him. He wants consolation and solace. There have been film productions of the story of Job in the twentieth century. McLeish's version is a famous one. It captured a large audience. However, the painful fact is that modern man finds God's answer from the whirlwind farcical, unconvincing and bullying. He sees it as a display of might and not of love. The faith that kindles this great feat of human endurance has been noticed but by few. Modern man has turned away from God partly because he has watched suffering with such intensity and on such a scale that he feels there is hardly any reason, any design, any soul making involved. He suffers as Job suffered for no sins of his own but he is, unlike Job, defeated by it. He is overwhelmed by the devil. He sees no ray of hope, no sunshine of faith. The clouds of gloom, sin and guilt have darkened his horizons; he is only capable of "unyielding despair." (Russel 1919: 48) Jung, in his *Answer to Job*, has critiqued what he calls the dualistic conception of Satan in Christianity. He points out that Job asked God to help him against God! His treatment of the theme has great psychological insights to offer and to clarify our relation with the evil one, the *nafs-i-amara*. However, the way he tries to argue for fusing God with Satan will not work. The Prophet of Islam did recognize the presence of the devil in our psyche or in our very blood but he did not ask to somehow integrate him but to convert him, to make him Muslim. It is our fight against the devil, who is our deadly enemy, that really toughens our moral fibre. This is what the mystics call crossing the dark night of the soul. The devil can be conquered and it is reckoning with and fighting against him that constitutes our trial on this vale of soul making. Satan is in us as scriptures affirm (and the Sufis have especially emphasized this point). He needs to be subdued. However, he is ruling the roost in modern times. The Antichrist has plunged modern man into the hell of disbelief and thus despair and absurdism. Modern man feels powerless against him. It is this obtrusiveness of evil in modern times and consequent apostasy and despair that bedevil modern life, which philosopher C. E. M. Joad identifies as the great and tough challenge to belief in modern times. Theodicy thus becomes vitally relevant today. I will present here Maqsood's appraisal of Job's answer to the problem of evil and offer my comments so as to identify the outlines of the Koranic approach to evil.

Maqsood rightly presents Job as the model of Islamic patience. Job's is a classic case of unjust suffering, the suffering of innocent man. Dostoevsky's Ivan could well have presented Job as a test case for all theodicy. Camus too could have pointed towards the plague that afflicted Job while arguing against Christian theology. Scripture has already dealt with the problem of innocent children's suffering. It has already provided the answer to it and this answer is so profound that it usually escapes the full comprehension of many a theologian and their critics. Its answer is that there can be no answer! And there need not be one! The question is not valid! How this is so has been argued by such perennialists as Marco Pallis in *A Buddhist Spectrum* and Frithj of Schuon (Isa Nuruddin) in *Islam and the Perennial Philosophy*.

Job's experience is presented in the Old Testament as that of a good man who suffered terribly, and could think of nothing that he had done to deserve it, simply because Satan saw how devout he was and requested God for permission to test him. He was afflicted with terrible sickness, his children died, he lost all his health and possessions and was rejected by his wife. He was virtually deprived of everything. The wife suggested that he "curse God and die!" but Job, who was the model of Islamic patience, replied: "Shall we receive good at the hands of God and not accept the evil" (Job 2:9 [*The Holy Bible* 2007]) This is one of the key statements of Job. The traditional Islamic affirmation of faith has a clause, "both good and evil are from God." This is the key to theodicy in Islam. This point is well argued by the Sufis and has been well discussed in the chapter on the Sufistic solution to the problem of evil by Mir Valiuddin in his *The Quranic Sufism*. The religious concept of God is not some anthropomorphic Being who is anxious to arrange things in the right order for humans. To attribute only goodness to God and yet to conceive of Him as the creator of evil is a contradictory position only if one has humanized and anthropomorphized the concept of God and attributed to a simple divine subject cosmic effects that are related to different universal sources. There is a contradiction or irresolvable dilemma for theology vis-à-vis evil only if Beyond-Being is subsumed in Being. Beyond-Being is indifferent to good and evil;

it has nothing to do with humans and their predicament. It is Being that creates, reveals and saves. Beyond-Being or Godhead is best referred to as Nothing. Nothing can be predicated of it. It is attributeless. It is not good. It is not evil. It does not plan. It is not wise. It is not omnipotent. It is wholly impersonal divinity, *Nirguna Brahman*, the darkness of *Dhat*. This qualityless Godhead is the true Ultimate, the Absolute rather than the personal creator God who is omnipotent and wise and good as ordinarily understood in theology. This qualitied God is "lower" in the scale of existence and is no more than the first manifestation of the Absolute. It is overemphasis on what Stace calls the "positive divine" to the exclusion of the "negative divine" (Stace 1952) in the exoteric theological tradition of monotheistic religions that makes the problems of evil insoluble. Other traditional religions like Buddhism and Hinduism have paid due regard to the tradition of negative divine with the result that there is no problem of evil vis-à-vis the Absolute for them (although sometimes it too gets overemphasized, especially in Buddhism, so that the positive divine and personal dimensions of the Absolute are compromised). It is mysticism or esotericism that provides a corrective to exotericism and that is crucially important in properly approaching the issue of theodicy. God's answer to Job has been found unconvincing primarily by those who do not see through the Biblical narrative, who approach it from the vantage point of dualistic exotericism. God's answer to Job could be best understood in the tradition of negative divine in monotheistic tradition that has usually been marginalized despite the protest of mystics. God gives no logical rational explanation of His doings. He need not! Why? Because He is not a being among other beings, a personal power whose omnipotence extends to His nature. He is not an interested party at all. He transcends both good and evil. God's infinitude and all-possibility necessitate radiation of the good or creation or manifestation, which is situated in *Maya* or divine relativity, a realm of contrasts, separation, disequilibrium and thus evil and suffering. To better appreciate the Muslim solution to evil or theodicy, this tradition of the negative divine needs to be foregrounded. This is attempted in the following discussion.

For a more explicit formulation of the concept of the negative divine, Buddhism and Hinduism can be cited. The distinction of Being and Beyond-Being or personal God and impersonal Godhead is explicit in Indian religio-mystical traditions. If the mystical approach to religion is correct and thus the perennialist vision of transcendent unity of religions granted there should be no problem of orthodoxy of the tradition of negative divine in monotheistic religions. The greatest Muslim perennialist scholar, Frithjof Schuon, has forcefully argued that nirvana and God are identical. Such mystical philosophers as W. T. Stace have also reached the same conclusion, though through a somewhat different approach. Meister Eckhart could be cited as a representative of the tradition of negative divine in Christian mysticism. Eckhart's assertions are quoted in Stace (1953: 10). "God," he says "is as void as if He were not." In another place he says, "Thou shalt love God as He is, Non-God, a Non-Spirit, Non-Person, a Non-Form." He terms divine being as "the nameless Nothing", "the still wilderness." Using the metaphor of darkness, Eckhart says, "The end of all things is the hidden darkness of the eternal Godhead." In a similar fashion Tauler describes God as "the divine darkness, the nameless, formless nothing, the wild waste" (quoted in Stace 1953: 11). Dionysius the Aeropagite speaks of the "divine darkness" (quoted in Stace 1953: 11) and he preaches the method of abstraction, which consists in denying all predicates of God. Even the great Augustine asserts that God is best described by negatives (Tarsicius 1993: 73–97) Speaking of the medieval mystics and their absorption in the negative divine, Dean Inge observes, "The words nakedness, darkness, nothingness, passivity, apathy, and the like fill their pages" (quoted in Stace 1953: 11) In Jewish mysticism the conception of God as Nothing finds frequent and explicit expression. "In the depths of His Nothingness" is a favourite metaphor of the thirteenth century Kabbalistic and Hasidic mystics. Many examples can be cited.

Now I turn to Islam. Is there a tradition of negative divine in Islam? Stace examines the question and answers in the affirmative but refers to Sufism and not to the Koran for example. I think that I can refer to the Koran also in this connection, without needing to resort to Sufi authorities. There is no denial of the fact that the Islamic conception of God is deeply anthropomorphic, and the notion of His personality and consciousness belongs rather to the positive rather than to the negative conception of divine, as Stace (1953: 25) rightly notes. However, Stace's generalization that "it is always the positive rather than the negative conception of the divine which is emphasized in Islam" (Stace 1953: 25) is not warranted. The Koran and the prophetic traditions have in their own way strongly and forcefully emphasized the negative conception of the divine. One of the most frequently quoted chapters of the Koran (which is recited in Muslim ritual prayer most frequently) is the 112th chapter, named Ikhlas. It is usually presented as defining the Muslim creed of *Tawhid* by Muslim theologians and it contains the clearest statement of the negative divine. I quote Abdullah Yusuf Ali's translation (*The Holy Qur'ān* 2001): "Say: He is Allah the one! Allah, the Eternal Absolute! He begetteth not, nor is He begotten! And there is none like unto Him." There cannot be

Islam and Theodicy 51

more emphatic denial of anthropomorphism. Here is clearly discernible the Upanishadic *neti–neti*. Here the impersonal aspect of the Absolute is emphasized. Attributes that could be anthropomorphically applied are here clearly negated. The mystics have quite justifiably appropriated this chapter in their Unitarian interpretation. The conception of God as the Absolute, the Pure Being or Beyond-Being, Supraformal Essence of which nothing can be predicated in positive terms could be easily derived from this chapter. It is no wonder that Abdul Karim al-Jili, Ibn Arabi and other great mystics and mystical philosophers have based their basic ideas on this chapter. Nothing is like Him, asserts the Koran. It also says no vision can grasp Him (*The Holy Qur'ān* 6:103) and He is free of all wants (*The Holy Qur'ān* 31: 26). The Koran's rejection of idolatry logically implies its transcendence of human conceptualizations of the positive divine.

Islam's rejection of idolatry resembles in many ways negative theology's problematization of all representations, constructions or conceptualizations of God. Islam resembles deconstruction in this respect as has been well argued by Ian Almond in *Sufism and Deconstruction* (2004). Both are anti-idolatrous. The deepest insight of Islam concerns its identification of the truth (*al-Haqq*) with God and its uncompromising stance on God's transcendence, inscrutability and otherness. The deconstructionist project (that essentially resembles the tradition of negative divine; it is Buddhism and its tradition of the negative divine that has influenced deconstructionist postmodernist philosophers) also consists essentially in recognizing this truth of the utter transcendence, inscrutability, otherness, incomprehensibility of the suprarational, supralinguistic and ever differing and deferring nature of the truth. Islam's uncompromising stance on God's transcendence could be interpreted in terms of the negative divine. Islam dismisses the possibility that one could have a vision of God in all its nakedness in this world (and one school of theology denies its possibility in the next world also). Ibn Arabi, one of the greatest Muslim mystics, thus expressed his conception of the negative divine:

> It is necessary that you know Him after this fashion, not by learning nor by intellect, not by understanding, nor by imagination nor by sense, nor by the outward eye, nor by the perception.... His veil, that is phenomenal existence, is but the concealment of His existence in his oneness, without any attribute. (Quoted in Stace [1953: 26])

Here the absence of attributes in God as He is in Himself is equivalent to the negative concept of God. One could multiply such quotes indefinitely from Sufistic literature. It is not necessary to comment further on the Islamic warrant of the tradition of negative divine; once this is granted, Islam's solution to the problem of evil can be easily understood.

Muslim scholastic conception of God has been critiqued for His capriciousness. He wills what He wills. He grants his favours and withdraws them for no reasons whatsoever (as humans would like to know or understand them). The Ash'arites are correct in a way for emphasizing the point that God owes no explanation to humans. He leads astray whom He wills and guides whom He wills. He afflicts with suffering whom He wills and showers unlimited bounties and blessings on whom He wills. He has decreed both good and evil and nothing happens except as He wills. If there ever was a righteous man, he was Job and if anyone was afflicted with the most terrible sufferings, it was He. God is above law. He is, in a way, indifferent to the fate of humans. He flouts all expectations of humans. God knows and we do not know. Evil arises because of Beyond-Being's indifference and remoteness from the world. It is not a personal entity to be personally interested in the fate of humans. Maqsood, in her analysis of Job's story, reaches a similar conclusion without resorting to these notions. She writes, "His story as presented in the Old Testament in fact gives a striking reminder of the inadequacy of human horizons for any proper understanding of the problem of suffering except that counselled by Islam." She elaborates that since human beings are not in a position to know God's will, it is their duty to submit and accept. She quotes Job's 'comforter' Elihu in chapter 35 (Maqsood 2000: 35: 7):

> if you do evil, you only harm yourself and not God. What are your sins to Him? Similarly, if you do good, you do not give anything to Him, and He does not receive from your hand. The good and evil that you do concerns only yourself.

She rightly defines a saint as a person who can accept whatever life places in front of him without complaint. Complaint against God is losing faith in God—the position finally arrived at by Job after he works through a time of great depression. Islam, like the Old Testament, counsels acceptance. A Muslim must submit to God's will. He is not a rebel. He resents only resentment. His will merges with God's will. This is the heroic posture attained at the most sublime peak of human endurance. It does involve a tragedy. The tragic sense of life is there to stay. There is no cure for pain. In a world where rebellion fetches nothing the only wise course is to be true to love, love, whose object is the whole universe and God, with all our heart and mind and might. Ivan's is not the solution. It leads to self-defeating despair. We cannot return the ticket of life to God. No one can take it back. There is no point in returning it. It is an inauthentic posture. It is bad faith. It is ingratitude. It is *kufr* (disbelief) in the Koranic perspective. What cannot be cured must be endured. Complaining against God, who is not malevolent (or benevolent in the anthropomorphist sense of the term) and who cannot interfere as we may wish Him to, is meaningless.

God's pen having written the decree cannot be persuaded to cancel it. Stoic resignation, acceptance, submission and *raza* are what are asked from the Muslims. This is the import of the Book of Job also. No one has solved the problem of evil in the sense critics of theodicy present it. We should not expect any solution at the rational plane according to all traditional religions. To the conceptualizing intellect the road to God and understanding His ways are barred. God is known by the heart, not the head. Reason may not justify His ways to men. However, it is not a sign of worry for believers. The intellectual—the philosopher and the theologian—is denied the vision of God. It is to intellectual intuition that the certainty of God's existence and His goodness is revealed. Reason's wings are clipped to approach God's throne. God's *sirr* (secret) is contained only in a *Mu'min*'s (believer) heart. Reason and theology (understood in the sense of science or knowledge of God discoverable by conceptual intellect, as distinct from gnosis or the esotericist approach to it wherein God is directly intuited by heart) have failed to make plain the meaning of God's doings. Reason or ratiocinating intellect is simply humbled before the mystery of God. God's wisdom is utterly unfathomable. There can be no theodicy on a purely rational plane. Stace's conclusion in this regard is essentially correct and theologians, much more than their critics, would concede its truth: "All attempts to show that God's omnipotence combined with perfect goodness are compatible with pain and evil—although they fill countless volumes—are patent frauds" (Stace 1953: 57). All the force in the Epicurean formulation of the problem depends on all the words in it being taken literally.

Maqsood considers various classical solutions to the problem and dismisses most of them and selectively appropriates a few in her Islamic perspective of it. She straightaway dismisses the solutions that compromise God's omnipotence. Mill's solution is critiqued without duly presenting his case. The author does not criticize it on rational philosophical grounds but dismisses it on Koranic grounds. Since it does not conform to the Koran, it is not worth reckoning. However, she does recognize the problem of free will versus predestination in this connection and discusses it later in the book.

Maqsood dismisses as nonsense another solution that posits that God exists, but is not to be characterized as supreme Good. She quotes the Koran (6:133 and 5:171) that says that Allah cares very much about the fate of his servants and also quotes the verse (Koran 27: 73) that declares that Allah never enjoys watching people suffer. Again, she does not offer a philosophical critique of this position. She also considers the possible solution that proposes God's impersonality and denies Him personality and thus any role of providence. This position takes God to be an impersonal force or some sort of inexorable cosmic law. She rejects this view as she considers it against the revealed books. She provocatively asserts that according to the revealed books God is intimately concerned with every detail of His servant's lives, and knows each one personally. She quotes certain verses and interprets them, perhaps not without sufficient warrant, to argue the case for special providence. She, as usual, does not reckon with various philosophical and theological critiques of this position. Then she takes on the thesis of Gnosticism, which states that God exists, but is not the creator of the universe, and belongs to a realm of pure spirit, and has nothing whatever to do with the physical universe. The being we think of as God was not really the creator at all. The realm of the matter is the creation of a lesser and inferior demigod whose object was actually malignant—it was to trap free spirits into the world of matter, where they certainly would suffer. The only way to conquer evil is to search for enlightenment and the finding of a saviour who would bring us back to the spiritual home. Needless to say, Maqsood casts aside this suggestion because according to the Koran Allah alone was responsible for creation, and is in command of all knowledge about it. Here it needs to be pointed out that she presents only a caricature of Gnosticism. She creates binaries where there may be none. She sees conflict or disparity between Islam and ancient wisdom traditions. Such a search for pure Islam ultimately results in creating a closed universe. Not only modern thought, but the whole corpus of mysticism and wisdom traditions is dubbed *jahiliya* (pre-Islamic paganism in Arabia), *shirk* or paganism from the vantage point of 'pure' prophetic Islam. These comments are relevant in our discussion of the pantheistic solution to the problem of evil that Maqsood next considers for criticism.

She links the pantheistic solution to reincarnation systems of Hinduism and Buddhism. In such systems, everything is part of a whole and in the end returns to source. In such systems evil is regarded as part and parcel of physical existence altogether. Through repeated rebirths all souls are absorbed back into the Godhead. Maqsood sees pantheism, reincarnation and return of all souls to God as fallacious ideas from the

Koranic perspective. No human soul can ever "become" God, or has ever been part of God (Koran 43:15 and Koran 43: 86–87). She emphasizes the fact that the Koran (43:59–60) considers even the most perfect of human messengers, the Blessed Jesus as "no more than a servant." The Quranic insistence on transcendence of God is stated quite emphatically in its chapter number 112.

Maqsood then considers the dualistic Manichaean solution. She says that dualism overemphasizes the contrast principle in the constitution of the universe and considers the devil another superpower besides God. She dismisses dualism as the Koran rejects it unambiguously. The Koran makes it clear that the devil is not equal to God. The Koran is also explicit on the point that there is no symmetry between good and evil (5:103). She notes the fact that Christians also accept the notion of an evil force opposing God, but that God is by definition supreme and that God will triumph in the end. She adds an objection (and does not proceed to answer it), "Naturally, there is no way of proving this (i.e., meliorism) and it does not explain the reason for the existence of the Devil in the first place! Why if God created the universe, did He create the possibility of evil at all?" (Maqsood 2000: chapter 2: 19–22).

Next is regarded another classical solution that posits Satan to be part of God. She thus presents the position: "Some people believe that since God includes everything that exists within Himself in some way, then we should also be bound to accept that the Devil is also part of God" (Maqsood 2000: chapter 2: 22).

The author dismisses this position in no uncertain terms. "This is shown in the Quran to be a nonsense, the Devil is God's sworn enemy, and not in any way a 'part' of Him (4: 45 and 2: 98)" (Maqsood 2000: chapter 2: 22).

However, what follows seems in plain contradiction to her avowed position. She writes (Maqsood 2000: chapter 2: 23):

> God is the sole source of all that is created, whether visible in this world or invisible. A lovely passage in the Old Testament, revealed by Allah to the Prophet Isaiah reads "I am the Lord, there is no other; I make the light, I create darkness, author alike of prosperity and trouble, I, the Lord, do all these things" (Isaiah 45: 6–7 [*The Holy Bible* 2007]).

Maqsood explains, "God is beyond all description, even the categories of good and evil" (2000: chapter 2: 23). While on the one hand, she rejects the position that the devil is in any way part of Him, she also describes God as the only source of all that there is, author alike of light and darkness or good and evil. I am not asserting that the devil is part of

God but wish to point out what a mess is created by indulging in what Schuon (1976) would call bad metaphysics. Here are contradictions exposed that necessarily infect all exoteric theologies. To account for the devil is one of the most difficult tasks of theodicy. To posit a devil that is eternally damned and to posit an eternal hell (as exotericists do) creates insoluble problems for theology. Without integration or dissolution of the evil principle in the good, monotheistic position is problematized. Jung's "monotheistic" conception of Satan against what he calls exoteric Christian theology's dualist conception is to be seriously reckoned with or appropriated, although his primarily psychological approach, coupled with his bias against metaphysics, makes his position heterodoxical and that cannot be accepted as such. It needs to be emphasized that Islam, like all traditional religions, does not posit the dualist conception of Satan. This follows quite plainly from the orthodox formulation of the Muslim creed though it is best understood through the metaphysical or esotericist exegesis. The Sufis have consistently proposed what Jung calls the monotheistic conception of Satan. God undoubtedly transcends the categories of good and evil but the personal God is good and not evil, although He is the creator of both. It is indeed a very tricky affair (only an astute metaphysician like Schuon sees through it well) to avoid contradictions when reckoning with all this.

Maqsood easily dismisses the suggestion that evil is only a subjective phenomenon and therefore meaningless illusion and thus all *privatio boni* arguments. She also refers to another solution that takes evil to be useful. It is rightly critiqued on the ground that not all pain is useful or produces a greater good.

Strangely, she seems to subscribe to Spinoza's theory of necessary evil as part of the 'complete' universe as she approvingly quotes and appropriates certain Koranic verses in her appraisal of it. She presents Spinoza's solution thus (Maqsood 2000: 27):

> If the complete reality was just one perfect system, in which every single thing followed its course by logical necessity, then obviously nothing existed by accident, but everything was determined by law according to the will of God ... everything that seemed to be bad or evil was just due to our lack of awareness and understanding, the fact that our minds and our knowledge are limited and that it is not possible for us to understand the infinite perfection of the system. Good and evil, then, do not exist as such, but are ideas in our minds by our habits or comparing the goodness or usefulness of things for ourselves.

Islam and Theodicy 57

She quotes verses 5:19 and 6:17 from the Koran that assert that nothing happens by accident. She also notes that limitations of our knowledge are stressed in the Koran for it is a human weakness to wish to know the reason why everything is as it is and why people should have to suffer. The Muslim (as Spinoza) is expected to accept whatever God sends with patience and endurance, and not to waste time seeking to understand the reasons, which are beyond us. She also approvingly refers to Spinoza's view that we are quite wrong to imagine that everything was made for our benefit.

It needs to be pointed out that Spinoza's pantheism is incompatible with the Islamic theism and thus their perspectives on evil, though seeming to converge, are basically divergent. Maqsood does not recognize the wide divergence in the background metaphysical assumptions of Spinoza and Islam.

She then takes on the suggestion that God's justice works out in another world. She considers an objection that the idea still haunts us that there could have been different way of arranging things, that surely it was unnecessary to evolve rational beings out of a material world with all attendant sorrows in the process. "Why God was not content just to have made us for that world in the first place and not ploughed us into the maelstrom of this life" (Maqsood 2000: 33). She doesn't let this thought disturb her as she has already made some remarks on the futility of asking such whys and the impotence of reason to comprehend everything.

Lastly, she critiques evolutionist approach to the problem (associated with Tielhard de Chardin and others) on moral grounds. She says: "What is morally intolerable in this argument is that in order to produce the end-product of enlightened conscious beings, untold millions of animals and species have had to fight and die and suffer on behalf of an end-product they could not conceivably value" (Maqsood 2000: 34).

Now I turn to Maqsood's ideas on what she takes to be the Islamic answer to the problem of evil. She refers to the Koranic version of Genesis. Crude exotericism and naïve psychologizing underlying in what Schuon calls bad metaphysics characterize her appraisal of Islamic theodicy although there are certain admirable insights here and there. First of all, she discusses why man chose evil in the Garden of Eden. Her answer is that the human *nafs* or soul could be influenced towards evil by the whisperings of evil spirits or jinns. It is her understanding of jinns that needs to be critiqued. She locates them in a realm that is not usually considered as belonging to or integral to man. Satan is an external agency of evil. It is difficult to see how he could be in our very blood veins as the Prophet said.

She seems to reject both mystical esoteric as well as modern appropriations of this mysterious power. As she puts it (Maqsood 2000: 58):

> According to the Quran, the urge to do evil was not caused by the weakness of humanity, or by their greed or lust, or by their disobedient nature. It went back beyond these things; humans were indeed weak but they were unwittingly being used by Satan or *Iblis*, the Devil.

The origin of the devil's animosity towards humans she traces to a simple historical event (it does not appear as a metahistorical event with a metaphysical import) when Satan refused to obey the command of God to bow down before Adam. She is quite content to take the forbidden fruit and the tree literally. She regards the Christian conception of Satan and original sin quite mechanically.

Maqsood rejects the traditional concept of predestination or fatalism but safeguards God's omniscience also. Many details she leaves out of the scope of predestination (God knows only universals not particulars). She offers an ingenious argument that the creator did not exercise His power to foreknow all the details. She sums up (Maqsood 2000: 82):

> Therefore, it is surely not a question of God's ability to foresee, foreknow, foreordain, for all things are possible to God. The question is rather God's will—what He chooses to foreordain!.... He examines a situation, considers, knows, and then He comes to decision.

She argues that God certainly chooses to exercise His infinite ability of justice and foreknowledge in a selective way to the extent that is His will. She oscillates between emphasis on God's omnipotence and foreknowledge, and justice and human freedom. However, it is voluntarist theology with its problematic conceptions that colours her overall perspective.

She deliberates more on moral evil and ignores the physical evil more or less. This is the usual strategy adopted by Muslim and most Christian theists. The question of useless pain in the animal kingdom and the question of large-scale disasters (such as the one described by Camus in *The Plague*) remain unanswered. She does not consider the possibility and the fact that suffering may often degrade rather than ennoble. She does attempt a philosophical theodicy but then she shifts to religious theodicy (that presupposes rather than explains evil, and is ultimately concerned with transmutation of evil or its defeat by good). It is no answer that God withheld the dispensation to interfere in the scheme of things as it pleased His sweet will. She is unable to account for what appears by all accounts a very capricious character of His will as revealed in history. On the one hand, she asserts that God knows and we do not know and that there is great wisdom in what He wills and does; on the other hand, she argues as if she knows that there is wisdom in the acts of God. This is not a rational argument but purely a faith-based approach. She proposes to answer the problem of evil but ends by advocating some sort of optimistic or melioristic faith.

Maqsood restricts her theodicy to the human world only. She argues that much of suffering could be understood as God's test and this also explains its use value. She reckons with the question of why God wants to test us. She answers as follows (Maqsood 2000: 96):

> It is because from these tests we grow out of weakness and selfishness, and become strong, understanding, compassionate and faithful people sometimes, the suffering and pain that burden the dark events of our life, such as severe illness, redundancy, bereavement, betrayal, can be authentic healing agents in their own right. Anything that deflects a person from a previously heedless way of life and causes him or her to think about the deeper issues of existence, perhaps for the first time in his or her earthly career, is potentially an agent of healing.

She cashes on the traditional free-will argument. To quote her (Maqsood 2000: 99):

> Human beings do have freewill, and Allah, in bestowing this freedom, would be grossly inconsistent if He were forever interfering with it to prevent particular evils. And what would the freedom to only do good amount to? If there is a temptation to which I have no chance of falling for because of my constitution, how can it really be called a temptation? Those who had been programmed so that they could never choose evil would be harmless. But could they really be called 'good?' Their goodness would be of no credit to them—praise and blame would not come into it.

This echoes Iqbal's free-will defence in his *The Reconstruction of Religious Thought in Islam* which has been critiqued in my previous works ('Islam and Theodicy: A Critique of Iqbal's Approach to the Problem of Evil' and *Problem of Evil in Muslim Philosophy: A Case Study of Iqbal*. Like

Iqbal, she admits limitation (though self-imposed) on God's power and freedom. She says, "In creating us with freewill He is in a way limiting Himself; although He can continue to guide through various means" (Maqsood 2000: 102) She defends the great price of evil that the boon of freedom necessitates. She asks whether an innocent victim (of moral evil) is not entitled to protest against God. It is in handling this question that she captures the essence of the great theological genius of Islam. This shows the Islamic response to the situation of hopelessness, despair and absurdity. She says (Maqsood 2000: 101):

> Such a victim might well cry out and accuse God of callousness and injustice. However, if in submission to the will of God, the victim can substitute a new moral attitude for the sense of injustice at his or her suffering then perhaps the will of God really may be done.

It is this response of love and submission that is the essence of both Islam and Christianity. It is the only way out of despair. Submission, acceptance, resignation and firmly believing that God somehow accomplishes His purpose through this travail are the elements of Islamic response to evil. It is not the justification of God's ways that is the question but our salvation or seeing our way through the evil. Religion is not very interested in the question of philosophical theodicy. It is a practical way of responding and ultimately conquering evil without bothering about the why and rational metaphysics. God in the Bible did not give rational answers to Job's questions. It is Job's freely given love and humble submission that God wants and that is the salvation of Job. A Muslim accepts God's will and surrenders his will and ego and thus harmonizes it with God's will. And in God he finds the end of sorrow and the peace that passeth all understanding.

Notes

1. Eastern traditions know nothing of the dualistic mentality that created Satan. Job expected help from God against God. Jung solves problems arising due to the dualistic Christian conception of Satan in his *Answer to Job* by resorting to an essentially mystical conception extrapolating from the Cusean notion of God as *coincidentia oppositorum*. He approvingly quotes Saint Clement of Rome that God rules the world with both the right and the left hands, with the right belonging to God and the left to Satan. Clement's view he sees as monotheistic as it unites opposites in one God. However, it needs to

Islam and Theodicy 61

be pointed out here that Jung's is a very crude appropriation of certain insights of metaphysics to the problem. His primarily psychological approach cannot do justice to the complex metaphysical problem. Although the purport of such mystics as Ibn Arabi, al-Jili and Rumi is essentially similar, they identify Being with goodness. It is the problem of divine nature that needs to be clarified. Maqsood, by accepting the problem of evil in the classical Epicurean format commits implicitly both these errors. It would be an offensively heterodoxical position to claim that the devil is part of God but God's infinitude must be taken into account in any theodicy. One must counter dualism or Manichaeism without sacrificing the goodness of Being. All this involves transcending the simplistic notions of both the personal God (who personifies good) identified with the Absolute and the devil (who personifies evil and suffers eternal damnation).

2. Schuon (1969: 153), true to the spirit of Orthodox Islam, rejects this binary of *creatio ex nihilo* and creative emanation. He points out that the doctrine of creative emanation is not opposed to the theological idea of *creatio ex nihilo*, but in fact explains its meaning.

References

The Holy Bible: English Standard Version. 2007. London: Good News Publishers.
The Holy Qur'ān: Text, Translation and 2001. Commentary, (Wordsworth Collection) translated by Abdullah Yusuf Ali, London: Wordsworth Editions Ltd.
Almond, Ian. 2004. *Sufism and Deconstruction*. London: Routledge.
Al-Arabi, Ibn. 2004. *The Ringstones of Wisdom* (also translated as *The Bezels of Wisdom*), or *Fusus al-Hikam*. Trans. Caner K. Dagli. Chicago: Kazi Publications.
Camus, Albert. 1960. *The Plague*. Trans. Stuart Gilbert. London: Penguin Books.
Dostoyevsky, Fyodor. 1976. *The Brothers Karamazov*, Trans. Ralph E. Matlaw. New York: W.W. Norton.
de Chardin, Tielhard. 1976. *Phenomenon of Man*. Trans. Bernard Wall. New York: Harper Perennial.
Iqbal, Muhammad. 1997. *The Reconstruction of Religious Thought in Islam,* Ed. and Annot. by Mohammad Saeed Sheikh. Delhi: Adam Publishers and Distributors.
Jung, Carl Gustav. 1952. *Answer to Job*. Trans. R.F.C. Hull. Princeton, N.J.: Princeton University Press.
Maqsood, Ruqayyiah Waris. 2000. *The Problem of Evil*. New Delhi: Adam Publishers and Distributors.
Pallis, Marco. 1980. *A Buddhist Spectrum*. London: George Allen & Unwin Ltd.
Russell, Bertrand. 1919. *Mysticism and Logic and Other Essays*. London: Longmans, Green and Company.
Schuon, Frithjof. 1969. *Dimensions of Islam*. London: George Allen & Unwin Ltd.
———. 1976. *Islam and the Perennial Philosophy*, p. 141. London: World of Islam Festival Publishing Company.
Shah, Mohammad Maroof. 2005. 'Islam and Theodicy: A Critique of Iqbal's Approach to the Problem of Evil', *Journal of Indian Council of Philosophical Research*, 22 (3): 13–26.
———. 2007. *Problem of Evil in Muslim Philosophy: A Case Study of Iqbal*. Delhi: Indian Publishers' Distributors.

Stace, W.T. 1952. *Time and Eternity: An Essay Concerning Philosophy of Religion.* Princeton, NJ: Princeton University Press.

———. 1953. *Time and Eternity: An Essay Concerning Philosophy of Religion.* Princeton, NJ: Princeton University Press.

Tarsicius Jan van Bavel.1993. *God in between Affirmation and Negation According to Augustine.* New York: Peter Lang. pp.73–97.

Tom McLeish, Why is Science Such a Pain?—a film available at www.youtube.com/watch?v=ZpD2X-qqL8o, *Accessed on 2nd November, 2012.*

Valiudin, Mir. 1987. *The Quranic Sufism.* New Delhi: Motilal Banarsidas.

5

Suturing of Selves Past

The Body in Revolution

Anirban Das

I

An exact rendering of events: one can mean so many things by the expression. It's too difficult to resolve. Better to concede, there is nothing like that, never. Though a mortal hankering for the exact account never comes to an end. A sieve of destruction, and omissions born of indifference do invade this piece of writing.

In diverse ways, they continue to disturb, instigate. Then again, words fall short, too. Such is the texture of memory, to weave its yarns is so simple and complicated at the same time, that maybe it is impossible to translate that into language.... I cannot give in to a dissection of events. As past realities are distilled through the breweries of memory, they become somewhat brittle, partial. In those hypnotic times, no one noticed the trifles. So the details escaped the memory that is indisciplined, too much scattered. Only some faces, the lightning-streaks of some events, take possession to fill up the scattered space.

Raghab Bandyopadhyay, *Journal Sottor* (translated by the author).

Looking about forty years back into the past, one sees fragments of one's selves vying for eternity. Haltingly he gathers, trying to breathe meanings into them. Memories and forgetting interweave to forge pasts that creep innocuously in to structure one's 'here and now'. Suturing of past selves becomes a commentary on the present—an act of 'dis(re) membering'—"decompos[ing] the present that the past composed" (Ellman 1981: 191). Memories, written and written about, have this quality of being a history of selves, an ongoing note on the multiple stories of the individual, the individual shaped and made and brought into being through the forces and processes of larger histories.

Reading memories written as texts brings out certain itineraries of the acts of writing. As one goes on to produce (write) new texts in reading the earlier ones, one becomes—yet one more time—aware of the infinitude of the radical act of producing supplements. The importance of the literary reading as descriptive and productive acts becomes once more emphasized in such a process of readings/writings. The search for a social scientific description of phenomena gets supplemented by acts of ethical and political readings. As always, the supplements—dangerous—disrupt the descriptions. Memories of revolution exceed the history of revolution. Memories of the body of the revolutionary, inscribed upon by events and ideologies, interrupt these ideologies and produce events that go beyond the structure of the earlier ones. It is worth remembering that all writings of memories do not enact the breaks. Such enactments need ideological work. That work involves the descriptive of the social sciences and the performative of the literary (of course, empirical instances at both ends of this analytic binary combine the descriptive and the performative). The force of a responsible writing/reading pries open (im)possibilities in unanticipatable ways.

Histories, even the minutest ones, have ultimately to work within a secular telos of reason. A history of beliefs, superstitions, religions or 'unreasons' of any sort, can hardly work within the tenets of those very beliefs, religions or 'other' thought systems. To quote a brilliantly simple instance from Dipesh Chakrabarty (1998: 476), as he speaks of Ranajit Guha's exceptionally perceptive analysis of the Santhal rebellion of 1855 (Guha 1983), "The historian, as historian, and unlike the Santhal, cannot invoke the supernatural in explaining/describing an event." This happens because the historian, qua historian, has compulsively to work with "a narrative strategy that is rationally—defensible in the modern understanding of what constitutes public life" (D. Chakrabarty 1998: 476). Dipesh Chakrabarty would tentatively grope for the "subaltern pasts" that act as a 'supplement' (in a Derridean sense) to the historian's pasts. These, he argues, "enable history, the discipline, to be what it is and yet at the same time help to show forth what its limits are" (D. Chakrabarty 1998: 476) If one retraces his arguments as to how it becomes possible for 'history' to be aware of, even if unable to grasp or assimilate in cognizance, this supplemental 'otherness', the partial commensurability between the past and the present becomes a symptom of the incompleteness of the present. The 'inherently fraught and fragmented nature of the present' looks closely at one's gazing face. Fraught in the dimension of time as it is in that of space. "[The] writing of history must implicitly assume a plurality of times existing together ... what allows medievalist historians to historicize the medieval or the ancient is the very fact that these worlds are *never completely lost*," Dipesh Chakrabarty (1998: 478) (italics added) asserts. The junction of the other time with the time of the now points at disjunctures in the 'now'. The non-contemporaneities of the present with itself are the "time-knots" (D. Chakrabarty 1998: 479) he speaks about.

Reversing, yet wholly within the spirit of, Benjamin's (1992: 255) comment on the site of history being "not homogeneous, empty time, but time filled by the presence of the now"; one could look at 'now', the 'present', being 'filled up with the chips of a blasted, non-continuous history'. In a way, one thus arrives at the conception of the present as the 'time of the now', "shot through with chips of Messianic times" (Benjamin 1965: 45). Memories—written and written about—can, at times, convey this sense of fractured histories, their rough edges fitting uneasily into a blasted present.

One important offshoot from Dipesh Chakrabarty's insight is the recognition of the element of a sensitivity to and a bearing of, the 'presence' of the 'past' in all 'History', even in its most formal or disciplinary enunciations. This leads to an understanding of the sheer impossibility of a 'complete' objectification of the past by the present (history). Objectification of the past occurs, but fails, remains incomplete to the extent that the past is conceived as 'understandable', the element of commensurability forming the indestructible hiatus 'in' the object that (paradoxically) connects it with the subject (of history). In other words, objectification in history occurs not in the act of truncating the past, but in the act of reaching out to it. Not in the act of 'forgetting' (elements of the past), but in the act of 'remembering' (in terms of the present). For the presence of the 'pasts' in the 'present' is always already mediated by the terms of the present. Terms, lest one forgets, are forged—among other things—by these very pasts. The cycle of causality revolves eternally, until, maybe, one reaches the 'time-knots' where the pasts and the presents, the causes and the effects, coexist.

Disciplinary 'Histories' try to straighten things up. Unwinding the knots put 'pasts' and 'presents' in their respective assigned locations. They inexorably fail in (completing) their project(s). The unwindings reveal hybridities, mutual constitutivities that resist separation. As 'History' broadens its reach, goes out into the nether lands of othernesses, of victims, mads or un/pre-civilizeds, it carries on with its (ever) unfinished task of unwinding the time-knots. It seems it gets more and more wound up. But as Dipesh Chakrabarty convincingly asserts, the purported task remains the same. Minority histories, despite their seeming resistance to the discipline of 'History', retain their tours de force. 'Subaltern pasts' is the name he chooses for the radical alterity of 'History', an alterity that definitionally brings the practices of historicization to a crisis, a crisis unfolding in the very workings of the practices, yet bearing traces of a fundamental elision.

How to conceptualize a radical alterity to history? Dipesh Chakrabarty, in a Derridean vein, does not indulge, at least in the said essay, in any discussion regarding the possibility of a 'positive ontological dimension' to this alterity. Elements that interrupt the narratives of History cannot be defined except in terms of those narratives. Interruptions to history are defined as interruptions with regard to history, and not in terms definable fully beyond history. Zizek (1989), who speaks of a positive ontological dimension in his concept of symptom ("as sinthome" [Zizek 1989: 75]), poses the possibility of an ontic alterity. Yet, it seems to me that this positivity of the symptom does not reside in its own positive onticity. Rather, this dimension of the 'symptom' flows from its making possible, bringing into existence, of a 'certain positive entity', the being in the symbolic. Symptom remains the 'only point that gives consistency to the subject' (Zizek 1989, 75)—its positivity residing in its quality to provide consistency to the subject. I do not go into the theoretical intricacies of the problematic of naming, of choosing between the 'supplement' and the 'symptom'. Instead, I would like to speak of the (im)possibilities of an element of onticity in the category of a radical alterity to history. I want to speak of a certain kind of memory—and I emphasize, only a certain kind—in this context. I speak of a slender literature in Bangla on the memories of the Naxalite movement in the 1970s in India, written by some of its active participants in West Bengal.

I deal mostly with a single book, *Journal Sottor*, by Raghab Bandyopadhyay (2000), with occasional references to one other (*Karagare Athero Bochhor* by Azizul Haque (1991) and some pieces from a third (*Sei Doshok* edited by Pulakesh Mandal and Joya Mitra (1994). I have deliberately left out writings by women activists.[1] This 'gender bias' is self-imposed. I wanted to focus my attention on a very small problematic, without going into the profoundly interesting aspect of gendering[2] of memory–discourse except in a cursory and cavalier manner as it stands now in this chapter.

A note of caution and clarifications: disclaimers to the 'disciplinary' 'commonsense' of history have become commonsense assertions in many varieties of history writing. They search for the "small voice in history" (Guha 1996), alternative histories, or some other similar category with claims to an alterity. This mode of historiography has borne rich, variegated and brilliant results in certain traditions, like that of the 'subaltern studies' group emanating from India. They focus on the power differentials acting between the dominant, 'statist' view of history and the 'other' forms of remembering and retelling of the pasts. This preoccupation with the element of 'power' in strategies of representation and narration, an important dimension to be incorporated into the modes of historiography, may have resulted in a certain reification of the subordinated (narratives) as the 'others' to a dominant one. In this narrative of power play between 'History' and the 'rest', History may paradoxically have emerged to be the one to set the tone, the terms of reference and discourse. "To open up the area of historical enquiry" (Pandey 1999: 49) seems to be the project. The others lose their onticity. More importantly, when they retain the ontic element, it happens to be 'essentialized', defined in terms of the dominant. Memory, as one of the others, has probably had the same fate. Let me elaborate.

To understand memory as a 'positive substance', as not being solely definable in negativity (from history), there should be an assertion of the positive onticity of the phenomenon. This assertion may very well flow from the positive onticity of its phenomenal other. The onticness remains a mirror image of the 'authentic' onticness of History. Like the 'sheer presence' of the exotic other, this exotic onticness of memory may serve the causes of History, an instance of commodified symbolic capital. This 'reified presence' of memory may very well dispose of the criticalities in certain forms of history—turning more coercive than the master (narratives of history). The 'memories' of the Jews, reified to serve the state of Israel, have been effective in erasing memories of Palestinians (Said 2000) and even the criticalities in a disciplinary history of the region. Nearer home, purported 'memories' of the Hindus might be equally functional in the destruction of a mosque, straightening out the criticalities of a non-conforming 'history'. "Welcome to the memory industry," Klein (2000: 127) had his opening lines speak eloquently of the predicament. The aura of 'immediacy' that seems to authenticate the 'presence' of memory, as posited vis-à-vis the 'writing' of history, might very well turn out to bear ineradicable traces of this very writing—the privileging of memory over history may parallel a similar assertion of the primacy of the speech over writing, a guised phono- and logo- centrism.

How then, can one think of memories in a way that pushes history into a crisis, yet not renounce the criticalities of historicization?

II

> We have not seen the tiger
> We have seen only them who saw the tiger.
>
> Ranjit Gupta, *Mayabi Tantuja* (translated by the author).

Partha Chatterjee (1993), in his discussion of the 'women and the nation' in India, speaks about two genres of autobiography in nineteenth-century Bengal. One of these is the *atmacarit*, which most of the male writers of autobiographies resorted to. These deal with the growing up of the 'individual' personality of the protagonist, though as Chatterjee argues, remaining intimately related to the 'making' of the nation. The other genre of writing is the *smritikatha*, which has been used by almost all of the women writers. *Smritikatha*, the genre of 'memoirs' or 'stories from memory', "was not the life history of the narrator or the development of her 'self' but rather the social history of the 'times'" (Chatterjee 1993). The writings I am going to deal with belong neither to the one genre nor to the other. Written in a different time and social space, they in a way combine the qualities of both. These are memoirs in a very 'thick' sense of the term, putting together and grappling with slices of time and space, faces and events, forging histories out of the fragments. The individual pieces of the collage retain a sense of palpable 'presence', of an immediacy. Yet the marks of the effort in putting them together remain evident, belying any such gesture of authentication. The work of suturing—of times, of selves—creating intricate patterns of truth and fiction, memory and history. Nostalgia, which in other contexts has been indicted as "mourning for what one has destroyed," (Rosaldo 1989: 107) acquires a different texture in this setting. The objects of nostalgia are, here, one's own selves, emotions and rationalities. What one decries today are what one had loved, maybe never did cease to love. What one had destroyed were pasts of one's being, never 'others' except in a very 'intimate' sense.

Suturing of Selves Past   69

A quilt of tenderness wraps each moment of remembrance, even when it is being dismembered.

> Now the beard has reached the chest.... Rage, pain, disgust and the burning questions, all have been extinguished. In slow yet steady steps, the tender instinct of Bangladesh has taken hold of me. The locks of the prison-gate were undone, the bolts moved noisily.
> Outside, a white image of Annapurna. Mother's eyes were fixed on my face. How keen! How penetrating the gaze was!
>
> (Bandyopadhyay 2000: 63)

The mother's gaze—loving, tender, yet penetrating—maybe the metaphor for the memories I write upon. The figure of the mother remains central in Bandyopadhyay's narrative. His account almost starts and ends with his mother—her life, her aspirations, how her imagined future had shaped his own imaginations and his own futures, the tensions between her projected dreams of super-human living and sacrifice, and the middle-class ambitions of an insecure Bengali mother, the sweet self-contradictoriness born of "parental affection, family prestige and a terrible fear ... a fear of the subaltern life" (Bandyopadhyay 2000:11)—the tensions that rent his own self into a plurality, the same tensions that goad him on. Arguably, these are the tensions that drive him today to look back and re(dis)cover fragments of those very selves. This feminine figure of love, care and ambiguity, this (re)figuring of the 'mother' as the 'other' within, calls for a meticulous and sensitive study of gendering that I do not go into in this chapter.

Remember, even before the mother, in the very first utterances of the narrative ordering of the memoir emerges the almirah full of books "Dust, soot, cobwebs, insect-shit, spittings and fossil. Soiled pages of brittle books too. The disgrace which this book-filled almirah evocative of nineteenth century colonial furniture had to face, was the first thing that comes to [my] mind" (Bandyopadhyay 2000: 9). This was the repository of knowledge, the signpost of educated middle classness that the author and his mother carried with them, amidst the base rabbles of the urban bustees. This was the space where the memories of the gentile past resided. The police, when they came, did not fail to recognize where to strike. For they came to strike the person. The person who is the most resilient site to keep memories alive. They hit the almirah. When they went away, it was in a shambles, reduced to planks of wood—"As if, destruction of memory is the reason for which the facts, the signs and the evidences were erased. Those turbulent eventful years of terror and revolution, of self-annihilating courage and extreme madness, is a black hole. A lost man" (Bandyopadhyay 2000: 9). The almirah in its very absence, still remains the strongest evidence to evoke memories, memories of erasure and void. The theme of emptiness recurs throughout the book. Emptiness on different registers. Like a gap between one's multiple selves—the crucial moment when, following a party meeting where the author fails to voice, even utter, his own convictions against the party line, he feels divided into two separate halves. Suddenly, the possibility of a doubt-ridden journey in revolution leaps up before him. And then—the emptiness of discontinuity, of a break in the rational concatenation of thoughts. The emptiness born of the 'event', the event of his arrest—"all of a sudden, the chain of logic breaks down. Succession fails; and a gap, a hole, a void is born" (–Bandyopadhyay 2000: 46). Remember, the event qua event, transcending the boundaries of rational causality, could also work the other way round. A Kafkaesque phone call from some superior official saved the author from being killed by the officer in charge. To kill the only child of a Brahmin widow on the auspicious day of *navami* was deemed somewhat improper. Radical unanticipatability that marks the structureless structure of the event is the abyss that one crosses in the everyday existences of being. It is in the times of revolutions when this structure gets accentuated. To be more apt, the memories of revolution focus on the unanticipatability of events, blowing them up to characterize the event called revolution. The fullness of reason in the Marxist–Leninist revolution is remembered as the emptiness of the event. The void remains, yawning.

As it engulfs him, the ultimate eventuality of the 'absence'—the absence from the revolution, absence from the daily movements, absence from the society of humans, shifted to being a number, to the *nadaan*, the naïve, to the convict squatting in a file before the jail authorities—an absence from sentience, strikes home. Paradoxically, this emptiness might be a continuation of the 'nowhere' called 'underground' where the revolutionaries stayed when they were free. This was a space that was in the city, yet outside. An unseen protective ring of confidence and unformed beliefs surrounded them. The 'nowhere' was immune to the vagaries of the risky space of the city. As this ring broke down with the event of arrest, a different 'no where' engulfed their absent beings. This non-space made them vulnerable.

The void has yet another, a fourth, register. The dimension of corporeality, of 'the body'. This corporeal emptiness, present only as a possibility, looks him straight in the face. This bodily nonexistence, to me, it seems, haunts the book in the form of its other, in the ever-present ever-resilient primeval 'body'.

> To see one's own body being tortured was only a part. A sense of deep and widespread insult combined with the pain and suffering that emanates from torture. The body then was a stray dog; slaps, clenched fists and kicks were wrenching out such pain-shot inarticulate sounds from a structure of blood, flesh and bones that they belonged, far beyond the limits of the language of speech, reading or writing, to some animal. Yes, an animal.
>
> (Bandyopadhyay 2000: 49)

This body—of which the visionary revolutionist was hardly aware in his grand utopic world, extending *ad infinitum ad absurdum* the Cartesian split between the mind and the body, where the mind reigned and the body was almost absent—this body returned to him in vengeance, returned him to (corpo)reality. In another short piece, Bandyopadhyay (2000: 91) asserts:

> A surprising(ly) complex time. Completely divided into two. The present and the future are flowing in separate streams, without even touching one another.
>
> Those dedicated to the future do have nothing but the brains. The head, growing in size, had engulfed the body....
>
> About those whom the police murdered before everyone's eyes at dawn in the premises of Beliaghata CIT building, there was no doubt that till then the bodies of these youths had borne their heads. But not for their heads, nor for their thoughts, the thick mourning that descended in Beliaghata, was for those fresh youthful bodies. For the(ir) lives.

If memory is to be related not only to writing but also to 'inscriptions', one has to pay attention to what Said (2000: 180) has termed, "the extraordinary constitutive role of space in human affairs." And, to think of space in relation to memory, what inscriptions are more resilient, more intimate, more evocative, than those carved out in the space of the body? The body that, in a way, always already bears the marks of other spaces and other times, both literally and figuratively. As the repository of individual and social memory—to mark its inclusion or exclusion from the society, or to act as the bearer of social norms and values[3]—the body, in memorialising, may act as a heterotopia that "juxtapose[s] in a single real place several emplacements that are incompatible in themselves" (Foucault and Rainbow 1984: 181). Indeed, it is remarkable how 'the body' would fit as a heterotopia, in almost all its specifications.

The body of the revolutionary interrupts, even when it constitutes, the call for revolution. This is not the disruption of the mediated by the immediate, not the disruption of the abstract by the concrete. For the body, even when thought of as the space where memory is inscribed, is not immediate. As space is also not the passive substratum of immediacy that gets marked by events of torture, or death, or pleasure. Yet, there is something in the ideological making of the body that enables it to enact the disruptions in the ideal of revolution. One has to be very careful here. For the idea of revolution itself is construed to be disruptive of a dominant order. Yet, it repeats the fixity of the dominant structures in many of its articulations. The body of the revolutionary, in the memories that are textualized, interrupts such articulations of the concept of revolution. Maybe, the purported immediacy of the body—if not reduced to a move that authenticates the presence of the body—lends the body its possibility to interrupt the mediations of the ideal of revolution. Immediacy, as beyond mediations, has the ability to interrupt mediatory principles.[4] Again, the 'body' has the possibility to enact such an interruption. It may also not enact this move. Embodiment per se is not radical. Such an interruption is an ideological task that has to be enacted in writing. The act involves ethics and politics. It does not flow spontaneously from a certain ontology. *Journal Sottor* as a text enacts the ethics and politics of a productive disruption of the ideal of a certain form of revolution.

But, let us halt and think in a different vein. Is not this positing of the body as the repository of memory a simple reversal and not a working through, of the mind–body dichotomy with now the body as its favoured pole? And does not this run parallel to another presupposition? That, in a progressive dialectic of reason and emotion, the latter had been active in making one an activist 'then', which he can see for his rational self 'now'. Subhendu Dasgupta says in so many words (1994: 137):

> Maybe it is true that the movement would have taken a more correct course if reason had buttressed emotions at that time. But those who relied solely on reason, when rationality exposed the errors of the movement, drifted away from it.
>
> My primary attachment was through emotion. Now, when in the light of reason I judge the doings of the movement, I understand its faults. But I

cannot tear off the emotional attachment. Now I think and work rationally. That does not take me away from the Naxalbari movement.

For Raghab Bandyopadhyay it is somewhat different. He visualizes, from a certain distance, the logics of his then self. 'Now', he sees through them, brings out their 'irrational kernel'—how what seemed rational were the results of the dynamics in the social environment, of personal psychic patterns, of tall dreams and oppressive presents, of experiences lived and configured—a 'false consciousness' about one's own conscious rationality. "I didn't think for myself. It was not my search through roads that brought me where I stood. Yet how deep the hypnotism was! It seemed it was me who had thought. Yes, this was my *own* opinion" (Bandhopadhyay 2000: 9). In yet another frame of looking back, Mihir Chakrabarty still subscribes to the rationale that drove him to his decision and activities, given the circumstances leading up to these. He says (1994: 113):

> The young man standing on the pavement that day had an analytical and sensitive mind, and maybe, he had a certain sense of honesty.
>
> His surroundings were offensive, tyrannical, and rebellion was in the wind.
>
> The individual rebel of the 50's had now before him, instead of a disembodied adversary, the state—taught, in its own stale pedagogy and its universities, to be the country—armed to the teeth.
>
> The traditional left had reached its limits of inanity and itself was following the rules of "power".
>
> At this juncture, the "peal of spring thunder".
>
> What else could the boy do?

Even Azizul Haque, who almost fully stands by his political activities while writing his memoirs, works within the dichotomous division of reason and emotion. Most of the episodes he recounts are eloquent testimonies to his own vulnerabilities to emotions. He sees his past and present selves as one, reacting in a hypersensitive way to these inputs, to the extent of acting in opposition to the demands of reason. Even when he is perfectly aware of the 'call' of rationality. This task of ferreting out reason from emotion remains forever incomplete. Bandyopadhyay's account is the one to make this felt in a nuanced narrative of events and reasonings, the one flowing into the other with and without sudden jerks. The inalienable uncertainty that haunts a project of understanding, understanding reasonings of past selves across the hiatus of commensurability, a commensurability tenuous yet unmistakable in its presence in the selves of the present, marks his efforts throughout. What if what I now think to be the cause was not really so? What if I make it up now, as an afterthought? And maybe today's me cannot ever (re)cognize yesterday's—

> It is very difficult to answer these questions. The answers are never correct. What I think, I cannot put it down. When I write I find something has gone wrong. It is not possible to get hold of the mind as it was twenty-five years ago. Not possible to understand those passions with today's mind and rationality. I cannot make "today" comprehend the time and surroundings of those days.
>
> (Dasgupta 1994: 134)

To write about those days is nothing but such a failed effort. To make 'today' comprehend 'yesterday'. And writing about memories, somewhat disjointed yet adding up to a narrative structure, remains at least as effective in the process as 'history'. Specially when, popping in fragments of memories into the writing, one keeps in mind the impossibilities of a total understanding, yet keeps on disrupting standard narratives, or at least gives new twists to the existing ones.

Standard versions of the accounts of the Naxalbari uprising[5], in newspapers or official and institutional documents, mark it as a disruption in 'normal' life. A break in the 'peaceful' natural flow of daily activities, a 'calamity'. *Journal Sottor* does not contradict this view in a general sense. It speaks of the disruptions and the destructions involved. But differently.

The 'normal' flow of events turns out to be stultifying, stale, tyrannical. The hypocrisy inherent in and the insecurity of the living make the disruptions seem natural. Natural and just. Yet, a complete reversal of the orders that be appears too simplistic. For, this same course of orderly events that calls for the tyrannical regime of the police–army–prison institutions to support its continuation, is seen to carry within itself, streams of affection, likings, aspirations and a hankering for peace that borders on selfishness or insensitivity. Little streams, of which neither the institutions nor the revolutionists seem to be aware. In a way the destructions flow from this order of living, flow as being disruptive. And though the author occasionally drops in a comment that has a sense of regret for the forms that the revolutionary activities had taken, an unmistakable note of tragic inevitability regarding these very forms accompanies his utterances—

> They were (also) fugitives. Denying and wiping out the present. The present that was their life, their daily living—they were cursing, spitting on it. This man from Bengal was an enemy of Gandhi, a hardened, merciless critic of the non-violent movement; they do not have the time at hand or the patience at heart to examine any matter with circumspection. In passing judgements on national politics, they are not ready to take the care that is needed to separate the bones from a fish. Uttering obscenities at the father of the nation, they might even, if possible, hit the corpse of the man—struck dead by Nathuram's bullets—with worn out shoes. (Bandyopadhyay 2000: 13)

The account comes from a participant in the events, an active participant. Unlike most of the recent studies on memory and memorial accounts, the author is not an 'abject victim', nor does he read written/oral records of the victims from a distance. His separation from the event in time and space remains forever incomplete through the mediation of his self-hood. Not that selves are continuous and authenticating in an absolute sense. Yet, at least for Bandyopadhyay, there seems to be a sincere reaching out into the past that bridges (again, partially) selves through empathy. Here, the sense of being 'caught unawares' by the 'calamity', the bewilderment of "how inexplicable it all was" (D. Chakrabarty 1996: 2144) is seasoned by an effort to make sense of one's own thoughts and activities, of the rationale that had 'activated' one's self. 'Making sense of the inexplicable' becomes an active process of introspection 'and' retrospection, active in a way less spontaneous and unanalytical, less a reflex and more reflexive, than the passivity of victimhood would call for. The narrative hardly waits for the analyst or critical theorist for meanings to be rendered multiple. Not opting for a totally comprehensible rational historical account of the events (that many of the other 'memories' have attempted at, and I have not dealt with them here), it also shuns the authority/authorization of an 'otherness' to history flowing from an unreflexive immediacy. It leaves its reasons incomplete, and incomprehensibility is seasoned with causality. The rootedness of past selves of the narrator in the (re)constructed events, his onticity, does not try to authenticate a counter-history with its sights, in and out, its purported (incomplete) 'presence'. The radical unanticipatability of embodiment produces the politics and the ethics of a rupture in the reasoned progress of the purported revolution. It, at the same time, does not let go of the tentacles of a revolutionary utopia. At least, it leaves room for me to make such a reading. For a critical theorist who had dabbled, for a couple of years, in the political projects of the movement after about twenty-five years of these events, it can hark back in, some of the senses of dissatisfaction and rage, loss and void that he (re)collects.

> It was a small lane in Tollygunge. It was night. It was dark. The room was dark. There were about five families huddled in the single room. The little boy of four was there too.
>
> He had come up from the ground floor with his parents. Someone was saying, today the police would turn this place into Baranagar. He overheard.
>
> The next day, the police vans went away. The boy felt empty. The joy of living perhaps. They had killed Rabi, the one-legged chap, someone was telling. "Rabi uncle," the boy muttered.

Notes

1. These include pieces by Minakshi Sen (1993) and Mary Tyler (1977).
2. Not that I conflate the concerns of gendering with the question of women. To deal with both men's and women's writings on the subject would make a discussion of gendering central in a way that this chapter does not aspire to. Swati Ghosh (2001), Srila Roy (2007) and Mallarika Sinha Roy (2011) have dealt with these issues in different yet related ways.
3. For a detailed discussion on the multiple aspects of inscriptions on the body by the marks of society, see Das (1995).
4. The dynamic of such a possibility is worked out in Das (2010).
5. By the expression 'Naxalbari uprising', here I mean a whole spate of revolutionary movements that occurred at the turn of the 1970s, of which the incident of killings in the wake of a peasant uprising in Naxalbari was a single yet iconic episode.

References

Bandyopadhyay, Raghab. 2000. *Journal Sottor* (Journal of the Seventies). Kolkata: Mitra & Ghosh.
Benjamin, Walter. 1992 (German 1950). 'Theses on the Philosophy of History' in *Illuminations*, ed., Hannah Arendt, tr., Harry Zohn, 245–255. London: Fontana Press.

Benjamin, Walter. 1965. *Zur Kritik der Gewalt und andere Aufsätze* (nachw. H. Marcuse). Frankfurt: Suhrkamp Verlag.
Chakrabarty, Dipesh. 1996. 'Remembered Villages', in *Economic and Political Weekly*, 31 (32): 2143–2151.
———. 1998. 'Minority Histories, Subaltern Pasts', in *Economic and Political Weekly*, 33 (9): 473–479.
Chakrabarty, Mihir. 1994. 'Ei Mrityu Upotyoka Amar Desh Na' in volume 'SD': 105–113.
Chatterjee, Partha. 1993. *The Nation and Its Fragments*. Delhi: Oxford University Press.
Das, Anirban. 2010. *Toward a Politics of the (Im)Possible: The Body in Third World Feminisms*. London, New York, Delhi: Anthem Press.
Dasgupta, Subendhu 1994. 'Naxalbari: Nijer Kotha Nijekei Bola', in volume 'SD'.
Das, Veena. 1995. *Critical Events: An Anthropological Perspective on Contemporary India*. Delhi: Oxford University Press.
Ellman, M. 1981. 'Disremembering Dedalus: A Portrait of the Artist as a Young Man', in *Untying the Text: A Post-Structuralist Reader* ed. R. Young, 189–206. Boston, Massachussetts: Routledge & Kegan Paul.
Foucault, M. 1998. 'Different Spaces', tr., Robert Harley in *Aesthetics, Method, and Epistemology: Essential Works of Foucault 1954–1984 Volume. 2*, ed., James Faubion, 175–185. London, New York: Penguin Books.
Foucault, Michael and Paul Rainbow. 1984. *The Foucault Reader*. New York: Pantheon Books.
Ghosh, S. 2001. 'Prison Memory: Retrieval of the Silent Other', in *Margins* February, 50–63.
Guha, Ranajit. 1983. 'The Prose of Counter Insurgency', in R. Guha (ed.), *Subaltern Studies II*. Oxford University Press.
———. 1996. 'The Small Voice of History', in S. Amin and D. Chakrabarty (eds), *Subaltern Studies* Vol No. IX. Delhi: Oxford University Press.
Gupta, Ranjit. 1999. *Mayabi Tantuja*. Calcutta.
Haque, Azizul. 1991. *Karagere Athero Bochhor* (Eighteen Years in Prison). Kolkata: Deys Publication
Klein, K. L. 2000. 'On the Emergence of *Memory* in Historical Discourse', *Representations*, 69.
Mandal, Pulakesh and Jaya Mitra (eds). 1994. *Sei Dasak*. (That Decade). Kolkata: Papyrus.
Mitra, Jaya. 1989. *Hanyaman* (Being Killed). Kolkata: Anyadhara.
Pandey, G. 1999. *Memory, History and the Question of Violence*. Kolkata: K. P. Bagchi.
Roy, Mallarika Sinha. 2011. *Gender and Radical Politics in India: Magic Moments of Naxalbari (1967–1975)*. London and New York: Routledge.
Roy, Srila. Unpublished MS. 'Remembering Revolution: Gender, Violence and the Production of Identity in Naxalbari', Ph.D. Thesis submitted to the University of Warwick, UK in 2007.
Rosaldo, R. 1989. 'Imperialist Nostalgia' in *Representations* 26, 107.
Said, E. 2000. 'Invention, Memory and Place', *Critical Inquiry* 26 (2): 175–192.
Sen, Minakshi. 1993. *Jeler Bhitor Jel*. (Prison within Prison). Kolkata: Pratikshan Publication.
Tyler, Mary. 1977. *My Years in an Indian Prison*. Bombay, Calcutta, Delhi, Madras: B. I. Publications.
Zizek, S. 1989. *The Sublime Object of Ideology*. London: Verso.

6

Literature, Society and the Calling of Creative Public Spheres

Beyond Adaptation and Meditative Verbs of Transformations

Ananta Kumar Giri

> The work makes public something other than itself; it manifests something other; it is an allegory. In the work of art something other is brought together with the thing that is made. To bring together is, in Greek, *symbalein*. The work is a symbol.
>
> Martin Heidegger, 'The Origin of the Work of Art'.

> We seek certainly for that sort of expression which is self-expression. When an individual feels himself hedged in he recognizes the necessity of getting a situation in which there shall be an opportunity for him to make his addition to the understanding, and not simply to the conventionalized "me".
>
> G. H. Mead, *Mind, Self and Society*.

> Writing is a question of becoming, always incomplete, always in the midst of being formed.... It is not the first two persons that function as the condition of literary enunciation; literature begins only when a third person is born in us that strips us of the power to say "I".... *To write is also to become something other than a writer*.
>
> Gilles Deleuze, 'Literature and Life'.
> (Italics added.)

> The genuinely committed writer is never on the side of the Establishment. His voice is always a powerful protest against arbitrary power. He is always on the side of man, of the future and of truth in spite of the pretensions that seem to rule all around.... A writer is always on the side of affirmation, on the side of love.
>
> Chitta Ranjan Das, *A Glimpse into Oriya Literature.*

Introduction and Invitation

Exploring the relationship between literature and society is an adventure in co-realizations and transformations going beyond the logic of the fields of both literature and society. It also calls for understanding their manifold conceptualizations and realizations. The conventional understanding of literature is that it is created by men of literature. It is not always realized that literature is part of life and society; when it is, it is usually conceptualized and represented in a language of mirror and adaptation: literature is either a mirror of society or it adapts to the logic of society. But literature is not only a mirror of society but also a field of creative expressions and confrontations—which breaks existing mirrors of society and creates new languages of self—and social realizations and new landscapes of imaginations. Both literature and society are not only fields of adaptation but also fields of transcendence and transformations in which individuals and groups strive to go beyond adaptation and create new conditions of self-, co- and social realizations. These are fields in which there is interrogation and confrontation of the existing logic of literature and society.

In exploring the relationship between literature and society the language of interdisciplinary transaction is not enough. A new language and practice of transdisciplinary cultivation is needed, beyond adaptation and meditative verbs of transformations. In this striving for a new language and relationship, realizing the distinction between noun and verb is crucial. In conventional languages, literature and society, as well as such important terms of personal, cultural and national identity as person, nation, writer, India, Shakespeare, etc. come as nouns which one also uncritically uses, adopts and adapts to. These nouns from the beginning are imprisoned in a logic of possessive pronouns—this is 'my' self, this is 'our' literature—and any foundational critique of such possessive pronouns are met with resistance and sometimes violent annihilation. But literature and society, as well as such fundamental fields of life as self, are not only nouns but also verbs. They embody verbs of unfoldment, emergence and realizations.[1] As verbs they are not only activistic (which is the way verbs are constructed and realized in modernity) but also meditative. But these meditative verbs of action, expression, communication and co-realizations are manifold—sitting, walking, as well as dancing, verbs of life. Literature and society are verbs of co-realizations and meditative transformations involving walking, sitting and dancing verbs. The public sphere is an important sphere in which such verbs of co-realizations and transformations are at work.

In such transformative co-realizations the nature of 'and' plays an important role. If one conceptualizes 'and' in a logic of juxtaposition, as it mostly happens in the logic of interdisciplinarity, the terms and fields on both sides of 'and' do not get mutually interpenetrated and transformed. 'And' becomes a helpless presence repeating the logic of 'end' (which simultaneously means end of the meaning of as well as ultimate end or purpose). But if one's conception and realization of 'and' is mutual interrogation, transmutation and mothering bridge then one's inhabitation, meditation, dance, walk and work in the space of the 'and,' the space of the middle, becomes a work of transformation, transforming a one-sided conceptualization, realization and organization of fields such as literature and society.[2] While one conventionally understands and works in the space of 'and', reproduces a logic of 'end' and 'noun', in beyond adaptation and meditation, interrogating and mothering verbs, 'and' is a space of transformations. 'And' is a space of quest for infinity from the actors and fields on its two sides rather than a reiteration of the totalizing logic of totality of either of them.[3] 'And' is a mothering ground and bridge of quest for and embodiment of responsibility.

The public sphere helps in realizing such meaning of 'and' beyond the adaptive, already determined and ultimate logic of 'end'. Literature helps express 'ourselves to ourselves' as well as to the others and the public. Expression in the field of literature is simultaneously self, mutual and public and helps in the creation of public spheres in societies. In the creation of modern public spheres, as Jurgen Habermas (1989) himself says, literature has played an important role. He calls it literary public sphere. But it is one thing to talk about the literary public sphere as a type of public sphere or even as a segment of public sphere and it is another thing to realize the integral literary dimension of the public sphere itself.

In later conceptualizations and realizations, literature becomes an integral part of the public sphere through the work of rhetoric, language, style of argumentation and mutual co-presence in such modes as co-walking and co-labouring.[4]

Unfortunately an understanding of the public sphere in social sciences does not fully appreciate its literary dimension and constitution. It has a very prosaic and intellectualist rendering of the public sphere without realizing the public drama and public poetry in it. The other limitation of contemporary social science understanding of the public sphere is that it is part of an uncritical telos of modernity; originating in modernity, it can only become part of an unfinished agenda of modernity. Such conceptualizations of the public sphere do not help to realize the work of the public sphere in pre-modern and non-modern societies (cf. Giri 2002; Giri 2008; Uberoi 1996). But literature in all societies has created public spaces and public spheres for mutual communication, though depending upon the nature of the social arrangement and mode of government the nature of such social manifestation of creativity has varied. In societies where creators of literature seeking critical public dialogue with their literature of protest and alternative imagination are not tolerated, humiliated and killed, meditative verbs and streams also dry up and die. Such conditions existed in the past in many societies, especially those under authoritarian regimes, and they do continue to exist even in liberal modern democracies.

Literature and Society: Beyond Adaptation and Dynamics of Creative Expressions

In order to understand the relationship between society and literature, one needs to understand the transformed understanding of both these fields. Society is a field that helps individuals to come together and express themselves. In sociological theorization of society, there is an acknowledgement of the fact that society is not just a field of *a priori* determination and embeddedness but also a field of self-realization, co-realizations and creative emergence (cf. Sunder Rajan 1998). G. H. Mead, one of the pioneers of modern sociological thinking and author of *Mind, Self and Society* helps in realizing the limits of the social and urges, "neither I nor me is a reiteration of the existing conventions of society." As Mead (1934: 209) tells us:

Me may be regarded as giving the form of the "I". The novelty comes in the action of the "I", but the structure, the form of the self is one which is conventional.

This conventional form may be reduced to a minimum. In the artist's attitude, where there is artistic creation, the emphasis on the element of novelty is carried to the limit. This demand for the unconventional is especially noticeable in modern art. Here the artist is supposed to break away from convention; a part of his artistic expression is thought to be in the breakdown of convention.[5]

From contemporary philosophers and sociologists one gets an intimation of a post-conventional and post-social conceptualization of society. Jurgen Habermas (1990) states that morality is not just reproducing the conventional logic of society; rather, it is to learn how to think and act in post-conventional ways taking into consideration the calling of universal and universalizable justice. Alain Touraine (2007) talks about sociology beyond society, which explores the way individuals become subjects. For Touraine, becoming a member of society is integrally linked to the process in which one becomes a subject but to be a subject is to have the ability to say no to the existing logic if this does not allow creative self-realization. What Touraine and Habermas have not explored sufficiently however is how by cultivating the literary field on the part of self and society one can realize the post-conventional dimension of society, have the capacity to say no in the face of an overwhelming compulsion for yes, and go beyond the logic of an *a priori* social. What they have not explored is how the practice of creative literature can contribute to co-creating society as a field of creative expression and co-realizations.

From the field of literature also, one has a connected move to realize society as a field of self-expression and co-realizations. One finds it, for instance, in the work of Chitta Ranjan Das (1923–2011), a creative seeker, writer and experimenter from Odisha. Das emphasizes that society has been built by those who do not conform. Personality and self for him is not just a logic of adaptation and socialization; it is a field to realize an emergent wholeness, building upon one's quest for self-realization, co-realization and world realization (Das 2010). Touraine's appeal for sociology beyond society finds a creative resonance in Das, who explains how boundaries of sociology are now being transcended in creative experiments and adventures.[6]

Literature and the *Tapasya* of Transformations: A Glimpse into the Creative Worlds of Chitta Ranjan Das[7]

The space of the 'and'—the space in between, is a space of *tapasya*—where one strives to go beyond the existing logic of closure and realize openness and beauty, dignity and dialogue in self, society and the world. Here one can discuss in some detail the work of Chitta Ranjan Das, who is an embodiment of this reality and possibility in each one of us.

Das believes in *tapasya* as a mode of being in a world where one patiently labours to take existent reality to a new evolutionary height as well as make the descent of a higher level of consciousness and a more dignified and qualitative relationship into existent self, culture and society. Literature as *tapasya* makes possible many new beginnings. First of all, it enables one to blossom, to grow, become capable of more sharing, giving and love. The *tapasya* of literature is a *tapasya* of self-transformation. In literature, one is familiar with experimentation with styles and techniques, but for Das the most important experiment in literature is to experiment with one's life, to carry out manifold 'experiments with truth' in one's life, as Gandhi, another creative interlocutor of our times with whom Das had carried out a lifelong dialogue, also emphasizes. But self-transformation and world-transformation go together. Literature must contribute to the transformation of the world—from its ugliness and many indignities—literature must help the world be a more dignified place to be and become. The institutional moorings of the world—its politics, economy and education—must be changed in order that the dignity of the human person is at the centre of one's scheme of things. Literature must contribute to the building of such a world and the transformed consciousness that makes this possible.

As a *tapasya* of social transformation, literature has to take part in people's social, cultural and moral struggles. Literature as *tapasya* is a field of compassion and confrontation. It has to give expression to people's creativity and aspirations as well as pain and suffering through compassionate identification with them as well as through confronting systems that produce suffering. For this, poets and writers must write in the language of the people without unnecessary ornamentation. The dominance of ornamental language, as it occurred in the era of *Ritikavya* of medieval Indian literature, and as it happens in certain fields of modern poetry are signs of decadence for Das. One of the animating chapters in Das' (1981) magnum opus *Odia Sahityara Sanskrutika Bikashadhara* (the cultural development of Oriya literature) is called 'The conflict between *Reeti* (style) and *Preeti* (love)'. Das is for life-affirmative love in literature, a love that is expressed in the clarity of one's language. Writing in alienating language, whether it is Sanskrit in the medieval world or English in contemporary India, is an expression of one's alienation from vibrant links with people around. It does not make literature part of the creative public spheres of society.

But to write in the language of the people requires courage. One of the heroes of such courage for Das is Sarala Das, the maker of the Oriya *Mahabharata*. In the fourteenth century, when poets were writing in Sanskrit, Sarala Das chose to write in Oriya. This was a protest as well as a creative affirmation. Similar courage was shown by Achyutananda and the Panchasakhas—the famous five friends of fifteenth century Odisha, Balarama Das, Ananta Das, Yashovanta Das, Jagannatha Das and Achyutananda Das—who refused to write in Sanskrit and translated many epics and Puranas into Oriya. Das helps us understand that the Panchasakhas were people's leaders and chose this wider calling for themselves rather than the more secure one of being a court pundit. It has to be noted that the birth of mother languages in India is connected to the courage and creativity of such pioneers in every modern Indian language who chose to write in their mother languages rather than in the language of the courts. For Das, as a writer, one must have the courage to be on the side of the people rather than sing ballads for the kings and queens and loiter in the corridors of power.

Speaking of language, Das (1982a) believes that the written language in literature derives nourishment from the spoken language. The debate on the written and the oral has a contentious history and for Derrida, while the written fixes and binds one's thought, the oral gives unrestricted freedom to it. But Das is not obsessed with the issue of the comparative significance of the written and the oral. His main point is that users of the written must have the humility to realize that the written is nourished by the oral and have the readiness to learn from the oral. After a while, however, Das' meditation on language and literature goes beyond the conventions of the written and the oral. For Das, literature must be a mantra in life. Taking inspiration from Sri Aurobindo, another seeker who had been a constant companion of Das in his life's pilgrimage, Das believes that the language of literature should be the language of mantra. It must have the illocutionary power to transform. Das also suggests that alternative literature must have an alternative language because the existing language is inadequate to describe and express the horizon of emergence. Therefore when Das argues that one must write in the people's language, it is not an exercise in populism alone. In the evolutionary unfoldment of a writer, there have to be moments when the writer presents a new language to the people in order to describe the emergent world she has envisioned, strives to create or has created.

For Das, literature must have commitment but this is not necessarily expressed through commitment to political parties and ideologies. For Andre Béteille (1982), commitment does not mean commitment to an ideological orthodoxy alone; it also refers to the moral commitments of the actors. Das' concerns are similar and, at the same time greater, as he urges the ontological depth of moral and social commitments. For Das, one cannot be committed to society if one is not committed to oneself. But self-commitment here does not mean commitment to one's ego-aggrandizement but to the calling of the universal self within each individual. Das (1992) makes a distinction between ideology and devotion to an ideal life. Ideal life is not just a romantic utopia for Das but is the design of an ideal relationship of dignity which one continuously seeks to realize in the life of self, other, culture and society.

But what happened to the devotion to an ideal life in post-independent India? Das (2000) is pained by the death of ideals in this period and looks at it as an era of *prabanchita biplaba*, an era of "betrayed revolution." The Indian freedom movement wanted to realize both political freedom and social revolution. But after the realization of political freedom, the agenda of social revolution was hijacked by the powers that be. Das condemns the writers of the country for so easily and willingly becoming a party to this political conspiracy. For Das, poets and the litterateurs quickly forgot the dreams of the freedom movement and soon sang eulogies of the holders of power, even surpassing the court pundits of the medieval world. They forgot the language of *tapasya, sraddha* (transformative love), social struggles and social transformations. Thus the so-called modern era in a field like Oriya literature for Das is a field of decadence where writers became clinically preoccupied with styles and techniques. As Das (1982a: 242) writes: "The-so called modern movement in literature soon came to mean the movement for new styles and techniques, not often harping in a bizarre sort of way, on new lethargies and therefore also new eccentricities." While "literature could have given a leadership and provided an alternative," it compromised and declared its "insolvency" (1982a: 245). Furthermore, he says (1982a: 243):

> When there was this fundamental incapacity to face the real issues and the real privations, the writers ran away and took refuge in gimmicks and skills. One can say without exaggeration that in Oriya poetry at least there was a regression to the *Reeti* phase of its history in the 17th-18th centuries where the poets of the courts overdid the structure of poetry to conceal the fact as it were that they had nothing more important to say. Thus, as far as range is concerned, the poets remained very closed and cornered in spite of the avowed modernity of their styles.

For Das, literature in post-independent India should have been a literature of protest and of seeking new affirmations. The burgeoning body of post-colonial criticism has not really embodied this sensibility deep enough. Literature should have confronted the brutality of the post-colonial state and its dehumanizing configuration of power with love, courage and *sraddha*. These days, critiques of modernity under the rubric of varieties of postmodernism are still confined to the safe institutional corridors of modernity, but Das' critique of modern literature is inspired by an identification with the pangs and hopes of ordinary people who have been victimized by the processes of modernization. In a poverty-stricken society such as India, modernization has been the other name of elite domination. In another context, liberation theologian and critic Felix Wilfred (1997) has argued that a critique of modernity should be attempted taking into account what processes of modernization and the condition of modernity have done to many of its victims. Das' critique of the modern phase of Oriya literature is guided by similar concerns. Modern literature has forgotten that it is a dialogue with people and is a partner in their pangs, aspirations and many strivings for a more dignified future.

Rethinking Literature and Society: Chitta Ranjan Das' Perspectives on Poetry, Literature and Criticism

In order to understand the creative relationship between literature and society, it is helpful to get a glimpse of Das' perspectives on poetry, literature, culture and criticism. For this, the discussion shall be confined to a few of his texts, namely an essay by him on the new horizons of poetry called *Ethara Udiba Neta* (Now the flag shall fly) (1989b) and his collection of essays called *Sahitya O* (Literature and..) (1989a). It must be mentioned that his theoretical statements on literature are also presented in his other collections of essays such as *Ma Nishada, Jatire Mu Jabana* (1979) and *Pashyati Dishi Dishi*.

Ethara Udiba Neta is a unique and inspiring meditation on poetry and poets. It is a long essay on poetry written along with another inspiring poet of contemporary Oriya literature, Srinivasa Udgata. In this work Das (1989b: 2) begins by stating: Poetry is not primarily a *kruti*; a work: it is a *drusti*, a vision, a perspective, a way of looking at oneself and the world. *Drusti* gives rise to creation, *srusti*. This creation is fundamentally meant to take one from what one is to what one ought to be. But poetry is not meant to take one away from reality. Poetry makes bridges, establishes many threads. In the evocative words of Das (1989b: 7), which are difficult to translate into English:

> Poetry makes bridges, it conquers hopelessness by making bridges; by itself becoming a bridge, it establishes victory over all *asammati* (hesitation to consent) and *anamaniyata* (stubbornness). After this everything looks beautiful here.... Once the ladder is there, loneliness departs and the unreachable reaches us as our very own.

Poetry establishes a bridge between time and timelessness, history and eternity and reality and possibility. It is also a creative and transformative link between *bhumi* (ground) and *bhuma* (beyond). A poet stands on the ground but is continuously after a *bhuma*, a beyond. For Das, *bhuma* is such a constant attraction and appeal that while standing on the present and the past it continuously draws us to a future. For Das, to live with poetic sensibility is to live in continuous touch with what psychologists call the peak experience of one's life. Peak experience is a spiritual experience, an integral experience that makes the poet a traveller. In Das' words (1989b: 10):

> The real poet never situates himself at the center. He does not hide himself for a catch like the spider of a web and does not wish to sell his *tapasya* and get the fortunes of an Indra (The King of Heaven). He traverses his path with all his sufferings, sympathy and determination, the path which connects the ground with the peak.

For Das, to touch the peak while standing on the ground is called *utkranti* in the Indian *Sastras* and poetry is an embodiment of this *utkranti*.

Das draws attention to the distinction between the language of power and the aspirations of a poet. According to Nietzsche and Foucault, it is the human will to power that has dominated the way one thinks about poetry, literature, criticism and society. But Das provides an alternative language and an alternative world. While the man of power runs "to bring the entire world inside his closed fist," the urge of poetry ("*kabira basana*" as he calls it) brings one's consciousness to an intimacy when one feels at home with the entire world. At that time all fears vanish. There is also no hatred. The Upanishadic aspiration of life, "*tato na bijugupsate*" (no hatred), then becomes a way of life. In the poetic words of Das (1989b: 7), "[..At that time..] the bird inside comes out silently with all the achieved aspirations and urges of one's life. Once she starts coming out the door which had remained closed for centuries spontaneously gets opened."

But for Das, the man of power does not want to open his doors. He is afraid of expansion, he is afraid that he will be lost in the process of expansion. In the words of Das (1989b: 10),

> The man of power is not able to give himself. He is not able to open his many knots. The knots open and hesitations go away only when we discover the poet within us; we are then able to realize that our greatest way and dharma is to expand ourselves. When we look at the world through the eyes of a poet, we realize that our threads are connected with all this (with everybody in the world).

Thus for Das, poetry is continuous with expansion of consciousness, which while establishing a bridge between the outer nature and inner nature takes both to a new height. Taking inspiration from Biswanath Kaviraj, the great theoretician of poetry, Das calls this *chaitanya tanmayata*, expansion of consciousness. The creative imagination, which is the mother of this expanding urge, knows no bounds, accepts and acknowledges no limitation. For Das, this is the stage of "self-creation" in one's life where one strives to continuously create and recreate oneself.

In his earlier reflection on poetry and prose reflected in *Jatire Mu Jabana* Das (1979) had looked at poetry in a narrower way. For him, modern prose is closer to reality than poetry and thus he declares the present age as an age of prose. But in the present treatise Das has no such parochialism.[8] Rather, he challenges one to realize the blurring of genres between prose and poetry in one's creative works. In this essay, Das also invites one to transcend the distinction between poets and critics. In the integral unfoldment of her life, while a poet goes up step by step and is worthy of critical observation and presents the picture of a possible world as a critic of the existent world, a critic in the same trajectory of integral unfoldment is capable of touching deeper and deeper and is able to look at the world through the eyes of a poet (1979: 43).

Thus, central to the overcoming of the distinction between prose and poetry and poetry and criticism is the creative travel, creative immersion and creative evolution of the maker of literature. In fact, Das establishes an intimate connection and transformative link between criticism and creativity, deconstruction and reconstruction. He demonstrates this link in both his life and letters. In fact, one can use this issue of creativity to move to a discussion of another of Das' treatise on literature, *Sahitya O* (1989a), which is a collection of his sixteen essays on literature. All these essays have the connecting term 'O' ['and'] in the middle such as 'literature and commitment' and 'literature and creativity', which is probably meant to bring home his conviction that to think of literature is only to think of it in conjunction with life. For Das, literature alone is not enough; it is a means to leading a more dignified and qualitatively different life.

In his essay, 'Sahitya O Srujanasilata' (Literature and Creativity) Das argues that behind creative literature stands a creative person. While contemporary interlocutors such as Foucault (1977: 107) announce the 'death of the author' and argue, "if we wish to know the writer in our day, it will be through the singularity of his absence and in his link to death, which has transformed him into a victim of his own writings," Das brings to the fore the creative subjectivity of the writer. Of course, even for Das, all that one writes in the name of literature is not creative literature but one cannot be creative in literature if one is also not creative in one's life. For Das (1989a: 157), "a divided life is a diseased life and a diseased life can never be creative."

Das believes that in literature one cannot be confined either to truth or beauty. Das has a relational approach to aesthetics where aesthetics is part of the quality of life that constitutes the total context. In a recent essay he talks about two wings of aesthetic consciousness—food and freedom, and both the wings are animated by a desire to build bridges across the divides by oneself becoming a bridge (Das 2007). Das believes that adoration of beauty must have within itself, a fight against ugliness and a satyagrahic quest for truth. If one starts with either truth or beauty, then in the characteristic unfoldment of one's life one inevitably meets the other. The literature that adores truth is the literature of courage but those who adore beauty in literature may not necessarily be the bearers of courage and the determination to struggle.

As Das argues (2007: 148): "Those who are only aestheticians in literature are afraid of struggle, and are afraid to come down from their *palankas* [luxurious beds]; they are afraid that if they come down then they would fall down to an abyss of mud." Das wonders how such fearful aestheticians can ever create a literature of beauty! For him, beauty cannot establish itself by denying the truth and ignoring the courage and struggle that is required to protect, preserve and nurture both truth and beauty. Literature can then transcend the many distances between the few who consume literature only as beauty and the many who are condemned to remain at the margins of the world of aesthetics. Recently many critics have drawn one's attention to the dangers of an aestheticization of life (see Harvey [1989], for example) and Das contributes to this critical perspective of the times. But Das does not belittle the significance of beauty in purifying one's desire and making one's life artistic. What he wants is an integration of truth and beauty. In the words of Das (2007: 133),

> The person who realizes that he is also nearer to truth while having made one's life beautiful and more beautiful, he alone enters inside the real creative and artistic domain of one's life. The person with the love of being nearer to Truth also feels nearer to beauty and washes the many dusts which have gathered around his eyes, makes his life truly artistic. He elevates and expands himself to such a level that he sees both truth and beauty inside one gestalt plane.

Whatever Das has written about poetry and literature applies to his views on criticism as well. Criticism should help one be a more genuine friend of life, hold the hands of authors and people and take them to a new height. In a remarkable essay of his, 'Sarjantmaka Sahitya Sameekhya: Abhimukhya O Angeekara' (Creative literacy criticism: Objectives and commitment) Das clearly states this position. Das presented us two important monographs of criticisms quite early in his life—namely, *Odisara Mahima Dharma* (1952) and *Achyutananda O Panchasakha Dharma* (1951). In his work on Mahima dharma, while discussing the spiritual aspirations of prophets and seekers such as Mahima Gosai and Bhima Bhoi, Das discusses their work in a global context. He provides examples from other religious and philosophical traditions of the world while discussing the message of Mahima dharma. In this book, Das (1952) writes more than half a century ago, "Bhakti is a global urge which has manifested itself in many religions. This urge has also strongly manifested itself in Mahima dharma. So the critic would fulfill his duty if he can show the link between Mahima dharma and other dharmas." Das has carried this wide-ranging exploration in all his critical works, thus breaking the walls of parochialism that afflict us.

As far back as 1968, in the year of the worldwide student movement, Das wrote an essay entitled, 'Utsa Nirupanara Roga' (The disease of determining sources) (1977b), in which he urges one to overcome one's obsession with sources. But at the same time, Das (1977b: 121) makes clear, "I am not condemning history, I am only pointing to the limits of history in the discussion of literature." For example, he argues that if during the discussion of a maker of literature such as the great Sarala Das one is concerned only with whether "he belonged to this caste or not" (1977b) and whether he was one or many [like Shakespeare] and "whether he was born in this village or not," then one forgets the creative Sarala Das. Understanding the creative subjectivity of Sarala Das as expressed in his work is as important as understanding his many historical determinants. Criticism of literature has to be as creative as literature itself and for Das an uncritical bondage to the power of history in literary criticism often makes one forget this.

Das' *A Glimpse into Oriya Literature* (1982a) and *Odiya Sahityara Sanskrutika Bikashadhara* (1981) suggest some other methodological and perspectival insights as well. Das writes (1982a: 35):

> Periods in literature do not come in terms of one exclusively following the other. We study a literature in terms of a few periods solely for reasons of convenience. These periods do not really give into another which succeeds them. They just evolve into another and thus depict a process of development that is always there. The history of any literature, therefore, should be looked at and conceived as a continuum and unending chain of challenges and responses.

The above again illustrates Das' dissatisfactions with a mere historical approach. When a critic is looking at the history of culture and literature, his probing also carries the questions of the present. In the words of Das (1982a: 35): "The contemporary society determines to a very great extent the nature in which the challenges are served and emphases given."

Another insight gained from Das is to look at literature as a bearer of the cultural imagination of a group, a society. Culture for Das is the eye of a society, an eye that looks at existent social reality creatively and critically. Culture is a perennial seeking of value and a striving for dignified human relationships. Culture is a source of inspiration and Das calls it *prerana*.

He discusses literature keeping this reality and aspiration of *prerana* in mind. He discusses literary work from this point of view of *prerana*, both at the level of an individual author as well as the creative literary expression of a group. His *Odiya Sahityara Sanskrutika Bikashadhara* (1981) shows the dynamics of this *prerana* of culture throughout its history and how literature has sometimes enhanced its flow and at other times obstructed it.

Das contrasts the *prerana* of culture with the notion of *sampatti*, property. Culture is an inspiration, a *prerana*, not a property, a *sampatti*. The *prenana* of culture and literature is to help one be and become, rather than just to have and possess. Das shows us in his history of literature what happens to a society when the *prerana* of culture and literature is treated as a property by both the poets and the holders of power. It speaks of the death of the human person and creates obstructions in the flow of culture as well, which looks for the coming of a Bhagiratha, a Bhagiratha who makes the river Ganges flow from the mountains by the dint of his *tapasya*. For Das, the *tapasya* of the Bhagirathas is facilitated and strengthened by different social, political and cultural movements as well.

Das's emphasis on culture can immediately make one jump to the conclusion that Das is also a postmodernist and post-structuralist, as these movements also reiterate the significance of culture. But while the postmodernist notion of culture is still very anthropological and anthropocentric, treating culture as a way of life and a mode of practice without understanding the transformative potential inherent in it and the *sadhana* which makes it possible, Das brings the dimension of continued seeking and self-transformation to the core of culture. Second, while discussing the work of culture Das does not remain at an ideational level alone despite the suggestion of idealism. Das looks at the base of culture in land ownership and the educational capability of a society. He says that when excellent ornamental poetry was being written in the royal courts of medieval India, a majority of people did not have ownership of land and were working as tenants. These vantage points of poverty and social death are as helpful to look at medieval literature as the creative literature and theoretical texts emerging from advanced industrial societies, the home of the postmodern and post-structural enunciations on the human condition today.

What blocks potential for realization, self-, co- and social, is a condition of pathology for Das, which needs works of compassion, confrontation and healing. For Das, literature is a field of not only murmuring but also grumbling, a field of higher grumbling.[9] Literature questions the existing logic of pathology in self and society and strives towards healing and creative therapy by making these fields of self- and co-realizations.[10] Literature is a field of both compassion and confrontation and a space for expressing luminous anger at the existing ugliness and indignities in societies. This has implication for one's theorization of literature and society in general.

The Calling of Creative Public Spheres

One usually looks at literary creativity in an individualized way but now one needs to link both to fields of creative public spaces and spheres. For the *tapasya* of creativity in literature and society, one needs the spheres of the creative self, intimate groups of mutuality as well as public spheres. But in each of these spheres, one continues the modernist logic of linearity. Despite the language of 'sphere' in public spheres, one's conceptualization and organization of it is linear. It is hardly a sphere where the spherical nature of one's being is at work or finds an expression.[11] In this context, one needs to conceptualize and realize public spheres as manifold circles and chakras. Public spheres as chakras, reminding one of such historic exemplars such as Buddhist *dharmachakras*, bring interested people together where they, through creative sharing as well as contestations, generate mutual energy. Literature can help realize public spheres as chakras where individuals and groups can express themselves—both their vertical aspiration for higher seeking as well as horizontal longing and commitment for solidarity—and through this, generate energy. Public spheres as chakras thus become an inviting and mothering space for intertwining the vertical and horizontal dimension of one's quest and seeking to integrate these in creative ways.

This challenges one to go beyond the dualism of the vertical and horizontal. The concept and organization of public spheres in modernity is bound to the logic of double contingency and dualism. For example, one looks at the self, other and society through the logic of what Strydom (2009) calls 'double contingency' of self and the other. This double contingency is also imprisoned within dualism. Now one needs to bring the concept of 'triple contingency' to each of these spheres. In triple contingency, along with self and other, there is also a public (Strydom 2009). But this public is not fixed, it is emergent, it is not only observing but also participating. Triple contingency does not lie only outside but also works inside. Triple contingency is also a bearer of transcendence as it transcends the dualistic logic of double contingency of the self and the other.

In literature, spiritual traditions and creative imagination, one is familiar with the concept and reality of the third eye. This third eye exists not only in Shiva, the conventional meditative *tapaswee* and dancer, but also in all. Triple contingency can be linked to the work of the third eye. Literature and creative public spheres can help one realize and cultivate not only the triple contingency of life, thus going beyond the arrogance and exclusionary assertion of either the self or the other and also develop and realize one's third eye, a challenge missing in contemporary theorization of society and public sphere. Public sphere and creative meditation can help realize both triple contingency and the third eye, and then move further to the fourth, fifth and further dimensions of contingencies, aspirations and struggles.[12]

Life Worlds and Living Words

Further, one needs to recreate the link between what is called life worlds and system worlds through the categories of lived worlds and living words. Lived worlds everywhere are multiplex and plural, but the language of life worlds and system worlds as it occurs in sociology and in the works of critical theorists such as Habermas usually presents a one-dimensional logic and rationality such as the primacy of rational in modernity and hierarchy in traditional societies. Life worlds everywhere are also subjected to the dominant logic of the system world such as market, state, caste and gender. In this context, to cultivate lived worlds with their creativity, courage, transcendence and multidimensionality is a challenge that calls for going beyond the existing logic of life worlds and system worlds. This challenge has been articulated and answered in the creative works and worlds of Chitta Ranjan Das. As Das would emphasize, literature can help society and the public sphere in this journey by cultivating what may be called living words. The challenge of creativity is simultaneous: simultaneously nurturing lived worlds of vibrancy, energy, soulful togetherness and meditative solitude and living words which move one not towards hatred and annihilation but to mutual blossoming and co-realization. Both lived worlds and living words do *tapasya* for and with beauty, dignity and dialogues in the face of and in the midst of ugliness, indignity and violence.

Living words work as new mantras of life, to put in the words of Sri Aurobindo and embody what Heidegger (1994) calls 'way making movement.' They just do not mirror 'forms of life' but create new ways of life. They just do not reproduce existing language but create new languages of self- and social realizations. They just do not reproduce the rationality of either tradition or modernity but possibly embody strivings towards what Enrique Dussel calls 'transmodernity.'[13] They are not just part of either the logic of transcendental awe in tradition or 'linguistification of the sacred' in modernity (Habermas 1990). While they seek to make the divine and nature part of the communicative field of humans and express it in ways understandable to the modern rational mind, they nonetheless do not reduce either of them only to what is comprehensible in the language of modern rationality. Transmodernity seeks to cultivate the ineffable in both lived worlds and living words while at the same time making them part of one's everyday conversations. Both lived worlds and living words become sites of courage, creativity and transcendence working in between and in the margins of fear, drudgery and pull towards an imprisonment in closed walls, which is justified in the name of immanence.

Going beyond the linguistification of the sacred in modernity and the consequent disenchantment and dualism between the religious and secular, both life worlds and living words embody new border crossings between the rational and emotional, religion and reason, nature and human, mental and supramental. The life worlds and living words embody such a new border-crossing language of human, nature and divine in continuously emergent ways.

Towards a New Art of Cross-Fertilization

Literature, society and public spheres are fields of living words and lived worlds. Living worlds and lived words can make one pregnant with a new creativity. While one's existing space and time are empty and continuously being emptied out with the logic of the system such as money, market and capital, life worlds and lived worlds help cultivate the regenerative spirit. Both lived worlds and living words work as seeds for a new cross-fertilization, thus helping to realize the concept of immaculate conception in new ways. Metaphorically it can be said that living words can impregnate, as one's lived worlds of *tapasya* can make each and all fertile, which is an embodiment of a new spiritual eroticism.[14]

Thus, the fields of literature, society and public sphere have become dry and deserted and one needs to make these fertile. For this, available fertilizers from the market and external world are not adequate. One needs to make them fertile through self-, mutual- and cross-fertilization in which one's quality of life, relationships and living words play a crucial role.

Again, metaphorically it may be said that earthworms make the land fertile and in present times one needs to be an earthworm to others as well as to one's own self. Once the land is fertile one would have to cultivate the land as a garden for which one also needs to be a gardener. But both earthworms and gardeners can remain bound only to the field, thus uncritically reproducing the logic of embeddeness, which also becomes hostile, opposed and violent not only to forces of emergence from the field itself but also to other fields. In this context the calling of cross-fertilization and cross-pollination calls us to grow wings and simultaneously be birds and bards, fly and sing together, wonder and wander.[15] Literature, society and creative public sphere can help one simultaneously become an earthworm, a gardener and a bird.[16] It can also help one to become a Socratic gadfly, as Socrates, Antigone, Gandhi, Das and many other seekers and fighters of humanity have embodied, striking the powers that hinder one's potential, aspiration and efforts for self-realization, mutual blossoming and world transformations.

Notes

1. It may be noted here that in different philosophical, cultural and spiritual traditions, body, mind and Being are considered verbs. As Tu Wei-ming (2000: 50) writes about body in Chinese culture and philosophy:

   There's a beautiful term, *ti*, which means the body. But, that word, *ti*, can also be used as a verb. It means just my body, but also to embody. The embodiment is a process of understanding other human beings experientially as well as intellectually and spiritually.

   In his *Art and Experience*, John Dewey also writes about mind: "Mind is primarily a verb" (quoted in Elbridge 2000: 244–45). And theologian and philosopher Raimon Panikkar (1995: 26) writes about Being: "Being is a verb, an action, and it has rhythm."

2. This is explored in two interesting creative works, one coming from the field of creative literary criticism and the other from poetry. In his work, *Sahitya O* (Literature and..) Chitta Ranjan Das (1989a) suggests such a transformative, interrogative and mothering meaning and realization of 'and'. This also comes out in a joint work of co-creation in

which the poetic critic and essayist Chitta Ranjan Das and poet Srinivas Udgata (1989) co-create poems and reflections on poetry together in the work *Ebam* which also means 'and'. (This is discussed later in the text.) So does poet and novelist Rabi Narayan Dash (2008) in his book of poems, *...Ebam Kadha* (...And buds).

3. This resonates with the thoughts of Emmanuel Levinas. Franson Manjali (2001) also explores such pathways in his *Literature and Infinity*.
4. While Habermasian public sphere is mainly one of argumentation I make it plural by bringing such activities as love and labour in to it; cf. Giri (2008).
5. As Mead (1934: 221; italics added) tells us:

    The value of an ordered society is essential to our existence but there also has to be room for an expression of the individual himself if there has to be a satisfactorily developed society. A means for such an expression must be provided. *Until we have a social structure in which the individual can express himself as the artist and the scientist does, we are thrown back on the sort of the structure found in the mob, in which everybody is free to express against some hated object of the group.*

6. Note what Touraine, a sociologist, and Das, a creative practitioner of literature, write about sociology. For Touraine, one of the main themes of sociology is therefore the reversal of the conception and role of institutions. These were defined by their functions in the integration of a social system. They defined and imposed respect for the norms and instruments for the defence of individuals that enable them to defend themselves against norms. Our society is less and less a society of the subjected and more and more a society of volunteers (Touraine 2007: 191). About sociology Das (2009: 579–80) shares with us the following:

    The story of all real sociology is one of breaking open the boundaries. The discipline was originally bound strictly to its specific lines and limitations, and it is great that transgressions have been happening all the time. It is becoming more and more clear that society, people, do always matter more than the study of society. The older definitions and contours are fast changing and there are more and more people who are less shy and hence willing to transgress the boundaries. More mature days are in the offing and the recluses till now working in the laboratories are becoming more courageous. Yes, courage, more than anything else, always helps us to ask questions and rewrite our canons of enquiry. Intellectuals are rethinking and as it were from within more ready to revise their roles. Albert Camus has once made a remark that the intellectual's role will be to say that the king is naked when he is and not to go into raptures over his imaginary trappings. And look, all around now there are hegemonies, kings all round who are visibly naked! The intellectual's laboratory has now to come down in proximity to people where they really are, move and have their beings, suffer all the time waiting for an appropriate remedy. The academics could not as a rule do that. Shri Ramakrishna of India had once observed, "some people climb the seven floors of a building and cannot get down." But some can, he did hope, really climb and then come down. They are always of greater worth.

7. This part of the chapter builds upon my earlier and existing work on Chitta Ranjan Das. See Giri (2002).

8. Though it must be noted here that when Das exclusively writes on prose—its nature and possibilities—such parochialism continues to haunt him, as is evidenced in a recent series of essays written on prose in the famous Oriya literary journal *Jhankara*.
9. In the seminar on "Society and Literature: Interdisciplinary Transactions" in Shillong, Professor Mrinal Miri, who presented the keynote address, presented the notion of language and literature as murmuring.
10. To be a person is not just to adapt to a society if it is sick and pathological, but to try to change it. Das challenges the acceptable definition of normality, pathology and therapy. Building upon Abraham Maslow's concept of metapathology and higher grumbling, he urges us to grumble at the existing ugliness, indignity and desecration of life. Das' call for a new realization of personality, which would also contribute to realization of society as a healthy wholeness by first realizing its pathology and sickness, also finds a resonance in many creative thinkers, for example, in the recent work of Axel Honneth of the critical theory tradition in Europe. As Honneth (2007: 34, 35, 37, italics added) tells us:

> In order to speak of a social pathology … we require a conception of normality related to social life as a whole. The immense difficulty involved in this project has been made evident by the failure of social-scientific approaches that have sought to fix the functional requirements of societies solely through external observations. Since what counts as a developmental goal or as normality is always culturally defined, it is only by a hermeneutic reference to a society's self-understanding that social functions of their disorders can be determined. Thus we may have a defensive possibility of speaking of social pathologies within a culturally contingent notion of normality, since we can limit ourselves to an empirical description of what a given culture regards as a disorder.... A paradigm of social normality must, therefore, consist in culturally independent conditions that allow a society's members to experience undistorted self-realization.... The question then becomes crucial whether it is a communitarian form of ethical life, a distance-creating public sphere, non-alienated labor or a mimetic interaction with nature that enables individuals to lead a well-lived life.

11. Philosopher Peter Sloterdijk urges us to realize the distinction between a spherical approach and a linear approach.
12. This calls for cross-cultural dialogue and border-crossing dialogue between critical theory and religious and spiritual ways of thinking. It would be interesting to explore further dialogue between the concept of triple contingency in critical theory and trinity in the Christian religious and spiritual tradition. For Panikkar, "Trinity is not a number but the depth and unfolding of the riches of reality, which is a living relationship.... Panikkar thereby seeks to move beyond a form of dualism, following the best *advaita* experience (of non-dualism), opening a way to dialogue" (quoted in Pikaza 2010: 119). In the same way one can realize triple contingency not as a number but as the depth and creativity of relationship beyond the dualistic logic of self and other. But triple contingency also urges one to realize that trinity, whether it is in Christian tradition or Hindu tradition, is also confronted with the challenges of the public—an observant and meditative public.
13. The following quotation from Dussel helps us to understand transmodernity:

> Europe began to function as the "center" of the world market (and therefore to extend the "world system" throughout the world) with the advent of the

industrial revolution; on the cultural plane, this produced the phenomenon of the Enlightenment, the origins of which, in the long run, we should look for (according to the hypothesis of Morrocan philosopher Al-Yabri, who we will discuss later) in the Averröist philosophy of the caliphate of Córdoba. Europe's crucial and enlightened hegemony scarcely lasted two centuries (1789–1989). Only two centuries! Too short-term to profoundly transform the "ethico-mythical nucleus" (to use Ricoeur's expression) of ancient and universal cultures like the Chinese and others of the Far East (like the Japanese, Korean, Vietnamese, etc.), the Hindustanic, the Islamic, the Russian-Byzantine, and even the Bantu or the Latin American (though with a different structural composition). These cultures have been partly *colonized* (included through negation in the totality, as aspect A of Diagram 1), but most of the structure of their values has been excluded—*scorned, negated and ignored*—rather than annihilated. The economic and political system has been dominated in order to exert colonial power and to accumulate massive riches, but those cultures were deemed to be unworthy, insignificant, unimportant, and useless. The tendency to disparage those cultures, however, has allowed them to survive in silence, in the shadows, simultaneously scorned by their own modernized and westernized elites. That negated "exterior," that alterity—always extant and latent—indicates the existence of an unsuspected cultural richness, which is slowly revived like the flames of the fire of those fathoms buried under the sea of ashes from hundreds of years of colonialism. That cultural exteriority is not merely a substantive, uncontaminated, and eternal "identity." It has been evolving in the face of Modernity itself; what is at stake is "identity" in the sense of process and growth, but always as an exteriority.

These cultures, asymmetrical in terms of their economic, political, scientific, technological, and military conditions, therefore maintain an alterity with respect to European Modernity, with which they have coexisted and have learned to respond in their own way to its challenges. They are not dead but alive, and presently in the midst of a process of rebirth, searching for new paths for future development (and inevitably at times taking the wrong paths). Since they are not modern, these cultures cannot be "post"-modern either. They are simultaneously pre-modern (older than modernity), contemporary to Modernity, and soon, to Transmodernity as well. Postmodernism is a final stage in modern European/ North American culture, the "core" of Modernity. Chinese or Vedic cultures could never be European post-modern, but rather are something very different as a result of their distinct roots.

Thus, the strict concept of the "*trans*-modern" attempts to indicate the radical novelty of the irruption—as if from nothing—from the transformative exteriority of that which is always Distinct, those cultures in the process of development which assume the challenges of Modernity, and even European/ North American Post-modernity, but which respond *from another place, another location.* They respond from the perspective of their own cultural experiences, which are distinct from those of Europeans/North Americans, and therefore have the capacity to respond with solutions which would be absolutely impossible for an exclusively modern culture. A future *trans*-modern culture—which assumes the positive moments of Modernity (as evaluated through criteria distinct from the perspective of the other ancient cultures)—will have a rich pluriversality and would be the fruit of an authentic intercultural dialogue, that would need to bear clearly in mind existing asymmetries (to be an "imperial-core" or part of the semi-peripheral "central chorus"—like Europe today, and even more so since the 2003 Iraq War—is not the same as to be part of the postcolonial and peripheral world). But a postcolonial and peripheral world like that of India, in a position of abysmal asymmetry with respect to the metropolitan core of the colonial era, does not for this reason cease to be a creative nucleus of ancient cultural renewal which is decisively distinct from all of the others, with the capacity to propose novel and necessary answers for the anguishing challenges that the Planet throws upon us at the beginning of the twenty-first century.

"*Trans*-modernity" points toward all of those aspects that are situated "beyond" (and also "prior to") the structures valorized by modern European/North American culture, and which are present in the great non-European universal cultures and have begun to move toward a pluriversal project.

14. Note here what philosopher Luce Irigaray (2002: 115–17) writes:

> Carnal sharing becomes then a spiritual path, a poetic and also a mystical path…. Love takes place in the opening to self that is the place of welcoming the transcendence of the other…. The path of such an accomplishment of the flesh does not correspond to a solipsistic dream … nor to a fin-de-siècle utopia, but to a new stage to be realized by humanity…. Nature is then no longer subdued but it is adapted, in its rhythms and necessities, to the path of its becoming, of its growth. Caressing loses the sense of capturing, bewitching, appropriating…. The caress becomes a means of growing together toward a human maturity that is not confused with an intellectual competence, with the possession of property … nor with the domination of the world.

> For Irigaray, "sharing breath" is an important aspect of this aspired-for spiritual eroticism, giving birth to life and each other and the making of a spiritual community. For Irigaray, "This proto-ethical plane of shared breath is the eternal germ of a spiritual community, i.e., a community of embodied individuals, caring for each other" (quoted in Skof 2011: 136).

15. A poem written by my friend Francis Regis Bouquizabout *Le Troubadour*, about the wandering musicians in medieval France, can be of interest. The following line from the poem in French tells us how the troubadour visits from place to place:

> "Je suis le troubader du chemin qui me mene vers Lui
> Et le passager des temps visibles, invisibles."

Also, the poem *On Wings* by Rabi Narayan Dash (2007) can help us realize many meanings of growing wings:

> When I emerged
> Broken and aimless
> She came out on to her terrace
> To ask if I had seen a flying cat
> And a little sparrow crying in sorrow
> If I knew leaves are already yellow.
> The world I came of, seeking
> Care, if I am I love with
> Money or work with a
> Passion for becoming
> Somebody and something

I have already read
"the child is the father to man"
Sharing her words and unending dream
I started to scream:
"God! Return me to her,
To child, the mother!"

About wings, Rumi tells us its significance in the following ways: "Something open our wings, something makes boredom and hurt disappear."

16. When I present these three modes of being, I always ask what the words are for them in local mother languages. While presenting it in Hanoi, my Vietnamese participants told me that the word for earthworm is *konchin*, for garderner is *kechia* and for bird *lantivuan*. During our conversation we created a symphony of *knochin*, *kechia* and *lantivuan*.

References

Béteille, André. 1982. *Marxism, Pluralism and Orthodoxy*. New Delhi: India Renaissance Institute.

Das, Chitta Ranjan. 1951. *Achyutananda O Panchasakha Dharma* [Achyutananda and the religion of the Panchasakhas]. Shantiniketan, India: Department of Oriya Research, Visva-Bharati.

———. 1952. *Odisara Mahima Dharma* [The Mahima dharma of Orissa]. Shantiniketan, India: Department of Oriya Research, Visva-Bharati.

———. 1977a. *Ma Nishada*. Berhampur: Pustaka Bhandara.

———. 1977b. 'Utsa Nirupanara Roga' [The disease of determining sources], in *Ma Nishada*. Berhampur, India: Pustaka Bhandara.

———. 1979. *Jatire Mu Jabana* [I am an outsider by caste]. Berhampur, India: Pustaka Bhandara.

———. 1983. Pashyati Disidisi. Berhampur, India: Pustaka Bhandara.

———. 1981. *Odia Sahityara Sanskrutika Bikashadhara* [The cultural development of Oriya literature]. Bhubaneswar, India: Orissa Text Book Bureau.

———. 1982a. *A Glimpse into Oriya Literature*. Bhubaneswar, India: Orissa Sahitya Akademi.

———. 1983. 'Gangadharanka Tapasya', in *Pashyati Dishi Dishi*. Berhampur, India: Pustaka Bhandar.

———. 1989a. *Sahitya O*. [Literature and...]. Berhampur, India: Pustaka Bhandar.

———. 1989b. '*Ethara Udiba Neta*' [Now the flag shall fly], in Chitta Ranjan Das and Srinivas Udgata, *Ebam* [And]. Cuttack, India: Books & Books.

———. 1992. *Shukara O Socrates* [The pig and Socrates]. Berhampur, India: Pusthaka Bhandara. Oidsha o Odiya Biswaku Gabakya [Windows into the World].

———. 2000 [1972]. "Prabanchita Biplaba [Betrayed Revolution]", pp. 22–35, in Chitta Ranjan Das, *Gandhi Gopabandhu*. Bhubaneswar: Pathika Prakashani.

———. 2006. *Prabandhara Pruthivi* [The World of Essays]. Cuttack: Mita Books.

———. 2007. *A Revolution in Education, Kristen Kold: A Pioneer of the Danish Folk High School Movement*. New Delhi: Shipra Publications.

Das, Chitta Ranjan. 2008. "Soundarya Bodhara Duiti Akhi [Two Eyes of Aesthetic Consciousness]." *Eshana* 56: 117–132.

———. 2010. *Byakti O Byaktitya* [Person and personality]. Bhubaneswar, India: Pathika Prakashani.

Das, Chitta Ranjan and Srinivas Udgata. 1989. *Ebam* [And]. Cuttack, India: Books & Books.

Dash, Rabi Narayan. 2007. *On Wings and Other Poems*. Huddinge, Sweden: Prima Verba and Balasore, India: New Race.

———. 2008. ...*Ebam Kadha* [...And buds]. Balasore, India: Samara Graphics.

Deleuze, Gilles. 1997. 'Literature and Life', *Critical Inquiry*, 23 (2): 225–30.

Dussel. Enrique. 2010. "Transmodernity and Transculturality." Paper presented in the seminar on "Research Across Borders." University of Luxembourg.

Elbridge, Richard. 2000. 'Dewey's Aesthetics', in M. Cochran (ed.), *Cambridge Companion to John Dewey*. Cambridge, UK: Cambridge University Press.

Foucault, Michel. 1977. 'What is an Author?' In M. Foucault, *Language, Counter-Memory, Practice: Selected Essays and Interviews*. Oxford, U.K: Basil Blackwell.

Giri, Ananta Kumar. 2002. *Conversations and Transformations: Towards a New Ethics of Self and Society*. Lanham, MD: Lexington Books.

———. 2008. 'Civil Society and the Calling of Self-Development', *Sociological Bulletin*.

———. 2009. 'Beyond Adaptation and Meditative Verbs of Co-Realizations: Toward Creative Nurturance of "I," "Me," and "You" and the Transformative Fellowship of Non-Duality', *Journal of Indian Council of Philosophical Research*, 26 (3): 109–30.

———. 2011. 'A New Morning with Chitta Ranjan: Adventures in Co-Realizations and World Transformations', *Social Change*.

———. 2012. 'With and Beyond Plurality of Standpoints: Sociology and the *Sadhana* of Multi-Valued Logic and Living', in Ananta Kumar Giri, *Sociology and Beyond: Windows and Horizons*. Jaipur: Rawat Publications.

Habermas, Jurgen. 1989. *The Structural Transformation of the Public Sphere*. Cambridge, MA: The MIT Press.

———. 1990. *Moral Consciousness and Communicative Action*. Cambridge, MA: The MIT Press.

Harvey, David. 1989. *The Condition of Postmodernity: An Inquiry into the Origins of Cultural Change*. Cambridge, MA: Basil Blackwell.

Honneth, Axel. 2007. *Disrespect: The Normative Foundations of Critical Theory*. Cambridge, United Kingdom: Polity Press.

Heidegger, Martin. 1994. 'The Origin of the Work of Art'. In *Poetry, Language, Thought*. Trans. Albert Hofstadter, pp. 163–86. New York: Harper and Row (1971).

Irigaray, Luce. 2002. *Between East and West: From Singularity to Community*. NY: Columbia U. Press.

Mead, G. H. 1934. *Mind, Self and Society*. Chicago, IL: University of Chicago Press.

Manjali, Franson. 2001. *Literature and Infinity*. Shimla, India: Indian Institute of Advanced Study.

Panikkar, Raimon. 1995. *A Dwelling Place for Wisdom*. New Delhi: Motilal Banarsidass.

Pikaza, Xavier. 2010. 'Raimon Panikkar (1918–2010)', *Concilium*, 5: 117–20.

Skof, Lenart. 2011. 'Pragmatism and Deepened Democracy: Ambedkar Between Dewey and Unger', in Akeel Bilgrami (ed.), *Democratic Culture: Historical and Philosophical Essays*, pp. 122–42. New Delhi: Routledge.

Sri Aurobindo. 1953. *Future Poetry*. Pondicherry: Sri Aurobindo Ashram.
Strydom, Piet. 2009. *New Horizons of Critical Theory: Collective Learning and Triple Contingency*. New Delhi: Shipra.
Sunder Rajan, R. 1998. *Beyond the Crises of European Sciences: New Beginnings*. Shimla, India: Indian Institute of Advanced Study.
Touraine, Alain. 2007. 'Sociology Beyond Society', *European Journal of Social Theory*.
Uberoi, J.P.S. 1996. *Religion, Civil Society and State: A Study of Sikhism*. Delhi: Oxford University Press.
Wei-ming, Tu. 2000. 'The Complex Bridges between China and the West.' In *A Parliament of Minds: Philosophy for a New Millennium* (eds.), Michael Tobias, J. Patrick Fitzerald & David Rothenburg, pp. 46–59. Albany: State University of New York Press.
Wilfred, Felix. 1997. 'Postmodernism and Critical Theory: Their Implications for Third World Societies', Paper presented at the National Seminar on Postmodernism and Critical Theory, held at the Radhakrishnan Institute of Advanced Study in Philosophy, University of Madras, August.

SECTION II
Textuality and Representations

7

Enugula Veeraswamy's Journal

A Study

Mohan G. Ramanan

In acknowledging the symbiotic relationship between the social and the literary, one has to also be conscious of the fictionality of fact and the facticity of fiction. By this is meant that all writing is in a profound way fiction, even historical writing. After all, writing implies selection of material and narrative deployment, emphases and foregrounding of one thing at the expense of another. Therefore history also is, because of these features common to all writing, a kind of fiction. To illustrate the point it might be useful to study a travel narrative by an early modernist called Enugula Veeraswamy, a Telugu gentleman. His journey from Madras to Kasi and back is the subject of this text, first written in the 1830s, and as it is an account of an event which actually happened it is a kind of history. I do not need to labour the point, well known, that diary writing, journal keeping, memoirs and confessions and the novel are all part of the modernizing tendency after the European Renaissance. Historical consciousness and self-consciousness are attributes of that intellectual movement and the writing of history and the writing of novels are part of the manner of articulating that new knowledge. Thus Veeraswamy, who precedes the Indian renaissance of the nineteenth century, is demonstrating dramatically in his Telugu narrative the tendencies that led to the renaissance in India a few decades later. These tendencies have to do with an acceptance of quotidian reality, a sense of fact, an uneasy sense of a future opening up in contention with a loyalty to the traditional verities and values. In Veeraswamy's narrative, therefore, one can see the working out of the encounter of a modern mind with reality, with history, and in sum, with society.

India has had a long and abiding narrative tradition, but the novel as we know it emerged in India as a result of English education and exposure to Western values. It enabled Indians to consider the quotidian and the contingent as worthy of description. It is not as if Indians always lived in some timeless realm and communed constantly with the transcendent. Romila Thapar (1996) has shown that when Indians wanted to come down from terrestrial heights to terra firma they could do so seamlessly. They had a dynamic conception of time and clearly the real, the contingent and the this-worldly were not absent from their scheme of things. But the fact remains that the dominant tradition of the Indian narrative was more than ordinarily engaged with the other worldly, the spiritual and the transcendent. Thus when Meenakshi Mukherjee (1996) famously spoke of the combination of *Purana* and *Nutana* with reference to the emergence of the Indian novel she was being acute and accurate about the main narrative tendencies of modern India. Just as in eighteenth-century England a Richardson or a Defoe had a sudden sense of the present but could not quite shake off the transcendental platonic ideal so visible in Dr Johnson and Oliver Goldsmith, so also in the Indian narrative in the nineteenth century one finds a seamless movement from the universal to the particular, the transcendental to the actual, the typical to the specific. In Enugula Veeraswamy's narrative *Kasiyatra Charitra* this symbiotic relationship of dual vision is dramatically embodied in the author describing in Defoe-like manner the minutiae of daily existence but constantly and inexorably framing this in a context of myth, Puranic narrative and cosmology. But of this a little later.

I will first explore the circumstances under which Veeraswamy wrote his journal and his travel narrative. I am also conscious of the school of thought represented by David Schulman, Velchuri Narayana Rao and Sanjay Subrahmanyam, which speaks of early Indian modernity and while I broadly accept this view it seems also necessary not to overly stress this fact at the expense of what is called colonial modernity. There is hardly any doubt that the British presence facilitated modernity in India and initiated a series of reform movements. There was a campaign against child marriages, the widow remarriage campaign, the campaign against Sati or concremation, the raising of the age of consent, the Indian Education Act, 1835 and of course its corollary, the founding of several colleges, and later, universities which imparted a modern English education to Indians. Veeraswamy was a *Dubash* (one who speaks two languages) and in the employ of the East India Company. He was educated and moved in terms of some intimacy with many Englishmen with whom he had a warm relationship, not unmixed with native pride in his culture and his country. He, in a way, speaks for the many, torn by dual loyalties to the literature of England and its variations, and their keen sense of being deracinated and wanting to connect with their roots. Time and again one sees Veeraswamy singing paeans to his land, its people, its customs and usages. He was also part of what today might be called the comprador intellectual, one sympathetic to British rule, indeed collaborating with it. His ethnographic exertions, his intimacy with C. P. Brown, which made him keenly interested in lexicography and grammar, his untiring and loyal service to the Company are very much in evidence in his journal. He was, after all, at the age of twelve an interpreter and a translator for the Collector of Tirunelveli. At fifteen, he became head interpreter to the Supreme Court of Madras. Evidence of this ethnographic imagination at work is visible when Veeraswamy characteristically refers to the ethnic and caste composition of the people of specific places visited by him, the customs and the usages, the rituals and religious practices. The journal is a mine of information about social, political and economic conditions prevailing in the land. He also acknowledges the British presence by repeatedly drawing attention to English friends from the Company or the government who help him with the arrangements for his pilgrimage. A quick list would include Davidson with whom he has a dialogue, Beular, Kifen Blake, and many others who engage him in discussions about customs, usages and religious beliefs. Why, one asks him is he like his country cousins in blindly accepting the superstitions of his race? A pilgrim tax used to be levied on Hindus even by the British and Veeraswamy was none too happy at this. But he controls his indignation because as a servant of the Company he knows better than to offend. Veeraswamy repeatedly stresses the benefits of British rule and clearly he enjoys basking in the sunshine of Pax Britannica, which makes his pilgrimage safe, and free from hazards both from men and nature. He is grateful that his livelihood has been ensured by the Company because without it he could not have made the journey. They, the British, have constructed *choultries* (rest houses) for pilgrims like him, cleared the paths and generally exercised control over the land and the people. For Veeraswamy the English are bound by their word and they are blessed souls of the gracious eye of God and as a result a city like Calcutta where there are many Englishmen is gravitated towards by rich Hindus who think that they can do their business well here and avoid the hardships of their own places. But Veeraswamy balances this kind of remark in an entry for 1 July 1831 where he states that the English government in Madras has treated Hindus with contempt. The English have made efforts to be comfortable themselves but when it comes to public interest they have neglected things and left it in the hands of God (Veeraswamy 2000: 198). And it does look as though the Brahmins have slowly come out of the tyranny of Mohammedan rule and the British have replaced the Muslims by the will of God. Apart from his resentment at the levying of the pilgrim tax he is none too happy with the opium trade that the British encourage, but on the whole he is not inimical to British rule. He is indeed complicit with that rule and he is a participant in the project of enlightenment that the British have initiated in India. Veerawamy was proficient in English, which he used well and to good effect. His proficiency was important for the Company, which involved him as an informant. Informants were crucial in the ethnographical and anthropological work being done by the Company. English grammarians like Brown, Pope and others gave a modern Anglo-Saxon grammar to Indian languages imposing a pattern on native tongues. They charted the land and the landscape taking in the flora and the fauna and the geology of the country. This was their effort at possessing the land that possessed them. The command of language modulated into the language of command, to use a catchy phrase by Bernard Cohn (1985) and Veeraswamy played his role in this historical process. Indeed his journal has to be seen as history in the making and Veeraswamy is both the writer of history and the maker of it. He is what one would today call a participant observer. He is both the describer of a journey and the chief character in that journey.

But then who is Veeraswamy with reference to the text under consideration? Veeraswamy was obviously a master of Telugu and Sanskrit. He does use archaic language and peppers his Telugu writing with Sanskrit quotations. His compound sentences are a distraction according to Telugu scholars. He has a subtle wit and can make pungent observations about men and matters. But this Veeraswamy to a large extent is only a latent presence in the English text that is considered here. In fact Veeraswamy wrote a number of letters to his friend Komaleswaram Srinivasa Pillai who had requested him to write about his travels. Veeraswamy apparently wrote detailed letters and Pillai compiled them, arranging the material chronologically, and omitting pleasantries and courtesies Veeraswamy indulged in as preliminaries. Pillai first got the journal published in Tamil, not Telugu. He engaged Panaguri Venku Mudalari to translate the journal into Tamil. Subsequently the Tamil text was translated into Marathi by Nagapuri Veerasami Mudalari. An initial English version by Veeraswamy himself is lost and this had been done because the British Resident of Nagpur had evinced interest in his work. It is this longish publishing history that culminates in the English translation that is used here. It is a translation that comes nearly a hundred years after the work was first written.

I will now look into the idea of the organization of this journal. In the Telugu text it had twenty-five chapters. Sitapati translated the first fourteen but expanded it to eighteen sections or chapters. When Vadreru Purushottham translated the remaining eleven chapters, a Telugu text of twenty-five chapters became an English text of twenty-nine chapters. It was also called a 'Journal' by Veeraswamy's English translators. Besides, the quality of the translations is an important point. There are marked differences in style. I have to mention these details relating to publication to make the point that what one is dealing with here (and I can say this of many novels of the nineteenth century translated into English, sometimes by more that one hand) is a highly unstable text. There is no integrity between the English and the Telugu of this text and while it may not have been mediated through Tamil and Marathi, it is a fact that the text being used is several removes from truth to use a Platonic expression. Sitapati, besides, omitted sections from the original in his translation of the first fourteen chapters. There are also as, Telugu knowing scholars assure me, some mistranslations. But the text one is dealing with in English exists and one has to make do with it in spite of its frequent unreliability. Besides, the English is at times archaic and one is often inflicted with details, much of them retarding the narrative and leaving the modern reader a little depressed and cold. But in spite of this one needs to see this journal as a document of culture and a valuable one at that. One may, therefore, properly speak of the English version as a text, leaving the question of the status of the text in its avatar as a work and its trace of authorship behind. One can, indeed, therefore treat the material as discourse and analyze the discursive text.

Why is this so? Veeraswamy (now one would have to put the name in quotes because of the uncertainty the name has acquired—it is a trace of the original) speaks of matters that all in all represent the nation. First is his concern for the imagined community that is his country. He charts the path he takes, gives details of the landscape, the people, the dresses worn, the food eaten, the vegetables grown, the grains produced, the birds and beasts, the soil and all kinds of curious information. It is this detail that convinces one that he is charting nothing less than India, which is no longer an idea or a spirit but a tangible quotidian reality. Incidentally his journey took him from Madras through Tirupati, Cuddapah, Srisailam, Hyderabad, Nirmal, Nagpur, Jabalpur, Mirzapur, Allahabad, Kasi, Patna, Gaya, Monghyr, Rajmahal, Krishnagar, Calcutta, Srikakulam, Rajamundry, Machilipatnam, Nellore and Tiruvallur. He almost does a round of India, though not quite. Here are two or three examples of the detail with which he speaks of places and terrains:

> I left Madras on the 18th, Tuesday of May in the year 1830 at 9 in the night and camped at Madhavaram village. This place is situated at a distance of about an hour's journey from my garden at Thandayaruveydu. A salt canal, which has been bridged, has to be crossed on the way. The water table is high in the soil here. Water is also sweet and plentiful. The *Dravida* Vaishnavas who reside here make a living by trading in *Samidhas* (Samidhas are pieces of wood that are offered to the ritual fire) and such other materials at Madras. (Veeraswamy 2000: 1)

In this passage one can see the specific details of the time and space contexts of the pilgrimage. It is the first journal entry incidentally and it sets the tone of the narrative. In subsequent entries one sees these features reinforced. Incidentally if the initial form of the narrative was epistolary it is remarkable that in the English version it now has a journal form—this mixture of genres is another feature of this narrative and in this it is close to the novel, that most gnomic of all literary forms. I will give one more example. It is the entry for 9 October 1830:

> Waking up at 5 hours in the morning of the 9th and covering a distance of 8 miles I arrived at Gopigunj at 11 hours. The river Ganga has to be crossed in front of Vindhya Vasini. The road has not been laid on the path here. The land here is comprised of [*sic*] white clays. There are villages for every foot here. Dry crops are cultivated here. A big "*vagu*" (a small canal) joins the Ganga here at the place where the Ganges has to be crossed. (Veeraswamy 2000: 85)

He also speaks about the quality of the soil in Cuddapah and the dress worn by the people of Gaya. He knows about weights and measures: "The weighing measures are like this: One seer is equal to 80, and it is equal to 18 *gandas* (a unit of measurement of grains) at some other places 25 *gandas* a seer and some other places 11 *gandas* are there" (Veeraswamy 2000: 144). He knows the caste composition of the district, which would match the capacity of latter-day politicians who win votes on the basis of that knowledge. He knows about currency and their value. He is aware of the linguistic diversity of the land and dilates on Farsi, Sanskrit and English. He is familiar with the almanac system and he is not immune to the gastronomic delights that the paan affords.

> Betel leaves are kept, preserved for 6 to 12 months and consumed by rich people here. Common people cannot get good betel leaves. According to the tradition here [Gaya] a roll of two or three betel leaves with a quantity of betel nut powder, lime, *catechu* (a yellow bitter powder that is used as an ingredient in *paan*) put in them is offered and it is consumed without opening and seeing the contents in it. Chewing of betel is very common here. (Veeraswamy 2000: 153)

He is a wayfarer and can give advice on what routes to take—"If we go to Baleswar without touching Medinipur we can save three halts on the way and hence we followed this route" (Veeraswamy 2000: 176)—and more in the same vein. He is also concerned that people in the country have contrary opinions of each other. The Bengalis who eat fish ask why South Indians do not eat fish when they are perfectly happy to use shell lime for their paan. After all as Veeraswamy states (2000: 179), "The shells are nothing but the outer body of the aquatic animals!" If people eat the bodies of fish as food, South Indians burn the outer shells of those aquatic animals. In engaging with these and other vexed questions of intra-national differences, Veeraswamy takes a metaphysical position. He writes (2000: 180):

> It is God's will and pleasure that different people should speak different tongues and when a Tamil and Telugu meet at a tank and with all the good intention of helping, the Tamil warns the Telugu not to enter it as there are leeches in the tank, unheeding the advice, the Telugu stays in the tank and is bitten by the leeches. Accusing the Tamil that he intended him to be killed the Telugu quarrels with the Tamil. The quarrel about customs of different regions is similar to the above incident. All these things are acts of God willed at his pleasure.

Such a statement can be read as Veeraswamy's attempt at national integration of sorts. Above all he is religious and his pilgrimage is a religious one, and so he tells us about the legends of the place and the temples and the religious customs, usages and rituals appropriate to each section of the people and the Brahmins in particular. While this solidity of specification is, as is well known, a feature of the novel according to Henry James, Veeraswamy is nonetheless a part of a culture, which is, for lack of a better word, transcendentalist. The reference is of course to the age-old Puranic tradition of narrative, which sees time not in quotidian terms but as part of a cosmic order. Space is not temporal and contingent but part of a larger scheme of things in which the earth one lives in is only a small part. In Veeraswamy's narrative one finds repeatedly a tendency to move from the actual to the transcendental, from the phenomenal to the noumenal. This is nowhere better seen than in his recounting of the *Sthala Purana* of a place. Here is the narrator on the Gaya *Sraadhdha* (an annual rite to propitiate ancestors) (2000):

> When I ponder over the greatness of Gaya I feel like this. In this world affection towards mother, father, and other near relatives will generally be great and it is not known when birth and death occur and so on, when such blood relations depart suddenly, it is but natural to feel that during their lifetime enough could not be done to them or whatever was done to them was not sufficient. It is for those people who feel that they are indebted to their departed kinsfolk, if they know there is a way they could make their souls attain salvation, to follow that way and achieve mental satisfaction and joy, that the Gaya *Mahatmyam* (the great qualities of) was created.

Then follows a long description of the intervention of God in the affairs of men and a suggestion is made that these holy places remind one of God in the form in which one would like to see Him or remember Him. The exemplary greatness of Gaya is written in the *Vayu Purana* and the *Garuda Purana*. Veeraswamy writes (2000: 131–32):

> The gist of it is this. Gayasura, a huge bodied demon, does penance for a long time and gets a divine gift that his body become [the] holiest of all the holy places on the earth. But due to the influence of his previous birth's associations of violence, he still acted wildly and was roaming about. In order to pacify him, Brahma, one of the trinity of Gods, approached him and requested Gayasura to allow him to perform a yagna on his body as his body is [*sic*] considered to be a [*sic*] holiest place. The demon readily agreed. He laid his head in this holy place and slept. Brahma created the holy priests to perform the yagna and the yagna was started. Then the head

of the demon started to move and when a few large mountains were placed on the head to keep it steady it never stopped moving and the mountains scattered away and the same mountains are called Rama mountain and Preta mountain now. Afterwards a stone supposed to be the personification of a *Pativrata* under a curse of her husband was brought and kept on his head. So in order to complete the Brahma Yagna all the celestials came down. This is in accordance to the sloka *yeesana Vishnu kamalasana* recited at the time of ceremonial rites. Lord Vishnu assumed the form of holding the celestial club and put his right foot on the head of Gayasura and the yagna was completed without the head moving anymore. At the request of all the celestials the disabled Gayasura and the *Pativrata* in the shape of a stone, Lord Vishnu the ocean of compassion who came and stood there in the shape of Gadadhara to save the yagna performed by Brahma, agreed to stay there in that image of shining glory. They also entreated him, and got a divine gift according to which whoever performs *Pinda Pradan* in accordance with the sloka *smamipatra pramena pindam dadyad gaya sire* of their clan will attain salvation. From that time it came to be known that Lord Vishnu stays always here and would be pleased and bless those who perform the *Sraadhdha Karma*s here. So right from morning till the evening pilgrims come in thousands and perform *Pinda Pradan* at the insignia of the footprint of Lord Vishnu. Though *Pinda* cannot be made without first performing the *Sraddha* ceremony, as it is mentioned in the legend of the place that offering of *Pinda* is important at this place, mostly people offer only *Pindas* here and hence I also did accordingly.

Veeraswamy, by recourse to Puranic narration enables the contemporary reader to see the geographical space now called India in relation to myth and legend and India gets a spiritual dimension with this account of spiritual geography. Passages like this come in frequent intervals and this is part of the spiritual discourse and narrative, which sets the tone for such a document to be read in conjunction with those nationalistic texts from the later part of the nineteenth century, which placed a premium on the nation as a sacred space.

Kasiyatra Charitra is a tirtha yatra, a pilgrimage. Pilgrimages and fairs or melas are related closely. The locus of both is devotion and both are associated with a tirtha. But in one, the tirtha is a place to which pilgrims resort in considerable numbers throughout the year, a place that has special religious sanctity of its own, apart from the occurrence of a holy day, and which it is the duty of the pious to visit at least once during their lifetime. Melas are different because it is not enjoined on any Hindu to visit one and usually it is incidental to the pilgrimage. It is, besides, blighted by entertainment. The tirtha is, to use Mircea Eliade's famous expression a hierophany, typically a ford or a crossing or a river where ritual baths and other observances can be done (Eliade 1968). A tirtha is one among Eliade's objects of nature where one gets a physical manifestation or revelation of the sacred. The mela, in contrast, is carnivalesque. Anthropologists have pointed out that pilgrimages begin as individual visions but soon modulate into sodalities and congregations. In *Enugula Veeraswamy's Journal* while the congregation is a part of his scheme of things, one sees much more of a loner and an individual effort to understand the country in religious terms. It is noteworthy that Veeraswamy is usually separate from his servants and retainers. His attention is given to places where Brahmins congregate and where food can be eaten in ritual purity. Also, Veeraswamy sees the English as allies in keeping his inner space pure because they have facilitated his pilgrimage by ensuring safety on the roads and rooting out Pindaris and thugs. Veeraswamy is also attentive to the system of patronage available for such journeys. His natural propensity is to allude to his contacts or meetings with zamindars. For example, he mentions Raja Mitarjit Singh of Gaya and the English officials who repeatedly come to his aid by providing him with material needs. Veeraswamy says little of other travellers and he is more concerned with the philosophical dimensions of the pilgrimage. Repeatedly he gets into a philosophical disquisition on spiritual matters. He has eloquent passages on ideas of dharma and karma, on religious customs and usages. He can even defend atheists because they are closer to intellectuals "who possess ideal vision, there is nothing like a masculine being the supreme ruler of the universe" (Veeraswamy 2000: 166). His point is that religious people give way to superstition and abuse atheists who after all speak with the voice of reason. They are closer to the thinkers. This, however, does not imply that Veeraswamy is an atheist himself because his entire journal is about a sacred pilgrimage and about the sacred geography of India. He is, to use Turner's well-known phrase, more concerned with his Brahmanic exclusiveness rather than taking the traditional route of a pilgrimage, where, as Turner (1969) has it, the pilgrim attempts to get into a state of liminality. Attaining a liminal state is in Turner's formulation "neither here nor there; [one is] betwixt and between the positions assigned and arranged by law, custom, convention, ceremony" (Turner 1969: 95). On this showing Veerasamy is nowhere near dissolving his social identity and attaining to communitas. He shows no kinship with the community. His is a frankly Brahminical world and he is much concerned with caste pollution and ritual purity. This manifests itself in his great concern for the right kind of food and the right way of cooking and eating. He is separate from his entourage. His pilgrimage does not entail divesting himself from his social structural role and relationship. If anything it underscored his social status and confirms him in his identity. Nowhere does one see in the text any anxiety about caste or gender roles. This still does not prevent him from evoking an imagined community and to see the pilgrimage as a remarkable and ancient institution sustaining a system of linked centres that helps bind together the incredibly diverse people of the Indian subcontinent. While Veeraswamy is always implying this larger community he himself is exclusive and individualistic. His quest is for personal salvation. He frowns on entertainments and melas, and shows no enthusiasm for *utsavams*. He has a single-minded desire to fulfil his pilgrimage and to take in, in the process, the lie of the land and the journey itself is an enabler of spiritual growth. His is a ritualistic approach to religion and he involves himself in every ritual a devout Hindu is enjoined to perform in the various tirthas. In a way Veeraswamy traverses the classic Hindu pilgrimage route but doing it as he does in the nineteenth century, and above all writing about it as he does, he gives the traditional route an added significance. He implies that the route defines traditional spiritual India. It is the essential India he is going around in.

However, the ambivalence of Veeraswamy comes through at crucial moments in the text. The otherwise exclusive Veeraswamy is also interested in medicine and when twenty of his entourage fall ill he administers to them a medicine prepared with the decoction of a herb called the "*Chirta*" in Hindi and bitter in English. This medicine was suggested to him by a native doctor in Gaya. When a palanquin bearer develops blood motions he administers a mixture prepared with potato juice and a few drops of sulphur essence. The patient is cured. The English Veeraswamy is of course familiar with English medicine. He refers to the European doctor Karbin who had written a book for children's treatment in Barrackpur. He had written another book for the treatment of vomiting and nausea. Is Veeraswamy not miming with great fidelity the ambivalence many of us demonstrate with respect to the allopathic form of treatment and our sometimes unstated preference for home remedies and alternative medicine?

Chapter 22 is a long and illuminating disquisition on the cosmogony of the Hindus. Now for a readership that understands Hindu ways much of the chapter would be a tiring repetition of information, which is rooted in its culture. But for an English readership, which includes many like the author, now far away from an appreciation of these Hindu ways, the chapter is bound to irritate, even though by itself the information is of some interest. But consider the manner of his approaching the issue (Veeraswamy 2000: 156):

> When I started enquiring about the existence of the 56 countries and 56 languages on earth and their location, I came to the conclusion from my personal experience and after an extensive travel around the whole country, that all these languages and countries are in the vast land that extends from Kanyakumari to Kashmir and that is known as India. Nevertheless, as the country was occupied by the Muslims and they ruled the country without any proper boundaries then, it is very difficult now to make out and write down all these 56 regions. But still we may be able to write down boundaries of these 56 regions.

This is Veeraswamy's sense of India and her linguistic plenitude, though from the perspective of hindsight one knows that there are more than fifty-six languages spoken in India and the fifty-six countries are the regions of the land as known to Veeraswamy's times. But the remarkable thing here is that Veeraswamy modulates into a cosmogony, which alludes to seven upper worlds and seven subterraneous worlds. His reference to the three worlds as heaven, earth and hell clearly takes him away from any kind of modern or scientific discourse. Yet Veeraswamy blithely goes on in this chapter to expound a traditional cosmogony, with appropriate references to Gods, demons, *pretas*, rakshasas and so on. The point of this exercise, as I see it, is that Veeraswamy is not content with contemporary modern knowledge and is asserting the importance of a nativist knowledge system covered as it is with symbolic language and myth and Puranic lore. He has similar statements about the soul, and other metaphysical questions.

In his narrative, Veeraswamy provides one with many ways of reading the soon-to-emerge Indian novel. If autobiography and memoir writing is seen as in some profound ways fictive—after all not everything about Veeraswamy is revealed—he exercises the privilege of letting you know only so much, of selecting his episodes, of colouring one thing and downplaying another—then the connection between a narrative like *Kasiyatra Charitra* and the novel becomes apparent. In novels like *Pratapa Mudaliar Charitram* (*The Life and Times of Pratapa Mudaliar* in English) by Vedanayagam Pillai or Veeresalingam Pantulu's *Rajasekhara Charitra* (The Story of Rajasekhara) (fortune's wheel) or Bankim Chandra Chatterjee's *Rajmohan's Wife* one sees the intrusion of the transcendental, the other worldly and the Puranic. While *The Vicar of*

Wakefield by Oliver Goldsmith was a popular model for Indian novelists so was *Rasselas* (1765) by Dr Johnson and between these models one can plot the typical trajectories of the genre as practised in India. However, it would be a mistake to think that Indian novelists did not have Indian models for their on occasion romantic, on occasion philosophic, novels. The Puranic tradition of the tale within the tale, the Urdu form of the *daastan* (romance)and the epic models in India are legitimate sources for the new Indian novel. One could suggest that a text like Veeraswamy's narrative with its mixture of memoir, confession, diary and journal, its fusing of realism with mythopoeic consciousness parallels uncannily the procedures of Indian novelists. Many of their novels have a broad affiliation to the realist tradition and are apparently close to history and quotidian reality. But like Veeraswamy's incursions into myth and Puranic narrative they too resort to those stylized conventions. *Indulekha* has any number of highly stylized passages when Sanskrit has to be evoked and this contrasts with the otherwise everyday Malayalam it seems to be using. In *Pratapa Mudaliar Charitram* one sees the tale-within-the-tale method of narration. This suggests that in the Indian context the mere reference to realism is not enough. It requires something more and in this one is helped by Romila Thapar's formulation of clock time and mythic time, mentioned earlier (Thapar 1996). Narratives freely move between these two and suggest that India is both a landscape and an idea, that the Indian nation is not just a child of colonial modernity but a value for which an acceptance of its glorious past is a sine qua non. Literature and society, I said earlier, have a symbiotic relation and in the negotiations Veeraswamy makes between his narrative and his society, one sees a prefiguration of the complex manner in which the novel in India imagines an Indian nation and a civil society.

References

Chatterjee, Bankim Chandra. 1969. 'Rajmohan's Wife', in Jogesh Chandra Bagal (ed.) *Bankim Rachanavali*. Calcutta: Sahitya Samsad.

Cohn, Bernard S. 1985. 'The Command of Language and the Language of Command', in Ranajit Guha (ed.), *Subaltern Studies IV: Writings on South Asian History and Society*. New Delhi: Oxford University Press.

Eliade, Mircea. 1968. *The Sacred and the Profane: The Nature of Religion*. Translated by Willard Trask. New York: Houghton Mifflin Harcourt.

Johnson, Samuel. 1765. *Rasselas: Prince of Abyssinia*. New York: Robert Carter and Brothers.

Mukherjee, Meenakshi. 1996. *Realism and Reality: The Novel and Society in India*. New Delhi: Oxford University Press.

Pillai, Vedanayagam. 2005. *Pratapa Mudaliar Charitram (Life and Times of Pratapa Mudaliar)*. Trans. Meenakshi Tyagarajan. New Delhi: Katha.

Thapar, Romila. 1996. *Time as a Metaphor of History: Early India*. New Delhi: Oxford University Press.

Turner, Victor. 1969. *The Ritual Process: Structure and Anti-Structure*. London: Penguin.

Veeraswamy, Enugula. 2000. *Enugula Veerasamy's Journal (Kasiyatra Charitra)*. Edited and translated by P. Sitapati and V. Purushottam. Hyderabad, India: Andhra Pradesh Government Oriental Manuscripts Library and Research Institute. Telugu original compiled by Sri Komaleswarapuram Srinivasa Pillai.

8

Kafka

Literature, Law and Language

Franson Davis Manjali

In one's contemporary frames of understanding, one no longer tends to see literature simply as a mode of representation, albeit of the aesthetic kind. One also no longer wants to see literature as what a writer says about the world, even if one understands by the word 'world' one's own social or cultural world. For many philosophers today, literature consists neither in the processing of facts that are submitted to a faculty of judgement, in the Kantian sense, nor in the manifestation of submerged and uncontrollable feelings of awe or fear with regard to that which cannot be expressed in ordinary language or in the given artistic field: that is, by invoking a feeling of the 'sublime'. One still tends to understand the aesthetics of the sublime, rightly or wrongly, in terms of the mediation between the world and the work of art in the human representational faculty.

While discussing the intertwining relationship between the 'social' and 'literary', it is useful to consider the two German words having significance for the study of culture, namely, *Gesellschaft* and *Gemeinschaft*, which may be translated into English as 'society' and 'community' respectively. It is easy to notice that these words are related to other English words, such as 'social' and 'socialism', in the case of the first, and 'communion', 'communication', and 'communism' in that of the second. The word "society", it seems, is suggestive of a 'cohabitation' or an 'association' of or a 'collaboration' between people while the word 'community' seems to involve the coming together of people into a unity, a fusion, a unification or even a 'communion' where individual variations are expected to disappear even if temporarily. What is to be noticed here is that these two terms have their distinct domains of use, though in ordinary language, one often tends to use them interchangeably.

It is worth asking what would be the relationship of literature to 'society' on the one hand, and to 'community' on the other. Much of the modern discussions of language, literature and art have spoken of these domains in terms of 'society'. 'Community' has been somewhat relegated to the background (that is, in spite of 'communism'; it is worth considering the more recent philosophical–literary revival of this term of medieval origin). For instance, in the classic work of modern linguistics, *Course in General Linguistics*, Ferdinand de Saussure speaks of language extensively in relation to society. As the founder of the modern fields of linguistics and semiotics, de Saussure (1978: 16) proposed the latter as *a science that studies the life of signs in society* (italics in original). Further, assuming a socially consistent knowledge of the system of signs, including the linguistic signs, de Saussure conceived of semiology as a branch of social psychology, which itself would pertain to a general psychology. Moreover, while modern nations are often spoken of as consisting societies, historian Benedict Anderson speaks of the emergence—largely linguistic—of modern nations in terms of 'communities' that were according to him, 'imagined into existence.'

What is of interest is the question of the coexistence as well as covariance of the elements of language and the elements of society or community. Following the emergence of modern nations, a language is taken to be coextensive with a society or a community. Thus, it is assumed that within a modern collectivity, national or social, individuals are supposed to be more or less equally competent in the same language and in the same discourses. That is, individuals are supposed to be linguistically and cognitively competent in the discourses of a nation or society more or less to the same degree. One thus (unquestioningly) speaks of a shared social knowledge in a shared language. Individual and social variations in use and in communicative competence are often (invited to be) ignored. What is not contested is the assumption of a coextensiveness of a fused society and a fused language and a corresponding fused cognitive competence. Surprisingly, some tend to have such wrong assumptions not only about small local communities, but also about the nation and what is supposed to be the 'global society'.

Once one is able to break out of the above frame, and is able to see that language of a particular collectivity of people is itself nothing natural but a contingent and historically continuous invention, then one is already on the way to understanding the relationship between literature and society.

Literature, paradoxically, is both an affirmation of the language of a given society or community, and a denial and a defiance of it. Literature is the transgression of and an invitation to transgress the boundaries that circumscribe the (coextensive) coexistence of language (discourse) and society. Literature is not a mode of repeating or replicating the discourse or the mode of knowledge that is present in the language of a given society. It is on the other hand, a mode of affirmation of the denial of what is discursively given to a society. It is not a mode of enhanced 'consensus' with respect to a society's given discourse, but rather the incessant creation of 'dissensus'. Literature, therefore, is not 'in' society or the language that is given to one, but is always 'outside' of them. It is in this sense Maurice Blanchot writes that literature was a mode of salvation for Franz Kafka.

Blanchot's early view on this problematic appears in his work, *La part du feu* (The work of fire), a collection of critical essays published in 1949. These texts, along with the essays in an earlier collection, *Faux pas* (1943) represent Blanchot's own transformation from a religious revolutionary and a Heideggerian existentialist to someone whose faith was in literature. His more mature work on literature was published in 1956 as *The Space of Literature*. Blanchot's primary interest is in an ontological enquiry about writing: What is writing? Why does one write? How does one go about the act of writing?

The primary condition for literary writing is the solitude of the writer, involving a retreat from language, which is perhaps accompanied by some sort of a cognitive void. It is the surrender of the language and the discourse that is given to him that makes a writer write. But paradoxically, "that which destroys language in him also makes him write" (Blanchot 1943: 2). In his solitude and retreat, the writer transports himself to the extremities of his world, where language and its signs are already annihilated. It is in that annihilated or 'neutral' space of literature that the writer affirms himself. And what he affirms in language is in fact no real thing. Literary discourse, like the religious discourse that preceded it, is the reaffirmation or affirmation of an alternative language, but it and its predecessor basically affirm nothing real. What it offers in this affirmation of otherness as nothing, which is nothing but another language, is a discourse other than what is 'socially' given. It is marked by the feature of the 'neuter' because it can be characterized as neither subjective nor objective.

Referring to Kafka's published diaries, Blanchot wants us to note that Kafka devoted, and self-consciously so, all his life to literature. Kafka writes: "All I am is literature, and I am not or willing to be anything else" (Blanchot 1995). In the midst of life's other difficult and banal chores, Kafka, in fact, had to struggle in order to stay in literature. He also writes:

"My situation is unbearable, because it contradicts my only desire and my only calling: literature" (Blanchot 1995). Being religiously involved in literature, his only inspiration and happiness came from literature. It, for Kafka, was a mode of being, and writing involved, one could say, using a Levinasian expression, the "otherwise than being" (Levinas 1991). And therefore, it was never a matter of mere aesthetic deliberation. Literature, for Kafka, is the mode that leads both being and language towards death, but in it, both being and language remain in a state of impossibility of dying. (In the banality of life, one 'survives' or 'lives on' through literature.) Literature opens towards the exteriority of the given being as well as to the otherwise than being as such. It becomes the in-between and the neutral space between the self and the other. It is outside of the desubjectivized or dead self, but it cannot cease to be or die. It is the dying–undying state of being in language.

Blanchot describes this movement as the movement from ordinary language to something like a pure or neutral language of literature. It involves the shift of the personal pronoun 'I' to 'he' or 'it' in literature. 'He' or 'it' is the pronoun of the neutral, abstracted from the transactions of everyday life. As he puts it (1949: 17–18):

> Literature consists of trying to speak at the moment when speaking becomes most difficult ... and consequently necessitates a recourse to a language that is most precise, the most aware, the furthest removed from vagueness and confusion—the literary language.... Literature thus becomes an "assault on the frontiers," a chase that, by the opposing forces of solitude and language, leads us to the extreme limit of this world, "to the limits of what is generally human."

Writing, like death, is thus characterized by a sense of the impossibility of possibility. (Contra Heidegger who sees death as the possibility of impossibility (Heidegger 2008). Both present themselves to one in their possibility only to let one encounter their impossibility. The existence of language, like death, is possible only in its impossibility. It is the impossibility of language that always makes it a language forever promised, just as it is the impossibility of death that makes possible one's survival. Blanchot says (1949: 20):

> If language and, in particular, literary language did not constantly hurl itself eagerly at its death, it would not be possible, since it is this movement toward its impossibility that is its nature and its foundation; it is this movement, that

by anticipating its nothingness, determines its potential to be nothingness without actualizing it. In other words, language is real because it can project itself toward non-language, which it is and does not actualize.

From Blanchot's perspective the trajectory that literature takes is very clear: a retreat from one's own subjectivity and the given language and discourse of one's culture, to the apparent possibility of another 'pure' language. But it is here, just as one's own death is an impossibility, that one encounters the impossibility of the language of literature, and of literature itself. This is where, literature can be spoken of as an 'incessant murmur' (Blanchot 1982b) in and of language, and this is where one can discern the movement of 'language to infinity.'[1]

The same ambivalence of an undying death is starkly present in Kafka's portrayal of his characters. According to Blanchot (1995: 81):

> Kafka, probably under the influence of Eastern traditions, recognized in the impossibility of dying the extreme curse of man. Man cannot escape unhappiness, because he cannot escape existence, and it is in vain that he heads toward death, that he confronts the anguish and the injustice of it; he dies only to survive.

And thus, says Blanchot (1995: 81–82):

> There is no actual death in Kafka, or more exactly there is never an end. Most of his heroes are engaged in an intermediate moment between life and death, and what they seek is death, and what they miss is life, in such a way that one does not know how to characterize their hopes, if they place their hope in the possibility of losing all hope, and how to appreciate their regrets, if these regrets eternalize the condemnation they undergo.

Kafka is known basically as a writer of fiction, short stories and novels, and as the author of his posthumously published *Diaries*. Blanchot, who drew much of his literary inspiration from Kafka (among other literary greats like Hölderlin, Mallarmé, Rilke, etc.), was no mean writer himself. Blanchot's initial writings were critical essays; later he wrote fiction, and went on to write texts referred to as *récits*, which are indiscernibly literature–philosophy–criticism. This shift in Blanchot's writing comes after having moved from philosophical criticism to philosophical fiction. It is as if Blanchot was reflecting on the ontology of writing, and simultaneously, also paying attention to the generic division of literature.

Blanchot's enigmatic text *The Madness of the Day* (1982a) (*La folie du jour* in French original) is an account of a man beginning to tell the story of his fall into a state of decrepitude. This is a short text that Derrida has subjected elsewhere to an extensive reading under the title 'The Law of Genre' (Derrida 1982: 221–252). In *The Madness of the Day*, the first person narrator barely speaks of his loss of faith in 'beings', and his simultaneous inability to die. The doctors try to treat his unspecified injury or illness, and later in his half-cured state, he sees 'behind their backs' the silhouette of law. The law, rather unexpectedly, is afraid of the man, it wants him to acknowledge 'her', and is strongly critical of his conduct, even when 'she' wants to remain close to him. The doctors remain attentive to the man, and they want him to continue narrating his story. However, when the man recommences his narration, he cannot go beyond the beginning. He realizes that he cannot relate his experiences in a narrative. His speech refuses to translate itself into the genre of a story, even if others presume that he has the competence for it. In his reading of the text, Derrida observes that this is a narrative that fails to be one. A failure, owing to the fact that both the narration and the narrator are heading towards their ends, and the law is unable to restore the generic character of either. *The Madness of the Day*, according to Derrida, narrates the necessary failure of the 'law of the genre.'

In another gesture, Derrida's essay, 'Before the Law' (1992) expounds Kafka's parable-like story, also bearing the title, *Before the Law*. The essay is a deep exposition of the relationship between law and literature. Kafka's story has appeared both separately and as part of his well-known novel *The Trial*. It is the story of a 'countryman' who sets out with many valuable possessions in search of the 'Law' and arrives in front of its gate, guarded by a tall and hefty Tartar with a thick moustache. The guard accepts all his gifts, but refuses to let him into the edifice of law, every time telling him that it is possible for him to enter, but 'not now.' The countryman is warned that the law is guarded by many guards inside, each more powerful than the preceding ones. He remains before the gate for the rest of his life and grows very old waiting for permission to enter. As he approaches his death, he wants to know from the guard why no one else has sought to enter it. "Everyone strives to reach the law; so how does it happen that for all these years no one but myself has ever sought admittance?" he asks. The guard replies: "No one else could ever be admitted here, since this gate was made only for you. I am now going to shut it."

Derrida reads this story as portraying the relation between literature and law in both directions: the law of literature as well as the literature of law. Or, better, literature as something legally conditioned, and law as something fictionally founded.

The two principal questions that Derrida poses in 'Before the Law' are the following: What makes a piece of writing literature? And, who decides? These questions are similar to the situation faced by the countryman before the doorkeeper of the Law: What makes him eligible to enter the Law? And, who decides? A corollary question that imposes itself is the following: can literature and the law be said to have surprisingly similar conditions of possibility?

As if to provide an answer to these questions Derrida makes an inventory of the formal–textual conventions employed in Kafka's story: its specific identity, for example its attribution to a singular author, and the title—also fictional—spatially separated from the text. And as for the crucial third question above, Derrida is of the view that both the story and the law are made to 'appear' before each other. In his words (1992: 191):

> The story, as a certain type of *relation*, is linked to the law that it relates, appearing, in so doing, before that law, which appears before it. And yet ... nothing really presents itself in this appearance; and just because this is given to us to be read does not mean that we shall have proof or experience of it.

Before the Law is a story about the fiction of law and the (non-existent) law of literature. The law is often assumed to be without a history, and not reducible to a story. The law excludes narrative. It takes itself to be universal, and it wants others to take it as universal, as natural. Derrida tries to see the interrelationship between law and literature (narrative) as being alluded to by the relationship between the doorkeeper and the countryman. Thus, the narrative wishes to enter the Law, assumed by the countryman to be a general law, and accessible to all. The narrative is before the law, like the countryman waiting for his entry. The Law keeps the narrative waiting, indefinitely. The law is inaccessible to the man in spite of the fact that the gate of the law is 'open as usual.' The law in the form of the presence of a series of progressively stronger doorkeepers described in the story, is also something frightening and fantastic, or 'uncanny'[2], in the sense of Freud. However, the first doorkeeper and the countryman are situated both 'before' and outside the law. Therefore, presumably there is no binary opposition, but only a difference ('*différance*'[3]) (Derrida 1992: 203) between the countryman and the doorkeeper, and thus between the story and the law. As to what exactly is the specific content of the law, the story does not permit us to know. Derrida says on this point, following a formulation of Heidegger, that like the truth of the truth that always remains hidden, the law has to always guard itself, its own fictional truth.

According to Derrida, it is the anonymity of the law that is particularly interesting from the point of view of literature. Besides, as Derrida says (1992: 207):

> It is neutral, beyond sexual and grammatical gender, and remains thus indifferent, impassive, little concerned to give an answer as *yes* or *no*. It lets the man freely determine himself, it lets him wait, it abandons him. It is neuter, neither feminine nor masculine, indifferent because we do not know whether it is a (respectable) person or a thing, who or what. The law is produced ... in the space of this non-knowledge.

The closing of the gate at the end of the story and the closing of the text are both abrupt and simultaneous. Just as the law talks only about itself, the text too talks about itself. In both the cases admittance is denied. Derrida views this as the unreadability of the text. Through its play of identity and non-identity, the law and the text neither arrive nor allow anyone to arrive (read). However, both claim absolute respectability. That the law and the text cannot be trespassed is something that is ensured by the concerned 'countrymen' (the readers) and 'doorkeepers' (the authorities of the literary institution: publishers, critics, professors, etc.) in the two respective cases.

Derrida's reads of the last words of the doorkeeper in the narrative, "I am now going to shut it [the gate]" as follows. By declaring itself as "I", the doorkeepers of Law as well as text show themselves up in their performatively constituted function of being in command of their respective domains. In this declaration, according to Derrida (1992: 212), "The text produces and pronounces the law that protects it and renders it intangible. It does and says, saying what it does by doing what it says." The performative 'I' is both inside and outside the text, as it is both outside and inside the gate of the Law.

As for the often-asked question, 'What is literature?' Derrida says that it cannot be answered in any general terms. Each text submits to its own conditions of possibility with its own implicit movements of 'framing and referentiality' (Derrida 1992: 213) In relation to these conditions of possibility, each text is surrounded by its own 'law'. And the site of this 'law of literature' is in fact external to literature. Thus, according to Derrida (1992: 214):

> The text (for example the so-called "literary" text and particularly this story by Kafka) before which we the readers appear before the law, this text protected by its guardians (author, publisher, critics, academics, archivists, librarians, lawyers, and so on) cannot establish law unless a more powerful system of laws ("a more powerful guardian") guarantees it, in particular the set of laws and social conventions that legitimates all these things.

In a similar vein, Deleuze has argued that literature cannot be understood in terms of any law of formation, well-formedness of language, but rather in terms of its permanent potential for transformation. Literature shuns the law of language, and "moves in the direction of the ill-formed or the incomplete" (Deleuze 1977: 225–230). Writing is to be located not in relation to already individuated beings of the world, but in relation to the process of individuation. Reflecting on the relation between literature and life, Deleuze (1977: 225) says:

> Writing is a question of becoming, always incomplete, always in the midst of being formed, and goes beyond the matter of any livable or lived experience. It is a process, that is, a passage of Life that traverses both the livable and the lived. Writing is inseparable from becoming: in writing, one becomes-woman, becomes-animal or -vegetable, becomes molecule, to the point of becoming-imperceptible.

Such a perspective on 'representation' of life in literature will of necessity have its consequences on the language of literature. Literary language is also something that is constantly becoming, existing only in the constantly deforming and zone of indiscernibility, both in relation to life and to itself. "Language must devote itself to reaching ... feminine, animal, molecular detours, and every detour is a becoming mortal" (Deleuze 1977: 225–230). Like Blanchot again, Deleuze holds that the language of literature exists only when it ceases to refer to real first or second persons, and begins to be associated with powerlessness of an impersonal third person. Following Proust, Deleuze (1977: 229) believes that literature "opens up a kind of foreign language within language, which is neither another language nor a rediscovered patois but a becoming-other of language, a 'minorisation' of this major language, delirium that carries it off, a witch's line that escapes the dominant system." Deleuze sees in Kafka's works this detachment from the fullness of the language that he is writing in, that is, the German language. The language of literature, according to Deleuze departs from the 'power' of its constant elements to the 'potential' of its variables, in creating a minor (literary) language from a major (official) language. It is in creating the minor German language of his writing, that Kafka can be called a minor litterateur. Minor and major languages, according to Deleuze are not two hierarchical forms of a language, but two different "usages" or treatments of the same. According to Deleuze and Guattari (1987: 104):

> Kafka, a Czechoslovakian Jew writing in German, submits German to creative treatments as a minor language, constructing a continuum of variation, negotiating all of the variables both to constrict the constants and to expand the variables; make language stammer, or make it "wail," stretch tensors through all of language, even written language, and draw from it cries, shouts, pitches, durations timbres, accents, intensities.

'Minor literature' exemplified in Kafka's writing, according to Deleuze, can be identified by three major characteristics. First, minor language is 'not' the language of a minority. It can only be a transformation wrought within a major language by a minority. What leads Kafka to construct a minor literature within the major national official language is linked to the inability of himself and of other Prague Jews to participate in the German national consciousness. Kafka's work represents the survival of language and literature against the oppressive and moribund legal and bureaucratic language of the German nation.

Second, it is necessary to notice the pervasively political character of minor literature. Rather than limiting the movement of literature from an individual–psychological level to a social-level as in the major literature, in the "minor literature" the individual is immediately in touch with the social and the political. For Kafka, as if evident particularly in *The Metamorphosis*, the familial is immediately political. The circle of the family intersects seamlessly with the circle of the bureaucratic in this story. As Gregor Samsa's life is metamorphosed into that of a beetle, the officials of his firm invade the privacy of his home, with the compliance of his father, and his sister begins to flirt with the strangers who come to lodge in their home. Gregor's body, meanwhile, becomes the object of ridicule, insults and assaults, and his voice is reduced to that of mere animal squeak and murmur.

The third important feature of "minor literature" is the "collective value" (Deleuze 1993: 153) of its statements. The author does not have the role of a master-narrator. This is because, Deleuze believes, an emerging collective consciousness is possible only through literature, and because "literature is the people's concern" (Deleuze 1993: 154) This is why the text of literature functions as a collective speech. And therefore, "there isn't a subject, *there are only collective assemblages* of enunciation, and literature expresses these acts insofar as they are not imposed from above and insofar as they exist only as diabolical powers to come or revolutionary forces to be constructed" (Deleuze 1993: 154). This is why it is possible to say that writing or literature takes place not within a community, but at its very limit. That is why it is possible to describe it as an "exscription", in the sense of Jean-Luc Nancy (2000).[4] Literature is always produced as that which ruptures the 'immunity' of a people with respect to its outside. It can only be the unworking of the 'community', which can exist only as its own contagion with respect to others and the outside, and the otherness 'to come' within itself and against its own immanence.

Notes

1. See for example, Foucault (1977). On the relationship between language and death, Foucault (54) writes:

    Boundless misfortune, the resounding gift of the gods, marks the point where language begins; but the limit of death opens before language, or rather within language, an infinite space. Before the imminence of death, language rushes forth, but it also starts again, tells of itself, discovers the story of story and the possibility that interpenetration might never end.

2. 'The Uncanny' is the title of an essay published by S. Freud in 1919. The German word used there is Unheimlisch. It refers to some thing or experience that appears familiar and foreign at the same time.
3. In Derrida's neologism, différance is meant to stand for both differing and deferring. The concept is discussed in detail in the chapter 'Semiology and Grammatology,' in his book *Positions*, 1981, (tr.) A. Bass. Chicago: University of Chicago Press.
4. 'Exscription' is Nancy's term for the material manifestation of writing, a sort of body-writing; the notion is developed in Jean-Luc Nancy, 2000. *Corpus*. Paris: Metailié.

References

Blanchot, M., 1982a. *The Madness of the Day*. Translated by L. Davis Barrytown: Station Hill Press.

Blanchot, M. 1982b. *The Space of Literature*. Translated by A. Smock. University of Nebraska Press.

———. 1995. *La part du feu* [The work of fire]. Translated by C. Mandell. Stanford: Stanford University Press.

———. 1943. *Faux pas*. Translated by C. Mandell. Stanford: Stanford Univesrity Press.

Deleuze, Gilles. 1977. 'Literature and Life', *Critical Inquiry*, 23 (2): 225–230.

———. 1993. 'Minor Literature–Kafka', in C. V. Boundas (ed.), *The Deleuze Reader*. New York: Columbia University Press.

Deleuze, G. and F. Guattari. 1987. *A Thousand Plateaus*. Translated by B. Massumi. Minneapolis, MN: University of Minnesota Press.

Derrida, Jacques. 1992. *Acts of Literature*. Edited by Derek Attridge. London: Routledge.

———."Before the Law," in D. Attridge (ed.) *Acts of Literature*. New York: Routledge, 1992. (pp. 181–220).

———. "The Law of Genre," in D. Attridge (ed.) *Acts of Literature*. New York: Routledge, 1992. (pp. 221–252).

de Saussure, Ferdinand. 1978. *Course in General Linguistics*. Translated by W. Baskin. Glasgow, UK: Fontana.

Foucault, Michel. 1977. 'Language to Infinity', in *Language, Counter-Memory, Practice*. Translated by D. F. Bouchard and S. Simon. Ithaca, NY: Cornell University Press.

Kafka, Franz. *The Metamorphosis* 1972. Translated by S. Corngold. New York: Bantam.

———. *The Trial, (Tr.) Willa and Edwin Muir. New York: Everyman's*

Heidegger, M. 2008. *Being and Time*. Translated by J. Macquarrie and E. Robinson, pp. 279–311. New York: Harper and Row.

Levinas, Emmanuel. 1991. *Otherwise than Being or Beyond Essence*. Translated by A. Lingis. Dordrecht: Kluwer Academic.

Nancy, Jean-Luc. 2000. *Corpus*. Paris: Metailié

9

Understanding Tribal World View

A Painter's Perspective

Sujata Miri

Philosophical work over the past few decades has been concerned with issues relating to understanding and not explaining forms of life which one frequently, unthinkingly designates as tribal. The distinction between understanding and explaining, to my mind, is all-important. To put it starkly, understanding has to do with making sense (as in understanding a poem, for example) and uncovering, and explaining, with finding causes and functions. While in the case of the more complex, for example, the so-called civilized societies, there is available, for social scientists to study, traditional written texts along with their 'hermeneutical' interpretations, the same is not true for most of the so-called primitive societies. The existence of a written intellectual tradition, however, should not lead one to the conclusion that the written word somehow lends an element of unchangeability to the tradition. A written tradition is just as vulnerable to historical contingencies as an oral tradition.

A world view represents a more or less flexible framework of concepts and a great variety of carriers of meanings (for example, symbols, metaphors, stories, songs, artefacts of different kinds, etc.) which offers answers to questions such as 'Who am I?' 'Who are others?' 'What is my relationship to others?' A world view contains guidelines about man–God, man–woman, man–child, man–nature relationships. Contrary to popular belief, tribal world views have a coherence and a completeness, which can be ascertained by gaining an access to the inner life of the people. All aspects of the life of a tribesman in his traditional system constituted by his language, custom and complex body of meaning-laden entities were covered in the wide framework of his religion. In one sense it can be said that religion was the centre of his cultural life. Most interesting to note is the fact that one can discover in traditional tribal religions strong sanctions for the preservation of their ecology; this is profoundly reflective of their unquestioned reverence for nature, man and animal. To take the case of the Khasis of North-east India, their world view seems to commit them to a belief in the existence of an all-pervasive order, *ka hok*, and a "law" operating in this world. There are intelligible connections between different courses and orders of events in the world. Human society also conforms to this all-pervasive order and human activities are regulated in terms of rules, which are expressions of the general order. Neither 'man nor bird' can deflect the course of law through their power.

Modern rationality demands unitary epistemologies and homogenization of evidence and the hope is that the acceptance of such an all-encompassing view of human nature will one day lead to the unity or oneness of the human world itself. Undoubtedly, universalism of any kind attempts to dispel the threat of cognitive anarchy, but there are underlying problems associated with it. No matter how attractive this conception is, it just so happens that there is such a variety of cultural systems in the world that anthropologists and others despair of ever finding any universal traits. The easier option is to conclude that the cognitive 'equipment' of other cultures, especially folk, tribal or indigenous cultures, is incomplete, if not totally erroneous. It is only in recent years with one's newly acquired respect for 'difference' and even 'incommensurability' that one has begun to take cultures other than one's own seriously. Prior to this academic journey one had the tribesman identified as an animist because he sees spirit everywhere, believes in ghosts, and generally lives in a world of fear and suspicions. The source of this misunderstanding is the failure to identify the vision of life a tribal culture represents. One would call it the traditional vision, which sees God, man and nature as inescapable parts of the great 'community' of beings. This vision, one wishes to emphasize, can form the basis of an authentic spiritual and moral experience. The tribal is concerned more with the well-being of the 'world' comprising man, animal and nature than with 'personal' salvation. This will be incomprehensible to someone who, schooled in modernity, places man at the centre of the universe, isolated both from God as well as nature. The first point to emphasize is the very different understanding, in tribal world views, of the notion of sameness that brings together man, God and nature in a profound unity. Indeed the image of creation speaks of the love between the pair of sky god and earth goddess. They willingly separate from each other so that there will be room for others to grow and flourish. Other legends describe mountains, rivers and clouds as beings who felt, thought, perceived and deliberated as persons. The Adis of Arunachal Pradesh, for example, identify the sky, the mountain, the earth and the rivers as the highest gods.

One's paintings may not provide crucial points of access to the very depths of the tribal world view. They may be seen perhaps as naïve attempts, at an appropriation of tribal traditions, as a sort of retelling and re-presenting. While looking at them however, one must stand guard against subsuming them hastily to one's own expectations of meanings. Only then can one begin to hear the traditions and their meanings.

A description of few of my paintings (Miri 2005) would elaborate the point. Among other things, these paintings, simply because the medium of painting is no respecter of the binaries of the Kantian (enlightenment) notion of rationality, show how, as narratives, they enjoy a special freedom.

In one of my paintings I have attempted to represent how according to a certain tribal belief, thunder takes place. The sky god has a frigid wife and whenever he tries to touch her, she runs and emits light to deter him, and that is how lightning occurs (Miri 2005: 12).

Some of my paintings describe the ethics of nature as understood in the tribal life-world. Two lovers are pictured and the man tells his beloved to be as faithful as the trees above and not like the unfaithful river, which has turned away. When two rivers flowing in the same direction are met by a third, there is turbulence, waterfall and so on. But in spite of the powerful water currents separating them, the trees are trying to reach out to each other. The trees are firm and erect.

Another powerful belief that informs and inspires tribal wisdom particularly is the idea that once you are dead you do not disappear altogether from the world. Almost all tribal communities talk of the protection that departed ancestors provide to living generations and I have attempted a visual rendering of this belief through my painting (Miri 2005: 40).

In the light of these narratives through paintings it may even be suggested that these paintings depict the general tribal theme of unity of the great community of beings—man, god, trees, mountains, animals, sun, moon, earth and so on.

The larger philosophical issues involved in understanding the tribal world view through these paintings are: What does it take for a human collectivity to count as a community? What constitutes the identity of a community? How is one to spell out the notion of a tribe? In what ways might the 'world view' of a tribe or a community be connected to its identity or at least to its sense of its own identity? Another set of issues arise from focusing on the term, 'the other' and the anxieties associated with its construction. The other could be a stranger in the community; it could be an alien community; and since 'alienation' is a matter of degree, it could be a community that is neither entirely alien, nor quite the same. In what ways can the idea of a stranger figure in the self-knowledge of a community? Can the 'stranger' ever become a participating member of the community? In what ways might the identity of a community be enmeshed in the identity of another community (for example, in what ways, if at all, is the identity of Dalits tied up with the identity of the caste-Hindu society)? If knowledge of the other in the case of individual human relationships is essential for self-knowledge, as many have argued, is the knowledge of the 'other' community also essential for the self-awareness and self-knowledge of a community? These are very interesting, and, in my view, very important issues.

Canonical philosophy would never attempt to understand the tribesman as an autonomous self or a subject of civilizational history. Therefore, philosophers generally do not consider tribal world views as deserving of much serious attention. The only interesting studies of tribal world views have been the ones done by anthropologists. But here the bounds of the discipline—even for scholars like Lévi-Strauss or Geertz—are such that world views or religions remain purely sociological or psychological phenomena: they are explored for what they have to teach one about the structure of the society and about how members of such a society relate themselves to the world around them or about the psychological determinants of individual and community behaviour. Tribal world views are never studied (as Hindu, Muslim or Christian world views are), as possibly more or less autonomous moral–epistemic frameworks in terms of which the question of truth and falsehood and good and evil can be explored and answered.

My contention in understanding the religion and culture of Khasi-Pnars, Adis of Arunachal Pradesh and of some of the Naga tribes has been that it is a grave mistake and injustice to treat these religions as mere devices—however clever and complex—to cope with the mundane predicaments of earthly existence. They must also be seen as possible embodiments and expressions of truths, which are beyond psychology and sociology—truths that are also the ground for a view of the world as saturated with values. Indian scholars working on the distant or early past of tribal communities developed a non-pluralistic (a modern though non-European) framework to unravel their metaphysics. Their endeavours were grounded in the philosophy of monism, which in large areas of the country derives its inspiration from teachings of the Vedas and the Upanishads, not to speak of the homogenising role of modern sensibilities. The overriding project of labelling tribal cultures as animistic is constitutive of a colonizing mind, which must be decolonized if one is to recover, even if partially, the authenticity of the tribal tradition.

Almost all introductory accounts of Indian philosophy, whether by M. Hiriyanna, S. Radhakrishnan or C. D. Sharma, talk of the early polytheistic beliefs of the Vedic period, which were replaced gradually with a kind of monotheism, on its way to the more sound monism of the Upanishads. The process of evolution from the former to the latter was for the better since monism as a philosophical system was healthier and more sophisticated. Hiriyanna repeatedly refers to the early Vedic religion, which he sees as a form of 'nature worship' (Hiriyanna 2008: 10). In this religion, according to him (Hiriyanna 2008: 10),

> the various powers of nature like fire (Agni), wind (*Vayu*) and the sun (Surya) are ... personified, the personification implying a belief that the order which is observed in the world, such as the regular succession of seasons or of day and night, is due to the agency of these powers.... The gods thus worshipped are very many.

In line with the above view, a contemporary Indian writer asserts (Hiriyanna 2008: 112), "In the later Vedic period there is a noticeable shift from plurality of nature gods within the universe to the supreme Transcendent Deity" (2008: 112). Professor Raju (1985: 9), an eminent Indian philosopher stresses the same: "Indian religion has had a gradual growth and development from very early polytheism to impersonalistic monism." He further says (Raju 1985: 10):

> The hymns of *Rig Veda* indicate that their religion was one of sacrifices—not necessarily of animals—addressed to various natural forces like the sun, the wind, the sky etc., understood as different gods.... It is said that for the early man, the child of the race, it was not easy to draw the distinction between spirit and body even in himself and he could not draw it in the natural forces also. His religion then was animatism. Both animatism and

animism are forms of polytheism. But when he began to draw the distinction within himself, he would draw it in the natural forces also and address his prayers to the spirits of the forces. His religion then is animism.

Professor Raju continues (1985: 12):

> When we trace the development of monism out of the polytheism of the Rigvedic hymns, we should note that the monistic god was gradually made inward to man. The inwardisation started with animism, that worshipped the spirits within the natural forces instead of the natural forces themselves. But these spirits are different from the spirit of man. But in the final stage, Brahman becomes the supreme atman (*Paramatman*) and is inward to the individual atman and yet transcends it.

H. S. Prasad says (1986: 43–44):

> The regularity of the natural phenomena, their predictability, and a design in them forced the early Vedic thinkers to conceive of an anthropomorphic divine principle as creator and regulator of the universe. At this stage, the tension created by the distinction between the singularity of such principle and the multiplicity of gods representing various natural forces remained unresolved. The anthropomorphic image of these gods became the foundation of man's relationship with them, which presupposes the elements of dispositions, will, agency on both sides.

People's faith remained steadfast and continued to be shaped by diverse configurations of this line of thinking; it was no surprise to find this belief controlling and influencing their everyday understanding of ancient or tribal India. Evidence for this can be found in the philosophical/ historical debates on the virtue of this goal, while it became the hallmark of social advance and institutional growth. An authority on what ought to be, it continues to be presented in idealized terms in academic as well as non-academic circles.

While reflecting on the tribesman's world, the modern intellectual has stopped short of the spirit of David Hume's masterpiece, *Dialogues Concerning Natural Religion*. Here Hume (X) reasons that it is not the order and unity of nature which first impresses 'the ignorant multitude' but rather 'some grovelling and familiar notion of superior powers.' Accordingly, polytheism is a more natural and a more primitive form of religious belief and should be regarded as such.

In short, it is not reason but fear of the unknown causes at work in nature, universally personified by uncritical minds, that produces the tribal deities of primitive men. That large-scale adoption of the motto, polytheism should be replaced by the more coherent monism, became a tool in the hands of a few. Inspired by such convictions, even if tacitly, books after books reiterated the same theme giving impetus to moves (religio-political) for urgently replacing the polytheism of, for instance, the Adi communities with a more logically consistent system of beliefs. The thrust of the attack by the demolition squad has been as follows: tribal religions are wholly beyond the reach of either support or criticism by rational means. The overwhelming probability of the laws of nature discovered by science and common sense is sufficient to establish that no power other than them is required to explain natural events. Thus the belief in the many gods of the tribal pantheon rests upon a mistake and is contrary to reason. The explanation by tribal elders of how the variegated tribal godheads were held together in a coherent whole was not heeded by the relentless critique. Nor was any need felt to spell out, in the context of cosmology and metaphysics, their ideas of human nature or some transcendental ontology informing their view of the moral world.

The urge to reduce tribal religion to infantile psychology (Freud) or to disguised sociology (Durkheim) is so great, and the need for recovery and emancipation so enormous that a mere philosophical exploration of the possibility of its autonomy is only the beginning. The process of recovery would require an attention to tribal religion, which, while combating the great hunger of different epistemic regimes to appropriate tribal religions, will bring a complex variety of considerations to bear upon the question of its autonomy. These considerations will draw upon all one's resources of intelligence, understanding and insight: perception, reason, imagination and emotional, ethical and the aesthetic, as integral to them. Another way of putting it would be to say that they will be considerations that will show the emotional and the evaluational in the tribal form of life to be constitutive of the epistemic. Reduction takes place only on the basis of the separation of the epistemic from the emotional and the evaluational.

The means employed in putting together such considerations cannot, from the nature of the case, be purely argumentative. The odds against such an approach succeeding are enormous. And so narrative means must include, apart from argumentation, other forms of persuasion, or as I may put it, other forms of truth, for example, stories and legends, dance and music, paintings and other forms of art. This approach to understanding the tribal world view is a by-product of my growing conviction of the relative futility of purely argumentative modes of persuasion. Take for instance the tribe's feeling of proximity to environment as depicted in one of the paintings above. As we are aware, a powerful constituent of a tribal form of life is a profound 'affective' bond (spiritual?) between man and everything around him. Now this affective bond is also constitutive of the unique kind of knowledge that the tribesman has of himself in relation to this environment. A purely discursive, philosophical account of this constitutive element in tribal episteme is beset with the following difficulties: (*a*) it immediately encounters powerful counter-traditions in the philosophy of knowledge; (*b*) the tribesman himself hardly uses a discursive mode to represent knowledge; therefore the question—almost impossible to answer—whose philosophy of knowledge are we talking about? will always be pertinent; and (*c*) the similarity between what in philosophical literature is called the "mystical" and tribal episteme is only apparent; in reality the two are profoundly different. And this difference is not always amenable to a discursive understanding. The perfect ordinariness of the tribesman's knowledge of the world within and the world without—this again is a distinction that is not really a part of his vocabulary—is conveyed best by means other than abstract argumentation. If one is serious about this venture, one will find how in actual practice a tribal religion can be wholly integrative and, at the same time, non-coercive, how virtues figure centrally in understanding human as well as non-human life, and how the affective and the pragmatic are constitutive of the cognitive, that is, how knowledge cannot be abstracted from the experience of good and evil and the ways of coming to terms with such experience.

Students of philosophy are familiar with the two, almost opposing, traditions of undertaking philosophy, that of the analytical and the hermeneutical. While the analytic tradition in philosophy finds in analytical social science the tendency to evacuate the local in favour of some abstract universal and to demystify 'ideology' in the pursuit of a just social order, it is the hermeneutical tradition that produces a loving grasp of detail in search of an understanding of the diversity of human life-worlds leading towards recognition of the innate heterogeneity, not oneness of social worlds (see Chakrabarty (2000). Unfortunately, it is the former and not the latter that has held sway over the researcher's mind, contributing to the complete neglect of tribal studies. One of course cannot ignore certain methodological issues that confront one when one starts to talk of tribal philosophy. If the tribesmen are Indian and shared a philosophy of life with the broad Indian tradition that has been studied in such great detail, what is the point of undertaking this separate study? One will have to go to great trouble, learn new languages, and deal with texts which are in most cases in quite bad shape. Once one turns to learning about their ways of life, that is, of their distinctive past, one gets pressured to become cultural historians and not philosophers.

One might admit that undertaking philosophy is first of all pursuing wisdom. Can there be a convergence of methods by which the philosophical aim of self-understanding and insight can be achieved by storytelling, metaphor and analysis, in combination and mutual dependence? Explorations of the forms of knowledge, the forms in which human life can be examined, take diffused forms but are no less philosophical than writings of a discursive and analytical kind. Philosophy is an activity akin to conversation that can also be represented in writing. In other words, as McGhee says (2010: 15):

> The term "philosophical" names a function or telos rather than a subset of the methods by which this telos or function might be achieved. What I have in mind in referring to this function or telos is a particular kind of moral endeavour that defines a philosophical community, at once revelatory and emancipatory, critical and constructive.

Contemporary philosophers wish to dismantle the delusion and ignorance of the past, a part of what they characterize as their philosophical endeavour. There is cruelty in simply dismantling a system of beliefs and after having destroyed it, simply discarding it to oblivion: this exhibits a callousness and moral insensitivity, particularly in light of the fact that the subject of investigation is a whole way of being human, profoundly different though it may be from the researcher's way of being human. It may be argued in his defence that it is in the very nature of philosophical activity that ignorance and delusions be dismantled. That dismantling is a very essential part of philosophical enterprise cannot be doubted. Surely the philosopher must, however, know the system prior to dismantling it. There appears no evidence either of his genuinely entering the system of beliefs of the culture under consideration or of his ability to discover a way of finding what Wittgenstein calls a 'perspicuous' representation, an understanding that consists in 'seeing connections' (Kober).

More importantly, there is a need, on the part of the philosopher, if she wishes to seriously study and understand tribal world views, to recover the naïve innocence with which traditional concepts were made to serve their thinking. The philosopher must be aware of her own bias so that the text can present itself in all its otherness. The labelling of tribal traditions as primitive polytheism is a consequence of a bias on the part of the philosopher, which urges her to project a meaning for the whole of a tribe's world view, as soon as some initial meaning emerges in her research. She is disinterested in carrying out constant revision of her early conclusion. If she were to do so she would find himself compelled to discover deeper meanings in the text undertaken. Can one learn to see the past in its own terms and not in terms of the contemporary criteria and prejudices, within its own historical setting? "If we fail to transpose ourselves into the historical horizon from which the traditionary text speaks, we will misunderstand the significance of what it has to say to us," says Gadamer (1997: 302). This should not lead one to the hasty conclusion, as Gadamer points out, that there are such things as closed horizons that are supposed to enclose cultures. The historical movement of human life consists in the fact that it is never absolutely bound to any one standpoint and hence can never truly have a closed horizon. Transposing ourselves consists neither, he goes on to say, "in the empathy of one individual for another nor in subordinating another person to our own standards, rather, it always involves rising to a higher universality that overcomes not only our own particularity but also that of the other" (Gadamer 1997: 304). Thus the horizon of the past out of which all human life emerges and which exists in the form of tradition, is always in motion. When one's historical consciousness transposes itself in historical horizons, it does not mean that it has passed into alien worlds unconnected in any way with one's own. The worlds of the past combine with querying and affirmation of concepts and entities in the present.

References

Chakrabarty, Dipesh 2000. *Provincializing Europe: Postcolonial Thought and Historical Difference*. Princeton.
Gadamer. 1997 *Truth and Method*. Translated by Joel Weinsheimer and Donald G. Marshall, p. 302 New York: Continuum.
Hiriyanna, M. 2008. *The Essentials of Indian Philosophy*. New Delhi: Motilal Banarsidass.
Hume, David 1953. *Dialogues Concerning Natural Religion*, p. x. New York: Hafner Publishing Co.
McGhee, Michael. 2010. 'Philosophy as Poetry and Conversation', in A. Raghuramraju and Jyotirmaya Sharma (eds), *Grounding Morality: Freedom, Knowledge and the Plurality of Cultures*, p. 15. New Delhi: Routledge.
Michael Kober, *Grazer Philosophische Studien*, Volume 71, p. 28.
Miri, Sujata 2005 *A Book Of Paintings: On Themes From The Hills Of Northeast India*, New Delhi: Mittal Publications.
Prasad, H. S. 1986 'Buddhism and Marxism: Some Points of Difference', in *Buddhist Studies, Journal of the Department of Buddhist Studies*: pp. 43–44. University of Delhi.
Raju, P. T. 1985. *Structural Depths of Indian Thought*. New Delhi: South Asian Publishers.

10

Reiterating Stereotypes?

Assessing the Role of Women in Contemporary Jatra[1]

Somdatta Mandal

The privileging of the written word in general and the literary text in particular has led to the postcolonial condition being examined and theorized largely in relation to literature. As a consequence, the diverse cultural production of a large part of the postcolonial world falling outside the verbal—both traditional narrative and performing genres and the new electronically mediated arts—is excluded from the category of culture. However, in the age of new media dominated by the visual and the aural, representations of the postcolonial experience in film, television, music and theatre compete with those in literature. This chapter calls to attention the role played by women in the traditional performing art of *jatra* and shows the affinity of cultural production with similar roles in literary texts.

Jatra is the traditional theatre form of Bengal performed by travelling troupes. Though most *jatra* companies have their offices in Kolkata, particularly in a locality in the north called Chitpur, they usually perform more in the districts, in rural and semi-urban areas. The *jatra* of Bengal has always been looked upon as a poor cousin of the theatre but the city–village divide that affects many folk theatre forms in the rest of India is not particularly applicable to Bengali *jatra*. *Jatras* were usually epic four-hour-long plays featuring loud music, harsh lighting and dramatic props played on giant outdoor stages. They were often melodramatic with stylized delivery, exaggerated gestures and oration, accompanied by the overt use of traditional musical instruments. Originally the *jatra* had only themes pertaining to Radha and Krishna; today they are written by writers and dramatists of rural and urban centres and have also been modernized to feature contemporary crises through modern stories, bearing close resemblance to television soaps and serials and popular commercial films. According to the demands of the age, the budget and production of the *jatra* have also undergone changes.

The construction of female identity with its attendant cultural connotations; the fact that her position in society is lower in the patriarchal thought processes; the male value-orientation and cultural assumption about sex roles and sexual politics inform the theatrical world of the *jatra*. Historically speaking, female roles in the *jatra* until the mid-1960s were performed by male actors, often termed 'moustachioed ranis'. With the coming of the playback, microphone, and so on women performers entered the arena but they were either prostitutes or fallen women or women in dire need of economic stability as a result of post-partition migration. During that period people even had reservations about whether these women performers would be able to address the gathering of at least ten or fifteen thousand people with their soft voices. Another reason for this scepticism was the peripatetic nature of *jatra* performances. Moving from villages to small district towns each night without proper infrastructure, women often became soft targets for abduction and seduction. But since the early 1990s, the lure of the lucre has drawn a lot of actors from commercial Bengali cinema and theatre (including villains and starlets from Bollywood) to perform in the *jatra*—thus erasing the rural–urban divide to a great extent.

A close survey of the titles and advertisements of *jatra* being performed over the last four years in Bengal alone has revealed an amazing fact.[1] Without taking into consideration the sets, costume designs, cyclorama, playback music, dance numbers or anything else for that matter, it shows that more than ninety per cent of all *jatra* performances have women in central roles and titles. These show women in stereotypical roles, as mother, daughter, wife, lover and vamp (the other woman). Most of the time they are portrayed in extremes—they are either deified or demonized. It becomes clear why Indian traditional social structure, predominantly patriarchal, still portrays women in India in extreme stereotypical roles—the wife, the nourisher, the sacrificing mother, the scheming mother-in-law (something repeated ad nauseam in the *saas–bahu* serials and soaps on television); their position always lower in the social order, always conforming to the ideal roles. In the Western paradigm the list of female stereotypes and sub-types is long and varied on the surface, but it can be reduced to a basic core group—the virgin, the seductress/ goddess, the mother/wife and the old maid. Mary Anne Ferguson (1973: 5–11) speaks of several stereotypes: the mother, the wife, the mistress/ seductress, the sex object, the old maid, the educated woman and the lady. She goes on to delineate and break down these terms to include the submissive wife, the dominating wife and even the new form—the liberated woman. Among the constructions of female identity with their attendant cultural connotations in the Indian context, perhaps the most significant is the role of the dutiful, obedient, caring, self-effacing wife. In the world of *jatra*, the wife is portrayed in primarily three categories, namely (*a*) the sacrificing wife, (*b*) the rebellious/dominating wife and (*c*) the wise/intelligent wife. What follows in this chapter is an analysis of the titles that have women as their focal point.

The Wife as Homemaker (Operative Word is *Sangsar*)

Under the broad concept that considers the woman primarily as a wife, the first category revolves around the stereotypical role of the woman as homemaker—attributes desirable for all Indian women in the ideal family situation. So titles like *Ei Ghar Ei Sangsar* (This house, this family), *Rajar Ghare Rajlakshmi* (The Lakshmi in the king's house), *Sangsar Sukhe Hoye Romonir Guney* (The family is happy through female attributes), *Swapne Dehka Sukher Sangsar* (The happy family of my dreams) (see Illustration 10.1), *Sangsar Simantey Sita* (Sita at the periphery of the household), all primarily operate on the word *sangsar*—the family, the household, the home and the hearth.

The Bride (Operative Word is *Bou* or *Bodhu*)

This theme is closely followed by several productions that focus on marriage and the new bride (the *bou* or *bodhu*), where a romantic aura still exists in the psyche of the young woman at the threshold of a new married life. Titles, for example, are *Godhulilagne Mala Badal* (Exchanging of garlands at dusk), *Memsahiber Mala Badal* (A memsahib exchanges

Illustration 10.1.

Swapne Dekha Sukher Sangsar

Source: An advertisement in *Sangbad Pratidin*.

garlands), *Smashaney Holo Subhodrishti* (The eyes met only at the burning ghat), *Brishtir Aaj Subhodrishti* (Today Brishti will see her husband for the first time), *Saat Pake Bandha* (Entwined by seven *pheras*[2]). The word *bou* or *bodhu* is reiterated in many *palas*[2]—*Bonpolashir Notun Bou* (The new bride of Bonpolashi village), *Palkitey Bou Chole Jaye* (The bride goes away in a palanquin), *Buro Khokar Kochi Bou* (A young bride for an old boy) (see Illustration 10.2), *Dalanbarir Durga Bou* (The Durga-like bride in the big house), *Aami Rickshawalar Bou* (I am the wife of a rickshaw puller), *Bagher Khachay Balika Bodhu* (A young bride in the tiger's cage), *Gayer Bodhur Lojja Churi* (The shame stolen from a village bride), *Ghoom Kerechey Notun Bou* (The new bride has stolen sleep), *Rajbhikharir Patita Bou* (The fallen bride of a royal beggar), *Ray Barir Chhoto Bou* (The youngest bride of the Roy household).

Here a particular Hindu cultural marker like the sindoor, or the vermillion in the parting of the bride's hair pronouncing her married status, also becomes a significant operative word. So there are productions such as *Ashol Sindoor Nokol Bou* (Real sindoor but false bride), *Du Tookro Sindoor* (Two pieces of sindoor), *Harano Sindoor Firiye Dao* (Return my lost sindoor), or *Paaper Taka Punyer Sindoor* (Ill-gotten wealth but blessed sindoor), *Shob Sindoorey Sukh Melena* (All sindoor does not give happiness), *Sindoor Bhaggye Shoilo Na* (Fate did not permit the

Illustration 10.2.

Buro Khokar Kochi Bou

Source: An advertisement in *Sangbad Pratidin*.

sindoor), *Sindoor Diye Sita Haran* (Capturing Sita through the sindoor), *Sindoor Koutoye Kakra Biche* (A scorpion inside the box of sindoor), *Sithir Sindoor, Bagher Aachor* (The sindoor at the parting of the hair is like a tiger's scratch).

The Subservient/Self-Sacrificing/Suffering Wife

Once the new bride steps into her in-laws' home she is of course the stereotype of the all-enduring, suffering, submissive, totally dependent, sacrificing woman, someone who is more sinned against than sinning. So one finds a long list of titles such as *Aajke Debir Balidaan* (Today the virtuous woman will be slaughtered), *Aami Ki Fulshajjar Bashi Phool?* (Am I the Wilted Flower of the Bridal Night?) *Bou Katha Kao* (Bride, please speak), *Faashir Manche Debir Bodhan* (The virtuous woman at the noose), *Matir Ghorey Raj Protima* (A queenly goddess in a mud hut). As many titles show, the woman is deified as a goddess-like figure, a devi or a *protima*—a virtuous woman who is then mistreated by society and sacrificed either at the noose or the burning pyre. In the Indian marriage market the first attribute a woman should have is fair skin, otherwise she is unable to get a suitable groom. She becomes either the wife of a non-entity—*Aami Haridas Paler Bou* (I am the wife of a non-entity) (see Illustration 10.3) or has to remain content with a mentally challenged husband—*Kaalo Meyer Pagol Swami* (A lunatic husband for a dark girl).

Other titles are also significant because they highlight the helpless status of the wife or daughter-in-law in the household—*Jibon Chitay Jolchey Nari* (Woman burning in the pyre of life), *Protima Bisarjan* (The immersion of the goddess), *Ke Jude Debe Bhanga Churi* (Who will join the broken bangle?), *Maago Keu Bojhena Naarir Betha* (Mother, no one understands a woman's pain), *Chena Prithibi Achena Maanush* (The known world but the unknown people), *Dharitri Keno Lanchita?* (Why is Mother Earth suffering?), *Faashir Monchey Debir Bodhan* (A goddess worshipped at the guillotine altar), *Swadhin Bharate Paradhin Bhalobasha* (Subservient love in an independent India), *Choori Hoye Geche Swadhinota* (Independence has been stolen), *Bhalobashar Karagare Bandini Sujata* (Sujata trapped in the prison of love), *Kaandey Vishnupriya* (Vishnupriya weeps), *Lobhi Sosurer Lanchita Putrobodhu* (The tortured daughter-in-law of a

Reiterating Stereotypes? 149

Illustration 10.3.

Aami Haridas Paler Bou

Source: An advertisement in *Sangbad Pratidin*.

greedy father-in-law), *Maatir Gharey Rajprotima* (A goddess in a mud hut), *Polashpurer Protima* (The goddess of Palashpur), *Moroner Porey Bodhu Elo Gharey* (The bride comes home after death), *Nagna Samajer Lanchita Lakshmi* (The tortured Lakshmi in a crude society), *Purnimatey Chandragahan* (A lunar eclipse in a full-moon night), *Sukher Gharey Shanti Nei* (There is no peace in the house of happiness), *Tumi Amaar Jibon Songee* (You are my life partner).

The Rebellious/Domineering Wife

In spite of such suffering it does not take long for the demure new bride to become a domineering or dominating woman, perfectly fit for modern times—*Bashorgorey Bonnhisikha* (A firebrand woman on the wedding night) and declaring in a similar title, *Aami Bonnhisikha* (I am Bonnhisikha, a firebrand woman)[3] (see Illustration 10.4). She is a *Bidrohini Bourani* (The revolting daughter in-law) or a *Bidrohini Putrabadhu* (The Revolting Daughter-in-law), stating clearly—*Aami Bodhu Hote Ashini* (I have not come to be a bride). So the bride removes her veil, *Ghomta Khola Gaayer Bodhu* (The village bride without her veil), denies her lowly status—*Maatir Ghorey Poter Bibi* (A poster wife in a mud hut), *Ghor Jamaiyer Kelor Kirti* (The misdeeds of the house son-in-law), takes the *sangsar* under her control and thus emerges the sub-category of the empowered wife.

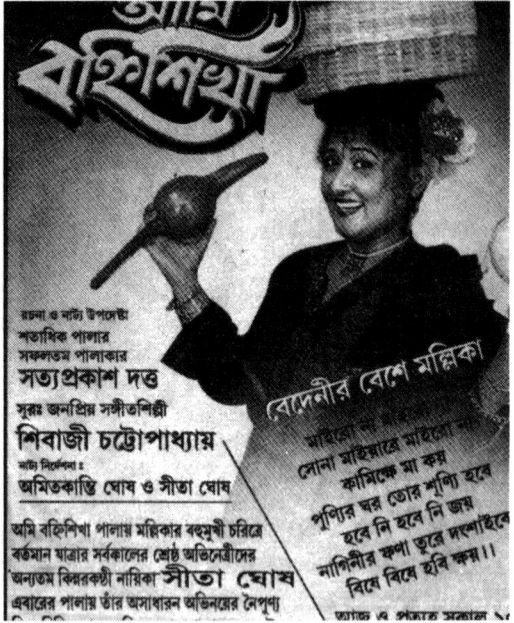

Illustration 10.4.

Aami Bonnhisikha

Source: An advertisement in *Sangbad Pratidin*.

The Empowered Wife

The actual empowerment or the desire to acquire it thus governs titles of several productions—*Lakshmir Haatey Trishul* (The trident in the hands of Lakshmi), *Roga Swamir Daroga Bou* (The matronly wife of a lean husband) (see Illustration 10.5), *Kaacher Ghore Lohar Bou* (An iron wife in a glass house), *Pagla Swamir Khooni Bou* (The killer wife of a lunatic husband); some even indicate revolts as a daughter in law—*Bahurupi Putrobodhu* (The chameleon daughter-in-law).[5]

The husband, often a henpecked has to then either declare, *Aamar Bou Shob Janey* (My wife knows everything), or lament on her indigestible quality, *Bou Enechi Boono Ole* (I have brought a wife like a wild tuber).[6] The family takes pride that they have a *Sikshita Bouma* (An educated daughter-in-law) or realizes her worth as *Boumar Daam Cheler Shoman* (The value of a daughter-in-law is the same as the son). After declaring *Nari Aami Khelna Noi* (I am a woman and not a toy), and becoming an

Illustration 10.5.

Roga Swamir Daroga Bou

Source: An advertisement in *Sangbad Pratidin*.

equal to her male partner in *Loafer Chheler Pocketmaar Bou* (A pickpocket wife of a loafer husband), one *pala* declares emancipation—*Banglar Bodhu Zindabad* (Bengali Bride, Zindabad).

The Mother

Like all Indian women the now-hardened wife turns into a mother. She has a stern exterior concealing a soft heart—*Baire Baghini, Antarey Jononi* (A tigress outside but a mother inside) or *Momotamoyeer Mostaan Cheley* (The disreputable son of a doting mother) (see Illustration 10.6),

Illustration 10.6.

Momotamoyeer Mostaan Cheley

Source: An advertisement in *Sangbad Pratidin.*

Kurukhetrey Kaadey Jononi (The mother cries at Kurukshetra), *Raktey Ranga Mayer Aanchol* (The mother's sari *pallu* drenched in blood), *Gandhari Jononi* (Mother Gandhari), *Maake Bachatey Manush Aschey* (A man is coming to save mother), *Firey Elam Mayer Koley* (I came back to the lap of my mother)—all exploring the different facets of the nourisher or the sacrificing maternal image.

The Mother-in-Law

Interestingly enough, compared to the stereotypical image of the mother-in-law as torturer that usually prevails in the Indian psyche and explored endlessly in television soaps and movies, there are very few *palas* directly focusing on her. One production that has a mother-in-law in the title is *Sashuri No.1* (Mother-in-law no. 1), another states *Shashuri Bhoyonkari Bouma Biswasundari* (The mother-in-law is dangerous, the daughter-in-law is a world-famous beauty), and a third one is called *Jamai Charsobish (420) Sashuri Unish Bish* (The son-in-law is a fraud (420), the mother-in-law almost the same). In an interesting role reversal the mother-in-law is seen begging for food in *Bouma Anna Bhiksha Dao* (Daughter-in law, please give us food), (see Illustration 10.7), with the realization that she will land up in an old age home, *Sesh Thikana Briddhashram* (The last address is an old age home).

Love or Lover (Operative words are *Bhalobasha, Prem* or *Pirit*)

There are a lot of productions that dwell on love, with the operative words *bhalobasha, prem* or *pirit*: *Ogo Amaar Praner Bodhu* (O my sweetheart wife), *Bhalobasha Ki Aage Bujhini* (I did not know earlier what love meant), *Bhalobasha Ki Aparadh?* (Is love a crime?) *Bhalobasha Keno Eto Asohay?* (Why is love so helpless?), *Bhalobashar Agnipariksha* (The trial of love by fire), *Bhalobeshe Ki Pelam?* (What did I get in return to my love?) and they slowly move the focus from the wife as the protagonist to the "other" woman, either a lover or a vamp. Productions such as *Moyna Bolo Tumi Krishna Radhe* (Mynah, sing of Krishna and Radha), *Kodomtolay Kolir Radha* (A modern Radha under the kadam tree),

Illustration 10.7.

Bouma Anna Bhiksha Dao

Source: An advertisement in *Sangbad Pratidin.*

Mirar Bodhua (Mira's Lover), *Mouboner Mayuri* (A peahen in the mahua forest), *Kestopurer Krishnakoli* (Krishnakali from Kestopur), *Ektuku Chhoyalage* (A little touch), *Hiyar Majhe Mor Priya* (My lover is in my heart), *Chirodinee Tumi Amar* (You are mine forever), *Golemaaley Pirit Korona* (Don't make love in times of confusion), *Footpather Rajkumari* (A princess of the footpath), *Premer Ghatey Noukadubi* (Boat wreck in the

Reiterating Stereotypes? 155

shore of love), *Ekdin Ratrey* (It happened one night), *Roopsagarer Rupashi* (A beauty in the beautiful sea), *Chokkhe Amar Trishna* (Thirst in my eyes), *Sobuj Dwiper Nayantara* (A beautiful flower in the green island), *Ke Tumi Nandini?* (Who are you, Ms Charming?), *Aami Kolkatar Rosogolla* (I am a rasgulla of Kolkata), *Nayika Niruddesh* (The disappearance of the heroine) *Swapnapurir Raajkanya* (The princess in a dream palace), *Rupashi Dohai Tomar* (For you, my beauty), *Nishidhha Premer Parinaam* (The fate of forbidden love) (see Illustration 10.8) are also supplemented with Bollywood-like titles, *Chameli 420[7]*, *Teri Meherbaniyan* (Your

Illustration 10.8.

Nishidhha Premer Parinaam

Source: An advertisement in *Sangbad Pratidin*.

munificence), *Sandhyaraater Lal Pari* (The red fairy of night), *Rangamatir Rangeela* (The fun girl from the land of the red earth), *Moner Manush Por Purush* (The desired person is another man), *Ruper Rani Swapner Raja* (The beauty queen and the dream king) (see Illustration 10.9), *Rang De Basanti* (Add colours in Spring), *Aami Ful Ganyer Fuleshwari* (I am Fuleshwari from Ful Village), *Aami Sandhyadiper Sikha* (I am the evening flame), *Chander Priya Chandramukhi* (Chandramukhi, the lover of the moon).

Illustration 10.9.

Ruper Rani Swapner Raja

Source: An advertisement in *Sangbad Pratidin*.

The Powerful Woman (Operative Words are *Konya* or *Meye*)

With the attainment of power the garb of the bride or *bodhu* is done away with and the woman becomes a *konya* or a *meye*—a daughter or girl. So one sees *palas* like *Nagna Samajer Agnikony*[8] (The firebrand daughter of a bare society), *Amar Adalat Raat 12 Taye* (My court begins at midnight), *Mahamanya Adalat O Ekti Meye* (The honourable court and a girl), *Aami Bangladesher Baghini Konya* (I am a tigress from Bengal), *Lalmaatir Dosshi Meye* (The naughty girl from the land of red earth), *Moila Samajer Meye* (A daughter of a dirty society), *Bostir Meye Parul* (Parul, daughter of the slums), *Meye Noy Jeno Aaguner Fulki* (Not a girl but a spark of fire). All these productions juxtapose the sexual/sensual femme fatale figure with that of the wifely/motherly image, but as the statistics reveal they are much less in number. The *jatra* industry is always very active in picking up themes related to contemporary affairs. And when the prime issue this season (2011) is the celebration of the most powerful woman (*meye*) in Bengal, it is no wonder that already ten *palas* have been composed on Mamata Banerjee, the present chief minister with her popular slogan, '*Maa, mati, manush*' (mother, soil and the people). So there is *Banglar Maa Mati Manush Kaadchey* (The mother, soil and people of Bengal are crying), *Agnikonya Aaschey* (The firebrand daughter is coming), *Bangla Amar Mamatamoyee* (Bengal is full of Mamata), *Banglar Khamataye Ebar Mamata* (Mamata is now in power in Bengal), *Banglar Mamata Dekho Taar Khamata* (See the power of Mamata of Bengal), *Banglar Masnade Mamata* (Mamata on the throne of Bengal), *Mahasangrame Jayi Mamata* (Mamata wins the great struggle), *Mukhyamatrir Khamatay Elo Mamata* (Mamata now in power as Chief Minister), *Swapner Netri Mamatamoyee* (Mamata now leader of dreams), *Didi Tomar Jobab Nei* (Didi, hats off to you) and *Lalgarer Chele Nandigramer Meye* (The boy from Lalgarh, the girl from Nandigram).

There are a few productions that dwell on 'the woman question' where the woman is usually portrayed as the protagonist but not strictly abiding to the stereotypes mentioned above. These relate to secular issues—*Jaat Nei Go Sujatar* (Sujata does not have any caste); Hindu–Muslim amity—*Abbajaner Hindu Meye* (The Hindu daughter of a Muslim father)[9] (see Illustration 10.10), brother–sister relationship—*Bhai Boner Sesh Dekha* (The last meeting of brother and sister), *Adalatey Dui Bon* (Two sisters in the court), *Aami Manush Khoojchi Babu* (I am looking for a human being, Babu).

Illustration 10.10.

Abbajaner Hindu Meye

Source: An advertisement in *Sangbad Pratidin*.

In most productions the homely *sati–sadhwi* wife (usually dressed in a traditional sari) is very carefully juxtaposed with a 'modern' woman (dressed in western clothes) who is usually the vamp, the dancer or maybe the villain. One might recollect how right from the 1950s onwards, popular Hindi films projected the westernized woman in modern outfits, just as the sari-clad *pallu*-over-the-head woman became the visual stereotype of the traditional *Bharatiya nari* image. This is a continuation of the *purab aur paschim* binary made popular by Saira Banu in the 1960s film of the same name. Apart from the dress codes, a close study of the women in the *jatra* advertisements reveals the impact of the visual images. In his seminal essay, 'The Rhetoric of the Image,' Roland Barthes (1977: 33) attempts to "submit the image to a spectral analysis of the messages it may contain." He turns to the advertising image, an image that, he argues, draws from "signs that are full, formed with a view to the optimum reading" (1977: 33) and which therefore is more frank and explicit in the information it conveys. Barthes wishes to use this clarity to move towards a clearer conception of how the image and its linguistic attendants produces signification. He proceeds by breaking this system of signification into three parts, that of linguistic message, the coded iconic message and the non-coded iconic message. He also argues that attention must be paid to the composition of an image as a signifying complex and to the naturalizing role played in photography, where the exact replication of reality "naturalizes the symbolic message ... innocent[ing] the semantic artifice of connotation" (1977: 45). The politics behind different *jatra* advertisements involve all the three different types of signification that Barthes talks of.

Before concluding, three things need to be mentioned. First, though the imaginative and often onomatopoeic nature of these titles is lost in translation, they reiterate several sociocultural issues of contemporary society and challenge the belief that all formulas come with an inbuilt expiry date. The second factor is that each of these *jatra* productions keeps in mind commercial viability and introduces song and dance sequences even in productions that have serious social issues to critique. If not directly related to the plot, these Bollywood-like song and dance numbers engaging young starlets (and most of the time mentioned separately in the advertisement), guarantee larger ticket sales and provide the entertainment quotient of the performance.[10] Third, evaluated from the perspective of culture studies, however much the city-bred individual might snicker at the titles, the charm, the attraction, the high-budget production (with many film stars and starlets performing in lead roles), the circulation, reception and preservation of the *jatra* are indeed crucial to the formation of 'modern' or 'national' memory and can delineate the ways in which one encounters social and cultural transformation vis-à-vis the position of women in contemporary Bengali (read Indian) society. A visit to McDonald's and multiplexes in urban Bengal is enough to gauge the change in contemporary society. But how can one measure the social change that is sweeping through rural Bengal? Entertainment in the agrarian belt, in spite of the easy accessibility to television soaps and serials, has not diminished the charm and attraction of the *jatra* performance. In fact as a recent newspaper report also highlighted, even urban people gathered in large numbers to see *jatras* at the Twelfth Jatra Festival held in Kolkata.[11] So though women are replicating the gyrating dancers of Bollywood culture even in a down-to-earth social drama set in Bengal, the thrust area of each tale still revolves around a stereotypical Bengali (Indian) woman, both critiquing and entertaining us. *Jatra* is alive and thriving in its own popularity and it would be wrong to consider it a devalued cultural form, inferior in taste. It is part of the socially accepted forms of normative behaviour and as the popularity charts and ratings prove, it is still the best medium to voice contemporary social issues.

Notes

1. This chapter is a revised and updated version of a presentation made at a seminar in ICCR (Eastern Regional Centre, North-Eastern Hill University, Shillong) in March 2010.
2. During the Hindu marriage ceremony, the bride and the groom have to go around the holy fire seven times together for the marriage bond to be eternally fulfilled. Each of these circles is called paaks or pheras. The term 'pala' (or 'palas' in the plural) is the actual word used for each *jatra* production. They are never directly called 'plays' to differentiate them from the ordinary theatre productions.
3. Each year the *jatra* season begins in July (on the auspicious day of the Ratha Yatra or Chariot Festival) and ends around February or March of the following year. The companies travel around the state, performing almost every night. During the rest of the year they rehearse new productions and some performers even shift contracts from one company to another. For the purpose of this survey I specifically studied the productions that began from July 2007 until 2011. This is not an all-inclusive list because I only followed the advertisements in one particular Bengali newspaper called *Sangbad Pratidin*. Many other vernacular newspapers also carry similar advertisements.
4. Loosely translated, the tagline of this famous production by Nattya Company reads: "Written in a new style, this tearful story speaks of the life struggle of a woman without a father and mother, who struggles against the injustice, terror and torture of society."
5. This production from Trinayani Opera has a rhyming couplet as its tagline: "*Jwalamoyee sashuri/Mukhe nei modhu/Protibader jhanda niye/Bahurupi putrabadhu.*" In translation this reads, the fierce mother-in-law without honey in her mouth is combated by the chameleon daughter-in-law who comes with a mast of protest.
6. The *ole*, or a large tuber, is a delicacy in Bengali household cuisine if cooked in the proper way. Sometimes a wild variety of this causes immense inflammation and itching in the throat. Here the daughter-in-law is compared to this second category—very hard to digest.

Reiterating Stereotypes? 161

7. The word Chameli is the proper name of a woman and 420 of course means a crook or dishonest person who is usually booked under section 420 of The Indian Penal Code. Hence the title could read as 'Chameli, the 420 Woman'.
8. The tagline of this Shilpitirtha production reads: "*Somajer ei koshaikhanay/Kanna Gham rokter bonnya/Badla nite aschey ebar/Nagna samajer agnikanya.*" Loosely translated, these couplets say, in the butchery of this society, full of tears, sweat and blood, a firebrand daughter of this naked society is now coming to take revenge.
9. This Rupanjali Opera production has two rhymed couplets as its tagline: "*Jaater cheye manush boro/Ei kothata beray geye/Ekla pathey egiye chole/Abbajaner Hindu meye.*" Loosely translated it reads, singing alone in the streets, the Hindu daughter of a Muslim father speaks of humanity, which transcends class and caste.
10. For instance, a new production entitled *Era Shotru* (These are the enemies) produced by Muktamanjari Opera and performed from August 2009 introduces a lady called King Fong Hung, who is claimed to be a famous actress and singer from China. Another social production *Ei Ghar Ei Sangsar* (This house, this family) produced by Debanjali Opera advertises an additional item called 'Dance Bangla Dance' and states, "*Ek jhak sundarider niye jatra seshe 30 minute byapi esho shobai dance kori*" (at the end of the *jatra* let all of us come and dance together for thirty minutes along with a whole bunch of beautiful women). Some *jatra* productions in Bangladesh that can be watched online on YouTube show how some of these dance numbers verge on crudity, where live performances of women strip teasing like girls in dance bars have the dubious distinction of demoting the original folk form to base or gross sleaze.
11. For instance, in an article published in *Hindustan Times* on 3 January 2008 entitled 'Festival Boost for *Jatra*, Funds for Needy Artistes' the correspondent reports that the West Bengal government has allotted ₹300,000 to organize that year's the *Jatra* Festival lasting for three weeks. According to the director of the Information and Culture Department, Anup Motilal, the folk theatre industry has started seeing better days after going through a very difficult decade. He states:

> Though there was always a rural audience for *jatras*, the folk theatre industry was getting an elite tag among the urban populace. But from last year, there has been a noticeable change in the character of the *jatra* viewers. Even urban people are gathering in large numbers to see *jatras*.

References

Barthes, Roland. 1977. 'The Rhetoric of the Image', in *Image, Music, Text*, pp. 32–51. Edited and translated by Stephen Heath. New York: Hill & Wang.
Ferguson, Mary Anne. 1973. *Images of Women in Literature*. Boston, MA: Houghton Mifflin.

11

The Reinterpretation of Historical Trauma

Three Films about Partition

M. K. Raghavendra

Cinema and Historical Trauma

The partition of India in 1947 was the most cataclysmic event in the modern history of South Asia. It is estimated that half a million people lost their lives in the ensuing riots and nearly fifteen million were forced to abandon their homes and become refugees. The aftermath of the partition of India perhaps occupies the same position in modern Indian history that the Holocaust occupies in the modern history of the West: a traumatic moment that must be relived constantly in order that the lessons learnt from it are not forgotten. The affirmative responses to the television mini series *Holocaust* (1978) stressed the positive effect of the intense emotional responses generated by the text and argue that *Holocaust* was instrumental in generating debates about the Nazi past (Landy 1997: 229–30) and the same viewpoint is perhaps held with regard to Govind Nihalani's television miniseries *Tamas* (1986) which deals with partition.

It has been suggested that the value of works like *Holocaust* lies in the paradigm of mourning, with its emphasis on the importance of replaying the past, of confronting loss and acknowledging guilt and responsibility. All this is rooted in a traditional notion of history associated with the elegiac tradition, enacting the mourning process and hence reaffirming beliefs about providence (Landy 1997: 230). While there is evidently emotional strength to be drawn from mourning, implied in its valorization is also an uncritical and ahistorical attachment to experience (Landy 1997: 230). It has been observed about films on the Holocaust in general (and this is as true of most Indian films about the partition) that the emphasis on mourning betokens a fascination with death as 'kitsch' (Friedlander 1982: 26–30); the mourning paradigm also leads to oversimplification, a denial of the dynamic nature of the past and the role the past plays in the present. With the passage of time, for instance, the Holocaust has come to seem the central event of World War II, with Hollywood (Doherty 1994: 51) becoming the instrument facilitating its recovery. This suggests that the past serves other purposes and is not merely being mourned. To illustrate the political uses to which the Holocaust is put today, after *Schindler's List* (1993) swept the Academy Awards, the editorials and commentaries made implicit and explicit connections between the film and concerns about the state of Israel, about conflicts between Israelis and Arabs, and about anti-Semitic statements by members of the African American community (Landy 1997: 256). Partition may therefore also have a covert political significance in Indian cinema that goes beyond grief at occurrences of the past.

Partition occupies the same position in the Indian consciousness that the Holocaust does in the consciousness of the West (Nandy 2001: 128–29) but mainstream Indian cinema has not given it the position that Hollywood has accorded the Holocaust. Still, Indian mainstream cinema has a singular relationship with history and I need to examine it before I actually discuss the films about partition.

Indian History and Mainstream Cinema

As demonstrated elsewhere (Raghavendra 2008: 31–41) Indian mainstream cinema does not acknowledge universal time. Not only is cross-cutting not in evidence, chronology and duration not strictly denoted but narratives also find it difficult to locate the action within the continuum of history. Only a handful of historical epochs provide it with subjects—chiefly the Mughal emperors Akbar, Jahangir and Shah Jahan but even these films are family dramas in costume and not historical inquiries. History creates few myths of its own and one is hard-pressed to find a film that uses even the Indian independence for its narrative thrust, despite the efforts of the state to build a durable mythology out of the freedom struggle.

Some cinema from the 1990s onwards—*1942: A Love Story* (1994) to *Lagaan* (2001)—appear to be departures but the films only use history as justification for patriotism; they do not pretend to 'interpret' history afresh even if for the contingencies of the present. This observation may also be made about *Gadar: Ek Prem Katha* (2001), an anti-Pakistani film with the Indian partition as backdrop. Other attributes deriving from this cinema's indifference to universal time is the closure through the family reunion (or the fruitful conclusion of a romance) and the impossibility of unknowns within the narrative, that is, no fate remaining unresolved. No character may walk away into the sunset secure in the knowledge of history continuing after the story.

A useful study of audience reactions to mainstream cinema testing several independent hypotheses on its social role concluded that it was largely an instrument of 'cultural continuity'. The films apparently stabilize the social system by representing new needs and mythologizing 'tradition'. Since new social needs are historically created, an 'instrument of cultural continuity' it can be argued, bridges the gap between traditional belief and the actual dispensation of history. What mainstream film narrative apparently does is problematize the experiences of history in a language acceptable to tradition and then provide 'traditional' solutions. The expectations of the immediate present are the key to what is problematized rather that a past occurrence (Raghavendra 2008: 237–38). The events regarded as violently cataclysmic do not produce a discernible impact upon mainstream cinema but the expectations deriving from them nonetheless do. The assassinations of Mahatma Gandhi (1948), Indira Gandhi (1984) and Rajiv Gandhi (1991) are not mentioned but the death of the Father of the Nation is followed by a proliferation of orphans in films like *Anokhi Ada* (1948). The anti-Sikh riots after Mrs Gandhi's death and the consequent alienation of the Sikh community are not acknowledged but Subhash Ghai's *Karma* (1985) introduces a gallant young Sikh who sacrifices his life for the nation at a critical moment. It can be argued that, generally speaking, mainstream cinema has been an instrument of reassurance, not simply representing or interpreting history but providing recompense—by sometimes anticipating it. This chapter examines three films with only two of them being from the mainstream. The first anticipates the partition of India and while the second responds to it as a contemporary event. The third film belongs to non-mainstream cinema and is the representative of a category of films about the partition that have received acclaim within India.

Anticipating Partition: *Anmol Ghadi* (1946)

After 1943, the Muslim question became gradually more important in India and expectations of partitioning India became unavoidable although until 1946 the Muslim League's definition of 'partition' was flexible and might have included autonomy within an Indian confederation. This led to Indian cinema explicitly affirming the Muslim ruler's place in India's tradition. The most important films to perform the function are *Tansen* (1943), *Humayun* (1945) and *Shahjehan* (1946). The above films are all nominally 'historical' but they are preoccupied with affirming the place of the Muslim in India rather than interpreting history.

Mehboob Khan's *Anmol Ghadi* anticipates the partition in a more covert and allegorical way. The film is about the childhood attachment between two children—the poor Chander and the affluent Latha. Latha presents Chander with a watch just before her family migrates to Bombay and Chander is left alone. Chander grows up and, thanks to his toiling mother, he acquires an education but continues to long for Latha until he also migrates to Bombay. A rich friend named Prakash induces him to move to that city, where he finds employment managing Prakash's business in musical instruments. A client named Basanti falls in love with Chander and Basanti is Latha's friend. Latha now writes bestselling novels under the pseudonym of Renu Devi and has herself still not gotten over Chander. Chander's mother is old and fragile and she falls ill but Chander is too preoccupied with finding Latha to attend to his mother. Prakash draws Chander's attention to the old woman's condition but Chander is still too taken up with finding his lost love. Chander and Latha finally meet but, by this time, Latha is engaged to marry Prakash. Chander is in despair and returns to his mother but the old woman is now gravely ill. Latha wants to follow him but other loyalties assert themselves and she resigns herself to her destiny. Chander takes his mother away from Bombay, and mother and son return to their village where Chander's mother goes to 'join her husband in heaven.' Before she 'goes away' Chander's mother reminds him of her earlier counsel—that the rich and the poor will always be removed from one another. Chander returns briefly to Bombay to attend Prakash's wedding and he presents Latha with the one gift he can afford—the watch she gave him as a child.

Anmol Ghadi is perhaps without parallel in Indian popular cinema in as much as it shows the male protagonist more attentive to the heroine than he is to his sacrificing mother. Chander's mother labours for her son's education but her toiling is shown in an unusual way—she mills wheat into flour so that he may not go hungry. There is also some dialogue in which the mother emphasizes the value of wheat, the way in which it becomes *atta* (flour) and then roti, and is therefore crucial to a person's sustenance. 'Bread-provider' is often a way in which the land is depicted to make it appear sacred. The motif of the mother-as-bread-provider can hence be read in a useful way and this is how *Anmol Ghadi* is equating the relationship between Chander and his mother as the one between a person and his land. The question to be posed is why Chander loses his mother and the answer is that it is because he follows 'rich people' whose loyalties are to their own class.

The political factor of pertinence here is that the Muslim community in India had a very small middle class and apart from medical doctors, lawyers or clergy, everyone of ability apparently gravitated to high posts in the government or the army (Spear 1970: 223). This meant there was a large class gap between the leaders of the Muslim League and their followers. Jinnah was himself elegant and westernized (Spear 1970: 228) and far from the devout Muslim that the future leader of a theocratic Islamic state could be, while the bulk of his following was different.

Anmol Ghadi appeared in 1946 when the Muslim League pressed for a second nation and *Anmol Ghadi* apparently addresses 'poor people' who would do better being loyal to 'their land' than follow the 'rich,' who have only their own interests at heart. Interestingly, Chander's song when his mother departs does not invoke a corporeal mother but simply inquires about "true kinship." It may be asked why Chander is not made a Muslim in the film and one explanation is that the director (Mehboob Khan) and the story writer (Anwar Batalvi) were Muslims and that they represent the protagonists simply as 'people' and not as 'Muslims'. It should also be noted that only in the genre of the 'Muslim social' (for example, *Mere Mehboob* [1963]) is a Muslim merely a 'person' and a Hindu, a 'Hindu'.

It is also significant that the 'rich' in *Anmol Ghadi* are not presented as self-seeking but sympathetically, as good people with loyalties only natural to them. My interpretation accounts for many things but it still leaves questions unanswered, and one of them is why Prakash is shown to be more attentive to Chander's mother than Chander himself is. The only solution to the puzzle is perhaps that Prakash's behaviour helps to give emphasis to Chander's own conduct and suggests that there is no inherent hostility between the rich and the poor. The rich may not be bad people but it will still be suicidal for the poor to forsake the land and follow them.

Partition in the Time of Partition: *Lahore* (1949)

M. L. Anand's *Lahore* appeared shortly after the partition of India and given the likely time lag between the conceiving of a film and its completion, it may be taken to respond to historical trauma as though it were immediate.

The story of *Lahore*, which begins with a nostalgic voiceover, is told in flashback and images of the streets of Lahore in 'the old days' fill the screen. As the story unfolds one discovers that Chaman and Leela live in adjoining houses, that they are to be married and that Chaman has an older brother, a wastrel, who spends his days playing with the children of the street or in a local restaurant. Chaman's father dies early in the film after confessing in court to some illicit activity and Chaman leaves for Bombay to study and also to work and support his family. The first part of the film is set immediately before 1947 but there is no episode in this part that may be said to contain a foreboding of the partition or its violence. If a comparison is to be made with a non-mainstream rendering of the same events, Deepa Mehta's *Earth* (1999) has a whole first part setting the mood for the violent climax. One has full knowledge of the film's intentions and also comes to understand that it is examining the relationships between its characters only in the context of what history is about to do to them. One sits waiting through the film's early parts (taken up with evoking the period) although no noteworthy event is scheduled to happen until history actually intervenes. Since the narrative of the film has its focus upon the historical moment of partition all personal anecdotes in it are, ultimately, details that add up to nothing more substantial than the recreation of a mood. It is only the events of partition that make a 'narrative' out of the assortment of incidents in the lives of the characters of the film.

The first part of *Lahore*, in contrast, is almost crowded with personal events and anecdotes that are inherently of interest. So many important things (important to the narrative) happen that one tends to forget the times in which story is set and the violence of 1947, when it comes, comes unexpectedly and abruptly. After dutifully sending money to his mother in Lahore every month, and having his money orders stolen by his older brother, Chaman returns home for a holiday during which he resumes his romance with Leela. It is during this holiday that the family is confronted by the reality of partition, its violence coming without warning. None of the violence is actually seen in the film—one hears it briefly on the soundtrack and sees documentary footage pertaining to its aftermath and a voiceover says '*Charon tharaf andhera hi andhera tha!*' (There was darkness all around!) Very soon after this Chaman and his mother find their way to refugee camps in India leaving the older son behind. Leela's whereabouts are not ascertainable although she is known to be in Lahore. The second part of Anand's film is taken up with how Leela is retrieved from Pakistan after she is forced to become the 'wife' of a Muslim in Lahore. Chaman also helps repatriate a Muslim girl Salma, who is in a similar predicament in India, to Lahore. The hero's older brother in Lahore is now also a model of responsibility and the film ends happily with the family being reunited in India.

Lahore keeps the riots and the trauma of the partition resolutely off-screen with the two parts of the narrative being arranged as separate tableaux, as distinct narratives belonging to different epochs, but carried over from the first part to the second is Chaman's enduring love for Leela. Partition does not stand out as a distinct occurrence among the episodes but takes the shape of an 'interval' separating a 'before' from an 'after' and this is reminiscent of the dissolve or the freeze that demarcates the prologue from the rest of a narrative in mainstream films like *Deewar* (1975). The two parts of *Lahore* stand clearly apart but they are not self-contained. Whatever is left incomplete in the first part is duly completed in the second. *Earth* concludes with the heroine's disappearance but *Lahore* cannot obviously end with Leela remaining lost; film convention dictates the impossibility of 'unknowns' in the narrative as well as the need for an appropriate closure.

As is customary in Indian mainstream cinema *Lahore* compulsively closes its universe but the film must nevertheless contend with the moment of partition representing a fragment of the authentic not explainable in the terms specified by its own melodramatic narrative logic and artifice. *Lahore* therefore declines to deal with the moment at the level of episode but turns it into an unprecedented 'interval' lying outside the purview of the narrative and which can be likened to a deliberate tear in its fabric. If interpreted as an admission that such an incomprehensibly horrific experience lies outside the capability of its own expressive powers and understanding, this aspect of *Lahore* may be regarded as a singularity in cinema. "A murderer's bloody fingerprint on a page says more than the words printed on it," proposes Walter Benjamin (1983: 94)[1] and the 'gash' or 'tear' in the narrative of *Lahore* is perhaps like a bloody fingerprint left by partition on Indian cinema.

Partition in Later Day Cinema: *Pinjar* (2003)

A characteristic of mainstream cinema is that it gives no indication that its myths are drawn from history. As Roland Barthes (1973: 143) phrases it, myth is a kind of language and a set of conventions by which the exigencies of a historical moment are sought to be given eternal justification. Due to its curious relationship with universal time and history, mainstream cinema does just the opposite. It responds to historical situations through familiar or timeless mythology. *Anmol Ghadi*, for instance, responds to the impending threat of partition by allegorizing it as a poor man forsaking his mother to follow a rich young woman. If *Lahore* appears different, history in the film makes a brutal intrusion into a still timeless tale. In contrast to these films Chandraprakash Dwivedi's *Pinjar* is actually about the partition of India and therefore needs closer examination. I would like to argue that it is not a mainstream film and belongs to a category that arose out of an entirely different, state-driven impetus.

While there the categories of Hindi language cinema outside the mainstream that go back much earlier—Bimal Roy and V. Shantaram's films, K. A. Abbas' *Dharti Ke Lal* (1946) are apparent examples—there is a hypothesis that the development of India's "art" and "middle" cinemas was largely facilitated by state interventionism and Mrs Gandhi's radical initiatives around 1969–70 and this eventually led to the segmentation of film audiences.[2] The Film Finance Corporation (FFC), which had functioned like any government institution, entered into competition with the mainstream industry. FFC policy was designed to promote a 'national cinema' through an emphasis on authenticity. Among the successful films financed and promoted by FFC were Basu Chatterjee's *Sara Akash* (1969) and Mrinal Sen's *Bhuvan Shome* (1969). While the movement lost steam around 1977 when Mrs Gandhi was removed from power, it can be argued that the virtues of non-mainstream cinema were still promoted in the state-owned television channel Doordarshan until well into the 1980s. Serials like *Hum Log* (1984), *Nukkad* (1986) and *Tamas* may be said, in a sense, to have subscribed to the aesthetic promoted by FFC policy. While the state no longer intervenes in the film industry, the idea of a national cinema has not been extinguished. The 'Indian Panorama' at the International Film Festival of India still showcases non-mainstream films and selection here guarantees telecasting on the state-owned Doordarshan as well as exposure to the rest of the world. Chandraprakash Dwivedi acquired prominence through his serial *Chanakya* (1990) on

Doordarshan and *Pinjar* may be regarded as brining the same perspective to the partition as the television serial by Govind Nihalani, *Tamas*, which is—and perhaps will remain—the definitive exploration of the subject in the medium of television.

Pinjar was nearly as expensive a film as the mainstream *Gadar: Ek Prem Katha* but the net domestic collections of latter film were more than sixteen times those of *Pinjar* (IBOS Network),[3] providing evidence that *Pinjar* targets a minority audience in the manner of art or middle cinema. The film begins with a brief prologue, a Sikh religious procession being attacked by an armed Muslim mob and the ensuing carnage, with a voiceover informing the audience of the times. It then shifts to the household of Mohanlal, his wife, two daughters Puro and Lajjo, and a son Trilok. The family is in Amritsar but they make for their estate in the west where the plan is to establish ties with Shyamlal's family by solemnizing marital ties between Puro and Shyamlal's son Ramchand. Ties are soon contracted between Puro and Ramchand and also between Ramchand's sister Rajjo and Trilok but, as fortune will have it, Puro is abducted by a Muslim named Rashid due to an old animosity. Although Puro escapes, her family will not have her back. She marries Rashid and is given the name Hamida after being forced into Islam. Rashid regrets his act and does everything possible to atone. He moves away from his family and lives a peaceful life with Puro in a milieu swiftly becoming polarized. But Rashid is not safe because Trilok searches him out and sets fire to his crops. Riots soon commence and the Hindu families try to flee but Rajjo is also abducted. Hamida/Puro and Rashid nonetheless seek her out and have her returned to her family. The film concludes with the Hindus returning to India but Hamida/Puro choosing to remain with Rashid in Pakistan although Ramchand offers to marry her and take her back to India.

Pinjar begins with a Muslim attack upon a Sikh procession but it still tries to divide its sympathies evenly. Hamida/Puro, for instance, adopts the child of a dead beggar woman but, after she has made the child her own, local Hindus take the child away because the beggar was a Hindu. Trilok's destruction of Rashid's crops is also the act of a vengeful person. On the other hand, the way the film treats family relationships points to another discourse. While the two Hindu families are always overflowing with cheerful women and children, Rashid's family is singularly without a feminine presence or the conspicuous presence of a child. Rashid has no mother and the only woman is a distant aunt who becomes friendly with Puro. More importantly, Puro becomes pregnant by Rashid but the child is stillborn. When Ramchand, Trilok and Rajjo take leave of Puro at the Pakistani border outpost, one senses an overwhelming sterility confronting Puro and Rashid in their future life. While the others seem to be brought together happily, there does not seem to be anything Puro and Rashid may look forward to. Since they remain in Pakistan and the others return to India, there is apparently a covert signification here of Pakistan as an infertile space.

Another item of significance is the absence of the mother in Rashid's family while both the Hindu families have mothers. The mother is the site of virtue in mainstream cinema (Vasudevan 2008: 110) and there is the celebrated sequence in the mainstream film *Deewar* in which the mother's association is with the virtuous son although it is her other son who is wealthy. This signifier apparently has deep cultural roots because it is sometimes employed in art cinema as well and in M. S. Sathyu's *Garam Hawa* (1973) about the travails of an Indian Muslim family during the time of partition, Salim Mirza's brothers leave for Pakistan one by one though Salim Mirza chooses to remain behind in India. His mother, importantly, also remains with him. In the context of *Pinjar*, one could say that the absence of the mother in Rashid's family can be interpreted as Pakistan being the less virtuous space.

Conclusion

Partition does not carry the same meaning for Pakistan that it does for India. There has apparently been only one film about partition coming from Pakistan[4] called *Kartar Singh* (1959). The film is about a Sikh miscreant at the time of partition who has a change of heart but is killed tragically when he is escorting a Muslim victim of violence across the border. According to a Pakistani critic, the film helps to reveal that Hindus and Muslims could have attained freedom without tearing each other apart if the political leadership of the three sides—the British, the Congress and the Muslim League—had had a better perception of the basic reality as it existed for most people in the subcontinent (Gazdar 1997: 81). What this suggests is that partition was inevitable for Pakistan but the bloodshed might have been avoided.

While for Pakistan, partition violence signifies the birth pangs of a newly emerging nation, for India, partition has tended to mean 'man's inhumanity to man' and this is the refrain not only of *Pinjar* but of *Tamas* and Pamela Rooks' *Train to Pakistan* (1998) as well. Deepa Mehta's *Earth* is different because it is based on a Pakistani novel by Bapsi Sidhwa and deals with partition violence being used to settle scores. It is significant that the vision of 'man's inhumanity to man' has largely ignored violence in Bengal which was nearly as great as the violence in Punjab though it was more sporadic (Guhathakurta 2003). One reason for the Bengal experience being sidelined is perhaps that its meaning is more complex—there was a clearer association between religion and class, and land went to the poor Muslims in the east (Shedde 2006)[4] when the Hindu landowners were dispossessed. Radical historians in India have attempted to look at partition through private memories and through personal narratives.[5] Both the received Indian and Pakistani historical interpretations attempt to give meaning to the events of 1947 by moulding them into a key moment in the realization of the destiny of the respective nation states. Oral histories and memoirs produced by those who lived through 1947 articulate a starkly different and competing vision of the period. It has been noted that survivors of the partition of India rarely separate the politics and violence of 1947 and for survivors "partition 'is' the violence" (Pandey 2001: 189).

While all this is undoubtedly true, the experience of *Pinjar* shows how an emphasis on the brutality and the violence can be used to privilege the Indian nation over the Pakistani one. India came out in 1947 as a secular nation, which means that—at least in theory—India is on the side of religious tolerance. Pakistan, on the other hand, is a theocratic state. Since 'India' is an ancient term and 'Pakistan' is a recent one, it is also difficult for Pakistan to dispute the notion that it was 'carved out of India' though both nation states came into existence together. It is perhaps these advantages that the Indian state covertly exploits when it promotes texts mourning the violence of partition through awards and acclaim. As long as this advantage remains, there will continue to be films made and novels written about the partition as another instance of 'man's inhumanity to man.'

Notes

1. In writing about the incorporation of real objects into a painting by the proponents of Dadaism, Benjamin (1983) has this to say: "The smallest authentic fragment of everyday life says more than a painting. Just as a murderer's bloody fingerprint on a page says more than the words printed on it."

2. See Prasad (1998: 115–23) for a useful summary.
   In terms of costs, *Pinjar* cost ₹130 million (Verma 2003), while *Gadar: Ek Prem Katha* had a budget of ₹180 million (Agarwal 2001). http://www.domain-b.com/companies/companies_z/Zee/2001630_zee_gadar.html Accessed 17th October 2012.
3. See Kapoor (2006), which reports on a talk by film scholar Ira Bhaskar.
4. Shedde talks to film scholar Moinak Biswas who says,

   But in East Pakistan, many of the Hindus were landowners. And according to scholars like Partha Chatterjee, with partition, there was expropriation of land by the tillers, leading to an agrarian revolution. The Bangladeshi poet Al Mahmood even says, 'Partition was a good thing.' It is mainly the Hindus who were traumatized and so don't want to talk about it. But for a generation of poor Muslim tillers, it was an escape from a life spent behind the plough.

5. See for instance Pandey (2001).

References

Agarwal, Alok. 2001. 'Will 'Gadar—Ek Prem Katha' create magic for Z' domain-b.com. Posted 30 June 2001. Available at: http://www.domain-b.com/companies/companies_z/Zee/2001630_zee_gadar.html (Last date of access: 17 October 2012).
Barthes, Roland. 1973. 'Myth Today', in *Mythologies*. London: Paladin.
Benjamin, Walter. 1983. 'The Author as Producer', in *Understanding Brecht*. Translated by Anna Bostock, p. 94. London: Verso.
Doherty, Thomas. 1994. 'The Americanization of the Holocaust', *Cineaste*, 20 (3): 51.
Friedlander, Saul. 1982. *Reflections of Nazism: An Essay on Kitsch and Death*. New York: Harper and Row.
Gazdar, Mushtaq. 1997. *Pakistani Cinema 1947–1997*. Karachi, Pakistan: Oxford University Press.
Guhathakurta, Meghna. 2003. 'Families, Displacement', in Ghislaine Glasson Deschaumes and Rada Ivekovic (eds), *Divided Countries, Separated Cities: The Modern Legacy of Partition*, pp. 96–105. New Delhi: Oxford University Press.
Kapoor, Rahul. 2006. 'Filmmakers Refused to Portray Partition.' Available online at http://www.realbollywood.com/news/2006/11/filmmakers-refused-to-portray-partition.html. (Last date of access: 2 February 2009).
Landy, Marcia. 1997. *Cinematic Uses of the Past*. Minneapolis, MN: University of Minneapolis Press.
Nandy, Ashis. 2001. *An Ambiguous Journey to the City*. New Delhi: Oxford University Press.
Pandey, Gyanendra. 2001. *Remembering Partition: Violence, Nationalism and History in India*. Cambridge, UK: Cambridge University Press.
Prasad, M. Madhava. 1998. *Ideology of the Hindi Film*. New Delhi: Oxford University Press.
Raghavendra, M. K. 2008. *Seduced by the Familiar: Narration and Meaning in Indian Popular Cinema*. New Delhi: Oxford University Press.
Shedde, Meenakshi. 2006. 'In East Pakistan, Partition Was Seen as a Good Thing', *DNA*, 7 July. Available at: http://www.dnaindia.com/mobile/report.php?n=1040148&p=0 (Last date of access 17 October 2012).

Spear, Percival. 1970. *A History of India*, Vol. 2. Harmondsworth, UK: Penguin.
Vasudevan, Ravi. 2008. 'Shifting Codes, Dissolving Identities: The Hindi Popular Film of the 1950s as Popular Culture', in Ravi Vasudevan (ed.), *Making Meaning in Indian Cinema*, p. 110. New Delhi: Oxford University Press.
Verma, Sukanya. 2003. 'Neither the Indian nor the Pakistani government will gain from Pinjar.' Available online at http://us.rediff.com/cms/print.jsp?docpath=//movies/2003/oct/22chandra.htm. (Last date of access: 12 February 2009).

Films and Television Series

1942: A Love Story. 1994.
Anmol Ghadi. 1946. Mehboob Khan.
Anokhi Ada. 1948.
Bhuvan Shome. 1969. Directed by Sen, Mrinal.
Chanakya. 1990. Directed by Chandraprakash Dwivedi.
Deewar. 1975.
Dharti Ke Lal. 1946. Abbas, K. A.
Earth. 1999. Directed by Deepa Mehta.
Gadar: Ek Prem Katha. 2001.
Garam Hawa. 1973. Directed by M. S. Sathyu.
Holocaust. 1978.
Hum Log. 1984.
Humayun. 1945.
Karma. 1985. Directed by Subhash Ghai.
Kartar Singh. 1959.
Lagaan. 2001.
Lahore. 1949.
Mere Mehboob. 1963.
Nukkad. 1986.
Pinjar. 2003. Directed by Chandraprakash Dwivedi.
Sara Akash. 1969. Directed by Chatterjee, Basu.
Schindler's List. 1993.
Shahjehan. 1946.
Tamas. 1986. Directed by Govind Nihalani.
Tansen. 1943.
Train to Pakistan. 1998. Pamela Rooks.

12
Identity and Politics in the Songs of Contemporary African American Women

Ellerine Diengdoh

The domain of folklore studies in general and African American studies in particular can be enriched by better examination of black female contributions in the field of music. But this is an area that has been sadly neglected, because scholars have been lax in mining black women's lyrics for the cultural and gendered values embedded in them. For example, before Angela Y. Davis' *Blues Legacies and Black Feminism* (1998), songs written and performed by black women were seldom contemplated in a theoretical context. The reason behind this is the belief that any analysis of popular songs lacked scholarly objectivity because songs are emotional, ephemeral, physical and accessible. In recent years however new disciplines like ethnomusicology and jazz studies have witnessed the proliferation of research dedicated to black music analysis, yet only a few published materials in these fields have focused on the songs or lyrics of African American women. The chapter is thus an attempt at interpreting the lyrics of black women and seeks to explore themes concerning self-actualization and the vindication of black womanhood. The chapter will also examine selected prominent themes in the lyrics of songs composed by Billie Holiday, Nina Simone and Tracy Chapman and also look at how these women have used music as a vehicle for social activism and cultural autobiography.

Holiday, Simone and Chapman are musical icons because of their unique vocal expressions, which come from a continuum of blackness and the blues. Black women have been central in maintaining, transforming and recreating the blues tradition of African American Culture (Davis 1998; Harrison 1990; Russell 1982). Angela Y. Davis, for example, while examining the lyrics of Ma Rainey, Bessie Smith and Billie Holiday, theorizes that the blues have "helped to construct an aesthetic community" that validates "women's capacities in domains assumed to be the prerogatives of males, such as sexuality and travel" (Davis 1998: 120). Michele Russell (1982) and Sandra Lieb (1981) argue similarly that black female blues developed at the turn of the twentieth century as a distinguishable idiom precisely because it enabled black women to own their 'past, present and future' by confiscating and reconstructing their identities (Russell 1982: 130). The blues have thus been used by black American women to achieve actual and symbolic liberation within the constraints of a white and male-dominated society.

African American women have had to deal with oppression encompassing "three interdependent dimensions" (Collins 1998: 4). According to Patricia Hill Collins, in her book *Black Feminist Thought* (Collins 1998: 4), the first is "the exploitation of Black women's labour essential to U.S. capitalism—the 'iron pots and kettles' symbolizing Black women's long-standing ghettoization in service occupations—represents the economic dimension of oppression." Second, the political dimension of oppression denied African American women their rights and privileges usually offered to white citizens. Black women were forbidden to vote, excluded from public office and were withheld equitable treatment in the criminal justice system. Finally, in the educational sphere, black women "were relegated to underfunded, segregated Southern schools [which ensured] that quality education for black women remained the exception rather than the rule" (Collins 1998: 4).

As a historically oppressed group, African American women have produced social thought intended to resist oppression. This thought takes on diverse forms from poetry to music to searing essays, each distinctly different, yet offering various ways to cope with or oppose prevailing social and economic injustices.

For African American women, music has provided a creative outlet, which facilitates their survival under oppression. As Angela Y. Davis (1998: 201) suggests, "Black people were able to create with their music an aesthetic community of resistance, which in turn encouraged and nurtured a political community of active struggle for freedom." Spirituals, blues, jazz and rhythm and blues are part of a "continuum of struggle which is at once aesthetic and political" (Davis 1998: 201).

The lyrical texts thus provide a fertile ground for the exploration of the lives of African American women and their attempt at self-definition as a means of coping with living on the social periphery.

Born on 7 April 1915 as Eleanora Fagan, Billie Holiday was gifted with a particular timbre and pathos-filled voice that inspired a generation. Her emotional connection with her songs came from a life of struggle against racism and sexism. Billie Holiday's lyrics are more than mere entertainment, and a cursory study would reveal them as a means for surviving, coping and even perhaps, social uplift.

Holiday was born in abject poverty and was raised by a single mother. She dropped out of school in the fifth grade and found a job running errands in a brothel. This was where she was exposed to blues and jazz for the first time, and she was particularly fascinated with Louis Armstrong and Bessie Smith. Their music helped her escape the poverty and hardship of her early years by inspiring her to dream. She moved to New York in 1928 and began working in small clubs as a singer.

Her popularity spread to black and white audiences and her soulful sound played a vital role in the influence of jazz on beat poetry, and writers such as Hettie Jones, Amiri Baraka, Jack Kerouac and Frank O'Hara all acknowledge the profound influence her music has had on their work.

Most biographies on Billie Holiday portray her as a sad creature, reminiscent of Griffith's tragic mulatto,[1] yet close to half her songs indicate positive emotions. She was also a woman of resilience, courage and hope and the songs that she wrote express a degree of optimism, assertiveness and self-empowerment. Holiday, as her lyrical narratives reveal, was a complex personality with insight, wit and a desire for a better life.

Racism was a serious problem for artists during this time and racism had a serious impact on Holiday's career. During her tours and radio broadcast with Artie Shaw's big band she was frequently forbidden to sit on stage with the rest of the band and some of her radio spots were cancelled. There was one instance when the band had a booking at the Lincoln Hotel in New York City, where Holiday was forced to use the freight elevator so she would not come in contact with the white people staying and visiting the hotel. Her encounters with racism took a toll on her spirit, but instead of distancing herself from these issues, she opted to take a stand, so that people knew her intention in matters relating to race: "I'm as good as a lot of people of all kinds—I'm proud I'm a Negro" (Purnell 2002: 458). While there are no known lyrics written by Holiday that specifically address the issue of race and though she did not write the song *Strange Fruit*, by all accounts it became her song.

The song *Strange Fruit* first materialized as a poem entitled *Bitter Fruit* written by Abel Meeropol, a Jewish schoolteacher. Meeropol wrote the poem after he saw the photograph of a double lynching that took place in Median, Indiana. He soon put it to music and thought that Holiday was the only person who would be able to bring the song to life. The song became one of the first and most important civil rights pleas, Meeropol and Holiday using their song as a form of social protest:

> Southern trees bear strange fruit,
> Blood on the leaves and blood at the root,
> Black bodies swinging in the southern breeze,
> Strange fruit hanging from the poplar trees.
>
> Pastoral scene of the gallant south,
> The bulging eyes and the twisted mouth,
> Scent of magnolias, sweet and fresh,
> Then the sudden smell of burning flesh.
>
> Here is fruit for the crows to pluck,
> For the rain to gather, for the wind to suck,
> For the sun to rot, for the trees to drop,
> Here is a strange and bitter crop.

The lyrics had an overwhelming impact on Holiday, sometimes causing her physical illness during the performance of it. Holiday had this to say about the significance of the song: "It means when the crackers are killing the niggers. It means when they take a little nigger like you and snatch off his nuts and shove them down his goddam throat. That's what it means" (Angelou 1981, cited in Gourse 1997: 173).

At a time when political protest was not often articulated in musical form, the song portrays lynching in all its cruelty. The three succinct verses are all the more powerful because the language that is used is understated irony. The juxtaposition of a beautiful landscape with the scene of lynching, the smell of 'magnolias' with that of 'burning flesh,' the blossoms typically associated with the climate of southern United States have now manifested themselves in the form of a 'strange fruit' produced by racial oppression—this imagery conjures up the essence of racist reaction. Racism in America stands indicted and exposed by these lines, with no need at all for a more moralistic or confrontational message.

The song was more powerful than any other song in mainstream America at that time. It was the first time any artist had had the courage to use music to stand up against a terrifying social and political institution. It thus became the first African American protest song that set the direction for future protest songs and begins the line into which Nina Simone and Tracy Chapman follow.

Eunice Kathleen Waymon was born in Tryon, North Carolina on 21 February 1933 and Eunice Waymon never intended to become Nina Simone, protest singer and social activist. She and her mother had in fact envisioned that she would become the first black concert pianist. As a child, Simone revealed an early inclination for music; she recalls an incident in her early life when her mother was "so surprised she almost died on the spot" (Simone and Cleary 1991: 15) as she witnessed her two-and-a-half-year-old daughter sitting at the piano playing her favourite hymn *God Be With You Till We Meet Again* in the key of F (Simone and Cleary 1991: 15).

Young Simone's exceptional piano playing earned her praise throughout the black community and with the white locals as well, including her mother's employer Miss Miller, who offered to pay Simone's piano tuition fee for a year. But Simone's rude racial awakening came early on when she was turned down by Philadelphia's prestigious Institute of Music and wondered if race was responsible for her failure to gain acceptance there. Gradually she began to see her life within the context of the Jim Crow South and the harsh reality of being black in America.

As Simone's political consciousness grew, she abandoned her usual formal performance attire for an exquisitely braided coif and an afro coupled with head wraps and caftans. There was a marked change in her music as well; she developed from singing jazz standards and love and folk ballads to protest music. Simone became one of the most outspoken and prominent musicians throughout the civil rights movement. Her music spoke to the hundreds of thousands of African American men and women fighting for their rights during the 1960s as she sang out against racial oppression, and gave voice to American apartheid.

Her most politically overt song *Mississippi Goddam* was written in response to the assassination of Medgar Evers and the church bombing that resulted in the deaths of four little black children in Birmingham. Simone explains how she took her first conscious step towards becoming a political artist (Neal 1999: 48):

> It was my first civil rights song, and it erupted out of me quicker than I could write it down. I knew then that I would dedicate myself to the struggle for

black justice, freedom and equality under the law for as long as it took, until all our battles were won.

Impelled by extreme rage at the loss of innocent lives to Jim Crow racism, Simone penned the provocative and irreverently titled *Mississippi Goddam*. The song expresses the feelings shared by many black Americans, who in Fanny Lou Hamer's famous words were "sick and tired of being sick and tired".[2] (Mills 1993: 108). Simone echoes this sentiment in the chorus,

> Alabama's gotten me so upset
> Tennessee made me lose my rest
> And everybody knows about Mississippi Goddam.

While 1964's *Mississippi Goddam* is a bold and direct statement against the repression of black people's freedom, *Four Women* illustrates the existing outcome of slavery, especially on black women. Simone uses a narrative approach where she uses black women to tell their stories in four distinct stanzas, exhibiting her familiarity with the African oral tradition where storytelling is an essential part of culture. In general, *Four Women* explores recurring themes that have been central to black women's narratives, including the pursuit for subjectivity and emancipation from both racist and sexist domination.

In this song, Simone sings of four black women whose experiences illustrate controlling images and well-worn stereotypes concerning black women. The predominant stereotypes categorize black women as being one or more of the following: mammies,[3] matriarchs,[4] coons,[5] toms,[6] tragic mulattoes, exotics and angry bitches with the politics of hair, colour and class as defining factors. In her autobiography Simone says this about the song (Simone and Cleary 1991: 117):

> The women in the song are black, but their skin tones range from light to dark and their ideas of beauty and their own importance are deeply influenced by that. All the song did was tell what entered the minds of most black women in America when they thought about themselves; their complexions, their hair—straight, kinky, natural which?—and what other women thought of them.

The writer Joel Siegel describes *Four Women* as "brief, incisive portraits reflecting the experiences and generational perspectives of a variegated quartet of black women" (Hampton and Nathan 2004: 27). The stories unfold as follows:

> My skin is black, my arms are long
> My hair is woolly, my back is strong
> Strong enough to take the pain, inflicted again and again
> What do they call me? My name is Aunt Sarah.
>
> My skin is yellow, my hair is long
> Between two worlds I do belong
> But my father was rich and white
> He forced my mother late one night
> And what do they call me?
> My name is Saffronia.
>
> My skin is tan, my hair fine
> My hips invite you, my mouth like wine
> Whose little girl am I? Anyone who has money to buy
> What do they call me? My name is Sweet Thing.
>
> My skin is brown, my manner is tough
> I'll kill the first mother I see, my life has been rough
> I'm awfully bitter these days, because my parents were slaves
> What do they call me? My name is Peaches.

Each woman's narrative features the horrors of slavery, torture as seen in Aunt Sarah's whippings on the back, rape which eventually produced an isolated Saffronia, the commoditization of the black female body and the myth of black female licentiousness exemplified by Sweet Thing's prostitution and finally anger, which is apparent in Peaches' vengeance and righteous fury. While the song is invariably a song of protest and an act of defiance against America's historical portrayal of black women, it is eventually an appeal to black women to reclaim themselves on their own terms and carry the cultural memory of slavery. Only then can the shackles of mental slavery be broken and black women can move beyond these particularly negative stereotypes.

While Simone remained steadfast in her dedication to the struggle for black liberation, Tracy Chapman, folk protest singer and activist responds by singing 'Talkin' 'bout a Revolution'.

> Don't you know
> They're talkin' 'bout a revolution

> It sounds like a whisper....
> Poor people gonna rise up
> And take what's theirs.

Chapman is thus carrying on the tradition charted by Simone, an artist who addresses the plight of the poor and downtrodden.

Tracy Chapman was brought up in a harsh, poverty-stricken black neighbourhood in Cleveland, Ohio. Being a bright student, she was awarded a scholarship to Wooster School, Danbury, Connecticut through President Kennedy's ABC fund for the disadvantaged. In 1982 she graduated and went on to attend Tufts University in Boston where she majored in anthropology. Chapman's personal experience of poverty, racial discrimination and humiliation coupled with insights gained from a university education moulded her into a socially conscious musician.

Chapman appeared in the 1980s and recreated the image of an artist isolated from the sexual imagery associated with music video entertainers popular in that era. Normally dressed in turtlenecks, sweaters and blue jeans with her trademark dreadlocks, she carries on the tradition charted by Nina Simone, to be an artist and a composer who addresses the plight of folk beyond the margins.

Chapman's self-titled debut album is a powerful social commentary, which draws attention to a country steeped in racial discrimination. As a dispassionate observer from the sidelines who bears witness to anomalies and atrocities that take place, she wishes to escape but is held back by "having mountains o' nothing at birth" ('Mountains o' Thing').

'Mountains o' Things' is a satire of the American Dream during the Reagan years, when rampant materialism and greed (as seen in the flourishing of big businesses) has created a growing chasm between the haves and the have-nots.

The narrator in the song is a daydreamer, who aspires to attain a life of ease that comes with being rich, but who eventually finds herself caught in a perpetual cycle of labour, serving to enrich the wealthy and established instead.

> The life I've always wanted
> I guess I'll never have
> I'll be working for somebody else
> Until I'm in my grave
> I'll be dreaming of a life of ease
> And mountains
> Oh mountains o' things

In most of her songs Chapman endeavours to bring to light the predicament of the invisible poor and the suffering of the minorities, but apart from these issues she also addresses the silence surrounding women's oppression, such as domestic violence. Rock scholar Ray Pratt (1994: 146) situates *Behind the Wall* (1988) as "the first song on any popular album ... that deals with violence against women."

> Last night I heard the screaming
> Loud voices behind the wall
> Another sleepless night for me
> It won't do no good to call
> The police
> Always come late
> If they come at all

Chapman liberates herself "from the silencing [that] occurs when Black women are restrained from confronting racism, sexism and elitism in public [discourse]" (Collins 1998: 50) Chapman speaks from a place that knows and sees, and in turn articulates on behalf of the increasingly disenfranchised and dispossessed Americans. Her observations are a documentation of the oppressive Reagan years and the growing consequences of capitalism.

While rallying out against the oppressive political machinery that threatened to engulf the poor and downtrodden, Tracy Chapman uses the motif of "flight" as an act of resistance. "Flight is a recurrent image in ... African American songs ... a symbolic opportunity for oppressed slaves to free themselves from the shackles of slavery" (Dunn and Jones 1994: 202).

From these circumstances came about the belief in 'Flying Africans', which has been thematically used throughout the black literary tradition. Virginia Hamilton (1993) further explains the motif and its pervasiveness in the black folk belief:

> There are numerous accounts of flying Africans and flying slaves in the Black folktale literature. Such accounts are often combined with tales of slaves disappearing. A plausible explanation might be the slaves running away from slavery.... Another explanation is the wish-fulfillment motif, a detailed fantasy tale of suffering, of magic power exerted against the so-called master, it was first told and retold by those who had only imaginations to set them free.

Two suggestions are offered by Hamilton to demystify the myth of the "Flying Africans", the first is that of mobility and action, the other imaginative but still resistive.

In the song *She's Got Her Ticket* (1988), a woman, perhaps Chapman in this case, is flying away from the urban ghetto, which stifles the development and potential of all young and talented black children. Angela Y. Davis (1998: 74) explains the significance of such a theme "for women especially, the ability to travel implied a measure of autonomy, an ability to shun passivity and acquiescence in the face of mistreatment and injustice and to exercise some control over the circumstances of their lives."

The song begins with the image of a woman who is determined to flee, but the woman's desired destination is left unknown:

> She's got her ticket
> I think she gonna use it
> I think she going to fly away
> No one should try and stop her
> Persuade her with their power
> She says that her mind is made
> Up

This flight to suburban community poses challenges for this young woman:

> Young girl ain't got no chances
> No roots to keep her strong
> She's shed all pretenses
> That someday she'll belong
> Some folks call her a runaway
> A failure in the race
> But she knows where her ticket takes her
> She will find her place in the sun

As evident in the above stanza, the 'flight' has broken the strong communal ties she once shared with her people and left a void. Having been uprooted from her community, she no longer has the support she needs and people are quick to condemn her, calling her "a failure in the race" as she goes against the prevailing norms of respectability. The song does not end in a bleak note; the woman 'knows' where her ticket will take her to 'find her place in the sun'.

Whether one takes the connotation of flight literally or symbolically, Chapman as a liberated, decolonized, radical black female has found her place in the sun. Her untiring commitment to social change does not end with her songs, for she continues to campaign against oppression and actively engages in activist and humanitarian causes.

As Chapman builds upon the legacy of Billie Holiday and Nina Simone, she in turn passes on a sustaining legacy of her own. Despite their commercial success, these artists have maintained a sense of personal and artistic integrity, addressing social concerns and bearing witness to the phenomenon of living and surviving as a black woman.

Notes

1. As seen in D. W. Griffith's film *The Birth of a Nation* (1915), the tragic mulatto is a woman of mixed-race marriage or sexual union. She invariably dies at the end of her story, as punishment for her 'sin' of being mixed race. (Henry 1999: 163).
2. For biographical material on Fannie Lou Hamer, see Lee (1999) and Mills (1993).
3. As seen in D.W. Griffith's film *The Birth of a Nation* (1915), mammy is an overweight black woman who takes care of the white master's children, without concern for her own. (Henry: 163).
4. As seen in D.W. Griffith's film *The Birth of a Nation* (1915), while mammy is considered to exemplify the maternal figure in white homes, matriarchs exemplify the maternal figure in black homes. (Henry: 163).
5. As seen in D.W. Griffith's film *The Birth of a Nation* (1915), the ineffectual and lazy coon stereotype is a foolish simpleton who would do anything to avoid work. (Henry: 163).
6. As seen in D.W. Griffith's film *The Birth of a Nation* (1915), female toms are presented as devoted servants totally absorbed in the lives of their masters and not caring for their own. (Henry: 163).

References

Clarke, Donald. 2002. *Billie Holiday: Wishing on the Moon*. New York: Da Capo Press.
Collins, Patricia Hill. 1998. *Fighting Words: Black Women and the Search for Justice*. Minneapolis, MN: University of Minnesota Press.
Davis, Angela Y. 1998. *Blues Legacies and Black Feminism*. New York, NY: Pantheon Books.
Dunn, Leslie C. and Nancy A. Johns (eds). 1994. *Embodied Voices: Representing Female Vocality in Western Culture*. New York: Cambridge University Press.
Gourse, Leslie. 1997. *The Billie Holiday Companion: Seven Decades of Commentary*. New York: Schirmer Books. Print.

Hamilton, Virginia. 1985. *The People Could Fly: American Black Folktales*. New York: Alfred Knopf.
———. 1993. *The People Could Fly: The Picture Book*. New York: Knopf.
Hampton, Sylvia and David Nathan. 2004. *Nina Simone: Break Down & Let It All Out*. London: Sanctuary.
Harrison, Daphne Dural. 1990. *Pearls: Blue Queens of 1920*. New Jersey: Rutgers.
Henry, Charles P. 1999. *Ralph Bunche: Model Negro or American Other*.
Hughes, Langston. 1974. *Selected Poems of Langston Hughes*. New York: Vintage.
Lee, Chana Kai. 1999. *For Freedom's Sake: The Life of Fannie Lou Hamer*. Athens, GA: University of Georgia Press.
Lieb, Sandra. 1981. *Mother of the Blues: A Study of Ma Rainey*. Amherst, MA: University of Massachusetts Press.
Mills, Kay. 1993. *This Little Light of Mine: The Life of Fannie Lou Hamer*. New York: Dutton.
Neal, Mark Anthony. 1999. *What the Music Said: Black Popular Music and Black Public Culture*. London: Routledge.
Pratt, Ray. 1999. *Rhythm and Resistance: Explorations in the Political Uses of Popular Music*. Washington DC: Smithsonian Institution Press.
Purnell, Kim L. 2002. 'Listening to Lady Day: An Exploration of the Creative (Re) Negotiation of Identity Revealed in the Life Narratives and Music Lyrics of Billie Holiday', *Communication Quarterly*, 50 (3/4 Summer/Winter): 444–66.
Russell, Michele. 1982. 'Slave Codes and Liner Notes', in Gloria T. Hull, Patricia Bell Scott and Barbara Smith (eds), *But Some of Us Are Brave*, pp. 129–40. Old Westbury, NY: The Feminist Press.
Simmon, Scott. 1993. *The Films of D. W. Griffith*. Cambridge, UK: University of Cambridge Press.
Simone, Nina and Stephen Cleary. 1991. *I Put a Spell on You: The Autobiography of Nina Simone*. New York: De Capo Press.
———. 2000. *Women and Popular Music: Sexuality, Identity, and Subjectivity*. London: Routledge.

Select Discography

Chapman, Tracy. 1988. *Tracy Chapman* (vocal performances). Electra/Wea.
———. 1989. *Crossroads* (vocal performances). Electra/Wea.
Holiday, Billie. 1958. *Lady in Satin* (vocal performances). Columbia.
———. 1959. *All or Nothing at All* (vocal performances). Verve.
———. 2000. 'Strange Fruit' (vocal performance). By Abel Meeropol. Recorded on *Billie Holiday*, Commodore.
Simone, Nina. 1964. *Folksy Nina* (vocal performances). Colpix.
———. 1964. 'Mississippi Goddam' (vocal performance). On *Nina Simone in Concert*. Philips.
———. 1966. 'Four Women' (vocal performance). On *Wild is the Wind*. Philips.
———. 1967. *Nina Sings the Blues*. RCA.

SECTION III

Societies, Literature and the Ethnic Life-World

13
Transcribing Orality
A Study of Ki Jingsneng Tymmen

Esther Syiem

At their creative best, *Ki Jingsneng Tymmen* (The teachings of elders) are a body of aphorisms that have been orally transmitted through the ages. They mark an important territory in Khasi thought for they capture the ambience of a culture with roots embedded deep in the oral practices of their ancestors, where the social and the metaphysical interpenetrate each other. The noted Khasi writer, Radhon Singh Berry, put them down in written form in a two-volume work first published in 1902, which will be continually referred to in this chapter. Although they are more than a century old, the two volumes—unedited—are still used as a literary text in schools and colleges for imparting Khasi culture to the present generation. Though repetitive to the modern reader, the very essence of the oral lies in just this. The paradox of *Ki Jingsneng Tymmen* lies in the fact that their interface with society is at the level of the oral. But for obvious reasons the discussion centres around the written version.

For purposes of the present study, this written rendition will be used as the primary, although not the exclusive, source. Within the scope of the discussion, the two volumes have been used as a means towards the larger end of understanding the structure of the Khasi belief and value system. One would, however, have to go beyond them and draw from the oral sources that have fed the very foundations of Khasi society.

One would look at *Ki Jingsneng Tymmen* as a vital extension of the social, an outgrowth of the oral that has defined the Khasi way of life. It serves as a coalescence of Khasi thought. Many of the dos and don'ts found in *Ki Jingsneng Tymmen* are still functional in modern everyday life, the anchor that, ironically, seems to assuage but not alleviate much of the confusion in an increasingly complex society.

Ki Jingsneng Tymmen reflect the vital chords of a society that has always believed in the existence of one supreme deity, *U Blei Nongbuh Nongthaw*, God the Creator and God the Maker, and the life concurrent with such a belief; that the Khasi has come to this world only to *kamai ïa ka hok* or to work for righteousness. The formulation of this body of sayings or proverbs and chants has been carefully shaped by a culture that has always preferred to explain its existence in mythic rather than in historical terms.[1] This is intimately connected with the elevation and installation of the oral to a position of centrality that was consequent upon the mythical loss of the written script.[2] The oral or the spoken word, *ka ktien*, rationalizes the ultimate meaning of existence in a way that is geared towards the preservation of a mystical sense of life where the *rngiew* or the aura that radiates from an individual and even the entire community must be kept alive (Giri 1998). The individual or community may be measured in terms of the *rngiew* that gives it distinctiveness.

The *rngiew* is a numinous extension of personality, a lighted area that is said to visibly encircle an individual, spelling out personality in several complex layers. Nourished by an inherent genius, which may be defined as racial wisdom, it is an unselfconscious recognition of one's multiple strengths. This in itself produces positive waves that communicate themselves to others in multifarious and intangible ways. The *rngiew* speaks of an inner force that is difficult to conceal. In maturity it is almost tangible and is a natural protection against all negative influences. Even a child may possess a strong *rngiew* or be *eh rngiew* and, therefore, be able to withstand the suppressive forces that may threaten it. Giving a child a name is the first step towards empowering its *rngiew*.

To be *jem rngiew* is to be opposite of *eh rngiew*; that is, to be abjectly prone to suppression or to be unable to contend with conflicting pressures of many kinds. In life one must make a conscious effort towards the development of a strong *rngiew*. The *rngiew* is an integral part of personality in a way that is difficult to peel off. It is an organic accumulation of the experiences that determine the inner core and outer layer that constitutes personality. Figuratively speaking, the person whose flag flies high at all times is the person whose *rngiew* remains uncontested, keeping marauders at bay.

At this point, an explicatory note is necessary to explain *Ka Niam Kur* or the clan religion originally practised by the Khasis. Dondor Giri

Nongkhlaw, a well-known geographer, has explained its origin and evolution in his article, "That Elusive Niam Kur (Clan Religion) of the Hynñiewtrep Geographical Landscape" (2007). Although it would not be possible to discuss this at length, the one indisputable fact that emerges is the respect that the maternal uncle in the Khasi matrilineal society evokes. Today, even in Christian families, he maintains an importance that is impossible to sideline. The appellation "orphan" for example cannot be indiscriminately used, if the clan uncle and grandparents are still alive. This effectively points to the indispensable role that the clan uncle has to fulfil in respect of his clan. All belief remaining the same in the various clans or *kur*, prayers, rituals and sacrifices were usually performed by the eldest maternal uncle of the clan. His esteem within the clan, and consequently within society, lies in his ability to negotiate the social and the spiritual, the physical and the metaphysical. He spells out the rationale for life by codifying existence for the clan and society at large.

As clan elder, Radhon Singh Berry perceives the value of the words that he transcribes, consciously aware that they will help in the maturing process of each individual *rngiew*. He must, therefore, take his role seriously in order to ultimately fortify the *rngiew* of the entire Khasi community. The motivating power of *Ki Jingsneng Tymmen* lies in the elder's consistent efforts to keep the symbolic Khasi flag flying high at all times, for the *rngiew* to be nourished and to grow.

Unlike the vast body of oral resources in African American literature that evolved as subterfuges to the white master, *Ki Jingsneng Tymmen* are straightforward, pithy reserves of philosophy and poetry, culture and literature. They come from a society that enjoyed the freedom of introspective and, especially, retrospective thought; the ancestors were unquestioned as the ideal repositories of wisdom and knowledge. They speak of the inevitable outgrowth of a society that has always placed great importance upon the spoken word, as it must continually harvest its own store of accumulated wisdom. This is both challenge and promise, for the spoken word has been perceived as a tool of immense potential, its full power understood only in maturity, hence it cannot be trifled with. Section 21 of Part 1 warns against the dangers of negating the word.

The antecedents of the written version of *Ki Jingsneng Tymmen* date back to a period when the evangelization of the Khasi and Jaintia hills by Welsh missionaries had gained momentum. As was inevitable in such cases, a number of Khasi intellectuals, having benefited from a Western and in some cases a Bengali education, fought hard to preserve the unwritten in the written form. One significant result of the preservation of Khasi literature and culture was the compilation of *Ki Jingsneng Tymmen*.

I have dwelt at length on the 'Invocation' as this forms a significant prelude towards the understanding of the Khasi belief and value system. The rest of the *jingsneng* grow from the argument that must be placed before 'God and man'. These *jingsneng* harvest the racial wisdom of the Khasis, which is communicated through chants or *ki phawar*, an inbuilt means of public communication. As a genre they form a vast store of undocumented knowledge. To some they come as naturally as speech itself. They use subterfuges such as humour and exaggeration to express themselves (War 1994). In *Ki Jingsneng Tymmen, ki phawar* are an inevitable outgrowth of a natural skill with words, wielded for the benefit of their audience. They display a sense of poetic propriety in their ability to combine the oral techniques of poetry with moral injunction.

The 'Invocation' is a request for empowerment from God. Three epithets have been used to describe Him: *"U Blei U Trai U Kynrad U Bastad,"* (Berry 1959: 1) or 'God the Maker, the Master, the All-Knowing One.' Although this is a formulaic beginning for all occasions, it is always at the altar of *U Blei* that the elder, the priest or the shaman invokes empowerment for the performance of his role. The four lines of the 'Invocation' sum up the Khasi world view, God above and supplicating humankind below. By virtue of his maturity, his position of responsibility and his contribution to society, the elder takes on the mantle of a higher responsibility to impart to a younger generation the values that must be nurtured for safeguarding a God-centred life.

When *Ki Jingsneng Tymmen* were first published, it may be inferred that Radhon Singh Berry was the ideal image of the Khasi elder, representative of a particular breed of Khasi men who have a manifest responsibility towards God and the younger generation. One must also see him within the perspective of the written version, as the poetic persona responsible for the projection of culture and religion. Upon him too, rests the ability to wield the spoken word with sharpness and insight. He is retracing a path that has been traversed several times over in the past by similar men of responsibility. The one significant difference lies in the fact that the path is now a 'written one'.

The verses resonate with accumulated voices from the past, repeating the essence of *Ka Akor Khasi* or the Khasi code of ethics. He emulates the spoken word through an oratorical display of language and maintains the formality reserved for occasions such as these, when the entire *kur* or clan gathers around the elder to be taught in its ways. Consequently, one must understand that the identity of the elder, of Radhon Singh Berry per se, is not as important as the ritual moulding of Khasi identity through the spoken word. This has been the compulsion of a society that perceives continuity primarily in its ability to impart, instil and teach its younger ones, in and through, the spoken word.

Hence the emphasis upon truth, *ka hok*, in the second line of the 'Invocation' as a way of life ordained by God, is also a metaphoric self-anointment by truth that elevates the elder to the position of seer. The second line envisions a generation that is made perfectible by its inner sighting of truth, equipping itself to lead the younger lot. The third line roots the race upon an important dimension, the clan, paternal relatives and the family: *kur, kha* and *ïing*. These have been crystallized and are reflected in everyday conversation in terms of *kamai ïa ka hok*, to earn (work for) righteousness, *tipbriew-tipblei*, to know man and to know God, and *tip-kur tip-kha*, to know one's maternal and paternal relations (Rymbai 1979).

In much the same way as caste is an all-pervasive entity in Hindu society (Kakar and Kakar 2008: 138), clan is in the Khasi way of life. These three cornerstones of existence for the Khasi find analogy in the three hearthstones that make up the Khasi hearth—*ki mawbyrsiew*. These special stones that ring the fire represent the strength and unity of a family and hence, of society. The glowing fire in the kitchen has been a cultural symbol of abundance and continuity, especially when a household can still boast of the presence of a member or members of the older generation who, in the literal sense, keep its embers alive by warming themselves around it. Ideally it is around the hearth, not in the shade of a tree, that character is formed and values forged, where the spoken word reigns supreme and wisdom is conferred to the eldest. Thus *sawdong ka lyngwiar dpei*, around the hearth, is an actual configuration of the oral-based foundations of the Khasi way of life.

The last line of the 'Invocation' completes the circle of life. While the third line is suffused with considerations of the present, family and society, the next line makes a vertical move back to God. Having fulfilled one's duty to family and society, one anticipates further guidance from above so that the respect of 'hearth and home', 'clan and society' may be kept intact. The elder also pleads before God not to bring humiliation upon the race. The 'Invocation' is a sensitive indicator of the priorities of a community, made clear in the written version of *Ki Jingsneng Tymmen*, through its elder, who is both the medium through which values are being processed and constantly refined and the prime actor in this public arena.

It must be emphasized that in Khasi society, gender roles are never ambiguous. The spokesperson for the clan and society, in most instances, can never be a woman. In Khasi matrilineal society at present, much debate has been generated over the equality of the sexes. Gender inequality is evident in all spheres, where many men and women, knowing that they have to move beyond their designated roles, are yet unable to disentangle themselves from the time warp that they are trapped in. However, Khasi society, in its ideal state as it flourished in a fairly insular set-up and as reflected in *Ki Jingsneng Tymmen*, is the subject of this discussion.

Thus the elder is usually the eldest clan uncle. He is the moral watchdog of the clan and of society. Among Khasis, male prestige has always been synonymous with the man's decision-making abilities, his capacity to shape and change society. A man who is *ksan rympei rem dorbar* becomes the object of ridicule. The phrase refers to a man who argues and debates only within the realm of the domestic, literally in front of the hearth, normally associated with women and children. At public meetings or durbars, however, in front of equals, he is incapable of expressing himself. As a consequence, his *rngiew* as a *rangbah* or a man is seriously challenged. Men have been identified with the public realm of policymaking whilst women have been identified with the private realm of the domestic, looked upon as custodians of society. According to oral sources, one of the reasons why men surrendered lineage to women was for safeguarding the clan name in that age when men constantly went to war. Hence it was for pragmatic rather than essential reasons that women were given custody of the clan name (Laloo 1970).

Ki Jingsneng Tymmen are steeped in the lore of a matrilineal society that gained strength from its oral deliberations. The word *sneng* in the third line of the 'Invocation' focuses upon the oral ability or the actual reaching out through the spoken word to one's relations, to advise, warn, teach, bring to consciousness; a responsibility that did not sit easy on the shoulders of many men. The compulsion to *sneng*, therefore, became the prerogative of a few who had the aptitude for keeping the channels of communication open, first with God and then with his fellow human beings. The emphasis even in the written version lies in this ability to shape character and reality using the spoken word.

The spoken word becomes a tool of great power and cannot in any way be trivialized. As inextricable as *Ki Jingsneng Tymmen* are from the oral, they are doubly dependent upon the oral discourse that must shape society in its continual evolution. There has, however, been a noticeable break in this discourse. In the wake of British colonization and the development of the Khasi alphabet by Welsh missionaries the compulsion to forge newer horizons of thought and fine-tune character has never regained its original impetus. In her book, *The Khasis under British Rule* (1998), the historian Helen Giri has discussed this impeded evolution at great length. Though not a conclusive factor, the very fact that *Ki Jingsneng Tymmen* have never been updated or revised says everything about the erosion of the oral and the failure of the written to replace it at this level of Khasi thought.

In his own way, however, Radhon Singh Berry has tried to stay the loss by crossing over to the written, thereby preserving whatever oral wisdom was accessible to him at that critical moment in Khasi thought. He is strongly grounded in the lore of Khasi life because he, like all his predecessors, experiences closeness to God and to people. This is a qualifying virtue that empowers him as it has others before him, with a strong sense of mission, to establish the two-way communication, both vertical and horizontal, that will enable him to interpret and clarify values for society in general. He closes the 'Invocation' by reminding everyone that once he takes on the mantle of elder in order to *sneng* others, God will henceforward preserve society from itself and keep disgrace away—an apt preamble to a discourse that has always been God-centred. One must keep in mind that the elder is not addressing himself to the reader but to a listening audience in which Radhon Singh Berry the author subsumes personal identity for a public and mythic role.

The opening line of the first verse calls up all the nieces and nephews, the clan at large, children and grandchildren, "*ko pyrsa ko iing bad ko khun ko ksiew*" (Berry 1959: 1), to pay heed to the words of advice to come. This roll call follows a precise order in a society that is *kur-* or clan-oriented. A sure sense of tradition is then evoked in the words that lead up to the next line where both boys and girls, "*shynrang, kynthei, ngan sneng eh rngiew*" (Berry 1959: 1) are expected to pay close attention to what is being imparted. In trying to understand *Ki Jingsneng Tymmen*, one must pause awhile to take in the ambience of a social situation in which nieces and nephews have taken predominance over one's own children (Chattopadhyay 1985).

The twin roles of the man, as clan uncle and as father to his children, follow this particular order. He fulfils his twin roles judiciously but sometimes with significantly more emphasis upon the former. There is a recognizable sense of continuity when plenty of nieces and nephews, children and grandchildren gather around the clan elder to listen to his words, ensuring by their youthful presence the growth of the clan as a whole. A balance is created whereby every clan uncle fulfils his duty to the clan, whilst the man as father has a supportive role to play in the clan of his wife and children (Chattopadhyay 1985).

The elder begins by cautioning the young against the ills of bad manners and a lazy lifestyle. Reprehensible habits are explicitly denounced, examples of which form the bulk of many verses. The poetry arises out of illustrations that reconstruct life in a chanting usage of idioms, *ktien kynnoh*,[3] that spill over into language thick with hyperbole, imagery and metaphor. The first book is lined with analogies taken from nature, illustrating the fallout of bad habits and an indolent mindset. Thus children are warned never to snatch things away "like a monkey," (Berry 1959) never to give or take anything "facing back" (Berry 1959) to someone, a taboo, much like the antics of a fleshless phantom from the underworld whose intentions are ambiguous. One is cautioned against recklessness towards nature and the elements, "*ka ding ka um, ka dieng ka maw,*" (Berry 1959) for this would definitely bring about accidents and ugly injuries of all kinds.

The path to be taken must be the middle one of moderation. In section 7 of Book 1, a litany of rhyming couplets explains the route to be taken in one's daily life. The justification for such a life lies in the elder's insistence that everything roots back to God Himself. The last couplet hones the litany back to a lifestyle that is based upon calculation and deliberation, "*da mut da khan, wat sarong, wat kyreit,*" (1959) free of arrogance, for this mars clarity of thought. These are fundamental to an existence that is oral-based.

A visible legacy of these moral precepts may be seen in the way guests are treated even today. *Kwai, tympew* or betel nut and leaf, must be offered after sometime; picking up a broom to sweep the room while they are still present is an insult, explicit in its message. And if one were to pass in front of them in order to leave the room or walk through to another room, one would have to walk bent from the waist down as a mark of respect and apology for entering upon the other's private space. Rules for hospitality are laid down in section 12 of Book 1 where specific instructions, for example, are given about the ways of serving extra lime when giving betel nut to others—not on the tip of a knife for this would seem like a ritual performed for the sacrifice of animals, an insult to others—on a betel leaf, the right way up.

Sections 29 and 30 of Part 1 and section 22 of Part 2 deal with marriage, an important milestone that must never be crossed impetuously. Family background and equality of social status are significant criteria as are the importance of informing both father and uncle. Nothing specific is said about marriages having to be arranged by them.[4] As love marriages have been the rule rather than the exception in Khasi society, utmost caution has to be exercised in any friendship between the sexes, so that should the friendship lead to marriage, it should not be a tabooed one, that is, exogamous.

Section 30 lays down six important guidelines for a responsible life, some of which are: never to enter into relationship that is taboo, never to lie as this will shorten one's life, the repercussions of embezzling money, the offensiveness of adultery, which may even lead to death. The list continues in other sections too, but the bottom line is that these excesses are taboo not only on earth, but also in the eyes of God: "*Baroh hynriew kim dei tang ha pyrthei/Sang bad pap ki long haduh khmat U Blei*" (Berry 1959: 19).

The *jingsneng* of the clan uncle are uncompromising and explicit. But before any further discussion and for the purpose of clarification, the difference between two concepts, that of *ka pop*[5] which is synonymous with *ka lait ka let* and *ka ryngkang ka palat* (mistakes of omission and commission) and *ka pap ka sang* (incest and taboo) must be explained.[6] As stated earlier, the clan is a pervasive entity that determines even the severity of sin. *Ka pop* is not as heinous as *ka pap ka sang*. *Ka pop* or *ka lait ka let* and *ka ryngkang ka palat* are human mistakes that are pardonable since they do not challenge the authority of the clan. Even if they do, they do not necessarily undermine it.

These may be petty instances of crime and in extreme cases, even murder,[7] but as long as motives are sufficiently understood as not impinging on the 'sanctity' of the clan, they can always be justified "in the eyes of man and in the eyes of God." The oral aspect has an irreplaceable role to play in all occasions. Cleansing rituals and supplications may be appropriately offered at such times and the reasons for such occurrences deliberated upon and closely weighed and examined in order to purge the cycle of any curse that may follow.

In *ka pap ka sang*, however, when the authority and sanctity of the clan is acutely jeopardized, the culprit or culprits must meet with dire consequences. Preservation of the clan in its sanctity has been the abiding concern of Khasi society. The individual has identity and significance only in respect to her position in the clan. Therefore a person's actions, good or bad, will always impact the family and the (maternal) clan to which the family belongs. Thus when a taboo is committed, the entire clan meets to deliberate upon it. Taboos such as the murder of an uncle by a nephew or vice versa, intra-clan marriage and incest demand immediate redressal because these violate the sanctity of the clan.

Actions such as these usually result in derecognition and expulsion from the clan. Meanwhile the information must be made public. The culprits have to set up a different life elsewhere, but their past will dog them as inevitable questions about their clans will always come up in their adopted place of domicile. In rare cases, the death sentence is pronounced and the entire clan engages in the communal killing. The act of killing is looked upon as a necessary evil in the interests of clan sanctity. The ritual process of purification requires intense effort and great oral skills on the part of the clan elders in order for the clan to be cleansed of the stigma of the taboo and of any boomerang effects thereof.

There are nuances buried in *Ki Jingsneng Tymmen* that may be understood only by a Khasi. In the course of my discussion I have attempted to bring them out bit by bit, but the *jingsneng* are layered with meanings that speak of a lifestyle with a thriving oral culture that has sustained itself for hundreds of years. Part 2 begins by explicating upon a social hierarchy based upon seniority. It exhorts all youngsters to take heed of the wisdom and instruction imparted by their elders. The clan elder is once again reinstated in his proper place for the discourse to continue. Verses leading up to section 7 weigh the priceless value of the spoken word: "*ap dngong ïa ka ktien ba kren ki rangbah*," (Berry 1959, Part II: 1) literally, to wait patiently for the word to sound from the elder.

This leads to a discussion on the verbalization of words: never to trivialize words by using them aimlessly, by name-calling, or when addressing others, to always use their full names in order not to mar their *rngiew*. Should one's name be heard in the distance, one must always wait for a second and a third call, for in the first instance, it might only be the beguiling call of a ghoulish spirit. Odd numbers spell trouble and people going about must walk in even-numbered pairs[8] to deter bad luck and harm. Section 10 spells out the ways in which people are to be greeted and *kwai, tympew* to be shared in a spirit of friendship. Section 11 elevates the priest and medicine man to a position of respect not to be taken over by anyone else, least of all one's parents. He is described as the arch debater, the necessary link to God who will speak on behalf of all humankind.

In Part 2, the elder continues his discourse, discussing serious issues related to life and death, sickness and sorrow, and the responsibilities, amongst others, that are related to marriage, clan and God. In sections 41–44 women are cautioned against excesses of behaviour, they are portrayed to be the intellectual inferiors of men and, all the similes used to illustrate them, describe them as 'custodians', '*ka lukhimai*',[9] or "*Ka nongri ïing, nonglum khih lum kamai*" (Berry 1959). In following a path replete with dangers of all kinds, there is a warning against allowing a woman to lead the way. In leading the way himself, the man symbolically obstructs danger and the enemy is deterred from attacking, knowing that the woman will "cry aloud for help", "*Man ka kam u shynrang uba haphrang, Man ka kam ka kynthei kaba ïap ang*" (Berry 1959). Men have always been perceived to be protectors and guardians. Men are also warned against a life of irresponsibility for it brings its own nemesis, examples of which abound in plenty.

A sense of retributive justice is inbuilt in Khasi thought. This is reflected in its mistrust of people with deformities (section 9 of Part 2), for the belief is that these are retributions for indiscretions of word or action. Consequently too, the razor-edged path that the elder has to traverse lies in choosing the right words and setting up the appropriate arguments "before man and God" so that they do not backfire or prove to be ineffectual.[10] The combinations and permutations that the argument takes has the ability to convict, condemn, cleanse or purge. The Khasi believes that it is humankind's (*u khun bynriew*) prerogative, at the altar of God, to 'argue and define,' 'disclaim and reclaim,' to 'erect' words of supplication or defence. The phrase *ïeng rangbah u briew, Ap jutang U Blei* depicts the archetype of the clan elder who literally 'stands before God as man' (as opposed to a child), knowing that God waits for him 'to speak so that the word be fulfilled.' The clan elder combines the dual role of priest and prophet, *u kñi uba sait uba pynkhuid* and *u kñi uba sneng uba kraw*. In his capacity as priest he 'expatiates and cleanses,' 'purges and propitiates'; and as prophet, he 'warns and denounces' and is the 'mouthpiece of God'.

Hence, the oratory that forms the backbone of *Ki Jingsneng Tymmen* stems from an intrinsic ability to communicate through the chants or *ki phawar* in a public setting. One must remember that only a few have the inbuilt ability to wield them. These are, therefore, special in terms of the 'chain of authority by which [they] are remembered.'[11] After the introductory dedication, where links are established and the pattern set, they navigate a metrical rhythm that occupies, especially in an earlier oral set-up, a mental space replete with the aesthetics of the moral and repeatedly expressed for a specific ethical purpose. They draw their inspiration from nature itself as they unravel the path to be trodden. These *phawar* negotiate time and space, faith and values and are entrenched within the racial psyche, from which they have always been culled out by the dedicated few. The written version of *Ki Jingsneng Tymmen* documents this constant process of redefining and reprocessing thought at a particular stage in the development of life in the Khasi and Jaintia hills.

Almost as a premonition of changes to come, the 'Epilogue' to Part 1 questions the fate of the Khasi code of ethics. And the question that arises as a consequence of reading these *phawar* is, since there has been no updating of these *jingsneng* have oral deliberations become defunct in a society that is pushing forward to meet the challenges of the day? How does one reclaim one's oral roots? Would it be in terms of the past or in the digitized terms of the global village? Questions relating to the future of Khasi morals are fired off by the elder in the 'Epilogue' to Part 1, but since he continues in the second volume, one deduces that he is forging ahead with the kind of zeal that comes only with the dedication of a bard or a seer who refuses to submit to alternative value systems. The foresight and dedication of the clan elder must always remain unimpeachable.

Notes

1. This refers to the commonly held belief that the Khasis, even today, refer to themselves as a group of the seven families who descended from heaven to settle on earth. The other nine stayed on in heaven.
2. According to oral sources the man chosen to receive the script from God was caught in a flood. Unlike his counterpart from the plains, the *dkhar*, who kept his within the safety of his knotted ponytail, the Khasi put his in his mouth. At the time of crossing the river, he swallowed the script, thus depriving his people of a written script.
3. The idiomatic speech of the Khasi.
4. Arranged marriages are rare, but not impossible, in Khasi society.
5. The word *pop* is a loanword and probably came into usage at a later time.
6. The clan still rules supreme in many families and the probability of killing by the clan, though rare nowadays, still exists.
7. This is the *tyrut* or the curse, which continues to have a superstitious hold on society.
8. This, according to oral sources, was what happened to inhabitants who were eaten up by the *thlen* or the serpent when they went marketing together in odd numbers.
9. *Lukhimai* is the spirit associated with wealth. Women are supposed to be of single strength whereas a man's strength consists of twelve layers. Another oral saying warns against such time when women would begin to 'crow like a cock', for it spells subversion of all kinds.
10. Diviners and priests have to be cautious in the way that they put up their arguments so that nothing backfires and no consequent destruction wrought.

11. Hugh Miles (2005) speaks about how the spoken word holds sway over the written and the importance attached to it in the Arab world. This is no different from many communities in the East. Amongst the Khasis, wedding invitation cards have no real creditability. It is the personal call at home that solicits a response from invitees. It is a commonly known fact that men were the original keepers of the clan name. See also Laloo (1970).

References

Berry, Radhon Singh. 1997. *Ki Jingsneng Tymmen* [The teachings of elders], Part 1 & 11. Translated by Bijoya Sawian. Shillong: Ri Khasi Press.
Berry, U Radhon Singh. 1959. *Ki Jingsneng Tymmen Shaphang Ka Akor Khasi ha ka Rukom Rwai Phawar* (Teachings of Elders About Khasi Manners in the Phawar), Part 1 and Part 11 reprints Shillong, India: Ri Khasi Press.
Chattopadhyay, S. K. (ed.). 1985. *Tribal Institutions of Meghalaya*. Guwahati, India: Spectrum Publications.
Giri, Helen. 1998. *The Khasis under British Rule (1824–1947)*. New Delhi: Regency Publications.
Kakar, Sudhir and Katharina Kakar. 2008. 'The Inner Experience of Caste', in *The Penguin Yearbook* (Complited and edited by Derek O'Brien) India: Penguin Books.
Laloo, Donbok T. 1970. *Ki Paju Lyngkot* (Small Narratives). Shillong, India: Don Bosco Press.
Miles, Hugh. 2005. *Al-Jazeera: How Arab TV News Challenged the World*. London: Abacus.
Nongkhlaw, Dondor Giri. 2007. 'That Elusive Niam Kur (Clan Religion) of the Hynñiewtrep Landscape', *Indian Theological Journal*, Vol. No. 1 (January–June): 54–74.
Rymbai, R. T. 1979. 'Some Aspects of the Religion of the Khasi-Pnar', in Hipshon Roy (ed.) *Khasi Heritage*. Shillong, India: Ri Khasi Press.
War, Juanita. 1994. 'The Khasi Phawar', in D. L. Kharmawphlang and Helen Giri (eds) *Lest We Forget*, pp. 24–34. Shillong, India: Seven Huts Enterprise.

14
The Interface of Mizo Society and Literature

Margaret Ch Zama

Society and literature are inseparable, for the former generates the subjects and themes of the latter. Taking a cue from this, the attempt here is to critique the interface of Mizo society and its literature after its transition from a pre-script culture to one that received what it did not have before—both script and institutionalized religion in 1894, through its first missionaries, all in one package as it were. The dominance of literacy and writing post-1894, which textualized Mizo literature through Christian-oriented discourse, reveals an interesting tension—first, the failure to diminish the influence and relevance of many of the oral folk traditions and cultural practices in spite of the new faith, and second, the convenient fusion of attitudes and mindsets of the old and new, on issues especially of gender and patriarchy. A look at two short stories *Chhingpuii* (1939) and *Lali* (1937)[1] later in this chapter will show how creative work can be seen as a social activity, as a receptacle of rich and old legacies, but more importantly, how this can be a thriving, alive technique for the exploration and depiction of the complex interface of contemporary issues as well.

One aspect of this complex interface to be touched upon with regard to the transition undergone by Mizo society from orality to literacy may be first taken to the very roots of what Ferdinand de Saussure (1857–1913), as referred to by Walter J. Ong (2004: 5), noted about language, that writing is a kind of complement to oral speech, and not a transformer of verbalization. Ong (2004: 15) adds:

Literacy, though it consumes its own oral antecedents and, unless it is carefully monitored, even destroys their memory, is also infinitely adaptable. It can restore their memory, too. Literacy can be used to reconstruct for ourselves the pristine human consciousness which was not literate at all.

The fact that the old Mizo societal set-up and its way of life was totally communitarian is borne out by its oral tradition, its many old beliefs and sayings, songs and tales, wherein the welfare and general good of the community took precedence over individuals and family units, and which to a great extent still provide the foundational basis of the present-day Mizo mindset and ethics, a case in point being the concept of *tlawmngaihna*.[2] Conspicuous too, was the ingrained male hegemony, long established in old sayings like 'old fences and old wives can be replaced', 'a woman's wisdom does not extend beyond the public water point', 'women and crabs have no religion' and so on. Such is the societal backdrop and ideological mindset that gets played out again and again within the framework of Mizo creative writings that have emerged, the bulk of which still remain untranslated.

That the examination of oral tales handed down through the generations could also be said to provide such an interface is also true. It has its own dynamics of knowing and evolving a world view depending upon the interpretations applied and providing one with a form of communicating the development of knowledge that a particular community undergoes. *Chemtatrawta*, a round (the tale ends where it begins) folktale of the Mizo contains much more than bawdy humour and sharp wit. It would not be too farfetched to state that a rereading of the tale throws up certain issues no less relevant today. The value and need for coexistence and respect for another's space is one such issue. None of the animals in the tale give a second thought as to how their actions might affect the welfare of others, just as Chemtatrawta showed his irresponsibility by reacting the way he did. He could have immediately addressed the culprit at hand instead of taking it out on the bamboo nearby which set off a chain of events that eventually went beyond his control. Another aspect is the importance of civic sense and cleanliness. The old lady's defecating at the village water source was unforgivable and not to be tolerated. She was therefore summoned before the people's court for questioning. The process of democratization of village administration appears to also have taken roots quite early.

The story *Chhingpuii* makes for interesting reading for several reasons, one being that it effectively utilizes the history and traditional life of the

Mizo forefathers as a backdrop for its tale, which is set in pre-Christian nineteenth century Mizoram. It tells of the tragic love story of Chhingpuii and her lover Kaptluanga, who is a noted *pasalthra*[3] of their village. But this tale also provides for exploring new possibilities of 'seeing' and 'reading' which open up a dialogic space for intellectual encounters and interdisciplinary transactions generating areas of study other than the literary. The tale contains a charming rendition of the old Mizo tradition of *nula rim* or courting of maidens. The sensitive reader can however look beyond the romanticization of such practices and read in it a powerful statement of deeply entrenched male superiority and chauvinism that is not only not contested, but considered a convenient tool by society to measure a maiden's fitness to be a suitable bride.

A brief description of this courting practice goes along the following lines: after a day of hard labour at the *jhooms*[4], both young men and women return home, but while the night offers rest and relaxation for the men folk, first at the *zawlbuk* and later at courting, the young woman, after completing all her household chores, starts work on her spinning even as she supervises and fuels the fire that cooks food for the pigs. At this point the young men arrive and gradually fill the house while being welcomed by the girl even as she offers to light their pipes with live embers from the fire. It is said that the mark of a truly worthy maiden is the manner in which she conducts herself throughout the long night. It would never do for her to reveal her preference for any of the young men, nor could anyone suspect her of harbouring special feelings for anyone in particular, even if she is indeed in love with one of them. She keeps all happy with her constant attention to the lighting of their pipes, laughing at their jokes and serving them cooked yam or maize as the case may be. Such is her discretion and diplomacy that with the first crowing of the cock that is referred to as *leng hawn ar*, which means the crowing that signals the time to take leave, the young men prepare to leave while the girl pleads that it is a crowing that signals them to take their time and remain, without once revealing her tiredness or irritation at their long visit. The long night does not deter her from rising early at dawn to perform her morning chores of fetching water from the stream, pounding paddy and cooking the morning meal, feeding the pigs and letting out the chickens from their coop.

Kaphleia depicts the practice more or less along the lines given above in the tale of *Chhingpuii*. We are told (Ong 2004: 249):

> Though she hardly spoke to Kaptluanga, Chhingpuii often stole a glance at him to see if he was looking at her. Pretending to be unaware of his

proximity, she spun skillfully, puffing away at her *tuibur* (a woman's smoking pipe) and listening to the chatter around her. Kaptluanga, seemingly deep in conversation, stole glances at her in turn.

When the first cock began to crow, "Those reclining on the floor sat up, lit their pipes and made to leave. Chhingpuii cajoled, 'Stay a while longer as promised'" (Ong 2004: 250).

Though such a practice has now been phased out, at least in the form described above, it is considered to have a unique charm of its own if one ignores the fact of the pressure on a girl to conform to a demanding social construct, failing which stories of her unsuitability and failure to conform would often be circulated out of spite.

Chhingpuii also provides an interesting vignette of the old Mizo life wherein *zu*, the traditional rice beer, was indispensable. *Zu* played a significant role not only during rituals and festivals for the quenching of one's thirst after a hard day's work or as a token of hospitality, but when proffered by the village chief or elders to a *pasalthra*, denoted the ultimate honour granted to a subject. Other than the obvious theorizations about change and transition that have taken place in most traditional tribal cultures of north-east India, brought on by the advent of Christianity and hence a new way of life and new societal values, there is to my mind, further scope for studying in the particular present day Mizo society and mindset vis-à-vis *zu*, now accepted by many as epitomizing social and moral evil. Post-colonial interpretations of how our "primitive" ways were condemned as the devil's handiwork by the white missionaries and were deeply entrenched in our psyche is definitely one aspect. But legitimizing this belief, which culminated in governmental imposition of the Mizoram Liquor Total Prohibition Act, bemoaned and cursed by many while seen by others as one befitting a 'Christian' state, reflects a much more complex interface of society, religion and tradition.

This interface is witnessed in *Lali*, claimed to be the first Mizo short story authored by Biakliana, the son of a Presbyterian reverend. Unlike *Chhingpuii*, this tale bears the stamp of Christian discourse throughout, reading somewhat like a sermon on the evils of an unchristian life, divine retribution and the rewards of a virtuous life. Though written over seven decades ago, the moral values contained in the story continue to be the yardstick applied for judging a good Christian in present day Mizo society—regular church and Sunday school attendance, Bible lessons, prayers.

And yet, this short story also offers scope for interpreting new nuances, one of which is the possibility of reading a subversive use of the teachings of the new faith to legitimize traditional male hegemony in the family and society, thus linking with and strengthening what the patriarchal Mizo culture had long established. The story of *Lali* is concluded with a reference to Genesis 3:15 in the Bible where the curse of God on the serpent for tempting Eve is referred to, but no mention is made of what the next verse says, which contains God's curse on the woman for the sin of disobedience—that she would greatly suffer the pangs of childbearing, yet her desire would be for her husband and that he would rule over her.

The scope for this reading is found in the story, which, besides its Christian theme of God's love and the repentance for one's sins, also focuses on the lot of women in a society that accepts their subservient role without question. Lali and her friend Thanmawii constantly refer to their many household chores like fetching water, weaving, rice pounding and so on, due to which they have no time to spare for themselves. Their condition causes Thanmawii to make a telling comment, "Perhaps it is our fate" (Ong 2004: 197). Though Lali has two brothers, she is without support and envies her friend, "You're lucky to have a younger sister.... It's very difficult being an only girl.... I wish I had a younger sister too" (Ong 2004: 198). The domestic violence and physical abuse that prevails at Lali's home due to her father's drinking is a situation they put up with to prevent further aggravation. Lali's father incidentally, is one who resists the new religion.

The sad and unfortunate lot of women is acknowledged and sympathized with by the author, but a justification for it is given at the story's end, along with Christian discourse—that the enslavement of women is the devil's work and it is only the good news of God's word that will set them free. The stamp of acceptance of an established discourse is glaring here; it is not the men who victimize women; rather, it is God's will and therefore reluctantly accepted as their fate.

The most striking note struck in *Lali* however, is the stance taken by the writer with regard to the lot of Mizo women. This may be seen as conflicting with the angle of interpretation just given. Mention should be made here that what follows is the view of the author or narrator in the story in the form of a direct address to the reader. When one considers the social history of the Mizo during the period in which the work was written, the sensitivity shown by the writer towards the cause of women is nothing short of radical and daring.

When Lali receives a proposal of marriage from a well-to-do prominent family of her village, both her parents, particularly her father, consider the match most favourably. Lali is not agreeable to it, her reason being that the proposed groom lives a decadent and an unchristian life, and even her father's threat to beat her into consent does not deter her. But the author's view with regard to the status of women and marriage is due to reasons that go far beyond moralistic preaching, and has closer affinity to the acceptance of the rights and dignity of a woman as a human being. Marriage for a woman is a curse inflicted by society that she has to endure. I quote (Ong 2004: 203):

> Our women bear the brunt of it, for they are sold off like cattle, and cattle buyers buy the best and the most hardworking of them all. It is as if we auction them off. And even after we possess them, the adage—Women and fences are but disposables!—still holds good. We men beat them and leave them at a whim.... Who shall lead Mizoram's enslaved women into the light of freedom?

Earlier in the story, the author's sympathy for women's plight in all spheres of life is seen in the lines that refer to the two friends, Lali and Thanmawii, "They walked along in silence contemplating the pathetic state of affairs and the wretched condition of women" (Ong 2004: 197).

It is apparent here that the stance taken by the writer goes beyond Christian discourse—it speaks of a progressive mindset way ahead of its times. That literature may serve as a vehicle for moral and social values is not a new thing, nor is writing with a social conscience confined to any particular literature. *Lali* is thus the first Mizo fiction work to highlight the lowly status of women in home and society but surprisingly did not, and has not, ruffled feathers, perhaps due to the foregrounding of religiosity in the work that overshadows other perceptions.

Notes

1. Authored by Kaphleia (1910–1940) and Biakliana (1918–1941) respectively, they were translated into English and published in *The Heart of the Matter: Handpicked Fictions from Meghalaya, Manipur, Mizoram, Assam and Nagaland* (2004).
2. *Tlawmngaihna* is a code of honour entailing selfless sacrifice and the giving of oneself to the service of others without expectation of recognition or reward for such acts rendered. The Mizo claim that this code is unique to their culture and that its flame is

kept alive today in particular by the Young Mizo Association (YMA), first established in 1935 as Young Lushai Association (YLA), following the end of the *zawlbuk* era (male dormitory system). The YLA was renamed the YMA in 1947.
3. *Jhoom* simply means the mizo cultivation on hill sides equivalent to rice fields found in the plains. The word 'jhoom' sometimes spelt as 'jhum' is not a Mizo word. It appears to be a term given by the colonists under British rule. This word is found in Dictionary of the Lushai Language by James Herbert Lorrain (Pu Buanga) 1940 by the Asiatic Society and again in 1975.
4. One who has proven his mettle as a brave warrior at war and his prowess in big game hunting, and who has earned the privilege of drinking *zu* (rice beer) from the *nopui* (horn of the gayal), usually proffered by the chief and his elders.

References

Biakliana. 2004. 'Lali' (Trans. Margaret Lalmuanpuii Pachuau), in *The Heart of the Matter: Handpicked Fictions from Meghalaya, Manipur, Mizoram, Assam and Nagaland*, pp. 196–214. New Delhi: Katha.

Kaphleia. 2004. 'Chhingpuii' (Trans. Margaret Lalmuanpuii Pachuau and Mona Zote), in *The Heart of the Matter: Handpicked Fictions from Meghalaya, Manipur, Mizoram, Assam and Nagaland*, pp. 247–275. New Delhi: Katha.

Ong, Walter J. 2004. *Orality and Literacy: The Technologizing of the Word*. London: Routledge.

15
Folklore and Folk Traditions as a Cohesive in Nepali Community in India

Utpala Ghaley Sewa

A prominent feature of modern reality today is communal mobility. This has evolved as a leitmotif of contemporary times within a globalized world where politico-cultural iconography is understood as a fluid rather than a solid entity (Bauman 2000; Castells 1998; Scholte 2000; Urry 2000). Bauman calls this a 'liquid modernity' that transforms even before gaining shape.

As several scholars have noted (Augé 1995; Malkki 1995), diaspora communities have become groupings who symbolize the fluidity and mobility of political and cultural identities. They occupy what Brah (1996: 209) refers to as a 'diaspora space,' located somewhere between the local and the global. Negotiating the problem of this 'diaspora space' and preserving and nurturing a sense of their identity poses a challenge today. Folklore and keeping extant folk traditions are offered as suggestions to this critical question (Bascom 1954).

William R. Bascom, American anthropologist and folklorist, states that folklore can serve four primary functions in a culture (1954):

1. Folklore lets people escape from repressions imposed upon them by society.
2. Folklore is a pedagogic device that reinforces morals and values and builds wit.
3. Folklore is a means of applying social pressure and exercising social control.

4. Folklore validates culture, justifying its rituals and institutions to those who perform and observe them.

It is these functions of folklore in a diasporic society that the present chapter proposes to explore with reference to Nepali settlements spread throughout India. The search for identity of this minority group, containing possibilities of some recreation through mythic revisiting of the imaginary homeland stands reinforced by their conscious and continuing practice of folklore and folk traditions. These practices have helped create in this diasporic, vastly dispersed, community the sense of cohesion that is both temporal as well as actual by locating the community in the imaginary homeland that centralizes, binds and keeps alive awareness of identity beyond the flux, confusion and loss of the actual homeland. It attempts to pre-empt forgetting and alienation from the remembered home through generations and so prevents sociocultural dilution where "being rootless, displaced between worlds, living between a lost past and a fluid present, are perhaps the most fitting metaphors for the journeying modern consciousness" (Rapport and Dawson 1998: 23).

History and politics both have had a very significant influence on the fate and character of the Nepali people in India, making it a community that is yet to formally receive a distinct place amongst the other Indian communities. This statement is especially true of the Indian Nepalis of North Bengal in West Bengal, namely the Darjeeling Hills, people who came with the land when it was annexed to India and made a part of West Bengal. However, that is not to marginalize the legitimate claims of the vast number of Nepalis who later migrated to Assam and the north-east of India either through the British (later, Indian) military recruitments, or as cheap labour under the The Indo–Nepal Peace and Friendship Treaty, Kathmandu, July 31, 1950.

To elaborate the above statements one has to turn some pages of history; see Pemble (2009) and Naravane (2006: 189–91). Rivalry between Nepal and British India culminated in the signing of the Treaty of Sagauli in 1816, ceding large parts of Nepali territories in Uttarakhand, Himachal Pradesh, the Terrai, the Darjeeling Hills and Sikkim (nearly one-third of the country) to the British in exchange for Nepali autonomy. As the ceded territories were not restored to Nepal by the British when freedom was granted to the people of British India, these have become a part of the Republic of India, Sikkim joining later in 1975.

The British, impressed by the valour of the Gurkha soldiers witnessed during the Anglo-Nepal War, incorporated into the nine articles of the

Treaty of Sagauli one that gave the right to recruit the Gurkhas as soldiers. The disbanded Nepali soldiers became the booty and were gathered by the British into a new force. Thus, on the ashes of defeat was born the first ethnically exclusive Gurkha Regiment, the very first to be created on ethnic lines in the Indian Army.

The third wave of migration came at the wake of the Indo-Nepal Friendship Treaty signed in 1950 that opened the doors of both countries to each other's citizens: the rich business houses from India set up shop in Nepal and thousands of cheap Nepali migrant labour became available in India. The migrants to India came looking for betterment, having escaped severe economic hardship in Nepal.

The Nepalis of India have any of these three reasons for being in India today (Kansakar 1984; Tyagi 1974).

Against such a historico-political context one seeks answers, futilely perhaps, for generations of voiceless, stateless people who are questioned about, and in turn question, their identity. Flung into distant corners of a land where their survival has depended on merging optimally with the local inhabitants, it is the folk songs, lores and practices that by keeping alive the practices of folk tradition, have nourished not just an awareness of the memory of a lost homeland but also helped delineate and keep alive a sense of their identity in the inevitable process of acculturation.

The practices of folk culture or tradition (ballads, riddles, stories) are those elements that help define the people to themselves by transmitting their values and their traditions, and thus help surmount the otherwise differentiating factors of spatial distances between the groups of settlements by clearly etching and reinforcing their sense of sameness and identity, despite and beyond the superficial differences due to variables of geographical, political and social factors. Remembrance of homeland, real and imaginary, and the wistful but unrealistic desire to return, are pivots on which the community's identity stands.

It is an accepted practice amongst Nepali folklorists, as no doubt with others, to group the oral tradition in terms of either their subject or form. Thus, *Lokgatha* are legends and stories, sung as ballads, of historical personages, heroes and kings and also include tales from religious epics like the Ramayana and the Mahabharata, and sometimes of ordinary mortals facing extraordinary human conditions. The strong Hindu feature of the community is not only reflected and reinforced, but also reflects the harmonious coexistence of the Buddhist or animistic beliefs of various ethnic groups of the community alongside the Hindu, insofar as the followers of Buddhist or of animistic beliefs too identify with, and weave into their value system, lessons learnt from the retelling of Hindu myths and tales. Likewise with animistic beliefs as also with Buddhist tales, primarily because for many ethnic groups who have adopted Hinduism, the animistic beliefs represent a part of their cultural roots, while the Buddha is held as yet another religious teacher or even an avatar of the myriad Hindu gods. This is perhaps an important factor behind the total lack of religious conflict within the community.

Bravery, the trait that, like a badge of honour, has been conferred on the community by the world at large, is unquestionably sown and nourished by innumerable ballads that sing of battles and victories, *Veergatha*, that include even comparatively recent subjects as the warrior Balabhadra, while filial devotion is nourished by ballads, for example, of Sravankumar. The pain of separation of householders forced by economic hardship to seek livelihoods outside their village, state or nation is delineated as a fact of Nepali life by ballads (for example, *Muna Madan*) and folk tales, but more so by folk ditties where it is viewed light-heartedly:

Ek dui paisa vyapar ma
Katuwa khanu paper ma
Switha Lahore ma

A bit of money through trade
Will buy me tobacco in a paper
Hence, off to Lahore

"Lahore" stands in metonymic relationship to places òf work outside the homeland, travelled to and lived in for economic reasons. Paper to roll tobacco in is a rare luxury for people who would normally roll it out in dry leaf, beedi-style. The ditty indicates that for economic betterment one needs to leave hearth and home and move to alien lands. The relating of the idea of leaving home to travel and live in often inhospitable lands to the idea of economic betterment for parents, wives and children left behind in the homeland is so deeply entrenched in the mind of the members of the community that travelling abroad for work is accepted as the norm. The profile of the Nepali people has developed as very adjustable, honest, hard working and non-threatening. Most also pick up languages easily, a feature that allows them easier existence and access in alien cultures.

They have a deep sense of their roots, never forget their identity and the folk customs and lore help them know themselves, vital in a diasporic community. Folklore shapes the perspective, morals and values of the community by delineating for them their own defining characteristics, and reinforcing them through multi-pronged repetitions: for instance, the same features may be stated in a ditty, again in a proverb, as well as figure in a ballad.

A feature that has helped keep alive the ballads through the centuries is not only, as with all verse sung, traceable to the rhythm and rhyme that are mnemonic aids, but also to the fact that the community has a separate caste, *gaienay*, of wandering minstrels who pass the oral tradition of *Lokgatha* from father to son and spread the stories far and wide as they roam with their sarangis. Even today the *gaienay* roam through villages giving life and longevity to their repertoire. They sing for their livelihood and often a village or a group may even today solicit their participation in celebrations and festivities. These folk minstrels enter the various pockets of Nepali settlements in India and bind them by giving a glimpse not just of a common heritage of culture but also indirectly by transmitting through them the mores and codes that have shaped the community.

Lokgeet, or folk songs, are often tribe or caste-specific. This group comprises such a wide variety of folk songs sung during various agricultural, domestic, religious and cultural occasions like Diwali, *bhai tikka* (ceremony for brothers' welfare) *teej* (festival for married daughters), *binyah* (marriage), *nauran* (naming ceremony), etc. that any discussion of it requires more space to do justice. Since these *Lokgeet* are sung at specific points of the celebrations, their importance in the cultural practices of the community living for generations with great spatial distances between them is obvious. Thus, a Nepali household in any part of India will during *Tiwar* (Diwali, or festival of lights) display a doorway garlanded by marigolds, cook *sel roti* (traditional Nepali snack made from rice flour) along with other regional food they have adopted like the Assamese *pitha* (a snack made rice) or Khasi *kwai* (betelnut). During *teej* the ladies will dance where steps and some parts of the attire are incorporated from the regional dances they are familiar with (for example, the Bihu dance).

As with most folk cultures, children are significant members of the family, often helping the parents economically, through child-labour, or otherwise through help in care of siblings or by undertaking domestic responsibilities. Their importance in the family fold is emphasized by the presence of a number of *Balgeet* and *Nininanee Geet*: they are children's songs that adults sing to children, songs that children hear from infancy. These songs generally are short ditties, often using nonsensical words in between for rhythm, rhyme and lightness of mood. Teaching, entertaining, play and evoking smiles and laughter are the basic aims of these songs. *Lohris* are cradle songs, lullabies sung to the flow of the melody to rock children to sleep in their small baskets or *kokro*, or in their hanging cloth cradles. These songs are not just catchy but very rhythmic, and not just reflect but perhaps are also the reason behind the community's love for music and dance. The love of rhythm and melody is, as it were, nurtured from the cradle itself to become an integral part of the world view. Most importantly it also defines the community to the individuals in it. Thus, despite the physical and economic hardship, practically every major festival and event in life is marked by singing and dancing; often the songs being event-specific.

As in all communities, marriage is always for the purpose of having children. Being barren is an unthinkable misfortune, and a man is expected to marry again for progeny. Male issue is desired, although the father is generally affectionate towards the daughters. The mother of a son proclaims her status by never plaiting her hair till the very tip, and is alone allowed to participate in some rituals.

A unique musical practice is the *Sareli*. Here a group of young men and women from one village is invited to stay from one festival to the next, usually the tenth day of *Dashai* (the ten days of worship of goddess Durga's return to earth, her parent's home) to the *bhai tikka*, by another village to participate in competitions and performances there. *Sareli* not only brings festivity to a fever pitch of competitiveness but also generates greater interaction between villages and often proves a fertile ground for romantic attachments, or carrying of information about eligible men and women for marriages to be arranged.

But the most interesting of the music-based oral traditions is the *Dohorie* or *Johorie*. This is a musical debate between male and female singers. It is staged as a performance to be watched by the village, or it can form a part of marriage festivities (the traditional Nepali marriage ceremony usually lasts three days, but sometimes five), and it can be incorporated into any social or cultural celebration. The participants, generally young men and women, seat themselves in two groups, gender-wise. Though a leader is chosen by each group, a few may legitimately intervene to help the leader. The subject is always love and the tone and mood playful. Wit is the essence of these songs. The attitude adopted by the leader of the male group is of a man desperately in love with a beautiful woman who is hard to woo. He uses arguments, flattery, promises and wit to woo her while the leader of the female group adamantly refuses to thaw and uses counter arguments, wittily expressed, to show the flaws in his promises. The banter between them is lively, and most significantly, it is impromptu. Each argument is sung in stanzas of four lines, with the main argument or punch line coming in the last one. The group echoes its leader's statement in the last line in a vociferous chorus. Simply accompanied with a *madal* or small drum, the *Dohorie* continues until a definitive winner emerges. Sometimes, it is said the *Dohorie* goes on for days. Legends and stories about *Dohorie* are numerous: such as one that lasted twelve days, or several where the winner won his competitor as his wife. Humour and wit make this love banter a much-loved folk tradition that is vibrantly alive and practised in the community even today.

Interestingly, this folk tradition has adapted itself facilely to the modern world of cable television. The language channels routinely telecast these musical competitions from the various villages or pockets of Nepali settlements to a vast and rapt audience. The cohesion that folk practices would generate generally is increased manifold in reach, spatial and numerical, and acceptance.

Romantic love is given respectability and its acceptance as an important aspect of life, although arranged marriages are generally more the basis of conjugal life, is engendered by popular and defining folk practices like the *Sareli* and the *Johorie*. The humour, the quick-wittedness, the repartee-based banter that Nepalis often indulge in amongst themselves even in daily communication is a rare distinguishing marker of the people that stands out all the more impressively in light of the hardships they live in.

Although *Ukhan* or proverbs are a feature of practically all languages, a mention of it is included here for an interesting reason. It is probably not known to those unfamiliar with the oral form of the Nepali language, that no conversation of some length is complete without at least one speaker using a proverb to bolster his point. Nepalis use proverbs copiously. They are innumerable, pithy, based on observations of common everyday life and striking in the worldly wisdom that is expressed so concisely and often with so much wit and humour. They inform and transmit to the hearers the worldly wisdom of the rural man who understood the ways of the world through keen observation, compassion, often humour and with a courageous acceptance. Examples of just a few from literally hundreds of them that illustrate the statement above are:

1. *Bhir jane goru lai Ram Ram bhanna sakincha, kandh halna sakinna.* Translated it says, the bull sliding downhill is one you bid farewell to, not attempt to lend a shoulder to save, which means that the unacceptable that becomes the inevitable must be accepted.
2. *Jasko tha sing chaina theysko naam theeko.* Translated it says, the bull with no horns is the one named Sharp, which means that there is no causal relation between merit and reward or that often the most inappropriate and inept actually walks off with the prize.

3. *Chinnu, na chinnawnu.* This is almost untranslatable, but generally means that one should aim to know and understand people but resist trying to pass personal opinions or knowledge to others where it may be transformed to mere gossip, be hurtful, inappropriate or cause harm to the subject; keep it as personal enlightenment about those around you.

These proverbs, shared by the community and the Nepali diaspora and used constantly in everyday communication, help shape the ethos by clearly etching the collective perspective and the general world view of the community.

A much-loved, and still flourishing, oral tradition is the *Gaon Khanay Katha*, literally, the village devouring stories. These are riddles that can be played at the domestic, familial level (between siblings, mothers and children: traditionally, the father is a patriarch who may look on indulgently, or help from the sidelines but often does not actively participate in games with his children) or in a larger group like the village. One person asks the riddle, in verse. The audience ventures the answer. They may try as many times as they like. The person who provides the answer then gets the chance to ask the next riddle. If the correct answer is not given, a whole system of negotiations comes into play. The audience offers various villages in mock trade for the correct answer. The quizzer thinks it over but may not accept the trade. Then another village, its beauties and worth exaggeratedly extolled, is offered. Should the quizzer accept it, he says so, but specifies what he accepts. Generally, he says that the dirty dogs, the stinking areas, the beggars and sick people of the village he wants to gift back to the audience, but in return for the answer to his riddle he will accept the better parts of the offered village. As the Nepali people are basically fun-loving, and wit is held in great esteem, the quizzer will use this trade to bring about laughter by specifying which areas, houses, and so on he or rejects and why. The one with the maximum number of villages in his kitty is declared the winner. A few examples of *Gaon Khanay Katha* are:

1. *Khai, khai dai/mo agay jao, kay ho?* Translation: Just a moment, brother, let me go first, what is it? The answer: A walking stick.
2. *Naam cha naari, stree haina/latta cha dhari, jogi haina, kay ho?* Translation: The name is Naari, but she isn't a woman, has dark coarse hair, but isn't a yogi, what is it? The answer: A coconut (*naariyal*).

3. *Agadi sankha, peechadi pankha, kay ho?* Translation: A conch in front and a fan at the back, what is it? The answer: A dog. (All passages from Nepali have been translated by the current author.)

Many pleasant, fun-filled evenings in the homes and villages owe their debt to the oral tradition of *Gaon Khanay Katha*. It is a cheap, entertaining pastime that not only bonds the family or the group together, but by providing wit at the heart of the riddles, gives its people the love, appreciation and practice of wit.

In keeping with the changing times, many websites on the Internet are devoted to this form of oral tradition (for example, the Nepali forum, www.Babbaal.com). Players from across the globe participate in these tournaments; along with having an interesting time, across the miles Nepalis bond through this traditional practice that keeps them grounded in their ethos, wherever they may be.

References

Augé, M. 1995. *Non-Places: Introduction to an Anthropology of Supermodernity*. New York: Verso.
Bascom, William R. 1954. 'Four Functions of Folklore', *Journal of American Folklore*, 67: 339–49.
Bauman, Z. 2000. *Liquid Modernity*. Cambridge: Blackwell Publishers.
Brah, Avtar. 1996. *Cartographies of Diaspora: Contesting Identities*. London: Routledge.
Castells, Manuel. 1998. *End of Millennium: The Information Age: Economy, Society and Culture*, Vol. 3. Cambridge, MA: Blackwell.
Kansakar, V. B. Singh. 1984. 'Indo–Nepal Migration: Problems and Prospects', *Nepalese Studies*, 11 (2): 49–70.
Malkki, L. H. 1995. *Purity and Exile: Violence, Memory and National Cosmology among Hutu Refugees in Tanzania*. Chicago, IL: University of Chicago Press.
Naravane, M. S. 2006. *Battles of the Honourable East India Company: Making of the Raj*. New Delhi: APH Publishing.
Pemble, John. 2009. 'Forgetting and Remembering Britain's Gurkha War', *Asian Affairs*, 40 (3): 361–76.
Rapport, N. and A. Dawson. 1998. *Migrants of Identity: Perceptions of Home in a World of Movement*. Providence and Oxford: Berg Publishers.
Scholte, J. A. 2000. *Globalization: A Critical Introduction*. New York: St. Martin's Press.
Tyagi, S. 1974. *Indo–Nepalese Relations 1858–1914*. New Delhi: D.K. Publishing House.
Urry, J. 2000. *Sociology beyond Societies: Mobilities for the Twenty-First Century*. London: Routledge.

16
Singing the Nation
Pratima Barua Pandey, The Princess of the Lost Lores

Jyotirmoy Prodhani

Folk art has an apparent innocence about it. There has been a subconscious anticipation for the exotic in our prospective encounter with folk culture. But Pratima Barua Pandey occupies a unique position for she is more than just a folk artist; she has been the provider of a cultural address to a community desperately seeking space of its own in the geo-cultural space of its habitation. The new awareness of a community as a nation, through its collective experiential understanding of the self, is essentially informed by its rediscovery of native cultural nuances.

The Rajbanshis, a major ethnic community living in west Assam and North Bengal in West Bengal, are a peculiar entity with odd historical compulsions to continually justify their own existence in the geopolitical context of the two territories. They had to opt for a voluntary revocation of their native selves. In the process they lost their tongue. Ironically, despite having a glorious history to look back to, they found it was not locatable in the official versions of history. In Assam, as Hiren Gohain (1998) mentioned once, the history of the Koch Rajbanshis is a truncated text as it remained in the history books only so long as it was relevant in relation to Sankardeva. And, since Bengal did not have any such stake on Sankardeva, it simply removed it from its official version of history.

More importantly, in Bengal, through a special mechanism of dispossessing the natives from their ancestral homestead, which was euphemistically termed 'land reform', the Rajbanshis found themselves been evicted from the geography of their own, their ancestral hearths. Being displaced from their own native space, they veritably became cultural nomads. Their claim in history became seemingly inauthentic; their political articulations provisional, which caused the dwindling of their cultural and social credibility following their dislocation from the most intimate physical locale—land. The aspirational middle-class Rajbanshis, with the obverse intention of gaining a respectable recognition in the altered context, jealously tried to sustain the façade of their acquired identity, forcing a state of cultural amnesia, resulting in the gradual receding of their cultural mores into the realm of almost an irrevocable dementia. At that time arrived Pratima Barua Pandey, like—as Sam Shepard, a radical American playwright, would put in a different context—"A rock n roll Jesus with a cowboy mouth" (Shepard 1971), a saviour with the reassuring comfort of the myths.

Pratima Barua Pandey (1935–2002) was the princess of the Gauripur Rajbari in west Assam. Being a member of a culturally illustrious family, young Pratima had rich exposure to various cultural forms from early childhood. She received formal training in classical music as a child and gained laudable mastery in *Rabindra Sangeet*. But she found the songs of the ordinary folks of her estate to be the most haunting and abidingly mellifluous. She responded to the dulcet appeal of these rustic songs with spontaneity. These were songs that did not have a name till Pratima gave them the status of a genre. She learnt the songs from her housemaids, who would sing those songs to toddler Pratima in the corridors of the Rajbari at Gauripur in west Assam. The resonance of the songs persisted in the young heart, which she would later pick as part of her vocation. Pratima Barua Pandey cannot be seen in isolation of the cultural legacy from where the songs emanated.

The Rajbanshi historiography has the uneasy legacy of being devolved from being a mainstream chronicle to a fringe narrative. The subordination of the Rajbanshi nation and its subsequent disfiguration as a marginal entity has effectively reduced its people into a culturally impaired 'disjunctive'. But the Rajbanshis found the possibility of retrieving the lost legacies of their identity through the evocation of their folk universe, which was still there in the recesses of their communal memory. Returning to the folk roots has become a means of regaining their lost consciousness.

The folk repository of the Rajbanshis is a rich treasure. But against the backdrop of the changed socio-political context, the cultural elements no longer remain neutral manifestations of folk innocence. The myths, the familiar images, the landscapes, the folk gods and goddesses, the banal body of the individuals and myriad other assortment of cultural references transform into chronotopic metaphors. They become potential catalysts for the evocation of a displaced nation's emotional geography. From the brink of near oblivion, the myths, the rituals, the lores and other intimate cultural ingredients find resurrection through the songs of Pratima Barua Pandey, and their temporal reconfigurations in her songs turned them into tangible artefacts of a culture's endangered historiography, as it were.

The songs that Pratima Barua Pandey retrieved were very much the part of the folk narrative of the Rajbanshis. There were singers who became quite eminent prior to Pratima. Some of them were the singers like Surendranath Basunia,[1] Tagar Adhikary,[2] and Abbas Uddin.

These artists and many more are some of the most respected names when one speaks of Rajbanshi folk songs. They are revered cultural figures for the Rajbanshis. Historically, they came to prominence when India was yet to be independent, states were yet to be reorganized on the basis of language and Coochbehar was yet to be annexed by Bengal despite huge public protest. Those were the times when the very notion of Rajbanshi nationality was yet to emerge though the social movement of the Rajbanshis had begun back in 1910 in the form of Kshatriya movement,[3] which evolved into a massive mass social movement in present Bengal and Assam under the powerful leadership of Thakur Panchanan Burma. Post-independent India brought a different urgency to the people in general and strengthened the idea of pan-Indian nationalism in the wake of which many micro-nations voluntarily suspended their claims of cultural sovereignty. But this gesture proved costly for them as they soon discovered themselves to be non-entities in the larger map of political and cultural transactions. This engendered a prolonged period of amnesia for such nations. The Rajbanshis became one such nation, agonized by this historico-cultural syndrome.

In the year 1955 when Dr Bhupen Hazarika heard the songs sung by young Pratima, who was then just twenty years old, for the first time in Gauripur Rajbari, he found them mellifluous but could not place them culturally. When he asked Pratima's father, Lalji, about the songs, he was informed that those songs had no names, that they called them *desi gaan* (country songs). The community to whom it belonged did not have a legitimate historico-cultural identity until that time; linguistically its people were devoid of their tongues, politically they were divided in such a way that they found themselves to be inhabitants of the fringes of both Bengal and Assam as well as Bihar and present Bangladesh, they were politically faceless; hence, their culture too carried no name. In Bengal they were called Bahès. It is ironical that they earned a provisional sobriquet in the land the history of which they had determined themselves in the recent past. This term is widely used even by intellectuals in a pejorative sense to describe native Rajbanshis in Bengal. The Rajbanshis address each other in informal conversations as Bahè, which has come into the Rajbanshi parlance as a popular term following its use by the Vaishnava saints in the late fifteenth century, who called each other *baap hey*, as a term to manifest both respect and affection.

However, it was Dr Bhupen Hazarika who gave the songs a name. He called them the Goalparia Folk Songs. He also recorded LP discs of Pratima's songs as *Goalparia Loka Geet*, which he used in two of his early films, *Era Bator Sur* (1956) (Tune of the abandoned roads) and *Mahut Bandhu* (1958). Though it was Pramathesh Barua who used one of these folk songs for the first time in a motion picture through his film *Mukti* (1936) (incidentally, according to Phani Talukdar, this was the first film where *Rabindra Sangeet* was used), Bhupen Hazarika turned these songs into characters. As he himself would say, "In my films the songs were the main attraction and in *Mahut Bandhu* the songs were the stars."[4]

Bhupen Hazarika sang duets with Pratima. That was a huge endorsement for the people of Goalpara; after all Bhupen Hazarika was the biggest cultural icon of Assam and his singing of the songs provided a legitimacy to the cultural expression of a confused nation. That famous ballad of the elephant damsel became a folk anthem in every household, *O Mor Hai Hastir Hanya Re*.[5]

In the context of Assam it was an urgent imperative to validate the cultural exclusivity of Goalpara, as the people had been subjected to humiliation because of their different mode of cultural and linguistic expressions. Assam resisted accepting the people of Goalpara as part of the Assamese fold. At the same time in Bengal, the Rajbanshis, in order to gain an entry into the realms of middle-class Bengal, uninhibitedly aspired to become a Bengali with very limited success. The Rajbanshis in Bengal are seen as a people belonging to a lower caste; hence, their social respectability happens to be limited.

It was Pratima Barua Pandey who had given the courage to the embittered nation to make its own cultural manifestations. The whole nation found in Pratima the realization of its collective desires and aspirations. Their deep-seated urge to redeem its collective identity obliterated history and transmuted memories. In 1962 Pratima's songs were broadcast by All India Radio, Guwahati. By that time songs of other communities like the Bodos, Misings and ethnic cultures were being broadcast. Bhupen Hazarika had to fight with Rudra Barua to have her songs broadcast. Finally, and all of sudden in 1962, people heard their songs floating on the radio waves. This changed the way the native people of Goalpara looked at themselves. She began a renaissance. Very ordinary folk instrument players, playing the *dotora*, *sarinda*, *khapi*, *jhumka* and *dhak dhol* became artists. The common Rajbanshis started learning their 'own songs'.

Pratima Barua Pandey had trouble bringing the songs onto the mainstream arena. It was not allowed initially because they were construed to be Bengali renditions and they were not broadcast in Bengal because they considered them to be Assamese renditions. In 1960, when she was performing in a programme organized by the All Assam Students Union, interestingly, they forced her to stop singing because they considered it to be Bengali songs. It was Bhupen Hazarika who had to intervene to make the irate students understand that Goalpara was, in fact, part of Assam and it had a slightly different cultural legacy.

Pratima Barua Pandey, the legendary folk artist that Assam has ever produced, was one of the most formidable cultural icons to have provided a historico- cultural address to the people through her songs. She was not only instrumental in the revival and consolidation of a folk form facing impending oblivion, but also became the subject of a vibrant folklore of our times. Her life reflects the various phases of Rajbanshi identity, and betrays how folk art is capable of acting as a syncretic energy for a community. Her songs, popularly called the *Goalparia Loka Geet*, are a part of a cultural community that has been historically dispersed around a vast territory including Assam, Bengal, Bihar, southern Nepal, the Bhutan foothills and Rongpur in present Bangladesh. When Pratima picked up the songs, they were seemingly in their last phase of life in public memory, for the history of the land had taken a sharp turn, forcing the communities living in the periphery to abandon their cultural moorings and acquire new identities to conform to the altered geopolitical legacy.

Pratima Barua Pandey emerged as the protagonist that revitalized the sagging vision of a community's self-identity. Her songs show how an apparently folk rendition can become a potential source of

Singing the Nation **223**

Illustration 16.1.
Matia Bagh Summer Palace: Where Pratima Barua Pandey Lived
Source: Prof. G.S. Pandey (husband of Pratima Barua Pandey) from his personal collection.

politico-cultural awareness of a community as well as how folk art can legitimize alternative narratives of history and expressions—both linguistic and cultural.

Pratima emerged as the cultural reference that the people were looking for. She retrieved the songs of the *mahouts* (elephant rider), the *maishals* (the buffalo herds), the *phandis* (trap setters for catching elephants), the boatmen, rural women, their private pangs and unexpressed desires, songs of the rituals like *Sona Rai, Hudum Deo, Kati Puja*[6] and myriad others. She made the continuity of a nation's cultural history possible. Her song, *Dine Dine Khasia Paribe Rangila Dalaner Mati*[7] became a haunting melody forcing the emotive evocation of people's receding history.

Without Pratima Barua Pandey the songs might have taken much more time to reach the position that they have today. Through her songs today the Rajbanshi nation's people become audacious enough to give a formative shape to their collective consciousness; they could at least get rid of the stigma of what they are—the Rajbanshis.

Illustration 16.2.

Pratima Barua Pandey (1935–2002)

Source: Prof. G.S. Pandey (husband of Pratima Barua Pandey) from his personal collection.

Notes

1. Surendranath Basunia passed the matriculation exam in first division in 1922 and joined Victoria College in Coochbehar. His father was a renowned lawyer, Dhirchandra Basunia, mercy pleader in the Coochbehar State Royal Council. Surendranath, instead of showing interest in carrying on the mantle of the family in the business of law, began to roam around in villages like Golakganj, Halakura and Bhandijealas in present Assam and Bengal in search folk music, to the great chagrin of his father who wanted him to become a pleader in the Royal Court of Coochbehar. In 1937 he recorded the first Rajbanshi *bhawaiya* songs with the gramophone company, HMV. At the time of the recording, eminent nationalist poet-singer of Bengal, Nazrul Islam, was associated with the studio and was of immense help to Surendranath in recording the songs (Adhikary 2006).
2. Among the icons of Rajbanshi folk songs, Tagar Adhikary is one of the most celebrated names. Born in 1914 (later coming to live at Kherbari village presently in Assam), he rose to fame when he went to Bombay in the year 1943 and won the prize for being the

most versatile player of the folk musical instrument, *dotora*. He later collaborated with the stalwarts like Sachin Dev Barman, Ravi Shankar and P. C. Joshi. He was also the *dotora* accompanist of Surendranath Basunia when he recorded his first disc of Rajbanshi *bhawaiya* songs with HMV. With the sheer mastery of his *dotora*, he came to enamour eminent people such as poet Sukanta Choudhury, Comrade Biren Dey, Salil Choudhury, and theatre personalities like Shambhu Mitra and Tulsi Lahiri when he became an integral part of Indian People's Theatre Association (IPTA) in 1948 (Aditya 2002).

3. The Kshatriya *andolan*, or movement, gained its formative shape in the year 1891 under the leadership of Har Mohan Ray, the widely respected zamindar of Shyampukur in Rongpur in present Bangladesh. The Rajbanshis were organized under the banner of Rongpur Bratya Kshatriya Jatir Unnati Bidhayani Sabha and presented a deputation on 10 February 1891 in front of the Rongpur District Magistrate to include the Rajbanshis as a separate ethnic entity in the census that was to begin that year. Later under the leadership of Thakur Panchanan Burma, the Kshatriya movement of the Rajbanshis took a more comprehensive shape. The first Kshatriya Sanmilani of the Rajbanshis was held on 1 May 1910 at the Theatre Hall of Rongpur. The session was presided over by an eminent lawyer, Madhusudhan Ray. The movement, for the first time, made the Rajbanshis aware, in a major way, of themselves as a distinctive social entity that needed to historically place themselves against a changed social reality in the wake of colonial rule in India, which made some different entities as the major players of administrative and economic activities (Roy 2009).

4. This was stated by Dr Bhupen Hazarika in the interview taken for the documentary film on Pratima Barua titled, *Hastir Kanya*, Directed by Prabin Hazarika, 1996. The film also got the National Award for the Best Biographical Film in 1997.

5. The song was recorded for the film *Mahout Bandhu* Directed by Dr Bhupen Hazarika. The LP disc was produced by HMV, 1958.

6. These songs are associated with the native Rajbanshi rituals for the indigenous Gods and Goddesses. *Sona Rai* is a folk god ritualistically worshipped in winter. *Hudum Deo* and *Kati* are the folk gods who symbolically represent *phallus* and are associated with fertility cult. In the rituals men are not allowed to take part only women are allowed to perform the puja with elaborate rituals.

7. *Dine Dine Khashiya Paribe Rangila Dalaner Mati*:

>It crumbles day by day
>The bright mansion moulders away
>For naught the house builds
>Futile stifles and bickering
>God it crumbles in its own way
>
>The bone house with the hide top
>Tied in knots and joints
>Underneath peacocks fan their feathers
>Mocking stars shine in the void
>
>Childhood spent. Fun and games
>Youth in enjoying
>Age in thoughts and worries
>Where is the time to worship
>God it crumbles in its own way.

(Translated by Pradip Acharya.)

References

Adhikary, Ramendranath. 2006. *Surendranath Basunia: Karma Jiban O Sangeet Sadhana* (Surendranath Basunia: His Life and Music) Coochbehar, India: Paschim Banga Adivasi O Loka Shilpi Sangha.
Aditya, Sudhanshu Shekhar. 2002. *Setu Bandhane Loka Shilpi Tagar Adhikary* (Folk Artist Tagar Adhikary in Building the Bridge). Boxirhat, India: Tagar Adhikary Memorial Cultural Committee (Toofanganj 2 Panchayat Committee).
Anderson, Benedict. 1993. *Imagined Community*. London: Verso.
Barman, Prafulla. 2004. *Axom Nandini Pratima Barua Pandey* (Assam's Damsel Pratima Barua Pandey) Guwahati, India: Vishal Prakashan.
Barman, Shanto. 2009. *Goalparar Jana Itihax* (The Folk History of Goalpara). Guwahati, India: Ashok Publications.
Barth, Fredrik 1969. *Ethnic Groups and Boundaries*. Boston, MA: Little Brown.
Bhakat, D. N. 2010. *Rajbanshi Bhasha Sahitya Aru Iyar Unnanyan* (The Rajbanshi Language Literature and its Development) Bongaigaon, India: All Assam Koch Rajbanshi Yuva Chhatra Sanmilani.
Brahmachoudhury, Suriti Sarma. 2006. *Ganor Pratima, Pranor Pratima* ([Pratima (Goddess)] of Songs, Pratima (Goddess) of Soul). Guwahati, India: Bina Library.
Chakraborty, Shyamal. 2005. *Mahut Bandhure: Pratima Barua Pandey—Jiban O Gaan* (Mahout Bandhure: Pratima Barua Pandey—Her Life and Music). Agartala, India: Gyanbichitra Prakashani.
Das, Dhiren. 1994. *Goalparia Loka Sanskriti Aru Loka Geet* (The Folk Culture and the Folk Songs of Goalpara). Guwahati, India: Chandra Prakash.
———. 1994. *O Mor Hai Hastir Kanya Rè* (O my, Daughter of Elephant) Gauripur, India: Jyotirmoy Prodhani.
Das, Dhirendranath (ed.). 2005. *Panchanan Smaranika* (Souvenir on Panchanan) Dinhata, Coochbehar, India: Thakur Panchanan Jagriti Mancha.
Gohain, Hiren 1998. "Axomot Koch Rajbonxor Gabexana" (Research on the Koch Rajbanshas in Assam), in *Romanthan* (Silver Jubilee Souvenir of Chilarai College, Golakganj, Assam), pp. 19–20. Golakganj: Chilarai College.
Shepard, Sam 1984. "Cowboy Mouth", *Fool for Love and Other Plays*, p. 157. NY: Banta Books.
Khan Choudhury, Amanatulla. 1991. "Rajbanshi Bhasha Tattva" (Facets of Rajbanshi Language), in the *Souvenir* of Uttar Banga Sahitya Sanmelan (North Bengal Literature Convention) Coochbehar.
Ray, Girija Shankar. 1996. 'Bhumika', (Foreword) in Binod Bihari Barman and Jatin Burma (eds), *Rajbanshi Kavita Sankalan* (An Anthology of Rajbanshi Poems). Kolkata: Anima Prakashani.
Roy, Dipak. 2009. *Manishi Panchanan O Asom* (Manishi Panchanan and Assam). Siliguri: Rajbanshi Academy.
Sarma, Shashi. 2006. *Goalparia Loko Sahityat Samaj Jibanor Protifolon* (Reflections of Social Life in the Folk Literature of Goalpara). Dhubri: Assam Sahitya Sabha.
Shepard, Sam. 1971. *Cowboy Mouth*. New York: Samuel French Inc.
Dhubri, India: Asom Sahitya Sabha, Dhubri Sakha.
Upasu, Shri. (ed.). 2004. *Manishi Thakur Panchananer Bani* (Words of Manishi Panchanan Thakur) Mathabhanga, Coochbehar, India: Jyotirmoy Prodhani.
Upasu, Shri. 2005. *Manishi Thakur Panchananer Jiban Katha*. Mathabhanga, Coochbehar, India.
Talukdar, Phani. 1990. *Pramathesh Barua*. New Delhi: National Book Trust.

17
The Revenant in Some Urban Legends of Shillong

Desmond L. Kharmawphlang

One of the most common aspects of urban folklore is the urban legend, which this chapter will primarily focus on, attempting to rediscover the supernatural beliefs of a modern urban community and also the rhetoric and other techniques through which those beliefs are presented. The study of two Shillong-based urban legends and their versions will be used to analyze the dynamics of what constitutes citylore. Urban legends are a genre of folklore consisting of stories often thought to be factual by those circulating them. Urban legends are not necessarily untrue but they are often false, distorted and exaggerated. Despite the name, urban legends do not always necessarily take place in an urban settir.g. The name is designed to differentiate them from traditional folklore created in pre-industrial and pre-modern times.

Collections of so-called modern, contemporary or urban legends are widespread phenomenon and the role of the media, Internet and movies has enhanced their exoteric features. Contemporary legends may be defined as stories dealing with unpleasant fearful stories or repressed subjects, which take some unexpected turns.

Urban legends are contemporary stories continually reinvented and shared among the members of a society. They contribute to the reconstruction and reaffirming of community identities and help reinforce social bonds through elaboration of the psychosocial communicational mechanism spawned at their narration.

Contemporary legends are widely regarded as the lore of modern society transmitted orally and electronically by young, school- and college-educated urbanites (Brunvand 1981: xvi). They are set in everyday life yet they are charged with a sense of peril that is often accentuated with an ironic twist. While these stories reside in the present and are regarded as disputable truth, they contain elements of ancient myths.

The study of urban folklore in the United States began in the late 1960s and 1970s, and the first occurrence of the term in its conceptual aspects was made by Jan Harold Brunvand in *Too Good to be True: The Colossal Book of Urban Legends* in which he collected more than two hundred of the most-repeated and best-known examples of modern folk-legends. This classic is not only a handy work of reference for scholars of narratives but also a good introduction to the study of urban folklore itself. This has attracted the attention of folklorists, anthropologists and culture specialists and made others pay more attention to the folklore of cities.

In the last thirty years or so, Shillong has undergone tremendous changes, the most noticeable being the explosion of its population as a result of the immigration of people from rural areas, and the influx of people coming from other parts of India and the neighbouring countries. As such, one can notice that there is widespread diffusion, assimilation and acculturation of different cultures, which has generated a great variety of folklore materials. The tremendous growth and pace of change that has occurred in Shillong city has produced social and cultural phenomena that can be considered and studied as representative examples of urban folklore. The processes of modernization coupled with the large-scale assimilation of peoples of diverse cultural, linguistic and religious backgrounds have made this city a teeming laboratory in which cultural dynamics can be examined minutely. On the streets, in homes and open spaces, in shops and stores, in schools and colleges, universities and different campuses (the list is inexhaustible!) new folklore is being created daily. To a conservative folklorist, this changed scenario would seem unfit for the generation and perpetuation of folklore but this perception has over the years changed. Folklorists now realize that such a mixture of traditions, customs, usages and beliefs produce vibrant and different kinds of folklore which reflect the contemporary life of the city.

These phenomena are of immense interest to the folklore scholar and the study of some of these aspects constitutes a very important task. In part, this chapter is also an attempt to indicate one of the concerns of folkloristics, in that the discipline is not to be viewed as a subject obsessed with the bucolic and the fanciful; rather, its strength lies in its ability to address modern-day issues and critique contemporary cultural dynamics.

The city of Shillong has undoubtedly generated urban folklore of various kinds and the concern of this chapter is to study the phenomenon as urban productions. Examples of the kind have been represented very artistically in innumerable modern creative writings, especially in novels and this corpus of material has indiscriminately made use of folklore. This wealth of material has not been studied except for their literary value. A proper analysis of this material would unearth and reveal the pervasive influence that folklore has had on these writers, thus establishing that society finds reflections in folklore.

When I was growing up in the early 1970s, there was an extremely popular story, which I shall call the 'Marina legend', revolving around the ghost of a woman of that name.

On the eve of Christmas or New Year, a young man went to a party at Pinewood Hotel where he met a beautiful woman whose name, he later came to know, was Marina. The two had fun, dancing and merrymaking till past midnight. When the party got over, he offered to drop her to her place which was somewhere in Upper Shillong. Seeing that the young woman was cold, he offered his jacket, which she gratefully accepted. On reaching the gate to her house, they bade each other farewell. The following day the man remembered about the jacket he had lent the woman and he decided to get it back. When he arrived at her house he knocked on the door and an elderly woman greeted him. When he introduced himself and stated the purpose of his visit, he was informed by the woman that Marina had expired three years ago. The man refused to believe this despite being repeatedly assured that this was the fact. Finally, in exasperation, the elderly woman offered to take him to the cemetery to which he also agreed. They went there and when they came upon Marina's grave he found his jacket hanging on the cross, on which was also inscribed the name Marina.

Folklore is replete with examples of the revenant phenomenon and surveys of documented folktales exhibit this. This reflects the working of the memorate or the personal experience story, which has great value in showing tradition actually in process, at work, shaping everyday experience. The process of traditionalizing and interpreting is accelerated when an experience is spoken of to others and this assumes the form of a narrative. From that point onwards, it becomes public, the account being, as it were, a 'discussion document'.

Folklorists have laboriously studied the socio-psychological factors of urbanization largely brought forth by massive social structure changes and folklore, being grounded in human experience, guides us to look at the ways that individuals deal with these experiences in a symbolic and expressive manner. At the core of this argument is the anxiety about resisting or coping with these changes. Taking the Marina legend, what can be detected is a subtle assertion of the way in which tradition can be interpreted through the prism of religious beliefs.

The arena where the most significant actions take place is the ballroom of Pinewood Hotel, a landmark known to most people of the city. The hotel strongly conveys a colonial heritage, both of the flattering kind as well as the dubious variety. A young man goes to a party and there he meets a complete stranger amidst possibly hundreds of other strangers in a neutral place bereft of personal and emotional ties. There, social transactions take shape in, we can assume, dimly lit circumstances. And of course, it is night-time. They get to know each other and the story suggests that they get along famously. There are also hints of familiarity if not intimacy. It is evident from the story that the couple engage in dancing and merrymaking and that their actions are not inspired by the solemn occasion of Christmas or New Year's celebrations. Traditionally, and especially on Christmas Eve, families spend time together, the more devout ones in prayer. There is also the singing of carols and feasting. All this suggests intimacy experienced in family and neighbourhood situations, the opposite of what we see happening in the story.

When the party breaks up and the couple goes on its way, the man, obviously thinks nothing of the fact that the woman, while being unaccompanied, is also hardly dressed to combat the wintry nights of Shillong. He offers his jacket, which she accepts and takes into her house when he drops her there. The following day, which was supposed to hold the promise of delighted expectation for the man, turns nightmarish and traumatic.

The legend seems to broadly hint at anxieties about transformed lifestyles when individuals are seen to abandon familiar and familial surroundings and display a readiness to fraternize with unknown people. The moving away from socially and religiously sanctioned traditions is also taken seriously with an even more serious penalty awaiting those who abrogate this coda. While analyzing the implications of the legend, we discover that its existence (or construction) is intimately linked to sociocultural factors. It is a response to the transformed lifestyles in Khasi society (at that point of time) when individuals are seen to abandon familiar and familial spaces, displaying a readiness to fraternize with unknown people. This interpretation particularly applies to the legend because the occasion of Christmas is normally associated with domestic celebration and is the one annual festival that brings most Christian families together.

As evident in the legend, the unnamed young man ventures out of home on Christmas Eve, thereby choosing the alien public sphere as a source of pleasure and entertainment. Moreover, the young man represents the Khasi youths' altered perspective, which looks at strangers and not family members as reliable and perhaps more 'exciting' counterparts. This development can be explained as a repercussion of pressurizing Western influences, making social interaction with complete strangers de rigueur in Shillong in the 1970s and 1980s.

The Marina legend also engenders multiple symbolic connotations. It is in the young man that the public and private, convention and change battle. By choosing to go to Pinewood Hotel instead of observing Christmas with his family, he is reprimanded through the traumatic experience. The traditionally sanctioned family gathering is superseded by the 'modern' gathering at a hotel with strangers. Thus, as opposed to the familial symbolism of life and regeneration, the young man who transgresses traditional practices encounters death. Hence, the crucial discovery of the death of Marina highlights the didactic nature of the story. Furthermore, the clothes and apparels of the two subjects of the story are also endowed with symbolic importance. As mentioned before, the woman is lightly dressed for a winter night in Shillong, thus prompting the young man to offer his jacket. The woman breaks the cultural dressing code by abandoning the traditional Khasi shawl called the *tapmoh*. In refusing this apparel, Marina also rejects notions of dignity and respect, which the *tapmoh* represents. Moreover, the spectacle of the young man's jacket hanging on the cross of Marina's tombstone carries the idea that the gesture of care and protection (offering the jacket to the woman) is now diverted to a stranger rather than to family. This is similarly met with a confrontation with death.

Another interpretation of the episode would be the unwelcoming attitude of society vis-à-vis the growth of private enterprises such as restaurants. Again, considering the occasion of Christmas being a domestically celebrated affair, the blooming fashion of 'eating-out' even on such occasions is received as a threat by the community in general. Now, we witness the transfer of domestic functions like cooking to private enterprises. Gary Alan Fine (1980) opines, "A recent societal change is that government and profit-making organizations have assumed social functions which formerly the family, neighbors or local charitable organizations handled." This is an overarching statement which underlines transformations even in the nature of family ties and threaten their closeness. A simple 'eating-out' on Christmas indicates the weakening family values as well as the limited (or lack of) communication within the family. Moreover, unlike homemade food, food from restaurants is looked at with suspicion, as the contents of the dishes are never known to the consumer.

The Marina legend, like several other urban legends, is born at the cusp of two consecutive (though conflicting) modes of sociocultural traditions. The variant parts, which constitute and mould the telling of the Marina legend, can be read as a reflection of the collective conscious or unconscious of the Khasi community. The inherent didacticism of the story is attributive of the existing anxieties of the community, when faced with cultural transformation, also resulting in changes in the social and familial structures.

An interesting feature of a certain post-cremation ceremony of the Khasis is the *pyngrei* which is performed a year after the cremation of a male member of a clan who died as a bachelor. The ceremony involves a mock marriage between two actors—a male and a female—who are hired for the purpose. The two actors are also required to eat rice from one common plate and jump over a mortar and pestle. It is only after the performance of this ceremony that the bones of the male member of the clan can be prepared for deposition in the clan *mawbah* or cairn.

It is interesting to draw an analogy between what happens in the legend and what constitutes the requirement of the *pyngrei* ceremony if one is open to see the paradigms constructed with inverse characteristics and features, which is a widely prevalent construction of folk psychology. The legend involves the relationship between an unmarried woman and man on an occasion, and in an environment, of celebration. They share drinks and meals and also participate in the merriment. However, there is no hint of resolution because the story produces a critical episode that culminates at the graveyard, a space usually associated with spectral experiences. This crisis is brought about by the man who is interested in sustaining his liaison with the woman and even when informed about her death years ago, refuses to believe it and insists on seeing the evidence of her death personally. The semiotic significance of the jacket being left hanging on the cross cannot be missed as it provides the more-than-expected evidence of her demise. The jacket proves that his one night's relationship or affair was with a revenant, a relationship that could not be contemplated as one is seen as belonging to the realm of the living and the other to the dead.

Pinewood Hotel, in the minds of many, represents a colonial or semi-colonial edifice. It is also my experience that structures associated with colonial times are believed to have an aura of supranatural characteristics. There are innumerable narratives about houses and sites used by colonial civil and military officers being haunted. There are still many of these houses in the city and also dotting across the length and breadth of the Khasi and Jaintia hills (many of which are lying in dilapidated condition). I have personally visited many of them and have collected anecdotes about abnormal happenings in many of them. A well-known Khasi novelist, Remy Phankon, has made use of such material to write a splendid novel entitled *Ka Dak Bangla* (1987). In the novel, contemporary characters have horrifying experiences during a night of revelry in one such house. While it is not one's intention to say that Pinewood Hotel is a site where paranormal things occur, one suspects that the creators of the Marina legend cycle cannot resist suggesting it as a place (because of its iconic position) where abnormal transactions may take place.

In 2004, a young pregnant woman whose name was Corphelia was brutally murdered by her husband. Five years later, immediately after the pronouncement of sentence for the accused (life imprisonment), the tale of a young woman hailing cabs and asking to be dropped at Riatsamthiah, a locality of Shillong, began to make the rounds in the city. What was strange was that on reaching a house in that locality, she would produce a five-hundred-rupee note and offer it as fare. The taxi driver would not have the necessary change and she would request him to wait while she got it from the house but she would not come back. The driver would go inside and be informed that the woman he described as the passenger died some years ago.

It would appear that belief in this type of reverent gains its impetus from experience of bereavement. Through the memorates (people) tell of this type of supernatural encounter, we are able to see tradition at work, interpreting and transforming experience, turning the strange states of mind and emotions common while grieving into objective encounters with the dead. This is especially true in the case of an unnatural death (murder, death by accident, suicide, etc.), which causes the coming into order of a phenomenon called *tyrut*. During my interviews with knowledgeable persons and those who have actually experienced its effects, the *tyrut* is described as an aura, a felt presence at a certain location of the most ominous kind (of evil), which threatens to unleash a repetition of the horrific acts of violence it is a product of. I know for a fact that homes and entire villages have shifted due to fears about the effects of *tyrut*. It is believed that on a particularly dark night, sounds of the agonizing torment of the dead are heard and this is referred to as the moaning of blood. It brings with it all the associations of the ominous and requires a cleansing ritual to stop its recurrence.

The concept of the revenant is not new to the Khasis and there are spectacular stories, both old and new, about them. What causes them to appear and negotiate the realm of the living is usually due to a sense of dissatisfaction of being denied something. In fact, those who die unnatural deaths are kept in a makeshift arrangement outside the house pending the funeral. It is also believed that those who perish in circumstances where their bodies are not retrieved, their spirits become disturbed and tormented. They may also trouble people. The reports of the sightings of Corphelia can be attributed to a host of factors which are grounded in folk belief and practice and one cannot downplay the role of the media in this because the gruesome murder and the protests and agitations it created were an important feature. The trial and subsequent sentencing of the murderer–husband was also followed up and reported in newspapers, on television and radio.

Bereavement, its physiology and psychology has been a subject of study by psychiatrists interested in pathological grief reactions. Researchers have noted that apart from the obvious physical and mental symptoms, what is also detected is the prevalence of hallucination, through intense and consistent memory sustenance of the dead person.

Modern study of the revenant, who is a victim or subject of unnatural death, has not been attempted much in Khasi folklore studies although substantial work has been done on the ancestor revenant phenomenon in ceremonies and religious practices of clans. This chapter is also an account of the work being done on urban legend collection, formulation of terms, definitions and creation of types and subtypes.

References

Brunvand, Jan Harold. 1981. *Too Good to be True: The Colossal Book of Urban Legends*. New York: W.W. Norton & Company Inc.
Fine, Gary Alan. 1980 'The Kentucky Fried Rat: Legends and Modern Society', *Journal of Folklore Institute*. Bloomington: Indiana University Press.
Phankon, Remy. 1987. *Ka Dak Bangla*. (The Bungalow). Shillong: G.B. Fancon.

18
Inter-Community Relations in Medieval Bengal as Reflected in Contemporary Bengali Vernacular Literature

Muhammad Shah Noorur Rahman

Medieval Bengal neither has any authoritative nor any continuous contemporary sociocultural historiography except Mirza Nathan's *Baharistan-i-Ghaibi*. This is a work on political history, which hardly throws light on the social conditions of Bengal. It deals with the expansion of the Mughal Empire in Bengal, Kamrup and Assam. Sir Jagadish Narayan Sarkar aptly describes the work as "an oasis in the desert of historical ignorance." Immediately after the British conquest of Bengal, the British administrators sought to collect all relevant details on the geographical, social and economic conditions of Bengal for the convenience of their administration. They also wrote history for the same purpose. Obviously the British historians were not free from bias. That is why Bankim Chandra Chattopadhyay declared.

> The works of history composed by Englishman are not true histories of Bengal....What is required is the history of Bengal; otherwise there is no hope for Bengal. Who will write it? You will write, I will write, all of us will write. Come, let us all write the history of Bengal.
>
> Translated into English by Jagadish Narayan Sarkar.

Even today there exists no standard full-fledged social history of medieval Bengal. Nevertheless, Bengali literature had attained its maturity and had definitely come into being during the period under review. Though no original work on the social history of contemporary Bengal exists, the typical Bengali mind was truly portrayed in the literature of this period. In this chapter an attempt has been made to focus on inter-community relations, mainly, Hindu–Muslim relations in medieval Bengal as reflected in the contemporary Bengali vernacular literature, namely *Mangal Kavya, Vaishnava Sahitya, Anubad Sahitya, Islami Bangla Sahitya, Purba Banga Gitika, Mymansingh Gitika, Punthi Sahitya, Atharo Bhatir Panchali, Sufi Sahitya, Pir Sahitya*, etc.

In studying the social conditions of medieval Bengal one has to bear in mind that the subject is very controversial. So I would have to critically examine different views on it. It will not suffice if one uses only one-sided materials, or if attention is focused only on one side of the picture. On the one hand, one has to admit that enmity existed in the political relations between the Hindus and the Muslims. The tradition kept the communal gulf wide open. The glory of one, for example, the stories of triumphs, the killing of Hindus and their slavery, constituted a source of shame and humiliation for the other. The breaking of idols and destruction of temples were proper and glorious to one but were to the other despicable, and considered to be a sacrilege of desecration. On the other hand, a different picture emerges if one turns from mere political relations and political history and from theoretical or legal works to study the life of the common man as depicted in contemporary literature.

As a matter of fact, from incidental references in contemporary literature one learns that the history of Hindu–Muslim relations is not a continuous and monotonous account of mere intolerance and different manifestations thereof. Even in literature one sees at times a bright picture and a reference to mutual influences in livelihoods. It is easily discernible from this that along with instances on blind bigotry a favourable atmosphere of mutual tolerance in society and culture was also developing.

First of all, one may use three distinct types of Bengali literature of the medieval period for the present purpose—(*a*) *Mangal Kavya*, (*b*) *Vaishnava Sahitya* and (*c*) *Anubad Sahitya*.

Mangal Kavya

The Muslim invasion hit the Brahmins severely. For this reason, a section of Brahmins revised their conservative stand and came to a compromise.

The Brahmins were proud of their position in society in religious matters and disapproved of the low-class Hindus and their ways of life. But after the victory of the Turks, it was no longer possible for the Brahmins to look down upon the lower-class Hindus and disavow their gods, goddesses and mythology. They had also to give them a place and niche in literature. This literature, composed mainly of the stories of Hindu and Buddhist goddesses, is known as *Mangal Kavya* (Haldar 2).

The *Mangal Kavyas* were composed in the fifteenth, sixteenth and seventeenth centuries. These three centuries witnessed the birth of *Bratagita Panchalis* (small poetic works with religious vows sung in honour of a deity). Jagadish Narayan Sarkar writes (1985: 81–82):

> In connection with narration of the greatness of the village gods and goddesses, based on a fusion of chronicle and fairy tale, these narrative poems fit to be sung were first composed on three deities. In chronological order these were *Manasa Mangal*, *Chandi Mangal* and *Dharma Mangal*.[1]

Manasa Mangal

A large number of poets of medieval Bengal wrote *Manasa Mangal Kavyas* one after another. Vijay Gupta was the most remarkable poet among them. He wrote his book during the reign of Sultan Jalaluddin Fateh Shah in 1494. He comments on the Sultan (quoted in Kalim 1988: 62–63):

> The king was as valorous as Arjuna in the battle and was as beautiful as the morning sun.
> He ruled over the world with his own prowess.
> The subjects were happy under the efficient administration of the king.

Here, the Hindu poet praises the Sultan for the happiness in the minds of his subjects and compares him with Arjuna, the hero of Mahabharata. Without a good environment of mutual living between the Hindus and the Muslims such a poem could not have been composed by a Hindu poet of contemporary Bengal.

Ksemananda composed his *Manasa Mangal* in the mid-seventeenth century. He writes that in the house of one of the poem's Hindu figures

(Laksmindhar, son of Chand Saudagar), a copy of the Koran was kept along with other charms for the purpose of warding off evil influence (D. C. Sen 1954: 674). A poet of Barishal, East Bengal wrote in 1494, "In this instance, the written word appeared not in a Hindu household but in the hands of a mulla. A group of seven weavers, evidently Muslims, since they resided in Husainhati" (Zbavitel 1976: 161–62), were bitten by snakes unleashed by the goddess Manasa and went to the court of the Qazi seeking help. The poet wrote (quoted in Eaton 1994: 294–95):

> There was a teacher of qazi named Khalas ... who always engaged himself in the study of the Quran and other religious books.... He said, if you ask me, I say, why are you afraid of demons (*bhut*), when we have got the religious books. Write (extracts) from the book and hang it down the neck. If then also the demons (implying snakes) bite, I shall be held responsible. The qazi accepted what the mullah said and all present to amulets from him (the mullah).

The above verse argues that in the society there was acceptability between the Hindus and the Muslims in times of danger. Richard M. Eaton (1994: 295) interprets this in the following manner:

> Here we see a Muslim ritualist meditating on the people's behalf with a class of ubiquitous spirits, *bhut*, that pervaded (and still pervades) the folk Bengali cosmology.... In modern times, too, one finds ritualists employing the magical power of the Quran for healing purposes in precisely the manner that mullahs had done three centuries earlier.[2]

This may be interpreted as an indication of mutual respect between the two communities.

Chandi Mangal

A few poems were composed during the sixteenth century using the background of the story of Kalketu, a hunter-cum-merchant, based on the greatness of the goddesses Chandi. Among all the *Chandi Mangal Panchalis*, Mukundaram Chakraborty's *Kavikankan Chandi* is the most famous. It was written in about the last quarter of the sixteenth century. Sukumar Sen (1948: 514) says:

It is doubtful if such a complete picture of Bengal and the Bengali people is available elsewhere in Bengali literature. His proficiency in Sanskrit literature and rhetoric, his knowledge and experience of customs and usages (*desi vidya* or *lok vyavahar*) and other matters are really surprising.

Translated into English by the author.

But the book is also valuable for the pictures in it draw on Hindu–Muslim relations. Kalketu, the hero, goes from Kalinga and builds the town of Gujarat. These might be imaginary towns, but the description of those Muslims who had left Kalinga and settled in Gujarat is not imaginary. It is a graphic representation what he actually saw in social life. As he writes (S. Sen 1992: 343):

> Leaving the city of Kalinga, the ryots of all castes settled in the city of the Bir [the hunter of the story] with their household goods. Accepting the pan [betel] of the Bir, as a token of their consent to the agreement the Mussalmans settled there. The western end of the town was assigned to them as their abode. Then came the Syeds, Maulanas, Qazis, mounted on horses, and the Bir gave them rent-free land for their houses. At the extreme end of their settlement they made their Hosenhati, a place of Muharram Tazia and they congregated all about the place.

Translated into English by the author.

Mukundaram Chakraborty suggests that the Hindus and the Muslims who live in the land as close neighbours should learn to live in amity. The poet had no sympathy with manifestation of haughty aloofness or the spirit of scornful nonchalance in one community towards the other. He implies that the Muslims lived in a quarter of their own, separate from that of the Hindus and refers, apparently regretfully, to the customs of the two communities.

In his work, Mukundaram Chakraborty also depicts a picture of the daily life of the Muslims in his time. He only expresses the attitudes and feelings of the Hindus towards the Muslims. He says (S. Sen 1992: 343–45):

> They rise very early in the morning, and spreading a red mat they offer their prayers five times during the day. Counting the *Sulaimani* beads, they meditate on Prophet Muhammad. Each of them contributes to the decoration of the *Mokam* [pir's house]—ten or twenty persons sit together and decide cases always referring to the Quran, while other sitting in the

marketplace distribute the pir *shirni* [the confectionary offered to the pir], beat the drum and raise the flag. They were very wise according to their own estimation, they never yield to anyone, and they never give up the *roza* or fast as long as they have life in them. Their appearance is rather formidable. They have no hair in their head but they allow their beard to grow down their chest. Travelling from one village to another, they offer prayers in every house as the disciples of spiritual guides or pirs. With beads in their heads some travel as leaders with black turbans on their heads as their symbols. They always adhere to their own ways. They wear on their head *topi* [cap] which has ten sides, and an *ijar* [pyjama] tied tight round the waist. If they meet one who is bare headed, they pass him by without uttering a word, but going aside, they throw clods of earth at him. Many *mians* [Muslims] with their followers sit there, they do not use water, but wipe their hands on their clothes after taking their foods. All four classes of Pathan sit there.... *Maktabs* also were set up where young Muslims were taught by pious Maulavis.

Translated into English by the author.

The salient features in the daily life of the Muslims depicted by the poet prove that he had close contact with the Muslims, otherwise such a description would not have been possible. Without good social relations between the Hindus and the Muslims how could a Hindu poet like Mukundaram Chakraborty know about the intricacies of the daily lives of the Muslims? The Muslims in the picture are represented as a highly devotional class of men. Mukundaram Chakraborty's account suggests that the education of the boys was not neglected by the Muslims of those days and the teaching imparted in the *maktabs* (elementary schools) could not have been altogether separated from religion. No communal sentiment in such a picture of society can be traced.

Dharma Mangal

The worship of Dharma Thakur or Dharmaraj (Raya) which had begun during the Sultanate period in Bengal as a result of the mixed practices of the Buddhists, Muslims and Hindus were also prevalent in Mughal Bengal. Many poets wrote *Dharma Mangal Kavyas*. Ghanaram Chakraborty is one of them. He completed his work in 1781. In his work (*Dhakurpala Part*) Ghanaram describes the settled locality of different castes, creeds and religions. He writes about the Muslims (quoted in Kalim 1988: 75):

In the heart of the town the Muslims settled themselves as a separate community. Many Mirs, Syeds and Pathans got high status there. The Mughals and the Shaikhs well versed in battle also settled there. They shared among themselves a piece of bread and were wholly absorbed in battle.[3]

Translated into English by the author.

One learns from the above verses that the poet had a good knowledge of the Muslim community and without close contact between the two communities the poet would not have been aware of the Muslims in such measure.

Ray Mangal

Ray Mangal is one of the important *Mangal Kavyas*. Here also one readily sees local cosmologies expanding in order to accommodate new superhuman beings introduced by foreign Muslims. *Ray Mangal*, a poem composed in 1686, celebrated both the Bengali tiger god Dakshin Ray (king of South Bengal) and a Muslim pioneer named Bara Ghazi Khan. This poem describes that the conflict between the two was resolved, not by one defeating or displacing the other, but by the elevation of Bara Ghazi Khan to the status of a revered saint, and by the peaceful co-existence of the two figures, who would thenceforth hold a dual religious authority over the Sundarban forests of southern Bengal. This dual authority was represented by the installation of the symbol of the tiger god's head at the burial mound of the Muslim saint. The two were not, however, fused into a single religious personage, but remained mutually distinct. The agent who resolved the conflict between Dakshin Ray and Bara Ghazi Khan was neither the Hindu god Krishna nor the Islamic Prophet Muhammad, but a single figure represented as half Krishna and half Muhammad (A. Bhattacharjee 1947: 49–50). That is why Eaton (1994: 270) comments: "Islamic super human agencies were thus associated with indigenous agencies at two levels, though not yet fully identified with them."

Annada Mangal Kavya

Bharat Chandra Ray, also known as Ray Gunakar, the court poet of Maharaja Krishna Chandra Ray of Nadia (one of the influential zamindars of the nawabs of Bengal) composed *Annada Mangal Kavya* in 1752. It throws light on mid-eighteenth-century Bengal (Bandyopadhyay and Das 1369 B.S.: 16).

In *Annada Mangal* there is an imaginary conversation between Emperor Jahangir and Bhabananda Majumdar, an ancestor of Krishna Chandra Ray. Jahangir criticized the customs and rituals of the Hindus before Bhabananda. The latter could not and did not tolerate these blasphemies. He retaliated by mocking at Islam. The fictitious dialogue merely suggests that religious difference could be discussed freely.

As *Annada Mangal* was recited with music in the court of the king, where the courtiers were both Hindus and Muslims (p. 13),[4] it may be assumed that the poet did not present anything which would go against either community or religion.

Poet Kalidasa says, "I don't consider my technique to be satisfactory until the experts are satisfied." Bharat Chandra Ray was perhaps cognizant of Kalidasa's dictum and tried to please both the Hindus and the Muslim courtiers.

Bharat Chandra Ray says, through Bhabananda Majumdar:

> For the Hindus, the Muslims and the other human beings and for the animals, God is for all and there are no two opinions in this. Is there anything different in the spiritual ruling in the Purana and the Quran? You, the Hindus and you also the Muslims, think over it. (p. 307)
>
> Translated into English by the author.

Here the poet preaches the ideal of one God for all. He argues from the theological point of view that God is singular to the Hindus and Muslims. There is no orthodoxy in the poet's mind. Rather, he tries to preach religious synthesis.

Vaishnava Sahitya

Sixteenth century Bengal witnessed a new wave of bhakti cult, better known as Vaishnavism. A new force arose during this period in Bengal with the philosophy of equality and brotherhood under the leadership of Sri Chaitanya (1486–1533) (Sarkar 1984: 103). The Bengalis became transformed into an entire and integrated nation by the cords of bhakti (devotion) of Chaitanya. He had a deep love and great sympathy for human beings. Many poets composed verses about him and his philosophy in Bengal. The poems versified by the love of God and Radha–Krishna love or dalliance are known as *Vaishnava Kavya*.

Brindavandas and Krishnadas Kaviraj were the two most famous authors of Vaishnava literature in Bengal during the Sultanate period. They wrote that the Qazi of Nabadwip tortured the Vaishnavas. They were not tortured out of communal feeling but for political reasons. The non-Vaishnavas like the Saktas and the Naiyaiks complained to the Qazi against the Vaishnavas to stop *namkirtan* (devotional songs). The qazi ordered the stoppage of *namkirtan* to avoid conflict between the Vaishnavas and non-Vaishnavas. But it is remarkable to note that there is not a single instance that proves that the Muslim masses opposed the Vaishnava movement in any way.

It is interesting to note that a large number of Muslim poets appeared with Vaishnava sentiment, in Bengal in general and Sylhet region in particular, during the period of review. They have become remarkable like their Hindu counterparts in the world of Vaishnava literature by writing some *padas* about the amorous dalliance between Radha and Krishna. They were professedly Muslims in religion and though there is no evidence that they ever embraced Vaishnavism, they actually wrote Vaishnava *padas*.[5] A mere perusal of the verses without knowing the names of their composers would not enable a reader to discover whether these were composed by a Hindu Vaishnava or a Muslim Vaishnava for these are full of Vaishnava spirit. They preach the message of religious synthesis and tolerance in their poems. Jatindra Mohan Bhattacharya has traced 162 Muslim poets with Vaishnava sentiments and a little above 900 verses in his recent book, *Banglar Vaishnav Bhabapanno Musalman Kavir Padomanjusha* (1984). Unfortunately their dates are not always available. However, irrespective of their dates, the sentiments underlying their writings are significant and point to valuable conclusions. While Sashibhusan Dasgupta holds that most of them belonged to nineteenth and twentieth centuries (Rahman 2001), it is quite plausible to hold, with Sarkar, that traditions of such mutual toleration can be traced much earlier in contemporary literature even outside Bengal as well as in *Islami Bangla Sahitya* (Sarkar 1985: 89–90). In the writing of Sufi pir Qutban of Northern India (*Mrigavat* 1512), and a few other authors such traditions are available. Malik Muhammad Jaisi's (of Awadh) *Padmavat* (1520–40), in Awadhi, also preaches the message of Hindu–Muslim fusion. Mian Sadhan's Awadhi *Meinsat* (*Mayna Sati*) also bears the clear impress of Vaishnava lyrics. This tradition was also followed in Bengal. Sarkar (1985: 98) says that even though most of the poets belonged to the eighteenth century, some at least belonged to an earlier period. Most of these Muslim poets were inhabitants of Eastern Bengal (now Bangladesh)—versifiers of Srihatta (Sylhet), Chittagaon, Tripura and Mymansingh exceeded in number than those from other places. Asim Roy (1983: 187) says, "Ranging from the sixteenth to the early years of the present century, these Muslim *pada* compositions have been gradually recovered and published in relatively old and recent compilations of Bengali padas." From these arguments one might hold that there were a few Muslim poets with Vaishnava sentiments during the period under review. It is needless to say that the cultural value of the poems and songs is very important and significant. Even though they are poems and historical sources, they are nonetheless valuable as factors throwing light on the mental outlook and approach of the composers. The trend of composing poems with Vaishnava inclination by Muslims is especially helpful in understanding the oneness of the Bengali people and broadness of their mind during the medieval period.

This literature can be divided into a six-fold category, following Jatindra Mohan Bhattacharya (1984: 15), which has been adopted by E. C. Dimock. The six categories are:

1. Pure Vaishnava poetry, in which the quality of devotion and poetic style make the poem indistinguishable from one written by a Hindu Vaishnava.
2. Philosophical poetry, in which ideas neither specifically Hindu nor specifically Muslim are expressed with the help of imagery drawn from the Radha–Krishna story.
3. Poetry that employs the names Radha and Krishna to designate not the Radha and Krishna of Vaishnava text and belief, but an abstract God.
4. A purely secular poetry of love.
5. Poetry on Chaitanya.
6. Poetry using subsidiary Vaishnava themes, but without clear mention of Radha, Krishna or Chaitanya.

However, Asim Roy is critical of this classification. One finds that this classification is diffused, overlapping and inadequate for providing for a clear basis of differentiation. Here, since the purpose is only to examine the Vaishnava sentiment of the versifiers in the verses, one may avoid classifying the verses into categories.

Inter-Community Relations in Medieval Bengal 245

Only a few Muslim poets with Vaishnava inclinations such as Daulat Qazi and Alaol, of the seventeenth century, will be mentioned here. A Sufi devotee, the poet Daulat Qazi, was at once the greatest Bengali Muslim poet and one of the most powerful poets of old Bengali literature. The poem *Sati Mayna*, which Daulat Qazi composed on the basis of Mian Sadhan's Awadhi *Meinsat* of the sixteenth century, is an incomplete *Panchali* poem. In *Sati Mayna* along with the adoration of Allah and Rasul (the Prophet) are mentioned the Dwarka of Krishna, dramatic performances of descriptions of twelve months (*baromasya pala*), various melodies, stories from the Puranas, Hindu dresses and *kirtan*. It also bears the clear impress of Vaishnava lyrics. The name of Alaol, an inhabitant of Faridpur district of eastern Bengal (now in Bangladesh), in the seventeenth century, is very important in this field. His best work is *Padmavat*, which was written in 1651 at the request of Magon Thakur, a minister of Arakan Raj. It is the Bengali adaption of *Padmavat* by the Awadhi poet, Malik Muhammad Jaisi (Rahman 2001: 73).

This work can rightly be considered as a bridge of Hindu–Muslim friendship. Alaol was a gifted Bengali Muslim poet. He adopted a pure Vaishnava theme for his lyrics. He writes about Radha's secret meeting with Krishna, going early in the morning and returning late at nightfall. For this, she is taken to task by her sister-in-law. Radha finds some excuses to tide over the dilemma and difficulty (Rahman 2001: 73). Such is the theme of the piece.

Most poems of the devout Vaishnavas can be regarded as Radha–Krishna allegories. The Sufi pir and Vaishnava poet Syed Murtaza prays thus (quoted in J. M. Bhattacharjee 1984: 317):

Carry me across, carry me across, oh boatman Kanai
Oh Kanai, do thou ferry me across.
Oh Kanai, thou art the custodian of the ferry ghat and the watchman of the path.
I offer my fresh youth as the ferry fare.
The market time is well past, but there is no transaction.
See the sun has reached the meridian.
Oh Radha, the milkmaid,
Lost are all the milkmaids in the market of Kanaiya.

Translated into English by the author.

Though Lal Mahmud was born in a Muslim family, he was a devotee of Krishna; he says of himself (J. M. Bhattacharjee 1984: 250):

> Though born as a Muslim, I do not ever think that I shall be deprived of the sacred feet [of Krishna].
> Now, Lal Mahmud has indeed accepted the name of Hare Krishna as his be all and end all.

He further says (J. M. Bhattacharjee 1984: 250):

> Whether a Hindu or a Muslim, it is all the same to you,
> Who considers the caste of one's own son?
>
> A bhakta [devotee] is the best of all castes whether he is a *chandal* [low caste] or a *chamar* [cobbler]
> Some call you Kali; some call you *banamali* [literally the gardener, here Krishna] and others call you Khoda and Allah; this is the secret [essence] of all secrets.

Chand Qazi says that Radha was very much devoted to the songs of Krishna's flute. He writes (J. M. Bhattacharjee 1984: 96):

> Chand Qazi says on hearing his (i.e. Krishna's) flute I cannot restrain my tears.
> In sooth, I will not live unless I see Hari.

These verses clearly demonstrate the cultural integration among the masses of Hindus and Muslims. It is evident from the above examples that it was in Bengal that at one time the message of Hindu–Muslim amity was uttered by the Muslims and the degree of emphasis laid on such a message.

The influence of the yoga system is also clear on the natural cultivation of love (*sahaj prem sadhana*). This is the common belief that the supreme beloved resides within our body, which is like a house. Sarkar says (1985: 101–2):

> The same sentiments of the same tunes run through the Sahajiya songs of the Buddhists, the Sahajiya songs of the Vaishnavas in the thought of the Sufi devotee in India. In practical sense in the eyes of the Bauls of Bengal the body itself is the temple. The same emotion pervades the description of the love sports by Radha-Krishna of the Muslim Vaishnava poets of Bengal, the poems and songs dealing with physiology-based relation of the individual and soul and the Supreme Being. One is the house (*ghar*) the other is the dweller (*gharani*). If Krishna represented the house Radha

Inter-Community Relations in Medieval Bengal 247

was the dweller. If Radha was the house Krishna was the house-holder. This dalliance between the *deha* (body, shape) and *dehi* (embodied soul) the *murta* (corporeal) and *amurta* (incorporeal), *sima* (limit) and *asim* (limitless) constitute the inscrutable mystery of the absolute.

Poet Shahanur describes the body to be the tryst between Radha and Kanu. According to the poet Radha is the body, Kanu or Krishna is the mind (here, soul). He further narrates that in Radha's abode of this transitory body, Kanu or the eternal soul is like a sojourner. Some poets say just the reverse. For example, we may mention a verse of poet Uchhman or Usman. He says (quoted in J. M. Bhattacharjee 1984: 317):

> Radha and Kanu reside together in the same room (in the same body), the two are not separate beings.
> The boat sails day and night taking the name of Radha.
> Kanu and Radha dwells forever in the same room (i.e. body).
> If cruel Radha deserts Kanu, he will surely be ruined.

Here Radha represents mind or soul, Kanu only the body. So if cruel Radha (*pran*) leaves, that is, if life becomes extinct, Kanu, the body, is destroyed.

In the songs composed by the Muslim poets on Radha–Krishna *lila* different sentiments and terms associated with the pursuit of yoga are often found scattered in various forms. It is quite clear from the song of Gholam Huchhan (Hussain) that the Muslim poets reached the very depth of yoga and that this would not have been possible if there had been no cultural synthesis between the Hindus and the Muslims. It is necessary to mention the time of Ghulam Huchhan (Hussain). The *pada* by Ghulam Hussain was published in 1854 Saka or AD 1776. in Abahan Patrika by Syed Hassan Ali in the Asomiya language. So I think that the poet's time was earlier than AD 1776. Ghulam Hussain composes:

> The boat built of unseasoned wood floats in mid-Jamuna and the pole for shoving the boat is made of unripe bamboo hence black-coloured is now the dress of Radha.
> Oh Rai! Look keeping your eyes fixed on (Har's) eyes.
> Hari is inside the boat, his feet adorned with anklet bells jingling.
> Set your ears on his ears and row the boat.
> Straight in front of the nose.

And drink the honey of Hari, by a mouth-to-mouth kiss.
The prow of the boat, Rai, moves ahead towards heaven.
By following the right path Radha will surely attain Hari.

Translated into English by the author.

A few Muslim poets with Vaishnava inclinations have described God by using the name of Radha–Krishna. To Hachhan Raja Chaudhury of Sylhet district there is no difference between Radha and Khoda. He addresses Radha as Rahim and Rabbani:

I long for you, oh! You beautiful Radha, I yearn after you.
For you Bengali Hachhan Raja roams with tears.
The Hindus call you Radha, I say you are Khoda.
If I invoke you as Radha, the Mullahs and the Munshis prevent me.
I will not allow this difference to exist.
Whatever the Mullahs and Munshis say is just nonsense.

(Quoted in J. M. Bhattacharjee 1984: 346)

He further says,

Oh my precious Radha, oh my precious Radha,
Why does my mind hanker after you?
Listen to me, oh Radha, you, the queen of the world.
I do not agree that only the Hindus invoke you as Radha.
Nothing exists except Allah, the rest is blank.
Repeatedly does Hassan Raja call you Rahim and Rabbani and also Subhani.
He calls Allah—Allah, I know not except one.

(Quoted in J. M. Bhattacharjee 1984: 346)

It is a wonder to see such a revolutionary change and radical shift in the field of literature on the soil of Bengal. This change was brought by the monotheist followers of Islam who were theoretically different from the Hindu idol worshippers. They broke the narrow limit of communalism, and casting all hesitations, composed books on the Hindu religion, wrote songs on mother Kali, described her greatness and wrote authoritative works on Natha literature. Sukur Mahmud's *Gopichander Sannayas* and Faizullah's *Goroksha Vijaya* may be mentioned in this context for their contribution to Natha literature. Even today, after taking a bath in the Ganges many orthodox Hindus recite the *Gangastak* (hymn to the Ganga), composed in Sanskrit by Daraf Khan, the Muslim poet of Tribeni. Daraf Khan's work proved his liberalism. It is very interesting to note that Daraf Khan was felicitated by the contemporary Muslims instead of scolding him for his pro-Hindu attitude. "At Tribenighat I adore Daraf Khan, whose water for ablutions was supplied by the Ganges" (Qadir and Karim 1945: 31).

The present subject matter is very important for the social and cultural history of Bengal. The united devotional exercises of the two communities helped the integration of Hindus and Muslims in Bengal during the period of review from which the contemporary world can draw lessons.

Anubad Sahitya

Neither the alien Muslim rulers nor the Muslim masses in Bengal had any knowledge of the Puranas and other classical works of the Hindus written in Sanskrit. In their quest for knowledge about Hinduism they desired the translation of the Sanskrit works into Bengali. There is also another opinion. During this period social conditions were not favourable for creating any type of literature, because uncertainty still reigned in the society, and literature supplied the only relief to mental liberation. For this reason the Muslim rulers were interested in translating works. The Bengali translations of the three holy scriptures, *Ramayana, Mahabharata* and *Srimad Bhagabata*, which started with the Iliyas Shahis and continued under the Hussain Shahis, fulfilled the mental urges of both the communities, Hindus and Muslims. This trend of undertaking translations was also followed by the Mughal rulers.

Had the Muslim rulers of medieval Bengal not offered help to translate Hindu religious texts, the Bengalis would have had to wait long to receive them. One may understand from these translations that the Muslim rulers were respectful towards Hindu religious philosophy as they took initiatives for such translations.

Islamic Bengali Literature

Though the process of Hindu–Muslim cultural synthesis began to be reflected in Bengali literature during the Sultanate rule in Bengal, Islamic

Bengali literature during the Mughal period too illustrates significant aspects of it. It is interesting to note that while the Hindu poets were primarily and mainly concerned with stories of the greatness of deities, the Muslim poets clung to the stream of romantic narrative poems and love songs. They also wrote numerous compositions regarding Hindu gods and goddesses. As regards Hindu–Muslim understanding, the writings of three Muslim poets of the seventeenth century, Sabirid Khan, Daulat Qazi and Alaol are very important.

A new tendency was seen in Bengali literature, namely, to write biographies of Prophet Muhammad and the Caliphs towards the end of the sixteenth century and the early part of the seventeenth century. Sayid Sultan occupies a distinguished place among the authors, with his poetical works, *Nabi-Vamsa* (Family of the Prophet) and *Rasul Vijay* (Prophet's victories). It is interesting that he composed two religious books of the Muslims and a tantric treatise on the science of yoga, named *Jnan Pradip* and *Jnan Chautisa*. The author consulted the Hindu Sastras, and the Sanskrit work *Hari-Vamsa* had been imitated in *Nabi-Vamsa*. That the author considered Brahma, Vishnu, Shiva and Krishna as Nabis (prophets) is a significant aspect to be noted in understanding religious practices of those times.

In the pir ballads, literature on the pirs, we get a blending of the Dharma Thakur of the Buddhists, the pir of the Muslims and the Narayan of the Hindus in the *Pir Panchalis* (poetical works praising the glories of the pir) composed in the seventeenth century, specially towards the later part.

Towards the end of the Muslim rule in Bengal, the first effort towards the fusion of religions between the Hindus and Muslims was made through the ballads of *Satya Pir* and *Satya Narayan*. Sukumar Sen (1948: 80–81) says that the scribes of the pir ballads were Hindus, the singers were Muslims, but their composers were poets of both the communities. He further states that numerous Hindu writers, from West Bengal to Assam, composed *Satya Narayan* or *Satya Pir Panchalis* by equating Rahim of Mecca and Rama of Ayodhya. There are considerable similarities between the ballads of Faizullah of West Bengal and the *panchalis* of Rameswar Bhattacharya. The story of Faizullah contains clear hints of communal synthesis. He salutes the adored deities of both communities in the beginning and then writes:

> You are Brahma, you are Visnu, You are Narayan
> Listen, O Ghazi, pay heed to yourself to preaching in the assembly (i.e. instead of fighting)

(Quoted in Sarkar 1985: 94)

As regards the contrariety between Brahmanism and Islam, the Brahmin says that one loses his caste by reading the Koran since at its very beginning there is the word 'bismillah'. In reply *Satya Pir* gives the following argument:

> Except one Brahma no two Brahmas exist, the Lord of all is one Niranjan Gosain, in whose name Brahma, Visnu, Maheswar utter prayers. In one pore of his skin lies the endless universe. Without hands, without legs, he holds the world. he has no mouth to eat; he hears without ears, sees without eyes. None can recognise him though he is omnipresent. Bismillah is but another name of that very same Niranjan; Visnu and Bismillah are not at all distinct.
>
> (Quoted in S. Sen 1948: 465)

So Satya Pir, Satya Narayan, Vishnu, Bismillah, Allah and Niranjan have all become fused into one. Hence the view of late Professor Ramesh Chandra Majumdar that Satya Pir was the god of the Muslims and Satya Narayan of the Hindus does not appear to be correct, at least at the time of the rise of this worship.

Of all the Panchalis composed by the Muslims this deserves mention most. This ballad is important proof of how closely the two communities had come into contact with each other.

Purba Banga Gitika and Mymansingh Gitika

During the medieval period a large number of poets, both Hindus and Muslims, from different places of East Bengal, composed lyric poems (*gitikas*) regarding the sorrows and joys of people in the villages. Collectors gathered preserved all of them with care. Dinesh Chandra Sen collected these *gitikas* from them, and edited and published them in books under the names of *Purba Banga Gitika* and *Mymansingh Gitika*. The exact date and year are not always available of all the *gitikas*. In spite of that these are very important source materials for the study of the social history of Bengal under the rule of the Mughals and the Nawabs of Bengal.

Purba Banga Gitika and *Mymansingh Gitika* manifest and witness the amicable relationship between the Hindus and Muslims in Bengal.

They refer to good mutual understanding among the votaries of the two religions during the Mughal rule. A Muslim poet wrote in the adoration of a ballad named *Nurunneha O Kaborer Katha*,

> The Hindus and the Muslims are a rope of a same bundle: someone says Allah Rasul, someone says Hari. Bismillah and Shri Bishnu are the same; when they are made different, they are called Ram and Rahim.[6]
>
> (Quoted in D. C. Sen 1954: 497)

The poet tried to unite the Hindus and the Muslims on the same platform. He did not find any difference between Rama and Rahman except that they were called by different names. Muslim pirs and Hindu gods are the same in his eyes. The poet's liberalism can be compared with the outlook of a great philosopher. These verses have a deep message for present-day India grappling with various divisive forces like language, province and religion. Another Muslim poet writes in *Pir Batasi Pala*,

> After adoring you, O brothers, Hindu and Muslim I extend my adoration for the Pirs and also I adore Mecca, Madina, Kashi and Gayathan.[7]
>
> (Quoted in D. C. Sen 1954: 539)

The above verse speaks of the cultural syncretism between the two communities, Hindus and Muslims, during the period under review.

A ballad named *Nizam Dacoit* is equally important to mention here. It is a ballad from Chittagong district, dating from the seventeenth or eighteenth century. The poet of this ballad says in the opening lines,

> First of all I bow down to the Supreme Deity (Prabhu), and secondly to (the same Omnipotent Being conceived as) the Creator (Sirajn); and thirdly to the benign Incarnation of Life. The Koran and other scriptural texts I regard as revelation—the sacred utterances of the Lord (Prabhu) himself.
>
> (Quoted in D. C. Sen 1954: 539)
> Translated into English by Richard M. Eaton.

It is very interesting to note that one can find in this literature a Hindu hero and a Muslim heroine in one *gitika* and Muslim hero and Hindu heroine in another. The heart of the poet was so clean that it did not ever fail to portray the true picture of the society and the real image of the characters of their times in contemporary literature. In fact these ballads tell us much about the religious universe of the unlettered audience to whom they were sung. Dusan Zbavitel has written of the ballads of Mymansingh and Purba Banga very aptly that they were "neither products of Hindu or Muslim culture, but of a single Bengali folk-culture" (quoted in Eaton 1994: 281), which may be justly said of medieval Bengali folk religion generally.

Punthi Sahitya

The value of *punthi* (manuscript) literature of Bengal can hardly be overestimated. Abdul Karim Sahitya Visarad collected *punthis* written by several writers of the eighteenth and nineteenth centuries by dint of his personal efforts from various sources. They were quite helpful for the study of Hindu–Muslim relations during the period under review. For example, a *punthi* entitled *Imam Churi* written by an unknown writer is mentioned. This is an imaginary story, written in imitation of the legend about Sri Chaitanya Deva, of how a merchant kidnapped the two grandsons of the Prophet, Hassan and Hussain (Sharif n.d.: 22). It indicates that one religion had regard for another religion.

Identification in Literature

One finds in Bengali literature dating from the sixteenth century— romances, epics, narratives and devotional poems—that the Muslim authors identify God and the Prophet using Sanskrit words. Haji Muhammad, the sixteenth century poet identified the Arabic Allah with Gosai (Sanskrit for master), Saiyid Murtaza identified Prophet Muhammad's youngest daughter Fatima with Jagat Janani (Sanskrit for mother of the world), and Sayid Sultan identified Adam, Abraham and Moses with Prabhu (Sanskrit for Lord), or more frequently, Niranjan (Sanskrit for one without colour, i.e. without qualities). Later, Ali Raza, the eighteenth century poet identified Allah with Niranjan, Iswar (Sanskrit for God), Jagat Iswar (Sanskrit for God of the Universe), and Kartar (Sanskrit for Creator). One sixteenth century poet wrote, "Muslims as well as Hindus in every home" would read the *Mahabharata*, the great religious epic of classical India. Another poet of that century wrote of Muslims being moved to tears on hearing on Rama's loss of his beloved Sita in the epic Ramayana. It is hardly surprising then, that romantic tales from the Islamic tradition drew on this rich indigenous substratum of religious culture. For example, an eighteenth century Bengali version of the popular Iranian story of Yusuf and Zulaikha employs imagery, clearly recalls Radha's passionate love for Krishna, the central motif of the Bengali Vaishnava devotional movement. These are some of the examples of local influence on the Bengali Muslims.

Conclusion

From the above discussion one can infer that there are numerous instances in medieval Bengali literature to show that during the period under consideration the relationship among the masses of the two communities was on the whole friendly and cordial. Both communities lived peacefully. The two communities lived side by side in amity as good neighbours, in perfect harmony and in a spirit of peaceful coexistence. There was hardly any communal clash between the two communities. Tension might have cropped up occasionally but that was confined mostly to the upper stratum and hardly affected the common people of the two communities. The tension, if any, arose more often out of the struggle for power or appropriation, and not necessarily out of communal animosity.

Notes

1. Apart from these there were also some other *Mangal Kavyas* (eulogistic poems about gods and goddesses), for example, *Shiva Mangal* or *Shivayan, Kalika Mangal, Ganga Mangal, Ray Mangal*, etc. may be mentioned.
2. See also Karim (1959: 171) and cf. Gupta (1962: 140).
3. In the introduction to the *Sunya Purana* Muhammad Shahidullah writes that the Brahmins regarded the Buddhist worshippers of Dharma and the Muslims in a uniform manner. So Dharma Thakur represented the joint remonstrance of the Buddhists and the Muslims against the Brahmins. Many Islamic rites and customs have merged in the system of Dharma Thakur.
4. Bharat Chandra Ray refers to the names of Muslim courtiers in Krishna Chandra Sabhabarnana, namely, Mahmud Jafar, the *jamadar* of sepoys, Habsi Imam Boxsh, head of the Habsis and Sher Mamud, the chief dancer, showing that the king appointed several Muslims in his court.

5. The Mughals of Sylhet also patronized Vaishnavas through grants called *vishnottar*, and Shaivas through grants called *sivottar*. For example, we can say that the Mughal government granted four *qulbas* (15.6 acres) of jungle and a house to Gobinda Das, a Vaishnava holy man (*bairagi*) described as *mustahaqq-i-wajibar-riyat* (worthy of honour), an Arabic-Persian phrase that would have befitted any accomplished Muslim scholar or Sufi. See Eaton (1994: 262).
6. Sir Asutosh Chaudhury collected *Nurunneha O Kaberar Katha Pala* in 1928. The *gitika* contains 632 lines. Chaudhury was told of the ballad by Sher Ali Khan, the zamindar of Bara Vathan, which lies under Diwang Hill. See D. C. Sen 1954: 497.
7. Sri Chandra Kumar Dey collected *Pir Batasi Pala*. He wrote that he tried for more than two years for the collection of this *gitika*. The major portion of this *pala* was collected from Brindaban Bairagi of Ajmer. The remaining part of this *pala* was collected from Sridan Patuni and Jagabandhu Gayan of Laxmiganj. See D. C. Sen 1954: 539.

References

Bandyopadhyay, Brajendranath and Sajanikanta Das. 'Preface to the Edition', in Brajendranath Bandyopadhyay and Sajanikanta Das (eds), *Bharatchandra Granthabali*. Calcutta: Bangiya Sahitya Parishad. 1369 B.S. (Bangla Sal).
Bhattacharjee, Asutosh. 1947. 'The Tiger-Cult and Its Literature in Lower Bengal', *Man in India*, March, 27 (1).
Bhattacharya, J. M. 1984. *Banglar Vaishnab-bhavapanna Musalman Kabir Padamanjusha*. University of Calcutta.
Chakraborty, Ghanaram. '*Dharma Mangal*', in Pijus Kanti Mahapatra (ed.), *Dhakurpala Part*.
Chakraborty, Mukundaram. 1992. *Kavikankan Chandi*. Edited by Srikumar Bandopadhyay and Biswapati Chaudhuri. Calcutta: University of Calcutta.
Chattopadhyay, Bankim Chandra. 'Banglar Itihas Samhandhe Kayakti Katha', Brajendranath Bandyopadhyay and Sajanikanta Das (eds), *Bibidh Prabandha*, Kolkata. Agrahayan (month) 1287 B.S. (Bangla Sal).
Dimock, E.C. Jr.1969, 'Muslim Vaishnava Poets of Bengal', in D. Kopf (ed,) *Bengal's Regional Identity*, pp. 25ff. Michigan.
Eaton, Richard M. 1994. *The Rise of Islam and the Bengal Frontier (1204–1760)*. New Delhi: Oxford University Press.
Gupta, Vijay. 1962. *Padma Purana*. Translated by Abdul Karim. Calcutta: University of Calcutta, Calcutta.
Haldar, Gopal. 1956. *Bangali Sanskriti Prasanga*. Orient Book Company: Calcutta.
Kalim, Musa. 1988. *Madhaya Yugar Bangla Sahitye Hindu-Mussalmaner Samparkhya*. Calcutta. Mallick Brothers.
Karim, Abdul. 1959. *Social History of the Muslims in Bengal*. Dacca, Pakistan: Asiatic Society.
Nathan, Mirza 1936. *Baharistan-i-Ghaibi* (written in Persian), (Trans. M.I. Borah). *Guwhati, Assam: Government of Assam*.
Qadir, Abdul and Rezaul Karim (eds). 1945. 'Jangnamah', *Kavyamalancha*.
Rahman, Muhammad Shah Noorur. 2001. *Hindu-Muslim Relations in Mughal Bengal*. Kolkata: Progressive Publishers.

Roy, Asim. 1983. *The Islamic Syncretistic Tradition in Bengal*. Princeton, NJ: Princeton University Press.
Raygunakar, Bharat Chandra and Annada Mangal. 1369 B.S. *Granthabali* edited by Brajendranath Bandyopadhay and Sajani Kanta Das. Calcutta: Bangla Sahitya Parishad, 3RD edn.
Sarkar, Jagadish Narayan. 1984. *Thoughts on Trends of Cultural Contacts in Medieval India*. Calcutta.
———. 1985. *Hindu-Muslim Relations in Medieval Bengal*. New Delhi: Idarah-i-Adabiyat-i-Delli.
———. 1948. *History of Bengal*, vol. II. P. 501. Dacca: Dacca University.
Sen, Dinesh Chandra. 1954. *History of Bengali Language and Literature*. Calcutta: University of Calcutta.
Sen, Dinesh Chandra (ed.). *Purbavanga Gitika*, Vol. 4.
Sen, Sukumar. 1948. *Bangla Sahityer Itihas*, Vol. 1. Bardhaman Sahitya Sabha.
Sharif, Ahmad. n.d. *Abdul Karim Sahitya Visarad Kartik Sankalita Punthi Parichiti*. No.18. Ms. 65.
Zbavitel, Dusan. 1976. *Bengali Literature*, Vol. 9. In Jan Gonda (ed.), *A History of Indian Literature*. Wiesbaden, Germany: Otto Harrassowitz.

Select Bibliography

Adhikary, Ramendranath. 2006. *Surendranath Basunia: Karma Jiban O Sangeet Sadhana*. (Basonia's Life and Pursuit of Music) Coochbehar, India: Paschim Banga Adivasi O Loka Shilpi Sangha.
Anderson, Benedict. 1993. *Imagined Community*. London: Verso.
Ao, Temsula. 2006. *These Hills Called Home*. New Delhi: Penguin Zubaan.
Augé, Marc. 1995. *Non-Places: Introduction to an Anthropology of Supermodernity*. London: Verso.
Ayyub, Abu Sayeed. 1973. *Poetry and Truth*. Kolkata: Jadavpur University.
Bandhu, C. 2002. *Nepali Loksahitya Nepali Folk Literature*. Kathmandu, Nepal: Ekta Books.
Bandyopadhyay, R. 2000. *Journal Sottor*. Kolkata: Mitra & Ghosh.
Baral, Kailash C. (ed.). 2005. *Earth Songs: Stories from Northeast India*. New Delhi: Sahitya Akademi.
Barman, Prafulla. 2004. *Axom Nandini Pratima Barua Pandey*. Guwahati, India: Vishal Prakashan.
Barman, Shanto. 2009. *Goalparar Jana Itihax* (Popular History of Goalpara). Guwahati, India: Ashok Publications.
Barth, Fredrik. 1969. *Ethnic Groups and Boundaries*. Boston, MA: Little Brown.
Barthes, Roland. 1977. 'The Rhetoric of the Image', in *Image, Music, Text*, pp. 32–51. Edited and translated by Stephen Heath. New York: Hill & Wang.
Bauman, Z. 2000. *Liquid Modernity*. Cambridge: Polity.
Benjamin, Walter. 1983. 'The Author as Producer', in *Understanding Brecht*. Translated by Anna Bostock. London: Verso.
———. 1997. *Ki Jingsneng Tymmen* [The teaching of elders], Part 1 & 11. Translated by Bijoya Sawian. Shillong, India.
Berry, U. Radhon Singh. 1959. *Ki Jingsneng Tymmen Shaphang Ka Akor Khasi Ha Ka Rukom Rwai Phawar*, Part 1 & Part 11. Shillong, India: Ri Khasi Press.
Béteille, André. 1982. *Marxism, Pluralism and Orthodoxy*. New Delhi: India Renaissance Institute.
Bhakat, D. N. 2010. *Rajbanshi Bhasha Sahitya Aru Iyar Unnanyan* (The Rise and Development of Rajbanshi Literature). Bongaigaon, India: All Assam Koch Rajbanshi Yuva Chhatra Sanmilani.
Bhattacharjee, J. M. 1984. *Banglar Vaishnab-bhavapanna Musalman Kabir Padamanjusha*. Kolkata: University of Calcutta.

Brahmachoudhury, Suriti Sarma. 2006. *Ganor Pratima, Pranor Pratima*. Guwahati, India: Bina Library.
Biakliana. 2004. 'Lali', in *The Heart of the Matter: Handpicked Fictions from Meghalaya, Manipur, Mizoram, Assam and Nagaland*. New Delhi: Katha.
Capra, Fritjof. 1989. *Uncommon Wisdom*. New York: Bantam.
Chakraborty, Mukundaram. 1992. *Kavikankan Chandi*. Edited by Srikumar Bandopadhyay and Biswapati Chaudhuri. Calcutta: University of Calcutta.
Chakraborty, Shyamal. 2005. *Mahut Bandhure: Pratima Barua Pandey—Jiban O Gaan* (Elephant Rider: Life and Music of Pratima Barua Pandey). Agartala, India: Gyanbichitra Prakashani.
Chanda, Rajat. 2009. 'Kabya O Bignaner Samanya—Rabindranather Bignan Manas', *Anandalipi*. Kolkata: PMG Publication.
Chattarji, Dipankar. 2000. *Rabindranath O Vijñân*. Calcutta: Ananda Publishers Private Ltd.
Chatterjee, P. 1993. *The Nation and Its Fragments*. Kolkata: Oxford University Press.
Chattopadhyay, Bankim Chandra. 1872. 'Banglar Itihas Samhandhe Kayakti Katha', in Brajendranath Bandyopadhyay and Sajanikanta Das (eds), *Bibidh Prabandha*. Kolkata.
Chattopadhyay, S. K. (ed). 1985. *Tribal Institutions of Meghalaya*. Guwahati, India: Spectrum Publications.
Choudhury, Amanatulla Khan. 1991. 'Rajbanshi Bhasha Tattva', in *Souvenir*. Coochbehar, India: Uttar Banga Sahitya Sammelan.
Clarke, Donald. 2002. *Billie Holiday: Wishing on the Moon*. New York: Da Capo Press.
Cleage, Pearl. 1993. *Deals with the Devil, and Other Reasons to Riot*. New York: Ballantine.
Collins, Patricia Hill. 1998. *Fighting Words: Black Women and the Search for Justice*. Minneapolis, MN: University of Minnesota Press.
Darwin, Charles. 1859. *The Origin of Species*. London: John Murray.
Das, Anirban. 2010. *Toward a Politics of the (Im)Possible: The Body in Third World Feminisms*. London, New York, Delhi: Anthem Press.
Das, Chitta Ranjan. 1982. *Balarama Das*. New Delhi: Kendra Sahitya Akademi.
———. 1989. 'Ethara Udiba Neta' [Now the flag shall fly], in Chittaranjan Das and Srinivas Udgata, *Ebam* [And]. Cuttack, India: Books & Books.
———. 1982. *A Glimpse into Oriya Literature*. Bhubaneswar, India: Orissa Sahitya Akademi.
———. 1981. *Odiya Sahityara Sanskrutika Bikashadhara* [The cultural development of Oriya literature]. Bhubaneswar, India: Orissa Text Book Bureau.
Das, Dhiren. 1994. *Goalparia Loka Sansrkti Aru Loka Geet* (Goalparia Folk Culture and Music). Guwahati, India: Chandra Prakash.

Das, Veena. 1995. *Critical Events: An Anthropological Perspective on Contemporary India.* Oxford University Press.
Dash, Rabi Narayan. 2007. *On Wings and Other Poems.* Huddinge, Sweden: Prima Verba and Balasore, India: New Race.
Dash, Rabi Narayan. 2008. *...Ebam Kadha* [...And buds]. Balasore, India: Samara Graphics.
Davis, Angela Y. 1998. *Blues Legacies and Black Feminism.* New York, NY: Pantheon Books.
de Sausssure, F. 1978. *Course in General Linguistics.* Translated by W. Baskin. Glasgow, UK: Fontana.
Deleuze, Gilles. 1993. 'Minor Literature—Kafka', in C. V. Boundas (ed.), *The Deleuze Reader*, New York: Columbia University Press.
Derrida, J. 1992. *Acts of Literature.* Edited by Derek Attridge. London: Routledge.
Deschaumes, Ghislaine Glasson and Rada Ivekovic (eds). 2003. *Divided Countries, Separated Cities: The Modern Legacy of Partition.* New Delhi: Oxford University Press.
Devkota, L. 2004. [1973]. *Gayienay Geet* (Minstrel's ballads). Lalitpur, Nepal, Darjeeling, India: Sahja Prakashan. Darjeeling.
Dufrenne, Mikel. 1973. *The Phenomenology of Aesthetic Experience.* Translated by Edward Casey et al. Evanstan: North-Western University Press.
Dunn, Leslie C. and Nancy A. Johns (eds). 1994. *Embodied Voices: Representing Female Vocality in Western Culture.* New York: Cambridge University Press.
Einstein, A. 1982. [1930]. *Ideas and Opinions.* New York: Crown Publishers.
Elbridge, Richard. 2000. 'Dewey's Aesthetics', in M. Cochran (ed.), *Cambridge Companion to John Dewey.* Cambridge, UK: Cambridge University Press.
Eliade, Mircea. 1968. *The Sacred and the Profane: The Nature of Religion.* Translated by Willard Trask. New York: Houghton Mifflin Harcourt.
Ellman, M. 1981. 'Disremembering Dedalus', in R. Young (ed.), *Untying the Text: A Post-Structuralist Reader.* Boston: Routledge.
Ferguson, Mary Anne. 1973. *Images of Women in Literature.* Boston, MA: Houghton Mifflin.
Friedlander, Saul. 1982. *Reflections of Nazism: An Essay on Kitsch and Death.* New York: Harper and Row.
Ganguly, S. N. 1977. *Tradition, Modernity And Development: A Study in Contemporary Indian Society.* Delhi: The Macmillan Company of India Limited.
Gazdar, Mushtaq. 1997. *Pakistani Cinema 1947–1997.* Karachi, Pakistan: Oxford University Press.
Giri, Ananta Kumar. 2008. 'Civil Society and the Calling of Self-Development', *Sociological Bulletin.*

Giri, Ananta Kumar. 2002. *Conversations and Transformations: Towards a New Ethics of Self and Society.* Lanham, MD: Lexington Books.
Giri, Helen. 1998. *The Khasis under British Rule (1824–1947).* New Delhi: Regency Publications.
Giri, J. D. 2001. *Loksahitya Ko Awolokan.* Kathmandu, Nepal: Ekta Prakashan.
Greene, Meg. 2007. *Billie Holiday: A Biography.* Westport, CT: Greenwood Press.
Griffin, Farah Jasmine. 2001. *If You Can't Be Free, Be a Mystery.* New York: The Free Press.
Guha, Ranajit. 1983. 'The Prose of Counter Insurgency', in R. Guha (ed.), *Subaltern Studies ll.* Oxford University Press.
———. 1996. 'The Small Voice of History', in S. Amin and D. Chakrabarty (ed.), *Subaltern Studies lx.* Oxford University Press.
Gupta, R. 1999. *Mayabi Tantuja.* Calcutta.
Gupta, Vijay. 1962. *Padma Purana.* Translated by Abdul Karim. Calcutta: University of Calcutta.
Habermas, Jurgen. 1990. *Moral Consciousness and Communicative Action.* Cambridge, MA: The MIT Press.
———. 1990. *The Structural Transformation of the Public Sphere.* Cambridge, MA: The MIT Press.
Haldar, Gopal. 2001. *Bangali Sanskriti Prasanga.* Calcutta.
Hamilton, Virginia. 1985. *The People Could Fly: American Black Folktales.* New York: Alfred Knopf.
Hampton, Sylvia and David Nathan. 2004. *Nina Simone: Break Down & Let It All Out.* London: Sanctuary.
Haque, A. 1991. *Karagere Athero Bochhor.*
Harvey, David. 1989. *The Condition of Postmodernity: An Inquiry into the Origins of Cultural Change.* Cambridge, MA: Basil Blackwell.
Heidegger, Martin. 1975. *Poetry, Language and Thought.* Harper Colophon Books.
Hiriyanna, M. 2008. *The Essentials of Indian Philosophy.* New Delhi: Motilal Banarsidass.
Honneth, Axel. 2007. *Disrespect: The Normative Foundations of Critical Theory.* Cambridge: Polity Press.
Hughes, Langston. 1974. *Selected Poems of Langston Hughes.* New York: Vintage.
Kakar, Sudhir and Katharina Kakar. 2008. 'The Inner Experience of Caste', in *The Penguin Yearbook.* pp. 25–40.
Kant, Immanuel. 1991. 'The Metaphysics of Morals', in H. S. Reiss (ed.), *Kant: Political Writings* Cambridge, UK: Cambridge University Press.
Kaphleia. 2004. 'Chhingpuii', in *The Heart of the Matter: Handpicked Fictions from Meghalaya, Manipur, Mizoram, Assam and Nagaland.* New Delhi: Katha.

Kargupta, Sourav. 2011. 'Jacques Derrida and the Gift of Translation', *Jadavpur Journal of Comparative Literature*, 47 (2009–2011): 97–113.
Karim, Abdul. 1959. *Social History of the Muslims in Bengal*. Dacca, Pakistan: Asiatic Society.
Keil, Charles. 1966. *Urban Blues*. Chicago, IL: University of Chicago Press.
Landy, Marcia. 1997. *Cinematic Uses of the Past*. Minneapolis, MN: University of Minneapolis Press.
Lee, Chana Kai. 1999. *For Freedom's Sake: The Life of Fannie Lou Hamer*. Athens, GA: University of Georgia Press.
Malkki, L. H. 1995. *Purity and Exile: Violence, Memory and National Cosmology among Hutu Refugees in Tanzania*. Chicago, IL: University of Chicago Press.
Manjali, Franson. 2001. *Literature and Infinity*. Shimla, India: Indian Institute of Advanced Study.
Maqsood, Ruqayyiah Waris. 2000. *The Problem of Evil*. New Delhi: Adam Publishers and Distributors.
Mead, G. H. 1934. *Mind, Self and Society*. Chicago, IL: University of Chicago Press.
Mills, Kay. 1993. *This Little Light of Mine: The Life of Fannie Lou Hamer*. New York: Dutton.
Mitra, J. 1989. *Hanyaman*. Kolkata Anyadhara.
Mukherjee, Meenakshi. 1996. *Realism and Reality: The Novel and Society in India*. New Delhi: Oxford University Press.
Nandy, Ashis. 2001. *An Ambiguous Journey to the City*. New Delhi: Oxford University Press.
Naravane, M. S. 2006. *Battles of the Honourable East India Company: Making of the Raj*. APH Publishing.
Neal, Mark Anthony. 1999. *What the Music Said: Black Popular Music and Black Public Culture*. London: Routledge.
Nongkhlaw, Dondor Giri. 2007. 'That Elusive Niam Kur (Clan Religion) of the Hynñiewtrep Landscape', *Indian Theological Journal*, 1 (January–June).
Nongkynrih, Kynpham S. and Robin Singh Ngangom. (eds). 2003. *Anthology of Contemporary Poetry from the Northeast*. Shillong, India: North-Eastern Hill University.
Ong, Walter J. 2004. *Orality and Literacy: The Technologizing of the Word*. London: Routledge.
Pandey, Gyanendra. 2001. *Remembering Partition: Violence, Nationalism and History in India*. Cambridge, UK: Cambridge University Press.
Panikkar, Raimon. 1995. *A Dwelling Place for Wisdom*. New Delhi: Motilal Banarsidass.
Pikaza, Xavier. 2010. 'Raimon Panikkar (1918–2010)', in *Concilium*, 5: 117–20.
Prasad, M. Madhava. 1998. *Ideology of the Hindi Film*. New Delhi: Oxford University Press.

Prasai, N. 2001. *Nepali Sahityaka Smalochak Ra Samalochana*. Kathmandu, Nepal: Ekta.
Pratt, Ray. 1994. *Rhythm and Resistance: Explorations in the Political Uses of Popular Music*. United States: Smithsonian Institution Press.
Qadir, Abdul and Rezaul Karim (eds). 1945. 'Jangnamah', *Kavyamalancha*.
Radford-Hill, Sheila. 2000. *Further to Fly: Black Women and the Politics of Empowerment*. Minneapolis, MN: University of Minnesota Press.
Raghavendra, M. K. 2008. *Seduced by the Familiar: Narration and Meaning in Indian Popular Cinema*. New Delhi: Oxford University Press.
Raju, P. T. 1985. *Structural Depths of Indian Thought*. New Delhi: South Asian Publishers.
Rapport, N. and A. Dawson. 1998. *Migrants of Identity: Perceptions of Home in a World of Movement*. Providence and Oxford: Berg Publishers.
Ray, Girija Shankar. 1996. 'Bhumika', in Binod Bihari Barman and Jatin Burma (eds), *Rajbanshi Kavita Sankalan*. Kolkata: Anima Prakashani.
Ray, Niharranjan. 1961. 'Rabindranath Tagore and the Indian Tradition' in *A Centenary Volume: Rabindranath Tagore*. New Delhi: Sahitya Akademi.
Roy, Asim. 1983. *The Islamic Syncretistic Tradition in Bengal*. Princeton NJ: Princeton University Press.
Roy, Mallarika Sinha. 2011. *Gender and Radical Politics in India: Magic Moments of Naxalbari (1967–1975)*. London and New York: Routledge.
Roy, Srila. Unpublished MS. 'Remembering Revolution: Gender, Violence and the Production of Identity in Naxalbari', Ph.D. Thesis submitted to the University of Warwick, UK in 2007.
Russell, Michele. 1982. 'Slave Codes and Liner Notes', in Gloria T. Hull, Patricia Bell Scott and Barbara Smith (eds), *But Some of Us Are Brave*. Old Westbury, NY: The Feminist Press.
Rymbai, R. T. 1979. 'Some Aspects of the Religion of the Khasi-Pnar', in *Khasi Heritage*. Shillong, India: Ri Khasi Press.
Sarkar, Jagadish Narayan. 1985. *Hindu-Muslim Relations in Medieval Bengal*. New Delhi: Idrah-i Adabiyat-i-Delli.
Sarma, Shashi. 2006. *Goalparia Loko Sahitya Samaj Jibanor Protifolon*. Dhubri, India: Asom Sahitya Sabha, Dhubri Sakha.
Scholte, J. A. 2000. *Globalization: A Critical Introduction*. New York: St. Martin's Press.
Sen, Dinesh Chandra. 1954. *History of Bengali Language and Literature*. Calcutta: University of Calcutta.
Sen, Sukumar. 1948. *Bangla Sahityer Itihas*, Vol. 1. Bardhaman Sahitya Sabha.
Sharma, Jyotirmaya and A. Raghuramraju (eds). 2010. *Grounding Morality: Freedom, Knowledge and the Plurality of Cultures*. New Delhi: Routledge.
Simmon, Scott. 1993. *The Films of D. W. Griffith*. Cambridge, UK: Cambridge University Press.
Simone, Nina and Stephen Cleary. 1991. *I Put a Spell on You: The Autobiography of Nina Simone*. New York: De Capo Press.

Skof, Lenart. 2011. 'Pragmatism and Deepened Democracy: Ambedkar Between Dewey and Unger', in Akeel Bilgrami (ed.), *Democratic Culture: Historical and Philosophical Essays.*
Spear, Percival. 1970. *A History of India*, Vol. 2. Harmondsworth, UK: Penguin.
Stace, W. T. 1953. *Time and Eternity: An Essay Concerning Philosophy of Religion.* Princeton, NJ: Princeton University Press.
Strydom, Piet. 2009. *New Horizons of Critical Theory: Collective Learning and Triple Contingency.* New Delhi: Shipra.
Subramanyan, K. G. 1987. *The Living Tradition: Perspectives on Modern Indian Art.* Calcutta: Seagull Books.
Sunder Rajan, R. 1998. *Beyond the Crises of European Sciences: New Beginnings.* Shimla, India: Indian Institute of Advanced Studies.
Tagore, Rabindranath. 1917. *Personality.* Calcutta: Macmillan.
———. 1994. *The Religion of Man.* Indus Publication.
———. 1978. 'The Real and the True' in Sisirkumar Ghose (ed.), *Angel of Surplus: Some Essays and Address on Aesthetics.* Calcutta: Visva-Bharati.
———. 1937. 'Visvaparicaya', in *Rabindra Racanāvalī*, Vol. 15. Calcutta: Visva-Bharati.
Thapar, Romila. 1996. *Time as a Metaphor of History: Early India.* New Delhi: Oxford University Press.
Turner, Victor. 1969. *The Ritual Process: Structure and Anti-Structure.* London: Penguin.
Tyagi, S. 1974. *Indo-Nepalese Relations 1858–1914.* New Delhi: D. K. Publishing House.
Upasu, Shri (ed.). 2004. *Manishi Thakur Panchananer Bani.* Mathabhanga, Coochbehar, India.
———. 2005. *Manishi Thakur Panchananer Jiban Katha.* Mathabhanga Coochbehar, India.
Urry, J. 2000. *Sociology Beyond Societies: Mobilities for the Twenty-First Century.* London: Routledge.
Vasudevan, Ravi. (ed.). 2008. *Making Meaning in Indian Cinema.* New Delhi: Oxford University Press.
Whitely, Sheila. 1997. *Sexing the Groove: Popular Music and Gender.* London and New York: Routledge.
———. 2000. *Women and Popular Music: Sexuality, Identity, and Subjectivity.* London: Routledge.
Zizek, S. 1989. *The Sublime Object of Ideology.* London and New York: Verso.

About the Editors and Contributors

Editors

Sukalpa Bhattacharjee teaches English at North-Eastern Hill University, Shillong. Her publications include *Postcolonial Literatures: Essays on Gender, Theory and Genres* (2004) and she has co-edited volumes such as *Human Rights and Insurgency: The North-East India* (2002) and *Ethno Narratives: Identity and Experience in North East India* (2006). Her review anthologies have been published in national and international research paper journals in the areas of critical theory, gender studies and multi-ethnic literatures of the United States. She is currently also working on a translation of partition narratives from the Barak Valley of Assam.

C. Joshua Thomas is presently the Deputy Director at the Indian Council of Social Science Research, North Eastern Regional Centre (ICSSR), Shillong. He is known for his pioneering research in diverse fields of social sciences in north-eastern India. His areas of research include issues related to ethnicity, peace process and border trade and displacement. Some of his earlier works include: *Dimensions of Displaced People in North East India* (2002), *Indo-Myanmar Border Trade: Status, Problems and Potentials* (2005), *Peace in India's North East: Meaning, Metaphor and Meanings* (2006) and *India–China: Trade and Strategy for Frontier Developments* (2010).

Contributors

Goutam Biswas is Professor of Philosophy and Pro-Vice-Chancellor (Humanities & Allied Disciplines) at Assam University. He is the author of *Art as Dialogue: Essays in Phenomenology of Aesthetic Experience*.

About the Editors and Contributors 265

Anirban Das is a Fellow in Cultural Studies at the Centre for Studies in Social Sciences, Calcutta. He shifted to the humanities (with a Ph.D. in Philosophy) after completing a bachelor's degree in medicine. He is the author of *Toward a Politics of the (Im)possible: The Body in the Third World Feminisms*.

Ellerine Diengdoh teaches English at St. Mary's College, Shillong and is a doctoral candidate at the Department of English, North-Eastern Hill University, Shillong.

Partha S. Ghose is a distinguished scientist and Senior Scientist Platinum Jubilee Fellow, National Academy of Sciences, India, Centre for Astroparticle Physics, Bose Institute, Kolkata.

Ananta Kumar Giri is currently on the faculty of the Madras Institute of Development Studies, Chennai, and has worked and taught in many universities in India and abroad including the University of Kentucky, United States, Aalborg University, Denmark and University of Freiburg, Germany.

Sourav Kargupta is currently pursuing a Ph.D. (through a programme affiliated to Jadavpur University) at the Centre for Studies in Social Sciences, Calcutta. He has worked on the project 'Nationalist Ideology and the Historiography of Literature in South Asian Cultures' at the Martin Luther University, Halle, Germany, funded by the Volkswagen Stiftung.

Desmond L. Kharmawphlang is Professor and Head, Department of Cultural and Creative Studies at the North-Eastern Hill University, Shillong.

Somdatta Mandal is Professor of English at the Department of English and Other Modern European Languages, Visva-Bharati, Santiniketan.

Franson Davis Manjali is Professor at the School of Language, Literature and Culture Studies, Jawaharlal Nehru University, New Delhi. He is the author of *Literature and Infinity* (2001) and *Language, Discourse and Culture: Contemporary Philosophical Perspectives* (2008).

Sujata Miri taught philosophy at Lady Sri Ram College and the North-Eastern Hill University, Shillong, from where she retired as Dean of

Humanities and Education in 2005. Her major areas of interest include the study and understanding of tribal cultures.

Jyotirmoy Prodhani is Associate Professor at the Department of English at North-East Hill University, Shillong. He is also the editor of an international research journal, *Protocol: Journal of Translation, Creative and Critical Writings*.

M. K. Raghavendra is a film scholar and researcher. He was awarded the Swarna Kamal, the National Award for the Best Film Critic in 1997 and a Homi Bhabha Fellowship in 2000–01.

Muhammad Shah Noorur Rahman is a faculty member at the Department of History, School of Social Sciences, North-Eastern Hill University, Shillong since 2003.

Mohan G. Ramanan is Professor of English and Dean, School of Humanities at the University of Hyderabad. He has written on modern poetry, Indian literature and culture and American literature.

Utpala Ghaley Sewa is Associate Professor of English at the North-Eastern Hill University, Shillong, and is the author of *Memory as Vision: A Study of the Poetry of Thomas Hardy*.

Mohammad Maroof Shah is a veterinary doctor by profession. He specializes in Sufi literature and philosophy and his papers have appeared in the *Journal of Indian Council of Philosophical Research*.

Esther Syiem is a bilingual writer and Professor of English at the North-Eastern Hill University, Shillong. She has authored two volumes of poetry, *Oral Scriptings* and *Of Follies and Frailties of Wit and Wisdom*, apart from numerous articles and poems in anthologies of poetry and literary studies.

Margaret Ch Zama is Professor at the Mizoram University, Aizawl. Her area of specialization and research interests are fiction, new writings, tribal literature, north-east Indian literature, cultural studies and translation works.

Index

Adhikary, Tagar, 220, 224n2
Adis of Arunachal Pradesh, 135–136, 139
aesthetics, xxxi, 13
African American women, xxxvii. *See also* Chapman, Tracy; Holiday, Billie; Simone, Nina
  oppression against, 176
Alaol, 245
anachronism, xxix
Anokhi Ada, 164
a priori 'social world', xxiii
  sense of literature and, xxv
art, xxxi
  distinction between science and, 3
  Tagore on, 14–16, 20–21
Atiyah, Sir Michael, 3
autobiographies, 68–76

Baharistan-i-Ghaibi (Mirza Nathan), xli, 235
Bandyopadhyay, Raghab, 73
Bandyopadhyay's narrative
  almirah full of books, 69–70
  mother in, 69
  revolution, 70–72
Banglar Vaishnav Bhabapanno Musalman Kavir Padomanjusha, 243
Barthes, Roland, xxviii
Bascom, William R., 209
Basunia, Surendranath, 220, 224n1
Before the Law (Franzz Kafka), 28, 126–129

'being-in-common' ontology, xxv
'being-in' ontology, xxv
Bengali literature of medieval period, xli
  Anubad Sahitya, 249
  bhakti movement and, 242–249
  biographies of Prophet Muhammad and the Caliphs, 250
  identification in, 253–254
  Islamic, 243–244, 249–251
  Mangal Kavya, 236–242
  Nurunneha O Kaborer Katha, 252
  pir ballads, 250, 252
  Pir Batasi Pala, 252
  punthi (manuscript) literature, 253
  Purba Banga Gitika and *Mymansingh Gitika*, 251–253
  Vaishnava Sahitya, 242–249
Benhabib, Seyla, 25
Berry, Radhon Singh, 192–193, 195
Bhattacharya, Jatindra Mohan, 243–244
Bhattacharya, K. C., 15
Bhuvan Shome, 169
Biswas, Goutam, xxx–xxxi, 13
black female blues, 176. *See also* Chapman, Tracy; Holiday, Billie; Simone, Nina
Black Feminist Thought (Patricia Hill Collins), 176
black literary tradition, 183–184
black music analysis, xxxvii
Blanchot, Maurice, 122
  Kafka's stories, 123–126
  The Madness of the Day, 126

Blues Legacies and Black Feminism (Angela Y. Davis), xxxvii, 175
Bose, Satyendranath, 5
Boyle, Sir Robert, 6

Chakrabarty, Dipesh, 64–66
Chakrabarty, Mihir, 73
Chakraborty, Ghanaram, 240
Chakraborty, Mukundaram, 239–240
Chanakya, 169
Chapman, Tracy, 175
   biography, 182
   as folk protest singer and activist, 181–183
   'Mountains o' Things', 182
   self-titled debut album, 182
   She's Got Her Ticket, 184
   'Talkin' 'bout a Revolution', 181–182
Chattopadhyay, Bankim Chandra, xli, 235
Chaudhury, Hachhan Raja, 248
Chhingpuii, xxxix
civilized societies, xxxv, 133
clan religion, 190–191
closed text, xxix
communication, idea of, xxxviii
community, 122
comparative literature, 25–26, 31
contemporary or urban legends, 227–228
cosmic religious feeling, 4
Course in General Linguistics, 122
creative subjectivity, xxiv–xxv

Das, Anirban, 63
Das, Anirbhan, xxxii
Das, Chittaranjan, 86–93
   approach to aesthetics, 89–90
   conception of normality, 98n10
   on culture, 91–92
   Ethara Udiba Neta, 87
   A Glimpse into Oriya Literature, 91
   Jatire Mu Jabana, 88–89
   language of power and poet's aspirations, distinction between, 88
   on literature, 89–90
   Odiya Sahityara Sanskrutika Bikashadhara, 91–92
   on poetry and poets, 87–88
   poetry as expansion of consciousness, 88–89
   prose and poetry, distinction between, 89
   'Sahitya O Srujanasilata' essay, 89
   views on criticism, 90
   on worldwide student movement, 91
Das, Sisir Kumar, 25
Dasgupta, Subhendu, 72
Datta, Sitanath, 5
Debendranath, Maharshi, 5
Deewar, 171
Derrida, Jacques, 23–24
Des Tours de Babel, 28–29
desubjectification process, xxix
Dharti Ke Lal, 169
Dialogues Concerning Natural Religion, 138
diaspora space, 209
Diengdoh, Ellerine, xxxvii, 175
discursive self-definition, xxvi
disjunction, xxix
Dufrenne, Mikel, 16

Eckhart, Meister, 50
Eco, Umberto, xxix
explanation, xxvi

Faux pas (Blanchot), 122
fee-for-credit educational service industry, xlii
'Flying Africans', 183–184
folklore, functions of, 209–210

Gadar: Ek Prem Katha, 164, 170
Ganguly, S. N., 17

Garam Hawa, 171
Gemeinschaft, 121
Gesellschaft, 121
Ghose, Partha S., xxx, 3
Giri, Ananta Kumar, xxxii–xxxiii, 78
Giri, Helen, 195
Goalparia Folk Songs, 221
Gramsci, Antonio, xxxi, 22
Gupta, Vijay, 237
Gurkha Regiment, 210–211

Habermas, Jurgen, 80
Haque, Azizul, 73
Hazarika, Bhupen, 220–221
Heidegger, Martin, xxxi, 13
Heisenberg, Werner, 7
hermeneutics, xxvii–xxviii
Hiriyanna, M., 137
history, xxx, 64–66
Holiday, Billie, 175
  biography of, 176
  encounters with racism, 177
  Strange Fruit, 178–179
Holocaust, xxxvii
Holocaust, 162
hospitality, 24–25
human freedom and texuality, xxix
humanities, 35
human sciences, understanding and
  interpreting, xxv–xxvii
Hum Log, 169
Hussain, Ghulam, 247

ideology, theory of, xxxi
implicit consciousness, 23
Indian Education Act, 1835, 108
Indian philosophy, 137
Indo-Nepal Friendship Treaty (1950), 211
Indulekha, 119
Inge, Dean, 50
inter-community relations, xli
interpretation, xxvi
intertextuality, xxviii

Islami Bangla Sahitya, 243
Islamic view on evil, xxxii

jatra of Bengal, xxxvi
  companies involved in, 143
  female roles in, 144
  modern concept, 159–160
  nature of performances, 144
  'pala', 160n2
  season, 160n3
  titles and advertisements of, 144
jazz studies, xxxvii
Joad, C. E. M., 48
Journal Sottor, 66

Kafka's stories, perspectives
  Blanchot, Maurice, 123–126
  Deleuze, 129–131
  Derrida, 126–129
Kant, Immanuel, 24–25
Kargupta, Sourav, 22, xxxi
Karma, 164
Kasiyatra Charitra, 112–116
Khan, Bara Ghazi, 241
Khan, Daraf, 249
Kharmawphlang, Desmond L., xxxix–xl, 227
Khasi-Pnars, 136
Khasi society, xxxviii–xxxix, 134, 191. See also Ki Jingsneng Tymmen (Esther Syiem)
  way of life, 193–194, 199, 230–232
  world view, 192
The Khasis under British Rule, 195
Ki Jingsneng Tymmen, xxxviii–xxxix, 189
  authority and sanctity of clan, 197–198
  eldest clan uncle, role of, 192–193, 195–196
  incests and taboos, 197–198
  'Invocation', 192
  ka ktien, 190
  ki phawar, 199–200

marriage, 196–198
moral precepts, 196, 198–199
opening line of the first verse, 195
process of purification, 198
Radhon Singh Berry, role of, 192–193, 195–196
retributive justice, 199
rngiew, 190
rules for hospitality, 196
spoken word, importance of, 194–195
supreme deity, 190
usage of idioms, *ktien kynnoh*, 196
written version of, 191–192, 200
Koch Rajbanshis, 218
Kristeva, Julia, xxxv
Ksemananda, 237
Kshatriya *andolan*, 220, 225n3

language, xxxiii–xxxiv
 lived experience of, xlii
 in relation to society, xxxiv
La part du feu (Blanchot), 122
law of the double, xxx
literary studies, xxix
 world-mediation-text model, 22
literature
 and arrogance of cartographic reading of, 33–34
 border crossing in, 26
 and cosmopolitan law, 24–27
 creativity in, 93–94
 Das' perspectives on poetry, literature, culture and criticism, 86–93
 Deleuze's views, 129–130
 in lived words, 94–96
 in living words, 94–96
 meditative verbs of transformations, 79–80
 from north-east India, xxxviii
 as a part of public sphere, 80–81
 'real' and 'representational,' dealing with, xxxi
 relationship with society, 79–82, 121
 representational mode between science and, xxx, xxxiv
 Spivakian collectivity, 31–33
 as a *tapasya* of social transformation, 83–86
 theoretical building blocks of a notion in, 27
 trajectory of, xxxiv–xxxv
 translation works, 28–29
lived worlds, 94–96
living tradition, 16
living words, 94–96

Mahmud, Lal, 245
Mahmud, Sukur, 248
Mandal, Somdatta, xxxv, xxxvi, 143
Mangal Kavya, 236–242
 Annada Mangal, 241–242
 Chandi Mangal, 238–240
 Dharma Mangal, 240–241
 Manasa Mangal, 237–238
 Ray Mangal, 241
Manjali, Franson Davis, xxxiv, 121
meaningful action, xxix
medieval Bengal, 235
 Bengali literature of. *see* Bengali literature of medieval period
 Hindu–Muslim relations in, 236
 social conditions of, 236
memories
 objectification of past, 65
 political activities, 70–75
 as 'positive substance', 67–68
 relationship between self and, xxxvi
 of revolution, 64
 as texts, xxxii
The Metamorphosis (Franzz Kafka), 130
metaphors, xxv
methodological consciousness, xxvi
Miller, J. Hillis, xxvii

Index **271**

Miri, Sujata, xxxv, xxxvi, 133
Mizo literature, xxxix
  Chemtatrawta, 203
  Chhingpuii, 202–205
  Lali, xxxix, 202, 206–207
Mizo society, xxxix
  Christian influence, 205–207
  concept of *tlawmngaihna*, 203
  societal set-up and way of life, 203, 206
Murtaza, Syed, 245
music
  Akash Bhora Surjo Tara (Tagore), 4–5
  black, analysis of, xxxvii
  Pratima Barua Pandey's, effect of, xl
  of Rabindranath Tagore, 10–12

Naga tribes, 136
Naxalbari uprising, 74
negativity of experience, xxiv
Nepali people in India
  Balgeet and *Nininanee Geet*, 213
  ballads sung, 212
  folk practices, 215
  Gaon Khanay Katha, 216–217
  Hindu feature of, 211–212
  historico-political context, 210–211
  Lokgeet (folk songs), 213
  love of rhythm and melody in ballads, 213–214
  marriage, 214
  music-based oral traditions (*Dohorie*), 215
  oral form of Nepali language, 215–216
  oral tradition of *Lokgatha*, 211, 213
  practice amongst Nepali folklorists, 211
  profile of Nepali people, 212
  Sareli, practice of, 214
nostalgia, 68

Oedipal law, xxx
Ong, Walter J., 202
open text, xxix
oral speech, xxxviii
oral traditions, xxxv, 211, 213–215
The Origin of Species, 4

Pandey, Pratima Barua, xl, 218
  biography, 219
  duets with Hazarika, 221
  film songs, 221
  Goalparia Loka Geet, 222
  songs of, 220–223
partition of India and cinema, 162–163
  1942: A Love Story, 164
  Anmol Ghadi, 165–166
  films and television series, 174
  Lagaan, 164
  Lahore, 167–168
  mainstream movies, 163–164
  non-mainstream cinema, 169
  Nukkad, 169
  Pinjar, 169–171
  Tamas, 162, 169
Peters, John Durham, xxxviii
Phankon, Remy, 233
Pillai, Komaleswaram Srinivasa, 110
Pratapa Mudaliar Charitrami (Vedanayagam Pillai), 118–119
primitive societies, xxxv, 133
Prodhani, Jyotirmoy, 218

Qazi, Daulat, 245

Radhakrishnan, S., 137
Raghavendra, M. K., 162
Raghavendra, S. S., xxxvii
Rahman, Muhammad Shah Noorur, xli, 235
Rajasekhara Chritra (Vedanayagam Pillai), 118
Rajbanshis, xl, 218
  in Bengal, 221
  conversational style of, 221

folk repository of, 219–220
historiography, 219
Rajmohan's Wife (Bankim Chandra Chatterjee), 118
Ramanan, Mohan G., xxxiii, 107
Rasselas, 119
Ray, Bharat Chandra, 241–242
Ray, Dakshin, 241
Ray, Niharranjan, 19
realism, xxvii
The Religion of Man, 8
Ricoeur, Paul, xxviii, xxxv
Rig Veda, 137–138
Ruqaiyyah Waris Maqsood's *The Problem of Evil*
  account of Christian theodicy, 45–46
  appraisal of story of Job, 47–48, 52–53
  approach to problem, 42–43, 57–58
  conception of God/divine, 50–54
  critique of the Biblical or Judeo-Christian approach to the problem, 43–45
  dualist conception, 55–56
  faith in God, 46
  God's nature, notions about, 43
  God's omnipotence and foreknowledge, 58–59
  Iqbal's free-will defence, 59–60
  pantheistic solution to reincarnation systems, 54–55
  Spinoza's theory of necessary evil, 56–57
  Sufistic theology, 48–49
  understanding of Satan, 45

Said, Edward, xxix
Sara Akash, 169
Sarkar, Jagadish Narayan, 237
Saussure, Ferdinand de, xxxiv, 122
Schindler's List, 163
Schuon, Frithjof, 50

science
  distinction between art and, 3–4
  frame of reference for, xxx
  and literature, representational mode between, xxx, xxxiv
  'self' and 'other,' temporal distance between, xxv–xxvii
  setting-into-work of truth, 13
Sewa, Utpala Ghaley, xl
Sewa, Utpala Ghaley, 209
Shah, Mohammad Maroof, xxxii, 41
Sharma, C. D., 137
Shillong-based urban legends, 227
  Corphelia legend, 233–234
  gesture of care and protection, 231
  Marina legend, 229–232
  process of traditionalizing and interpreting, 229–230
  pyngrei ceremony, 232
  socially and religiously sanctioned traditions, use of, 230–232
  symbolic connotations, 231–233
  transformed lifestyles, 230
  tyrut phenomenon, 233
Shillong city, modern, 228
Simone, Nina, 175
  autobiography, 180
  Four Women, 180–181
  Mississippi Goddam, 179–180
  piano playing ability, 179
  political consciousness, 179
smritikatha, 68
social, idea of, xxiv
social reform movements, 108
social relations, textual representation in, xlii
Spivak, Gayatri Chakravorty, 27
Sri Chaitanya, 242
subjectivity, xxiv
Subramanyan, K. G., 16
Syiem, Esther, xxxix, xxxviii–xxxix, 189
syncopation of creative consciousness, xxiv, xxv

Tagore, Rabindranath, xxx, xxxi, 34, 36–37
  approach to tradition, 16–17
  art activity, 14–15
  art objects, 15–16
  development of consciousness, 15
  discursive writings and artistic creations, 19
  distinction between 'true' and 'real', 15
  divinity of man, 14–15
  evolution, concept of, 15
  fascination for science, 5–8
  harmony, concept of, 19–20
  Hibbert lectures, 8–9
  Kakhon Baadol Chhonyaa Lege, 10
  meaning of 'modernity', 18–19
  meeting with Heisenberg, 7–8
  Mon Je Bale Chini Chini, 11
  nature of science in *Personality*, 6–7
  Nrityeara Taale Taale, 10
  philosophical anthropology, 18
  philosophy of art and literature, 20–21
  philosophy of literature, 14
  relationship between science and literature, 10–12
Taylor, Charles, xxvi
textual practices, xxix, xxv
  as "heterogeneous practice", xxxv
  literary text and representations of society, relation between, xxx–xxxi, 22–24
  'real' and 'representational', relation between, xxxi
  science and literature, representational mode between, xxx
  textual experience and ethical moment, xxvii–xxviii
theistic worldviews, xxxii
theory of ideology, 22

Too Good to be True: The Colossal Book of Urban Legends (Jan Harold Brunvand), 228
translation works
  and comparison, 29
  Derridean approach to, 28–31
transmodernity, 98n13
travel narrative (Enugula Veeraswamy), xxxiii, 112–116
Treaty of Sagauli in 1816, 210
The Trial (Franzz Kafka), 126
tribal world-views, xxxvi
  ka hok, xxxix, 134
  philosophical understanding, 140–142
  and religion, 137–139
  through paintings, 134–135

Uddin, Abbas, 220
understanding, xxvi
universal hospitality, 25
universalism, 134

Vaishnava Sahitya, 242–249
  categories, 244
  influence of the yoga system, 246–247
  Vaishnava inclination by Muslims, 243–248
Vedic religion, 137–138
Veeraswamy, Enugula
  on British rule, 110
  early years, 109–110
  narrative style, 119
  sense of India, 118
  travel narrative of, 112–118
  use of Telugu and Sanskrit quotations, 110–111
The Vicar of Wakefield (Oliver Goldsmith), 118–119
Visvaparichaya, 5

women, stereotypical roles of, 144–145

Bollywood culture, 160
as bride, 145–148
as empowered wife, 151–152
as homemaker, 145
as lover, 153–156
as mother, 152–153
as mother-in-law, 153
as powerful, 157–160
as rebellious/domineering wife, 150
as subservient/self-sacrificing/suffering wife, 148–149
Western views, 144–145
work, difference between text and, xxxiv–xxxv
written tradition, xxxv

Zama, Margaret Ch, xxxix, 202